MAXWOOD PUBLIC LIBRARY

W9-CER-126

# How and When to Be Your Own LAWYER

## A Step-by-Step Guide to Effectively Using Our Legal System

# Robert W. Schachner
## with Marvin Quittner, Esq.

AVERY PUBLISHING GROUP INC.
Garden City Park, New York

The information and opinions presented in this book are based upon the training, personal experiences, and research of the authors. The publisher believes that it is the right of citizens of this country to disseminate and obtain such information. Readers should understand that there is no guarantee that any one approach will always produce the desired outcome, for each person and situation is unique. It is therefore urged by the publisher and authors that people always use caution and responsibility in dealing with legal matters, including consultation with qualified professionals. Readers who are in any doubt about their legal situation should seek appropriate professional help. The publisher and authors take no responsibility for any misunderstandings or outcomes resulting from anyone's actions based upon the information and opinions contained in this book.

Cover designer: Richard Rossiter
Typesetter: Bonnie Freid

**Library of Congress Cataloging-in-Publication Data**

Schachner, Robert W.
    How and when to be your own lawyer : a step-by-step guide to
effectively using our legal system / Robert Schachner with Marvin
Quittner.
        p. cm.
    Includes index.
    ISBN 0-89529-523-7
    1. Civil procedure—United States.   2. Pro se representation
—United States.   I. Quittner, Marvin.   II. Title.
KF8841.S32 1993
347.73'5—dc20
[347.3075]                                          92-42909
                                                    CIP

Copyright © 1993 by Robert W. Schachner and Marvin Quittner, Esq.

All rights reserved. No part of this publication may be reproduced, stored in a retrieval system, or transmitted, in any form or by any means, electronic, mechanical, photocopying, recording or otherwise, without the prior written permission of the copyright owner.

**Printed in the United States of America by Paragon Press, Honesdale, PA.**

10   9   8   7   6   5

# Contents

*To Samuel Schachner; may he now rest in peace,
and to Alexander and Victoria with love.*

*And to Shelley, Lee, and Joy with love.*

# CREDITS

The opening quotation is from *A Report on Self-Help Law: Its Many Perspectives*, a report sponsored by the American Bar Association Special Committee on the Delivery of Legal Services © 1977 by the American Bar Association. Reprinted by permission.

The excerpts on pages ix, 7–8, and 163 from *Black's Law Dictionary* are reprinted with the permission of West Publishing Company.

The quotation on page 1 is from from the musical *Les Miserables*, by Alain Boublil and Claude-Michel Schönberg, lyrics by Herbert Kretzmer and Alain Boublil © Alain Boublil Music Ltd. Reprinted by permission.

West Publishing Company's key logo on page 44 is reprinted with the permission of West Publishing Company.

The excerpt on page 53 is from *Shepard's Southern Reporter Citations*, Volume 2 (Part 3) 1986. © 1986 by McGraw-Hill, Inc. All rights reserved. Reproduced by permission of Shepard's/McGraw-Hill. Further reproduction is strictly prohibited.

The excerpt on pages 227–228 is from *Resolving Your Disputes*. Reprinted by permission of the American Arbitration Association.

The excerpt on page 242 is from *Art of Advocacy—Jury Instructions* by S. Baldwin, E. Davidson, and J. Lynch, Jr. Copyright © 1992 by Matthew Bender & Co., Inc. Reprinted with permission. All rights reserved.

The excerpt on pages 243–244 is from *Florida Standard Jury Instructions in Civil Cases*, published by CLE Publications, the Florida Bar, Tallahassee, FL 32399-2300. Reprinted by permission.

The excerpts on pages 261, 280, and 281 are from *The Fundamentals of Trial Techniques* © 1988 by Thomas Mauet. Reprinted by permission of Little, Brown and Company.

The excerpts on pages 333–335 are from *Art of Advocacy—Preparation of the Case* by David Baum. Copyright © 1992 by Matthew Bender & Co., Inc. Reprinted with permission. All rights reserved.

The forms on pages 367–383 are from *Florida Rules of Court—State*. Reprinted with the permission of West Publishing Company.

# Acknowledgments

Acknowledgment is gratefully extended to the following attorneys, all of whom have had a profound influence on my life and thinking: Robert Raphael, Esq., who said after my first pro se appearance in court, "You won your first case"; George Hoffman, Esq., who taught me that David could slay Goliath; Vincent Bisogino, Esq., for teaching me that knowledge of the law does not automatically translate into success; Leonard Korobkin, Esq., who taught me that there is no honor among thieves; Harold Greenberg, Esq., who allowed me to work with him, side by side, 'til the wee hours of the morning; Melvin S. Slade, Esq., who taught me the meaning of "a captive of industry (or banking)"; Daniel Brashis, Esq., a lawyer who knows how to fly with hijackers, but not how to walk with clients; Irving Boigen, Esq., a gentleman and a brilliant and compassionate lawyer; Harvey Thomas McLain, Esq., a friend and true captain of industry and commerce; Robert Garven, Esq., for his knowledge of the appellate system; Jerry Pollack, Esq., for teaching me that I needed to develop the skills of self-help law; Martin Sandler, Esq., for teaching me the need to understand malpractice law; Wayne Carson, Esq., for proving to me that attorneys do not belong on pedestals; Robert Turek, Esq., for his help on this manuscript; Harry Averell, Esq., and Patrick Novak, Esq., for being there; and especially to my co-author, teacher, associate, and friend Marvin Quittner, Esq., for his faith, trust, and knowledge.

I must also acknowledge Barbara Klemm for her dedicated research and assistance; United States Congressman Thomas Bevill; Federal Judge (ret.) Miles Lord; Federal Judge Brian B. Duff; Judge Blanche Wahl; Judge Paul M. Marko III; Judge Barry Seltzer; Judge William H. Conner; Judge Robert C. Scott; Robert Coulson, President of the American Arbitration Association; a special friend, Clerk of the Broward County Court, Robert L. Lockwood; and the Nova University Law Library and staff.

I would also like to thank my editors, Joanne Abrams and Robert Weiser, for their invaluable help.

# Preface

"Sue the bastards" is a familiar cry voiced by many of us caught in some eminently unfair circumstance or situation. But when we examine the cost of engaging legal counsel to redress a grievance, our ruffled feathers quickly calm down. We are left with the frustration resulting from a lack of knowledge of the legal system and an inability to use that system by ourselves. There are, however, several options open to laypeople. One is to engage legal counsel on contingency, in which the attorney takes a percentage of the award, assuming there is one—and assuming you can find a lawyer willing to take the case on that basis. Another is to act on your own behalf, either for the entire proceeding or until you can find affordable counsel.

In legal terms, acting on your own behalf is known as pro se. *Black's Law Dictionary* defines the term as "for himself, in his own behalf, in person," and further, "appearing for oneself, as in the case of one who does not retain a lawyer and appears for himself in court."

This book uses a somewhat broader definition. This book will guide you through such complex legal areas as filing papers, drawing complaints, using a law library, and preparing for and conducting a trial. In addition, this book will provide you with the means to study, research, and understand these principles of law. *How and When to Be Your Own Lawyer* will discuss not only the risks and considerations entailed in undertaking a pro se action, it will also show you how you can take an active hand in your legal involvement even if you do retain counsel.

This volume will not discuss the criminal system, except to indicate that it is our opinion that an individual should not attempt to deal with criminal matters without the aid of a competent attorney. This opinion extends to appellate matters as well as matters that involve townships or local governments, such as zoning and municipal ordinance problems. However, the ability to take things into your own hands, to learn the system, and to research the law and the rules of practice will be immensely helpful in making you a better and more effective client when working in concert with an attorney.

When you finish this book, you should be more familiar and more comfortable with the legal process. We intend to strip away the system's mystique, and hopefully your fear of dealing with many of the system's practices. We will describe the court system, including traffic, small claims, and upper and lower courts; demonstrate the difference between equity and money damages; and help you understand dozens of legal terms that sound complex but are simple in concept. And, of course, we will teach you how to use a law library.

*Caveat:* Don't feel that you can take on the entire legal community after you have read this book, for this volume is no substitute for law school and years of experience at the bar. However, by becoming familiar with the practices and trappings of our legal system, perhaps you will be a step ahead of much of the field in your own legal involvement.

I once appeared before a trial court judge as a participant in a business-related lawsuit for which I had no counsel, the original law firm having withdrawn without affordable substitute counsel being retained. My opponent was a young attorney from a prominent law firm. The motion was set to be heard at 8:45 a.m. in the judge's chambers, along with numerous other matters scheduled for the same time. The judge assumed that those in the room knew that they were expected to announce their presence in approximately the same order in which they had entered his chambers, after making sure their opponents were also present.

As I pondered the details of my case, I noticed that some of the attorneys, including my opponent, were quite nervous. Just then, the current argument before the judge was concluded, and I announced my presence to his honor, who asked if I was appearing pro se. (I didn't look like an attorney that day.) I answered, "Yes, your honor," and proceeded to state my case. When the judge had ruled, I closed my file and said, "Thank you, your honor" (although the ruling went against me), and I left those sanctified chambers.

What stuck in my mind as I walked through the halls of justice was that I had witnessed my young opponent so nervous while performing in the environment in which he was trained to function. My next thought was logical: If some of the pros are intimidated by the courtroom environment, how could a layperson possibly deal with the situation—especially one who has not been fortunate enough to have thirty-odd years of exposure to the legal process, as I have? How could that person function, comprehend the procedures, understand the format of the documents, or even know when and how to address the judge? As an involved and interested businessman, I had learned much about civil process over the years preceding my pro se appearance that day. The need to help others who are naive about the system spawned the concept for this book—the need to unravel the jargon and decode the procedures of the legal system, and to enable the reader to defend or prosecute within the bounds of the system with or without the services of an attorney.

Unlike form books, dictionaries, and encyclopedias, this book tutors you in a step-by-step course of action to obtain an effective defensive or offensive posture. With the help of attorney Marvin Quittner, I have provided insights into our legal system and will guide you in how to use it realistically and successfully. Since a basic knowledge of key legal terms is essential to forming and following through on any legal strategy, simple and practical definitions of legal terminology are provided, not just as abstract concepts, but as current terms used in actions or procedures that you might be handling.

Stories and anecdotes punctuate the text to give perspective on the system. Basic procedures for taking action or preventing action, being heard, using a law library, and "stopping the clock" to gain time are all presented in simple-to-understand text, accompanied by helpful tables and sample forms.

Understanding our civil justice system will also help you better understand the work of an attorney if you choose to retain counsel to redress a wrong or defend a claim. This means you will be less of a burden to your lawyer, who works in a highly professional and technical field. The result will be a stronger attorney-client relationship, and savings of time and money.

At the very least, *How and When to Be Your Own Lawyer* should help you to fight back against your opposition, who will probably be pros. Lawyer Quittner, well-schooled in the tricks of the trade and with a lifetime of legal and courtroom experience, will give you insight into the thinking, attitudes, and direction of your opponents.

And just in case you're concerned about the attitude of the courts toward pro se litigants, we have included interviews with public officials and judges on the subject of do-it-yourself law, including an inspiring excerpt from an actual trial transcript of one of the most famous pro se cases in American legal history (see Chapter 19). Even the Supreme Court has addressed the issue, and has seen fit to support pro se litigants in their efforts, as this quote from Federal Civil Procedure Rule 11 shows: "The court has sufficient discretion to take account of the special circumstances that often arise in pro se situations." And again, after Section (d) of Rule 11: "parties appearing pro se are allowed greater latitude with respect to reasonableness of their legal theories (*Patterson v. Aiken*, 111 F.R.D. 354, 358 [N.D. Ga. 1986]). And the Supreme Court held in an Illinois case, "the pro se complaint . . . we hold to less stringent standards than formal pleading drafted by lawyers."

So if you are off to do battle in our civil justice arena, take heart! Despite its shortcomings, you will be heading into the most user-friendly justice system in the world. Good fortune!

R.W.S.

*"Self-help law [pro se] is here to stay. It is important that all parties involved recognize this fact. . . . self-help . . . provides a means through which consumers may gain greater access to the judicial system."*

—American Bar Association's
*A Report on Self-Help Law: Its Many Perspectives*

# CHAPTER 1

# Understanding the System

*Knowledge itself is power.*
—Francis Bacon

Our system of justice is based on centuries of efforts aimed at organizing society, "changing the chaos to order and light," as Jean Valjean sings in *Les Misérables*. After hundreds of years of barbarian behavior, conquests, inquisitions, and chicanery, the English royalty granted its subjects a form of constitutional law. Presented to the aristocracy in 1215 and confirmed in Parliament shortly thereafter, the document known as the Magna Carta (the "great charter") is now regarded as the basis for modern constitutional law.

For the first time, the subjects of an organized society were given certain inalienable rights. Within its eighty-two chapters, the Magna Carta defined rights of property, placed limits on taxation, and secured personal liberty. The document also established due process of law. Although these rights were granted only to the country's elite, the world finally had a model for a true system of justice, inscribed on paper, ratified by a political body of peers.

Despite this more equitable system of justice, political oppression and religious intolerance in England and Europe created groups of doubters, critics, and dissenters who were willing to colonize the New World as soon as the opportunity presented itself. In 1629, Charles I chartered the Massachusetts Bay colony and the American system was off to its start along the lines of its English parent. In the charter, Charles stated that the General Court (legislature) was authorized to create "all Manner of wholesome and reasonable Orders, Lawes, Statutes, and Ordinances, Direccons and Instruccon" as long as they were not "contrarie to the Lawes of this our Realme of England." In other words, the colonies were given the responsibility of establishing a system that mirrored the system codified in the Magna Carta, including the all-important concept of due process.

However, unlike England, which had five different professions involved in the practice of law (barristers, attorneys, solicitors, notaries, and scriveners), the colonies were short on professionals. Properly-worded legal documents and counsel were rare, because few individuals were trained in the law. Without a center of legal practice such as London, or even an appellate court to guide the legal system in its practice, the colonists began, out of necessity, to practice pro se; that is, to represent themselves without an attorney. One colonist, probably a lawyer, complained that the Massachusetts Bay colony actually discouraged the use of a paid attorney or advocate. However, since no society can survive and progress without the law, and since only a little education—along with the standing of a gentleman (a degree of wealth that many could earn in a short time in the New World)—was needed to practice pro se, most individuals represented their own interests. Also, not wanting to create a niche for another elite like that left behind in England, these gentlemen also represented those not able to act in their own behalf.

Prior to 1778, *The Constable's Pocket-Book* was the only book used by individuals acting pro se. This volume, named for the king's keeper of the peace, allowed the layman to do the work of the lawyer. But it was Sir William Blackstone's *Commentaries on the Laws of England* that contributed most to the flourishing of amateur lawyers in the early years of our country. If a gentleman in America could read and intended to own any books at all, the first two on his list were the Bible and Blackstone's.

The roots of the American tradition of legal self-representation are deep and as much a part of this country's history as the Pilgrims themselves. This is not to say that *How and When to Be Your Own Lawyer* is a twentieth-century Blackstone's, but it is clear that the concept of an individual acquiring the knowledge of the law—of society's rules in a particular jurisdiction—is as American as apple pie and the original thirteen colonies.

## THE FABRIC OF OUR LEGAL SYSTEM

Our legal system is based on four elements: Constitutions, statutes, decisions (including precedents and traditions), and rules. The system is constantly evolving through the interaction of the legislature, which makes the laws, and the executive branch, which enforces the laws. In addition, both of these branches act in concert with (and sometimes in opposition to) the court system. This evolutionary process reflects the growth and change of society and its needs (see Common Law, Equity, and Civil Law, page 3).

# Common Law, Equity, and Civil Law

*In the American legal system today, the cases heard in civil courts fall into two basic categories: Matters of common law and matters of equity.*

*Common law cases are decided on the basis of the body of law that is based on precedent, or decisions in prior cases, as well as interpretations or modifications of statutes enacted by legislatures.*

*Equity cases are decided on the basis of fairness, sometimes even in spite of statutes or precedents.*

*Common law cases heard by civil courts in the United States can trace their ancestry back to merchant law, a form of self-help law that was developed in England as a means of providing rules for commerce. These private rules were gradually incorporated into English common law, where they came to form the basis for the insurance law, negotiable instrument law, partnership law, and laws of sales we know today.*

*Equity law developed out of a system of law based on the power of the king, or his appointed officers, to be more flexible in administering justice by taking into account all of the circumstances surrounding a case, rather than being limited to the application of statutes or precedents. Equity courts could take preventive measures, such as issuing injunctions against a threat, and could settle matters of rights of all parties involved in a dispute. In the United States, elements of equity law have been accepted by the civil courts (in England, equity cases are still heard in separate courts, as they were originally).*

*Equity is what permits a court, in the interest of fairness to the parties concerned, to grant certain types of remedies when there is no other remedy available by law, or when the law is inadequate to provide justice. These can include:*

Accountings. *The court can call for the review of one party's books to enforce payment to the other party. This is often used in fiduciary matters, trust relationships concerning fraud, and in winding up partnerships.*

Partition. *The court can call for the fair division of property owned by two or more individuals.*

Specific performance.   *The court can enforce terms of a contract when the subject of the contract cannot readily be compensated by money.*

Clearing cloud on title.   *The court can rule on whether a lien or claim on a title is valid.*

Cancellation or reformation of contract.   *The court can cancel or reform a contract if a party entered into it because of fraud, misrepresentation, duress, undue influence, or mistake.*

Injunction.   *The court can restrain a party from committing an act that appears to be against equity or good conscience. This often is used in labor disputes, copyright issues, and monopolies.*

*The distinction between actions at law and those in equity remains, but the administration of the courts in the United States has been merged into a single, unified system. Hence, both equity and common law have a place in American civil courts. Civil courts should not, however, be confused with civil law. Civil law is a legal system based strictly on statutes—judges decide each case by applying the appropriate statute as it was enacted, without reference to precedent or fairness. This system of law originated in imperial Rome, and through the Napoleonic Code and French civil law came to form the basis for the legal system in a number of European and Latin American countries.*

Yet, despite a system that has grown so complex and has spawned so many specialties, flexibility and compassion remain for the individual who chooses to navigate his or her way through the justice system. Small claims court and do-it-yourself divorce and bankruptcy are all evidence of the system's acknowledgment of pro se action. On the other hand, a federal tax code of more than 2,800 pages in two volumes (U.S.C. Volumes 10 and 11) containing more than 7,700 different codes, may require a lawyer to devote a lifetime to its study. To better understand the structure of our legal system, let's look at each of its four elements.

## Constitutions

The Constitution of the United States, the document that reflects the agreements of our citizenry as to how society is to function, provides for a legislative body, Congress, with the responsibility to enact laws. There are also individual state constitutions, each of which permits a set of state laws to be enacted by a state legislature. Both federal and state constitutions provide for a court system to interpret the laws. State law must first be constitutional—that is, in conformity with the United States Constitution, and then consistent and in conformity with the law of the state in which it has been enacted and based on that state's constitution.

State constitutions also permit the establishment of a structure of cities, towns, municipalities, counties, etc., within the state. Each of these political bodies is able to enact certain laws, or ordinances. These ordinances must first be consistent with the United States Constitution, and then must be consistent with the state constitution. These local laws are overseen by the state court system. If called into question as to their validity in regard to the Constitution, local laws may be reviewed by the federal court system.

## Statutes

Statutes are the written rules and regulations that regulate the transactions of life. These are the laws our legislatures enact. Federal and state constitutions, respectively, are the bases for statutes on the federal and state levels. Each individual constitution, state or federal, establishes a legislative body that formulates the rules which govern our daily lives. The various statutes are then interpreted by the courts, often as a result of interactions with the executive and legislative branches of government. In reverse, a legislature may amend or override court decisions by changing laws or passing new laws.

## Decisions: Precedents and Traditions

The court system, along with the legislature, establishes the rules of the game. Almost every day, some appellate court somewhere in the United States is deciding an issue of law. This process of interpreting statutes and reviewing previous decisions, more than any other action by any branch of government, is responsible for the evolution of our laws and statutes.

A statute enacted with good cause on one day may not be valid the next day. A law enacted with all good intentions might be unconstitutional or even counterproductive to the needs of society. The process of judicial review is responsible for molding society's rules (its statutes) into a meaningful and cohesive body of law that has been tested in various cases against differing sets of facts and circumstances. Over time, these opinions tend to place the interpretation of a law or statute into a historical context. The result is a voluminous body of case law—precedents—that is a guiding light to others in their search for definitive answers to similar legal issues or questions.

An interesting precedent in the music industry illustrates the interpretation process. The test case of *King Records v. Mercury Records* came about when James Brown, the well-known rhythm-and-blues artist, was at the pinnacle of his career. Brown had just come out with one of his most successful hits, "Papa's Got a Brand New Bag," and was coveted by every major record company. However, he had signed an exclusive contract with King Records, the company that had originally discovered him. A competitor, Mercury Records, got the idea to record Brown as an instrumental artist instead of as a vocalist. Because Brown's contract with King Records referred to his exclusive personal services as a vocalist, the Mercury people thought they had a good chance of obtaining his instrumental services and thereby the use of his name. The Mercury moguls claimed that Brown was not and had never been a member of the American Federation of Musicians, in effect challenging King's definition of the contract that gave King the artist's services on an exclusive basis. King Records filed a lawsuit in federal court and asked for a permanent injunction preventing Mercury from selling their recordings. The court granted the injunction, and this was the last time a major record company tried to challenge the meaning of the term "exclusive services." The court's ruling set the precedent to which the music industry still adheres.

## Rules: Administrative Law and Procedures

Society has become so complex that another whole strata of law exists: Rules, or administrative law and procedure. Certain governmental bodies have been empowered to propagate rules and regulations within a relatively narrow area of society. Prime examples are the Federal Aviation Administration's rules and regulations for control of airspace and flight, the Federal Communications Commission's regulation of the transmission of radio signals and control of frequencies, the Federal Trade Commission's regulation of certain areas of business and advertising, and the Food and Drug Administration's control over food and drug substances. Fortunately, despite the power vested in these government agencies, their rules and regulations are all subject to review by the courts and thereby subject to the same evolutionary process (and safeguards) as are any legislative actions.

The courts themselves propagate rules and regulations that mandate procedure, form, and style to the conduct of the justice system. Although many states use the Federal Rules of Civil Procedure as a guideline for their own procedural rules, each state's situation is unique. Be careful when attempting to act in more than one state or jurisdiction. The rules may appear to be the same from state to state, but close examination exposes differences in the civil procedure rules as adopted by the individual states. For instance, the first sentence of New Jersey Rule 804.05 (depositions upon oral examination) is exactly the same as Ohio Rule 30(A) and its equivalent in Florida; then the changes take place that make each jurisdiction's rulebook a custom work to fit the need of its citizens and community.

There are also many thousands of rules that differ completely from one jurisdiction to another that can confuse even an experienced attorney, and that you must know if you are to practice pro se in any jurisdiction. For example, in Gila County, Arizona, the court has Rule IX regarding the suspension of its rules: "The Court may, in any matter, for good cause, suspend any local rule by an order entered in the minutes." This rule conjures up the days of the Wild West when the local marshal operated justice as he saw fit. And in Missouri, Rule 37.10 of the Traffic Court Rules states that the court is always open—"The court shall be deemed always open for the purpose of filing proper papers." As you read this book, you will appreciate how these seemingly insignificant rules can have great impact on your case.

The rules of the court work in tandem with the requirements and stipulations of the statutes of a given jurisdiction. One might even say the rules of a given court interpret or mandate the implementation of statutes, whereas case law-interprets the meaning and application of the statute itself.

## Statutes Versus Rules

Court-authorized procedures and rules, in addition to laws or statutes, may affect you as you proceed through the court system. You should understand these procedures before you take any action. For example, what papers (pleadings) should be filed at a particular point in a case is usually established by the court system, yet the appropriate venue, or where the case is filed and heard, is usually established by statute. Similarly, statutes usually establish the requirements of obtaining jurisdiction over a litigant. However, the form of the paperwork, such as the summons, used in that process, is usually established through court rules and procedures.

## THE COURT SYSTEM

In this book, we are concerned with the day-to-day operations of the working court system and how you might utilize this system, applying basic laws to a particular set of circumstances.

*Black's Law Dictionary* defines the court as "a body in the government to which the administration of justice is delegated." In an attempt to meet the special needs of our complicated and busy world, a system of courts has evolved on the federal, state, and local levels. Since a court is the ultimate arbitrator in a dispute, whether between an individual and the state (traffic ticket) or between two individuals (dissolution of marriage) or between a state-created entity, such as a corporation, and another individual and/or corporation, a working knowledge of the court system is important if you are contemplating legal action or are defending an action.

## The Federal Court System

First, a look at the federal system, which is made up of district courts, appellate courts, and the ultimate authority in our land, the United States Supreme Court.

Each district (see Table 1.1) has a number of judges appointed for life who conduct both civil and criminal matters. Some judges who are overburdened with cases have judicial assistants. Along with their law clerks, these busy judges may also have the help of a magistrate to hear cases or portions of cases. Since the federal courts are subject to rules that require criminal cases to move faster than civil cases, it is not uncommon for a suit brought in federal district court to get delayed, and to take up to two-and-a-half years or longer to resolve through trial and verdict by judge and jury.

When initiating or defending a matter in federal court, it is important to know the rules of practice in the court's particular district. Each district (as defined by the court) covers a certain geographical area, and procedural rules may vary from district to district, even though the districts are right next to each other. You must strictly adhere to the rules when appearing before the court. Generally, the federal court system is more concerned with detail and procedure than are local and state courts.

If you are dissatisfied with the outcome of a case brought before the district court and you have a basis for appeal, the next level in the system (see Chapter 17) is the appellate court. The costs are high and the rules exacting, but the panel of appellate judges that constitute the appellate court may, if they choose to hear your case, give it a thorough review. If you reach this level, you may make law; that is, if the decision is recorded and published in the books containing such decisions, the case may also be reviewed when a case of a similar nature is before another court, and your case may very well play a part in the decision based on the similarity of facts in the case. (More about case law in Chapter 2.)

From the appellate court, your only recourse is to petition (to ask) the

**Table 1.1.** United States Court System (1989)*

| State or Province | Courts of Limited Jurisdiction | Trial Courts of General Jurisdiction | Appellate Courts |
|---|---|---|---|
| Alabama | Probate<br>County<br>Justice<br>Recorder's | Circuit | Supreme Court<br>Court of Criminal Appeals<br>Court of Civil Appeals |
| Alaska | Magistrate<br>District | Superior | Supreme Court |
| Arizona | Justice<br>City and Town<br>Magistrate | Superior | Supreme Court<br>Court of Appeals |
| Arkansas | County<br>Municipal<br>Common Pleas<br>Justice<br>Police<br>City | Chancery and Probate | Supreme Court |
| California | Municipal<br>Justice | Circuit | Supreme Court<br>Court of Appeals |
| Colorado | Superior<br>Juvenile<br>Probate<br>County<br>Municipal | Superior | Supreme Court<br>Court of Appeals |
| Connecticut | Juvenile<br>Common Pleas<br>Probate | District | Supreme Court |
| Delaware | Family<br>Municipal<br>Justice | Superior | Supreme Court |
| Florida | County | Circuit | Supreme Court<br>District Court of Appeals |
| Georgia | Probate<br>Civil and Criminal<br>Justice<br>Small Claims | Superior | Supreme Court of Appeals |

*When the same judges preside over two or more classes of courts, only one of the classes is shown. Also, certain types of specialized courts, such as tax courts or industrial relations courts, have been omitted from this compilation.

| State or Province | Courts of Limited Jurisdiction | Trial Courts of General Jurisdiction | Appellate Courts |
|---|---|---|---|
| Hawaii | District | Circuit | Supreme Court |
| Idaho | Magistrate's Division of District Court | District | Supreme Court |
| Illinois | ——— | Circuit and Associate Judges | Supreme Court Appellate Court |
| Indiana | County Municipal Magistrate Probate Juvenile City and Town Justice of Peace | Circuit Superior Criminal | Supreme Court Court of Appeals |
| Iowa | ——— | District | Supreme Court |
| Kansas | Probate City County Juvenile Municipal | District | Supreme Court |
| Kentucky | County Justice Police | Circuit | Supreme Court |
| Louisiana | City Juvenile Mayor's Justice Traffic Family Municipal Parish | District | Supreme Court Court of Appeals |
| Maine | Probate District | Superior | Supreme Judicial Court |
| Maryland | Orphans' District | Circuit of Counties | Court of Appeals Court of Special Appeals |
| Massachusetts | Land Probate Municipal District Juvenile Housing | Superior | Supreme Judicial Court Appeals Court |

| State or Province | Courts of Limited Jurisdiction | Trial Courts of General Jurisdiction | Appellate Courts |
| --- | --- | --- | --- |
| Michigan | Common Pleas<br>Municipal<br>District<br>Probate | Circuit<br>Recorder's | Supreme Court<br>Court of Appeals |
| Minnesota | County<br>Probate<br>Municipal | District | Supreme Court |
| Mississippi | Family<br>County<br>City Police<br>Justice | Chancery<br>Circuit | Supreme Court |
| Missouri | Probate<br>Court of Criminal<br>  Correction<br>Magistrate<br>Municipal | Circuit | Supreme Court<br>Court of Appeals |
| Montana | Municipal<br>Justice<br>City<br>Workman's<br>  Compensation | District | Supreme Court |
| Nebraska | County<br>Municipal<br>Juvenile<br>Workman's<br>  Compensation | District | Supreme Court |
| Nevada | Municipal<br>Justice | District | Supreme Court |
| New Hampshire | Probate<br>District<br>Municipal | Superior | Supreme Court |
| New Jersey | Municipal<br>County District<br>Juvenile and<br>  Domestic Relations | Superior | Supreme Court |
| New Mexico | Probate<br>Municipal<br>Small Claims<br>Magistrate | District | Supreme Court<br>Court of Appeals |

| State or Province | Courts of Limited Jurisdiction | Trial Courts of General Jurisdiction | Appellate Courts |
|---|---|---|---|
| New York | Court of Claims<br>Surrogate's<br>Family<br>County<br>Civil (NYC)<br>Criminal (NYC)<br>District<br>City<br>Town and Village | Supreme<br>County | Court of Appeals<br>Appellate Division<br>of Supreme Court |
| North Carolina | District | Superior | Supreme Court<br>Court of Appeals |
| North Dakota | County<br>County with<br>  Increased<br>  Jurisdiction<br>County Justice<br>Municipal | District | Supreme Court |
| Ohio | Municipal<br>County<br>Court of Claims | Courts of<br>  Common Pleas | Supreme Court<br>Court of Appeals |
| Oklahoma | Municipal | District | Supreme Court<br>Court of Criminal<br>  Appeals<br>Court of Appeals |
| Oregon | County<br>District<br>Justice<br>Municipal | Circuit | Supreme Court<br>Appeals Court |
| Pennsylvania | Municipal<br>Traffic<br>Justices of the<br>  Peace | Courts of<br>  Common Pleas | Supreme Court<br>Superior Court<br>Commonwealth<br>  Court |
| Rhode Island | District<br>Probate<br>Family<br>Police | Superior | Supreme Court |
| South Carolina | County<br>Probate<br>Magistrate<br>City Recorder's<br>Family | Circuit | Supreme Court |

| State or Province | Courts of Limited Jurisdiction | Trial Courts of General Jurisdiction | Appellate Courts |
|---|---|---|---|
| South Dakota | Five law-trained magistrates and others | Circuit | Supreme Court |
| Tennessee | County<br>General Sessions<br>Municipal<br>Juvenile<br>Domestic Relations | Chancery<br>Circuit<br>Criminal<br>Law Equity | Supreme Court<br>Court of Appeals<br>Court of Criminal Appeals |
| Texas | Criminal District<br>Courts of Domestic Relations<br>Juvenile<br>County Courts at Law<br>County Civil Courts at Law<br>Probate<br>County Criminal<br>County Criminal Courts at Law<br>County Criminal Courts of Appeal | District | Supreme Court<br>Court of Criminal Appeals<br>Court of Civil Appeals |
| Utah | Juvenile<br>City<br>Justice | District | Supreme Court |
| Vermont | District<br>Probate | Superior | Supreme Court |
| Virginia | General District<br>Juvenile and Domestic Relations | Circuit | Supreme Court |
| Washington | District<br>Municipal | Superior | Supreme Court<br>Court of Appeals |
| West Virginia | Police | Circuit | Supreme Court of Appeals |
| Wisconsin | Municipal | Circuit<br>County | Supreme Court |
| Wyoming | Justice<br>Municipal | District | Supreme Court |
| District of Columbia | County | Superior | Court of Appeals |

| State or Province | Courts of Limited Jurisdiction | Trial Courts of General Jurisdiction | Appellate Courts |
|---|---|---|---|
| Guam | Traffic<br>Small Claims | Superior | Supreme Court |
| Puerto Rico | District<br>Municipal<br>Justice | Superior | Supreme Court |

Supreme Court to hear your case. At this level, you cannot act pro se, as the Supreme Court will allow only members of its Bar Association to represent themselves or anyone else before it. With the exception of certain original jurisdiction matters (see Chapter 3), in order for a case to be heard before the Supreme Court, the Court must issue a writ of certiorari, which is a request, by an upper court to a lower court, to review a transcript.

Sometimes law is made when the Supreme Court refuses to review a case. One interesting such instance was *Robert Olff v. East Side Union High School District*. The young lad, Robert Olff, was expelled from school for having long hair. The debate over the case raised the question of whether the school board could dictate what was considered an appropriate hairstyle. The Supreme Court refused to issue a writ of certiorari for this case. However, Justice William O. Douglas wrote in his dissenting opinion, "This court takes judicial notice that hairstyles have altered from time to time throughout the ages. Samson's locks symbolically signified his virility. Many of the Founding Fathers of this country wore wigs. President Lincoln grew a beard at the suggestion of a juvenile female admirer. Chief Justice Hughes' beard furnished the model for the frieze over the portico of the Supreme Court of the United States proclaiming equal justice under law."

Justice Douglas also defended the American concept of liberty: "The word 'liberty' is not defined in the Constitution. But as we held in *Griswold v. Connecticut* (381 U.S. 479, 85 S.Ct. 1678, 14 L.Ed.2d 510), it includes at least the fundamental rights retained by the people under the Ninth Amendment (Ibid., at 484, 85 S.Ct., at 1681). One's hairstyle, like one's taste for food, or one's liking for certain kinds of music, art, reading, recreation, is certainly fundamental in our constitution scheme—a scheme designed to keep government off the backs of people."

In the end, the school board prevailed and the grooming rule stood: "Hair shall be trim and clean. A boy's hair shall not fall below the eyes in front and shall not cover the ears, and it shall not extend to the collar in back" (Justice Stephen Johnson Field, Cal., 1879).

## State Court Systems

Most state court systems are divided into several levels, consisting of the trial (lowest) level, appellate level, and supreme level. The trial level may also be subdivided. In Florida, for instance, county court is the correct venue for evictions, traffic cases, and the lowest form of criminal cases, misdemeanors. Cases heard by county court have a $15,000 limit, and the small claims division handles cases concerning amounts of $2,500 or less. The small claims division is more accessible to the layperson, with preprinted forms and guidance from the court's personnel and often even the judge. Every effort is made to give individuals, especially those acting pro se, the opportunity to be heard and receive a fair measure of justice.

Small claims filing fees (and rules) vary from jurisdiction to jurisdiction. Amounts that are considered "small claims" also vary. For instance, in Fort Lauderdale, you pay $41 to file a claim of $99 or less, and $74 for a claim of $100–$2,500. Chicago has its own sliding fee scale. In New York City, the fee is $5.25 for a claim up to $2,000. Los Angeles is very different. Claims up to $2,000 cost $8 each, and that fee is good for twelve filings in a given year. For filings in excess of twelve, the fee is $16. (All figures are as of 1989.) Los Angeles also has a dispute settlement service (alternate dispute resolution, or ADR) that may be used to bypass the trial process (see Chapter 14).

A dry cleaner once lost the pants to an expensive suit of mine. After all else failed, I filed suit in small claims court. Following the usual delays and resetting of dates, I found myself with a major time conflict for the trial. Being late for the trial, I called the judge's secretary to explain I was on the way. She told me not to go to the courtroom when I arrived at the courthouse, but to come directly to the judge's chambers. When I reached his doorway, I was handed my long-lost pants, and then told to use his honor's bathroom for the fitting. If the pants were indeed mine, he was going to consider the case settled. They were mine, and the ends of justice were served right there in the judge's W.C.

The circuit court in Florida is not quite so informal, being charged with the responsibility to hear felonies, major contract disputes, and cases of $15,000 and more. It also hears cases having equitable jurisdiction. Equitable jurisdiction cases are not defined by monetary amounts, but by the fact that the court has to decide on the fairness of an issue, such as by reviewing documents or actions of individuals. A declaratory judgment is a form of equity decision that I have found to be helpful when, for instance, I am at odds over a contract with another business party. War is about to be declared, and inevitably one party or the other is going to file suit. In an attempt to have my interpretation of the conflict prevail, I file an action asking the court to declare the correct interpretation of the issue that is the basis for the disagreement.

If you have an adverse ruling, have retained the appropriate record, and have an appealable issue (see Chapter 17), you may be able to appeal to a higher court. In Florida, you may appeal from county court to circuit court, and from circuit court to the middle level, the district court of appeals. From that point, if statutes allow and the rules apply, a further appeal would go to the Florida Supreme Court.

## THE BOYS (AND GIRLS) CLUB

A fraternity exists in the legal world between judges (most of whom are lawyers) and the lawyers who practice before them. This part of the system is not usually spoken about; it could even be called America's underground justice system. Friendships may go back as far as law school or before, and this fraternity (with the support of the various bar associations) propagates a cartel in the legal system. (A local judge actually referred to my co-author as "one of the good ol' boys" during a conversation I had with him.) If you decide to appear pro se, you must realize that this good ol' boy (and girl) system exists and be prepared to deal with it. The system is maintained for a number of reasons. Lawyers negotiate with one another to bring about the most profitable solution to cases. This does not always hurt clients, but it sometimes deprives them of their day in court. It avoids or hampers malpractice suits—just try to find a lawyer willing to sue another "fellow" in the profession. It is used to make referrals and to collect referral fees (or forwarding fees), at the possible expense of the client. It may help lawyers receive certain protection from judges and vice versa. "Excusable neglect" is an example of a legal concept used to protect lawyers and litigants.

The judicial system itself may help foster the legal and economic power that lawyers (and the judiciary) wield in a community. For instance, courts may decree that certain basic legal functions, such as name changes and the like, may no longer be accomplished by a layperson, but must be accomplished by an attorney. Another favorite ruling in many states is that a nonlawyer may not represent a corporation or its shareholders (see Table 1.2).

If you are proceeding pro se, you must be especially careful to protect yourself from the club. You must function as professionally as possible, carefully document your position and/or case, and use all the tools at your disposal, including court reporters.

**Table 1.2**   States Where an Individual Can Represent a Corporation Pro Se

| State | Can an Individual Represent a Corporation? | Conditions | State Bar Association Telephone Number |
|---|---|---|---|
| Alabama | No | | (205) 269-1515 |
| Alaska | No | In small claims court by officer | (907) 465-3672 |
| Arizona | Yes | | (602) 252-4804 |
| Arkansas | No | | (501) 375-4605 |
| California | Yes | | (916) 561-8200 |
| Colorado | Yes | Depends on type of action corporation is taking | (303) 860-1112 |
| Connecticut | Yes | Only if shareholder | (205) 721-0025 |
| Delaware | Yes | In certain levels of court | (302) 658-5278 |
| District of Columbia | | | (202) 331-3883 |
| Florida | No | | (904) 561-5600 |
| Georgia | No | | (404) 527-8700 |
| Hawaii | No | | (808) 537-1868 |
| Idaho | No | | (208) 342-8958 |
| Illinois | No | | (815) 964-5152 |
| Indiana | | | (317) 639-5465 |
| Iowa | No | | (515) 243-3179 |
| Kansas | Yes | In small claims court | (913) 234-5696 |
| Kentucky | No | | (606) 781-1300 |
| Louisiana | No | | (504) 566-1600 |
| Maine | Yes | In small claims court | (207) 622-7523 |
| Maryland | No | | (301) 685-7878 |
| Massachusetts | No | | (617) 542-3602 |
| Michigan | | | (313) 961-6120 |
| Minnesota | | | (612) 333-1183 |
| Mississippi | No | | (601) 948-4471 |
| Missouri | No | | (314) 635-4128 |
| Montana | | | (406) 442-7660 |
| Nebraska | | | (402) 475-7091 |
| Nevada | Yes | Must be executive of corporation | (702) 382-0502 |

| State | Can an Individual Represent a Corporation? | Conditions | State Bar Association Telephone Number |
|-------|---------------------------------------------|------------|----------------------------------------|
| New Hampshire | | | (608) 224-6942 |
| New Jersey | | | (201) 249-5000 |
| New Mexico | | | (505) 842-6132 |
| New York | No | | (518) 463-3200 |
| North Carolina | Yes | | (919) 828-0561 |
| North Dakota | No | | (701) 255-1404 |
| Ohio | | | (614) 421-2121 |
| Oklahoma | Yes | Officer can represent corporation | (405) 524-2365 |
| Oregon | No | | (508) 620-0222 |
| Pennsylvania | No | | (717) 238-6715 |
| Rhode Island | No | | (401) 421-5740 |
| South Carolina | No | | (803) 799-6653 |
| South Dakota | No | | (605) 224-7554 |
| Tennessee | No | | (615) 383-7421 |
| Texas | No | | (512) 463-1463 |
| Utah | No | | (801) 531-9110 |
| Vermont | No | | (802) 223-2020 |
| Virginia | Yes | In small claims court | (804) 786-2061 |
| Washington | No | | (206) 448-0441 |
| West Virginia | Yes | In small claims court | (304) 346-8414 |
| Wisconsin | No | | (608) 257-3838 |
| Wyoming | No | | (307) 632-9061 |

I once sued an attorney in New Jersey for malpractice. The case had to do with a real estate purchase. The attorney, on my behalf, was supposed to hire an engineer to inspect the property, a 200-year-old dwelling, prior to the purchase. The engineer's work was slipshod, to say the least; he failed to find cracks in the foundation, a leaking and sagging roof, rotting beams, and more. The attorney also failed to protect me at the closing in the matters of the engineer's report, an escrow fund, and others.

I actually enjoyed serving papers on this attorney, a supposed pillar of the community. Unfortunately, I was not aware of the fraternity. The trial was held in a Morristown, New Jersey courtroom. When I began my direct examination of the lawyer, to my total chagrin and consternation, he conducted a whispering session with the judge. The fraternity was holding a social right in the middle of my trial. Needless to say, I lost the case.

In retrospect, I should have requested a court reporter, who is not usually present in lower civil court. That, and an expert witness—a third-party professional—would have made the fraternity a little more penetrable and the outcome of my case may have been different.

# CHAPTER 2
# Point of Decision

*You have to know the rules. It's got nothing to do with your case being
right. It's got to do with the rules.*
                                        —Judge Paul M. Marko, III

The decision to go pro se should not be made lightly. Under certain
conditions, such as criminal proceedings or appellate level matters, you
should not even consider handling your own case. However, some legal
situations dictate a pro se appearance; others may provide the opportunity to
participate in the system without a lawyer; and still others allow, or require,
your participation on a temporary basis.

The first questions you should ask yourself are, "What can I lose?" and
"Can I afford the loss?" If after serious consideration your answers are "a lot"
and "no," then get yourself the services of a competent lawyer. If your answers
are "not that much" and "yes," then you can consider your case a candidate
for a pro se appearance. Just be sure your decision is based on sound business
practice and not on anger.

One of the lessons I've learned in more than thirty years as a businessman
and after many legal involvements is what I call the first blush—that is, the
anger and emotional involvement that sends the adrenaline racing and goads
you into action—can involve you in needless (and costly) legal and/or judicial
entanglement. Deliberate carefully before taking action, with or without a
lawyer. Let your first blush cool before deciding to file.

Here's a case in point. Pennsylvania used to have a lower judiciary run by
aldermen and constables, permitting some interesting judicial manipulations.
At the time, I was producing the records of Harold Betters, a jazz trombonist
from Pittsburgh. ("Do Anything You Wanna" was number 74 on *Billboard*'s

Pop 100 in 1962.) Nightly, Betters was packing The Encore, a jazz club. The club's management was not thrilled with my success in having Betters perform on The Mike Douglas Show and other out-of-town venues. This attitude was reflected by the actions of Art, the ex-boxer and bouncer who controlled the doorway of the overflowing club. One evening, at the height of my struggle to get Betters released from the club for out-of-town appearances, Art took the opportunity of my being wedged in the doorway by the crowd to plant his fist squarely in my ribs. In my first blush of anger, I went right to an alderman and signed an assault and battery complaint. As an ex-boxer, Art's use of his hands was considered "deadly force." He was in big-time trouble (although I had no idea of the extent). So Art, to protect himself, marched right down to his alderman and signed a criminal complaint for perjury against me. Check . . . checkmate! Now I had to post bond or be arrested, as Art had to do when my constable reached him. With no witnesses, and a complicated and potentially expensive case, we both dropped our complaints. That ended the legal involvement on the matter. A little deliberation on my part prior to signing the complaint would have saved me the time and expense of that no-win situation.

Of course, you don't have to sit fuming while you wait for your anger to subside. If you have even a small suspicion that a lawsuit may be the outcome of an event, then thorough and immediate documentation to establish and prove the facts is necessary. Use your adrenaline to gather evidence, file a police report, interview or find witnesses. If after the first blush is over no case is mandated, so be it—the work you did to prove the facts can be considered insurance. And if a case does ensue, you or your attorney will be pleased with the preparation you've already done.

After your first blush fades and you have carefully considered the ramifications, costs, and possible outcome of a lawsuit, if you still want to redress a wrong, by all means do it. As to whether to act pro se or to retain an attorney to champion your cause, you should understand when it is important to seek competent counsel. Here are some things to consider when deciding the propriety of appearing pro se.

## COMPLEXITY OF THE LEGAL ISSUES

Involvement in the legal system ranges from simple traffic violations to complex constitutional issues stemming from questions of state and federal law. Obviously, the issue's complexity must be reviewed before decisions regarding hiring a lawyer, what level of the court to use, and the specialty area of the law that may be involved can be made.

For instance, in a federal court case against the Broward County (Florida) Sheriff's Office, I encountered a very complex issue that, on the surface, seemed to be a simple matter. I was involved in multiple businesses, all sharing the same building. The premises contained the inventory of three different corporations and my personal property. One of my trade creditors had won a judgment against one of my corporations that had a similar name to the one that used the building. A sheriff arrived at the building and proceeded to execute on (seize) certain property that did not belong to the corporation named in the writ of execution. (This is a legal document giving someone the right to execute a judgment.) I decided to sue.

When the situation was examined by a competent lawyer, part of my case against the Sheriff's Office hinged on whether that office was funded by the state or by the county; if by the county, the sheriff would be exempted from prosecution under Florida law. It took many hours for my attorneys to research the complicated legal questions regarding liability before any consideration could be given to the facts of the case. This was definitely not a situation for pro se action.

## PROTECTING YOUR RIGHT TO USE A HIGHER COURT (OR ALTERNATE COURT SYSTEM)

Another issue in my case against the Broward County Sheriff's Office affected the rights of multiple corporations to utilize a higher court, in this instance a federal court.

Interestingly enough, in an early stage of the case, one of my attorneys, while litigating in state court, attached certain documents to a motion that was filed before the court. More than three years later, a federal judge for the Southern District of Florida ruled that the case before the federal court had already been decided by a state court, thus denying me the right to a hearing in federal court because of a principle of law known as *res judicata*. This principle states that once a matter is judicially decided, it is finally decided. By attaching the documents used in a separate but related state court action, the attorney had inadvertently created the circumstances that permitted the federal judge to deny a hearing in the higher court. In effect, the plaintiffs were deprived of their right to utilize a federal court because the original legal work was not carefully handled before the state court. With no eye toward the future, the attorney involved in the case innocently precluded my right of appeal.

This is an example of an area of law so complex that if you are thinking of pro se action, you should first consider whether you want to preserve your right to appeal. If the answer is "yes," you should engage a competent attorney to handle the case.

Another area of law that is so complex that it may require the services of a lawyer is using an alternative court system. Most states offer the right of appeal (see Chapter 17) based on possible errors by the trial court. If an appeal is taken, the case is moved from the court of original jurisdiction to the next highest court. It is sometimes possible to "jump" from one system to another (i.e., from state to federal or vice versa, depending on the matter at issue). This is not an appeal in the genuine sense. The process may resolve the issue, but you will have to file new paperwork in the alternate court system. Keep in mind that a federal issue must be present in a case to allow resolution in federal court, while the state courts can decide federal issues when resolution is sought at the state court level. (A state court faced with resolution of a federal issue may at its option direct that the federal issue be removed to a federal court.)

## COST VERSUS POTENTIAL OUTCOME

Here are two more questions to ask yourself before making the decision to proceed.pro se. How much would it cost me to hire a competent attorney to accomplish my goals? Can I afford to lose this case?

A potential litigant must weigh the possible loss to lifestyle, assets, and family due to the legal action. In many situations, you can avoid the cost of a lawyer altogether by acting pro se. That is, after all, the thesis of this book. However, if the potential loss will disrupt your life, then it is better to opt for safety and retain counsel. If you represent yourself and the decision goes against you, you may need to hire an attorney at a later date at an increased cost to solve a more complex problem.

Here are some danger signals in contracts that indicate you should hire an attorney:

- Clauses including attorneys' fees and costs.
- Clauses specifying venue or jurisdiction.
- Clauses that waive notice.
- Documents that have a waiver of trial by jury.
- Documents containing binding arbitration.
- Documents or contracts setting a limitation on damages.
- Provisions that set or tax costs to one or more of the parties.

## LEGAL SPECIALTIES

A question frequently asked by people thinking of acting pro se is, "Do I need some special knowledge (of the law) to navigate to a successful conclusion?" Some areas of the law are just too complicated (or there may be too much at stake) for you to act on your own behalf. Form books are available for most matters and for most jurisdictions (see Chapter 3); however, there is no substitute for longstanding practice in such highly specialized areas as the following:

- Wills (other than the most basic ones).
- Trusts.
- Letters of credit.
- Real estate transactions and deeds.
- Adoptions.
- Bankruptcy (corporate).

## PAST THE POINT OF NO RETURN

Your legal needs may progress beyond self-representation. When that happens, the skills and experience of a competent lawyer are needed; in fact, a team of lawyers may be needed. For instance, garnishment of your property and/or wages and seizure of your property are matters that require the immediate attention of an attorney. (See Choosing an Attorney, page 26, for pointers on securing competent professional counsel.) However, as discussed earlier, an individual working in concert with an attorney can often accomplish what the lawyer alone cannot. Again, the rule of thumb should be to analyze the situation in the light of the risks and make the decision regarding representing yourself based on whether you can afford to lose the case.

## COURT COSTS

Costs will vary from community to community, and may be based on the size of the claim and the level of court the suit is brought in. Also, the ongoing legal process can get expensive, especially if discovery is involved (see Chapter 7). Service of subpoenas, witness fees (if applicable), and court reporters can make litigation an expensive hobby. If you decide to have a deposition transcribed, for instance, it may cost two to four dollars a page. Transcription alone can add hundreds of dollars to your costs, which, of

# Choosing an Attorney

*If you decide not to pursue your case pro se, you will have to select an attorney. The process of finding a suitable attorney should take a few weeks. If your legal situation is urgent, you'll need to find competent counsel much faster. See Chapter 5, "Stopping the Clock," for strategies you can use to gain time to find representation. If you cannot get enough time, you will have to accelerate your search by placing fewer candidates on your list, conducting interviews over the phone, and/or relying on the recommendation of someone whose judgment you trust. Another alternative is to ask a lawyer to handle a response to an emergency situation, with the understanding that you will soon find substitute counsel to manage the rest of the case.*

*The material in this book will help you to work well effectively alongside whomever you choose to represent you. Although you will have the final word on any decisions, an experienced, professional attorney will have a major influence on your thinking. You will have to trust this person to lead you through areas of which you have little knowledge. It is vitally important that you have an attorney in whom you have great confidence.*

*How do you find an honorable, compassionate, competent hired gun? With so many lawyers to choose from, how can you keep from being overwhelmed? To begin, decide on the area of the law in which you need special expertise. Although any lawyer can research laws, statutes, and procedure in any specialty, hiring a person with practical experience in the specialty you need will save both time and money, and may give you an advantage over your adversary (who may not have that practical experience). Following are some areas that lawyers may specialize in:*

- *Admiralty (ships, pleasure craft, cargo, navigation).*
- *Appellate (state, federal).*
- *Bankruptcy.*
- *Copyright and patent (including trademark law).*
- *Corporate (business and finance).*
- *Estate planning (wills, trusts, probate).*
- *International (trade, finance, other matters relating to affairs that involve two different countries).*

- *Labor relations (management, employees).*
- *Litigation (the courtroom phase of a legal matter).*
- *Malpractice (this may overlap with personal injury).*
- *Personal injury (including worker's compensation).*
- *Real estate (including zoning, planning, construction).*
- *Securities (stock and bond issues, high finance).*
- *Tax (local, state, federal).*

*Once you have zeroed in on the specialty, compile a list of attorneys with the experience you need. Seek recommendations from people you trust. Ask family and friends, but make sure they know what they are talking about and that their experiences are similar to yours. If your company has in-house counsel, ask that person for recommendations; if your company uses outside legal help, find out that attorney's name and ask for some suggestions.*

*Most law libraries, and many public libraries, have a copy of Martindale Hubble, a huge tome that lists most lawyers by location and firm, and provides a short biography of each individual, including education and past employment. This book will even give you the names of corporate clients the attorney or firm has represented.*

*Another way to add to your list of possible attorneys is to call the state bar association referral service in the state where you need representation. The bar will gladly give you the names of lawyers who specialize in the area you need. Be aware, however, that this will not be a list of all the lawyers in the area, nor necessarily of the best ones, as the service only gives the names of those lawyers who have registered with it. However, it is probable that if you do call one of these lawyers, he or she will explore the merits of your case for a token fee.*

*When you have your list of candidates, you must interview your choices (or, at the very least, discuss your case over the phone with them). This will help you narrow your choices to the individual or firm that you judge to be best suited to represent you. Remember, the ultimate decision is yours alone, so evaluate each candidate carefully. The following are some suggested questions to use as you interview each lawyer on your list:*

1.  *What is your fee arrangement—contingency, hourly, or flat rate (a set fee for the entire job)?*

2.  *How are expenses handled under a contingency arrangement?*

3. *What expenses should I anticipate?*

4. *Will you send copies of correspondence and pleadings to me as a matter of course? (With the knowledge of the legal process you gain from this book, you will be able to protect your interests by essentially looking over your attorney's shoulder.)*

5. *What is your background? Have you handled other cases like mine? How many?*

6. *Will my case require expertise that you (or your firm) do not have? If so, will you agree to consult with someone who has that expertise? Who will pay for this? (Some lawyers are so well connected in the legal community that they can call on friends or even judges for off-the-cuff help and advice.)*

7. *If litigation is even a remote possibility, are you an experienced courtroom advocate? If not, how will litigation be handled? Who pays, and how much? Who is responsible for trial preparation? (Sometimes a lawyer who does not handle litigation will do the trial preparation and then call in a "star" for the courtroom presentation. This may benefit you, as you will pay less for the lengthier preparation than you would if the star handled the entire process.)*

8. *If court action of any type is possible, do you know the judge involved? (A past social, business, or professional relationship with the judge may give you an edge. Ethically speaking, this should not be a factor; realistically, it may be.)*

9. *If legal research is needed, do you have your own law library? Who will be responsible for the research, and what will it cost?*

*If you have the opportunity to visit the lawyers on your list, notice the appearance of each one's office. Check for a neat, organized operation, and for personnel who seem happy as well as professional.*

*Finally, compare the answers the candidates give you to winnow your list. If you must, depend on your gut feelings and any first impressions the candidates make. Although there is no absolute guarantee that this kind of shopping will ultimately lead to a satisfactory outcome, you will have done your best to provide yourself with adequate representation. You will also have laid the foundation for a strong, safe relationship with your attorney of choice.*

course, do not include any possible adverse judgment or the costs of documentation, investigation, or expert testimony.

If you've checked the danger signals, analyzed the risks, and are ready to deal with "the club" and all its inherent prejudices, then go pro se.

## HOW JUDGES VIEW PRO SE

I have interviewed a number of judges who spoke candidly about individuals who practice pro se law. The higher the court, the more concern judges express regarding the procedural tangle that can envelop a case before the merits are argued. Judge Miles Lord, the outspoken, crusading federal judge of Dalkon Shield lawsuit fame, is adamant in his stance:

> I have in my time as a federal judge not found any pro se appearance to be satisfactory . . . even among attorneys. . . . The attorneys one may choose may not even be able to accomplish a proper result. In my broad experience as United States Attorney, Attorney General for Minnesota, and United States Federal Judge, I still find areas of the law that I would not touch with a ten-foot pole because I . . . do not know all the intricacies of the procedures.

The issue of procedure seems to be of central concern to judges. Judge Marko of the Circuit Court of Broward County echoes Judge Lord's statements regarding procedure, but from a slightly different angle: "I don't like people getting themselves involved and losing a case they should really win because of a technicality." Judge Blanche Wahl, of the District Court of Maryland, voices a similar concern: "How can an individual, unless he has a do-it-yourself book that he's using as a guide, be informed in procedure? I don't think he can. . . ." In discussing the procedural problems facing individuals representing themselves, Judge Marko voiced an alternative for those who don't want or can't afford a lawyer:

> Okay, if you don't want to have a lawyer and you want to do it yourself, do it yourself. There's a law library . . . open to the public. . . . Go down to the law library and start studying the law, because you can study and you can be as well versed as that lawyer is; all you have to do is read it, because we read it. . . . There are books on how to handle a divorce, how to handle a personal injury case, they have books on it. You can sit down and read the book. . . . I suggest very strongly that you do that;

but don't come in here and ask me to be your lawyer, because I am not going to be your lawyer.

Judge Marko's statement brings up the question of how much help you, representing yourself, can expect to receive from the bench. Judge Robert C. Scott, also of the Circuit Court of Broward County, says, "I can't help . . . very much, I have to remain neutral. . . . I can't take sides, I'd become adversarial. I can't end up being their lawyer."

However, when it comes to jurisdictions dealing with smaller amounts of money, the attitude softens. In Judge Wahl's jurisdiction, the court provides you with a booklet explaining your rights and obligations and what you must prove in order to win. When asked her position on helping a litigant, Judge Wahl said:

> Well, I do try to help, for example . . . if the other side asks him a question that's improper, that's not relevant, . . . I'll say . . . "You don't have to answer that. If you had a lawyer [he] would object and I would sustain the objection." I don't know if other judges do [that]. . . . I do.

County Court Judge Barry Seltzer of Broward County recognizes a clear difference and a responsibility when it comes to a pro se litigant:

> At the trial, a pro se litigant is treated somewhat differently. The judge wears the hat not only of the finder of fact, but also of the attorney for both the plaintiff and the defendant and will make the inquiry through the direct examination of the witnesses. The [small claims] courts were started initially to give laypeople an opportunity to come into court without the benefit of counsel and be able to represent themselves on a claim in which the amount in dispute could not justify hiring an attorney.

Judge William H. Cannon of the Township of Clinton (Michigan), gives another perspective on helping a pro se litigant:

> Well, I think certainly everybody has the right to represent themselves and should be allowed to do so. The problem it creates, an enormous problem for the judge because if you get both parties acting pro se, then that's one thing, but when you get an attorney on one side and somebody acting pro se on the other side, that's when you really have a headache. . . .

Here, Judge Cannon's opinion merges with the others concerning the layperson's involvement in procedure:

> Because the pro se individual doesn't know the rules of evidence, they don't know the court rules, they are at such a disadvantage, even though they may have equity on their side or they may have a better case, the fact that they can't articulate and they are not familiar with the rules puts them at a distinct disadvantage. . . .

Interestingly, the judges interviewed seemed less concerned about some items we thought would be of utmost importance to them. Here is Judge Scott on the subject of dress in his courtroom:

> Lawyers are supposed to be properly attired. . . . I wouldn't tolerate a contemporary bikini, or men . . . with athletic-supporter bathing suits . . . but I don't demand that they come in here elegantly attired . . . I would expect him [a pro se individual] to be conformed to some decree of decorum.

Judge Seltzer, on the subject of dress and cultural background:

> I don't have any dress requirement. . . . Certainly somebody who came into court dressed neatly is testifying by way of his demeanor and appearance. Somebody who comes into court dressed in a sloppy manner is also sending a certain message, which, . . . like it or not [judges] are receiving. . . . Profanity's an arrest. I think it would be inappropriate for a judge to cut the person off because of the manner of his speech, so long as they were being respectful in their ways.

Judge Cannon, on the other hand, warns of potential bias regarding appearance: "I don't put a lot of stock into people's speech, or dress, or appearance. I try to avoid that because it's too easy to stereotype."

When it comes to the concept of whether a client (of an attorney) should be passive or active in legal proceedings, Judge Cannon says, "I think that if you had to choose one or the other, I would choose that the person should be a passive client." On the other hand, Judge Seltzer, at his level, sees a distinct advantage to having a knowledgeable layperson in his courtroom: "I think people who are familiar with the procedure can help facilitate a smoother trial . . . certainly helpful to the ultimate determination. . . ." But he takes a more neutral position on whether a client should be passive or active with his attorney: "I think the lawyer and the client should work that out themselves. . . . If you're not happy with the lawyer, fire him and get another one." (Judge Scott indicated that there are almost 4,000 attorneys in Broward County. That means one of every 300 people you meet in Broward County will be a lawyer.)

In discussing the active or passive role of a citizen in the workings of government, as opposed to a legal proceeding, United States Congressman (and former practicing attorney) Tom Bevill of Alabama said, "As far as I'm concerned the man on the street can come in [to Congress] and testify—that's where he can speak." And Bevill expressed, most eloquently, one of the basic goals of this book: "I think the more knowledgeable the client is, the easier he is to represent. . . . I would much prefer to represent a knowledgeable person, one who is familiar with the legal system."

Here is what the judges have to say about whether there is a fraternity between judges and the rest of the legal community:

Judge Scott: "I have no comment. . . . Whatever they're called [the fraternity] is what I guess they perceive it."

Judge Seltzer: "There is a certain professional bond between or amongst members of the legal profession and officers of the court and it goes beyond just attorneys and judges and includes court personnel, clerks, probation officers, and the rest. . . . There is nothing improper with that. In my court . . . the identity of the attorney is wholly irrelevant to the manner in which the trial will be conducted and the outcome determined."

Judge Cannon: "I would be the last one to say there isn't a fraternity, but I will be the first one to say that it is not impossible to rise above that and make objective judgments."

Judge Marko: ". . . birds of a feather flock together. I usually don't hang around with ex-convicts, drug dealers, or auto mechanics. My friends have gone to college, they are friends of mine from church or they're friends from a group. You know, you get to meet people in college, they're your friends. . . . So, yes I think you do have a tendency to be fraternalistic in that fashion. . . . If you came in pro se . . . I wouldn't treat you any differently than I would treat him [opposing counsel]."

# CHAPTER 3
# Using a Law Library

*The knowledge of the law is like a deep well, out of which each man draweth according to the strength of his understanding.*

—I. Coke

There are many things that seem intimidating when you encounter them for the first time without knowledge or training, and walking into a law library is right there at the top of the list. The average well-stocked legal library—repository of our society's rules and regulations, precedents, constitutions, and ordinances, all cross-referenced and indexed—contains 200,000 volumes. The somber bindings of thousands of volumes from floor to ceiling presents an imposing and, to some, threatening wall of knowledge that may seem impenetrable. However, in order to proceed pro se, you must be able to use a law library. And take heart; it's not as impenetrable as it looks if you understand a few essentials.

Once the key to this vast storehouse of legal knowledge is presented to you, "learning by doing" becomes easy. You will learn the extent of your rights in society. You will possess knowledge of any area of law; you may even become an expert. No longer will you be intimidated, because now you know the law and how to use it.

Here's a case in point. I sued Equifax/CBI, pro se, for publishing inaccurate information in my credit report. This report affected my ability to borrow the money I needed to buy inventory for my record label. On the day of the trial, my adversary's attorney handed me a copy of a motion for directed verdict in favor of his client. (A motion requests that the court make a ruling based upon facts or pleadings.)

After hearing my side of the case, the judge was ready to consider my opponent's motion. However, he gave me ten days to respond with a memorandum of law supporting my legal position and opposing the defendant's motion. (A memorandum of law is a written memorandum setting forth appropriate background, research, citations, and other authorities that support your position.) The need to prepare a legal memorandum presented me with a major dilemma: Should I hire an attorney, at substantial cost, to research and write the memorandum, or should I do it myself? I chose to bite the bullet and learn once and for all how to use a law library.

Not every case or involvement in the legal process requires you to use a law library. If you are acting pro se, however, the library is an important tool, for that is where any research you will need will be done. Many law firms have their own well-stocked libraries that can provide forms, local procedures, statutes, and at least some of the precedents or decisions available on any given matter. A lawyer's ability to provide almost instantly accurate legal information is his or her stock in trade. Virtually all of this information is available to you at no cost at any law library in your community.

Before describing the contents of a law library, it's vital to understand what the law is and what it is not. As described in Chapter 1, the legislature in every jurisdiction enacts laws, statutes, and ordinances on specific subjects that society has agreed to legislate through its elected representatives. However, not every subject or circumstance can be anticipated by the legislature. Your representatives do the best they can, leaving to the courts the job of interpreting their efforts and ferreting out any missing details.

So what we laypeople call "law" is really a combination of a statute (statutory law) and a court's interpretation (decisions and precedents). A law is not simply a statute directing or prohibiting an act, but may be viewed as an entire system of interpretation—of court decisions interacting with other court decisions, statutes, rules, and regulations. This all-important concept might be diagrammed this way:

$$\frac{\text{Statutes}}{\underset{\text{(practice)}}{\text{Common law}} + \underset{\text{(interpretations)}}{\text{Court decisions}}} = \text{Law}$$

For instance, the practice of a property owner leasing space, land, and buildings or apartments is well established in common law. To clarify and equitably regulate this practice for all parties concerned, the legislature of a jurisdiction enacts a set of statutes under the heading "landlord/tenant." Section 83.56 part (3) of the Florida statutes deals with the notice that must be given in case the tenant does not pay the rent and the landlord wants to evict the tenant. It states:

> If the tenant fails to pay rent when due and the default continues for three days, excluding Saturday, Sunday, and legal holidays, after delivery of written demand by the landlord for payment of the rent or possession of the premises, the landlord may terminate the rental agreement.

The question of when the clock starts ticking on the three-days' notice now legitimately arises. What is the effective delivery date—the time the notice is written? When it's dropped in the mailbox? When it's stamped as certified mail? When it's placed in the recipient's mailbox? When it's handed to the recipient by the letter carrier? Or when it's signed for by the recipient as certified mail? This issue might be critical. The statute does not address itself to this issue, hence the law as to when the three-day period begins must come from precedent, or decisions reached by a trial court and affirmed by higher courts. To find the law, it's necessary to find cases that address as closely as possible the situation between the landlord and the tenant. When a decision on a case has such a set of facts, it's called *on point*. A judge will attach greater weight to a case that is on point than to one that falls short, regardless of the eloquence of the presenter.

A lower court first looks to decisions of higher courts in its own district for guidance, and then to decisions from outside of its district. How does the court decide which out-of-district decision to use as a guideline? It will consider the age of the decision, the number of courts for and against a particular position, and the validity of the legal opinion as perceived by the instant court.

Remember that the statute plus the case law on the issue equals the law for a particular set of facts. Thus, for the landlord-tenant dispute, case law shows that "when a party to a civil action conducts service by mail, an additional five days must be added to the period of time designated for response or compliance" (*Investment and Income Realty v. Bentley*, App. 5 Dist., 480 S.2d 219 [1985]).

When you understand that the statute plus the case law equals the "law," you will see why you need to avail yourself of the vast amount of statutory and case law found within a law library. The statutes of any given jurisdiction may take up only a few shelves in a law library; the recorded decisions of cases from as early as 1789—indexed and printed and bound along with commentary—take up most of the rest of the space. As of the 1970s, 4.5

million decisions had been published, with approximately 40,000 more being added each year.

Now that you know its purpose, let's look at how to use a law library. Dissecting its contents will help eliminate the intimidation caused by the sheer mass of material. By looking at the library's breadth and depth, we can begin to provide a more manageable view of its contents.

As shown in Figure 3.1 the material in a typical law library may be divided into four sections: Federal law, state and territorial law, specialty areas of the law, and general reference. Let us consider each section in turn.

## FEDERAL LAW

As previously discussed, the authority for and limitations on the lawmaking powers of Congress come from the United States Constitution. Most law libraries have copies of the Constitution and annotated volumes of decisions that interpret its provisions, complete with references (citations) to cases that brought about those decisions. Next on the federal shelf are approximately fifty volumes of the United States Code, which contain statutes as enacted by Congress. These volumes are arranged by subject, and the subjects are listed alphabetically in an index.

Alongside the United States Code you will find an annotated version of the Code. It follows the unannotated version, uses the same numbering system, and includes comments and references to court cases that have interpreted the particular law or statute. The annotation includes a brief summary of the point of law. The entire set is indexed by subject.

By far, case law takes up the greatest amount of space in the federal section. The publication of federal court decisions falls into three categories: (1) United States Supreme Court; (2) United States Court of Appeals (13 Circuits); and United States District Courts (96 Districts). Because of the tremendous number of cases that have accumulated since about 1876, when reporting of cases began in the United States, it became necessary to create an organized system for recording the cases. One of the first systems used indexes, or digests as they are called in the language of the law. These list each case by subject and provide a brief synopsis of the facts and findings of the case. Thus, the United States Supreme Court Digest is a complete, indexed compilation of decisions of the United States Supreme Court, and the United States Court of Appeals Digest similarly indexes all the federal appellate court decisions.

The decisions themselves are printed in a set of volumes called reporters. The majority of decisions in federal cases are printed in an extremely large

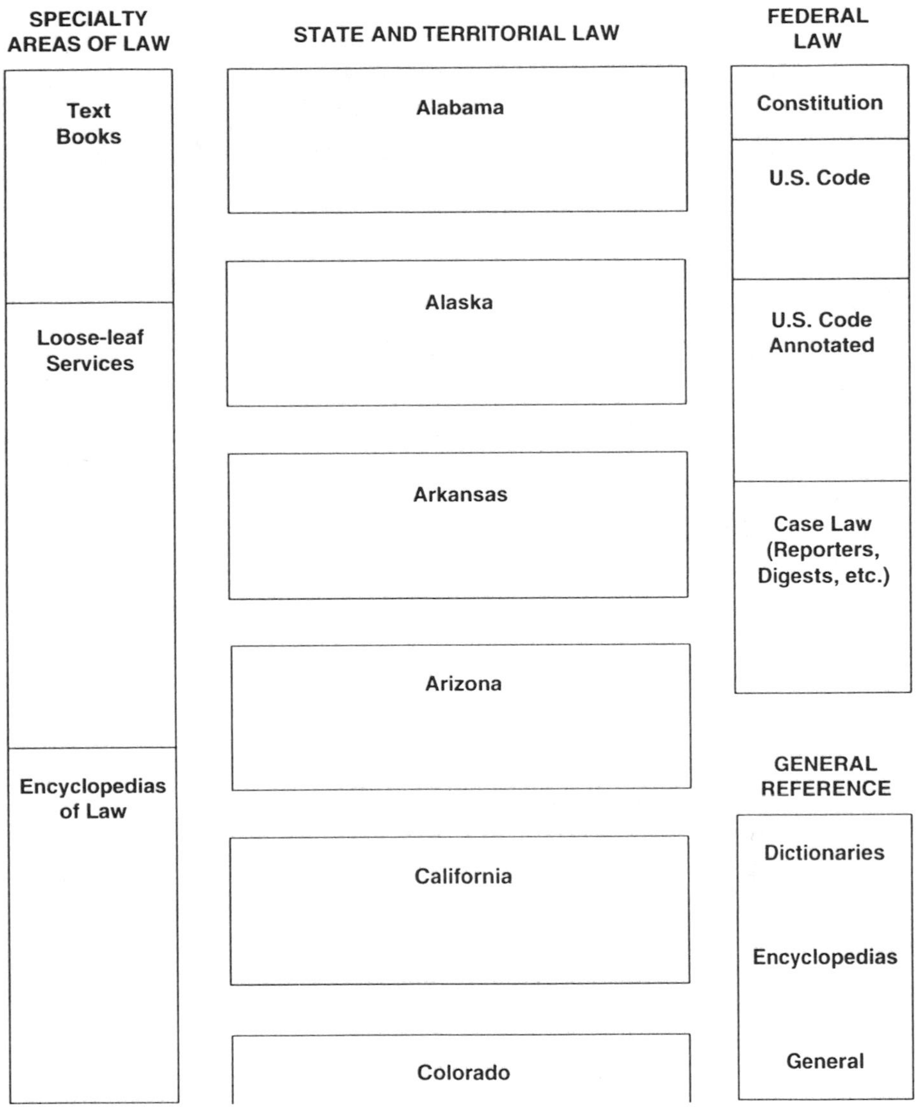

| SPECIALTY<br>AREAS OF LAW | STATE AND TERRITORIAL LAW | FEDERAL<br>LAW |
|---|---|---|
| Text<br>Books | Alabama | Constitution |
| | | U.S. Code |
| Loose-leaf<br>Services | Alaska | U.S. Code<br>Annotated |
| | Arkansas | Case Law<br>(Reporters,<br>Digests, etc.) |
| Encyclopedias<br>of Law | Arizona | |
| | | GENERAL<br>REFERENCE |
| | California | Dictionaries |
| | | Encyclopedias |
| | Colorado | General |

**Figure 3.1.** Diagram of a Typical Law Library.
Most law libraries are divided into four sections: Federal law; state and territorial law (in alphabetical order); specialty areas of law; and general reference.

**Table 3.1**   Reporting of Federal Court Cases

| Federal Reporter | Federal Supplement |
|---|---|
| U.S. Circuit Court | U.S. District Court |
| U.S. Commerce Court | U.S. Court of Claims |
| U.S. District Courts | U.S. Court of International Trade** |
| U.S. Court of Claims | Judicial Panel on Multi-District Litigation |
| U.S. Court of Appeals* | |
| U.S. Court of Customs and Patent Appeals | |
| U.S. Emergency Court of Appeals | |
| Temporary Emergency Court of Appeals | |

Effectively, the reporting of federal cases is contained in one continued set of volumes. However, there are different names assigned to the volumes for specific periods of time. *The Federal Reporter* picks up where a series called *Federal Cases* (St. Paul, MN: West Publishing, 1894) leaves off; and the *Federal Supplement* picks up where a series called Volume 60, Second Series (St. Paul, MN: West Publishing, 1924) leaves off.
*Formerly U.S. Circuit Court of Appeals.
**Formerly U.S. Customs Court.

set of books called *The Federal Reporter* (for appellate cases) and *The Federal Supplement* (for selected district court cases). Table 3.1 shows what types of cases and which courts' decisions are reported in these volumes.

Next comes the set of books that contain the rules of court practice, known as the *Federal Rules of Civil Procedure* (FRCP). When court decisions define and clarify issues involving civil procedure rules, these decisions are publish-ed in a set of reporters (originally in the *Federal Cases*). Since 1939, this set of books has been called *Federal Rules Decisions*. Many states have adopted all or part of these rules as their own court rules. It's interesting to note that portions of the FRCP will often be printed verbatim in the state's rules, and then the state's rules will go off in another direction, indicating the state's own interpretation and/or requirements on the subject.

Thus, the Constitution (authority), the Code (laws and statutes as enacted by Congress), the body of case law (decisions of the courts), and the courts' own rules and their interpretations are all found in the federal section of the law library. This complement of law books forms the basic tool for federal research.

There are, of course, additional useful volumes in the federal section. You will find that *Shepard's U.S. Citations* and *Shepard's Federal Citations* are extremely important to your legal research. (Their use is explained in the discussion of the volumes on state law in the library.) In addition to the Shepard volumes, the federal section will contain much of the following:

- Code of Federal Regulations.
- Federal Register.
- Bankruptcy Reporter.
- Bankruptcy Digest.
- Military Justice Reporter.
- Opinions of the Attorney General.

The following more specialized volumes will also generally be found in this section of the library:

- Civil Aeronautics Board Reports.
- Interstate Commerce Commission Decisions.
- Federal Trade Commission Decisions.
- Federal Communications Commission Decisions.
- Federal Power Commission Decisions.
- United States Maritime Commission Reports.
- National Labor Relations Board Decisions.
- Merit System Protection Board Decisions.
- Occupational Safety and Health Review Commission Decisions.
- Post Office Solicitor Opinions.
- Securities and Exchange Commission Decisions.
- Controller of the Treasury Decisions.
- Treasury Decisions.
- Immigration and Naturalization Administration Decisions.
- Department of Interior (Indian Affairs) Decisions.

## STATE AND TERRITORIAL LAW

The organization of the state section (which includes material for U.S. territories) parallels the basic organization of the federal section. The books are arranged in alphabetical order by state name, although the local state may be in a separate section.

In most law libraries, the inventory of material available for the home state far outstrips coverage of other states and territories. Using Florida as an example, here's what might be found in the home-state section of the library:

*The Constitution of the State of Florida.* Revised and amended, the constitution is published by the Florida Department of State and contains the constitution (indexed) without editorial comment or citations.

*Florida Statutes (laws).* These are published for each legislative session and are available from Florida's first General Assembly session in 1845 to the present, in their raw form, without commentary.

*Statutes Annotated.* The volumes of annotated statutes include the Florida Constitution with annotations and legal forms with comments. Here the laws and statutes are reprinted (using the same numbering system as in the statutes) with annotations. There are notes on court decisions with points of law indicated, historical notes, law review commentaries on the subject, and other references, where applicable. Appropriate case listings and citations are included for the points of law, each of which is printed as an individual paragraph. The citations provide case name and information so you may find the case that played an important role in the interpretation of the statute. The volumes of annotated statutes are indexed by subject to help you locate the appropriate section of the multivolume set of laws.

*Court Rules.* These are published for most states and usually cover, among other items:

- Evidence Code.
- Rules of Civil Procedure.
- Rules of Judicial Administration.
- Rules of Criminal Procedure.
- Worker's Compensation Rules of Procedure.
- Rules of Probate and Guardianship Procedure.
- Rules of Practice and Procedure for Traffic Courts.
- Small Claims Rules.
- Rules of Juvenile Procedure.
- Rules of Appellate Procedure.

The court rule book is the bible of every practicing attorney and judge, for it describes the day-to-day conduct of the business of most court systems. If you are acting pro se, it gives you the ability to act in a professional manner.

*Case Law.* The actual court decisions including an editorial comment are provided in bound reporters. Each case is shown with a heading including the plaintiff's name, case number, court name, and date. The editorial notes are divided into paragraphs relating to the points of law covered in the particular decision, and each specific point of law is assigned (in West Publishing's system of indexing and cross-referencing legal decisions) a "key number." This key number can be used to locate identical points of law in other cases. In addition to the key number, each point of law is numbered and coincides with the same number placed in the body of the decision as a reference. This makes it possible to read the synopsis on the point of law and then quickly locate the specific words the court used regarding that point of law, eliminating the need to read the entire decision to find the court's opinion on a specific point.

West Publishing puts out continuous volumes of reporters, which are geographically divided as follows:

- *The Atlantic Reporter*, which covers Connecticut, Delaware, Maine, Maryland, New Hampshire, New Jersey, Pennsylvania, and Rhode Island.
- *The California Reporter*.
- *New York State Reporter*.
- *The Northeast Reporter*, which covers Illinois, Indiana, Massachusetts, New York, and Ohio.
- *The Northwest Reporter*, which covers Iowa, Michigan, Minnesota, Nebraska, North Dakota, South Dakota, and Wisconsin.
- *The Pacific Reporter*, which covers Alaska, Arizona, California, Colorado, Hawaii, Idaho, Kansas, Nevada, New Mexico, Oklahoma, Oregon, Utah, Washington, and Wyoming.
- *The Southern Reporter*, which covers Alabama, Florida, Louisiana, and Mississippi.
- *The Southwestern Reporter*, which covers Arkansas, Kentucky, Missouri, Tennessee, and Texas.

*Digests.* These books provide a gigantic index describing, by subject, court cases that have been appealed. The digest itself is cross-referenced with a descriptive word index and a table of cases listing the plaintiff and defendant in all cases contained in the digest. To better understand the workings of the digest, let's look at a typical listing (see Figure 3.2).

Under the subject "landlord and tenant" and heading "premises and enjoyment and use thereof," is the topic or subheading "right of entry and possession of tenant." Under that subheading, the digest describes a case that might

specified right of way was not free from ambiguity, intent of parties was paramount consideration in determining whether words granting easement referred to width of way or were merely descriptive of property over which tenant might have way reasonably necessary to effectuate purpose of grant, and such intent would be ascertained by reference to surrounding circumstances.
Robinson v. Feltus, 68 So.2d 815.

☜124(3)-125.  *For other cases see earlier editions of this digest and the decennial digests.*

Library references
C.J.S. Landlord and Tenant.

☜125. Tenantable condition of premises.

Library references
C.J.S. Landlord and Tenant § 303 et seq.

☜125(1). In general.
Fla.App. 1981.  There was no implied warranty on part of lessor that demised premises were safe or reasonably fit for occupation.
Alvarez v. DeAguirre, 395 So.2d 213.

Lessees could not bring on theory of breach of implied warranty, action against lessor owner for fire that started in electrical box behind kitchen stove allegedly due to faulty circuit breaker which caused overload.
Alvarez v. DeAguirre, 395 So.2d 213.

☜125(2). Suitability of premises for the purpose for which they were leased.
Fla.App. 1980.  Where mobile home was not readily transportable and was on blocks with wheels removed, intent of parties was to rent mobile home and slab for use as residence for period of indefinite duration, and mobile home was sufficiently affixed to ground with proper sewer and plumbing connections, mobile home was "real property," and not chattel, for purposes of determining whether landlord could be held liable for breach of an implied warranty that mobile home was fit for specific purpose.
Solomon v. Gentry, 388 So.2d 52.

Landlord is not liable to tenant for breach of implied warranty of fitness for specific purpose based on fire which broke out in mobile home and destroyed entire contents of home.
Solomon v. Gentry, 388 So.2d 52.

(B) POSSESSION, ENJOYMENT, AND USE.

☜126. Duty of tenant to take possession.
Library references
C.J.S. Landlord and Tenant § 307.

Bkrtcy.Fla. 1982.  Where it was undisputed that premises were occupied and operated by wholly owned corporate shell created by debtor in Texas as convenience to satisfy legal requirement in that state, corporation name was trade name of all debtor's restaurants, funds and personnel involved in operation and all management control were provided by debtor, and landlord made no effort to dispossess corporation as interloper, debtor, and not third party, occupied premises in question.
In re Interstate Restaurant Systems, Inc., 26 B.R. 298.

☜127. Right of entry and possession of tenant.
Library references
C.J.S. Landlord and Tenant §§ 308, 309, 313.

Fla. 1942.  Where broker pursuant to authority given by plaintiff leased plaintiff's residence to defendant on conditions stipulated by plaintiff, and put defendant in possession with aid of a key made by a locksmith when plaintiff's friend with whom he left key refused to deliver it to broker, defendant was not guilty of an "unlawful entry" on which plaintiff could maintain action for unlawful entry.  F.S.A. § 82.01.
Caplan v. Burns, 6 So.2d 8, 149 Fla. 429.

Fla.App. 1979.  Lessor may retain an interest in leased realty sufficient to permit releasing of the same property on a nonexclusive basis.
Century Village, Inc. v. Wellington, E, F, K, L, H, J, M, and G Condominium Ass'n, 370 So.2d 1244.

☜128-129(1).  *For other cases see earlier editions of this digest and the decennial digests.*

Library references
C.J.S. Landlord and Tenant.

☜129. Actions for failure to deliver possession.
Library references
C.J.S. Landlord and Tenant §§ 314, 315.

**Figure 3.2.** Sample Digest Listing.
Digests list cases, by subject matter, that have been appealed. Looking under the subject "landlord and tenant," you would find the subheading "right of entry and possession of tenant," and information referring you to the case of Caplan v. Burns.

West Publishing Company materials reprinted with the permission of West Publishing Company.

have set a precedent on the subject of the listing (see inset, page 44). Cases may be similar, on point, relevant, or just helpful.

By finding the subject in its narrowest form possible in the digest, you can begin your research by reading the cases cited there. This listing opens the door to a particular research corridor because all cases brought before the higher courts on appeal cite cases with precedents that they believe are in their favor and contain facts as close as possible to the case being argued. Reviewing these cases will lead on to the next legal theory citing still more cases, and so on, all of which form the body of law on that particular subject. By following this line and not getting sidetracked by cases only marginally similar to yours, you should reach a conclusion; that is, you should accumulate a set of decisions that either proves or disproves your legal point.

*Encyclopedia.* This is a good place for you to start. A legal encyclopedia is similar to a digest except that it treats the subject as it might be treated in an entry in a general encyclopedia. It provides information, historical background, cases, and editorial comment on a particular subject of law.

*Shepard's Citations.* If you do any work in a law library at all, you will very quickly learn the name *Shepard*. This is a system of indexing cases that cross-references all reported cases and all existing points of law within those cases. In other words, Shepard's will provide the informational link between a case you are reviewing and other cases that have been cited by it or have some relevancy to it. Once you are familiar with the numbering system in a typical Shepard book, you will be able to trace forward the history of a case and similar cases up to the present through the entire court system. This is particularly important when you find a decision that supports your contention. Before you quote it in a memorandum of law, "shepardize" the case to be sure that it was not modified or overturned at a later date.

*Forms.* Books and sets of forms for a given jurisdiction provide standard pleadings, practice, and specialized forms for use in that jurisdiction. Form books can be extremely important to you when operating pro se. They may provide the outline of standard and accepted pleadings on hundreds of subjects, giving you an accepted plan of action to follow.

There are several other categories of books in the home-state section worth pointing out:

- Opinions of the Attorney General.
- Legislative history.
- Miscellaneous texts.
- Bar support publications.

🔑 127

🔑 **127. Right of Entry and Possession of Tenant.**

*Did you know that under Florida law if you lease a residence from a broker, who had the authority from the owner to make the deal (on conditions stipulated by the owner) and you had to break in or get a locksmith to let you in because the owner and/or broker could not or did not supply you with a key, you would not be guilty of unlawful entry? (See Figure 3.2.)*

*F.S.A. §82.01—Caplan v. Burns, 6 S.2d 8, 149 Fla. 429.*

*"F.S.A." stands for Florida Statutes Annotated; "§82.01" means Section 82.01 of the Florida Statutes; the name of the plaintiff (Caplan) and defendant (Burns) appear; "6 S.2d 8" is Volume 6 of the Southern Reporter, 2nd series, page 8; and "149 Fla. 429" refers to Volume 149 of the Florida Reporter, page 429.*

*The key number at the heading refers to the subject and is assigned by the editor of the volume. This number will refer to all other references in the entire digest to the same point of law.*

- Special legal topics (from corporate law to environmental regulations).

This area of the state section may also have continuing education materials from the bar association for the state's bar members and hundreds of specialized publications on very narrow subjects of state law. They are certainly worth reviewing if you're dealing with one of those narrow specialties of the law such as probate, juvenile, divorce, real estate, and worker's compensation.

The state section will obviously have a much fuller complement of law books on hand for the home state than for other states. Here's a typical listing of the volumes contained in a Florida library pertaining to New Jersey:

- New Jersey Constitution.
- *New Jersey Statutes Annotated* (including the Constitution).
- *New Jersey Court Rules* (with case synopses).

- *New Jersey Superior Court Reports*, which includes Appellate Division and Chancery Division (similar to equity).
- *New Jersey Law Digest.*
- *Shepard's New Jersey Citations.*
- The appropriate regional reporter (some libraries put all regional reporters in a separate section).

While this complement of books may be smaller than that for the home state, the basic tools are certainly available for research and case preparation.

## Pocket Parts

It is impossible for any publisher to bring out bound volumes, indexed and digested as we've described, without a lengthy editorial process. Therefore, the hardbound books on the shelves of the library are updated with softcover "pocket parts" (or even looseleaf pages) that are tucked away in the back of the hardcover volumes and updated periodically until new hardcover versions are available. *It is essential* for you to check these pocket parts for the most current information when working with a given set of law books. When I've hit a stone wall and can't find the case I'm looking for, it usually means that I haven't checked the pocket part for that particular case or subject heading. More often than not, that is where I find the missing item.

## SPECIALTY AREAS OF THE LAW

Referring back to Figure 3.1, you'll notice the specialty section of our prototype library. This section contains textbooks, looseleaf services, and general and specific books on various subjects of the law. You will find in this section legal specialties, such as tax law, probate, dissolution of marriage, and hundreds of others, along with legal books provided in looseleaf fashion that can be updated on a weekly or monthly basis.

## GENERAL REFERENCE

The general reference section in our prototype library contains standard dictionaries and general encyclopedias, as well as such books as *Gray's Anatomy* and other reference books that you might find useful or necessary when working on a case. If you are acting pro se, you will find this section of particular value when it comes to learning about some of the unfamiliar terms used in various areas of law and life in which you might suddenly find yourself.

**1** Begin in the *Digest's* index. Look up the general subject you are interested in, in this case, damages.

**2** Under damages, find the specific situation that applies (benefits incident to injury), and locate the key number (60).

# DAMAGES

References are to Digest Topics and Key Numbers

DAMAGES—Cont'd
MITIGATION—Cont'd
Benefits incident to injury. Damag 60
Breach of contract. Damag 62(4)
   For sale of goods. Sales 384(7), 418(7)
Breach of contract for sale of goods. Sales 384(7), 418(7)
Death actions. Death 91
Discharged fireman. Damag 62(1)
Dishonor of check—
   Payee's duty. Damag 62(1)
Duty of person injured to prevent or reduce. Damag 62(1–4)
Duty to prevent or reduce damage—
   Generally. Damag 62(1)
   Breach of contract. Damag 62(4)
     Buyer's duty to purchase similar property elsewhere. Sales 418(7)
     Seller's duty to resell goods. Sales 384(7)
   Discharged servant's duty to seek other employment. Mast & S 42

DA
OFF
  Ir
  P
OIL
OU1

PAI

PA\
PE(
PE(
PE(
  Ir
  N
PEﾄ

PEF
PEF
PH\

**3** Go to the *Digest* volume that contains the subject Damages.

**4** Under Damages, locate key number 60, and find the citation for the case.

# DAMAGES   ⬚⟿62(4)

ıld
its
ta-
ɪn,

ce
ch
ty,
en
aⶆ
in
of

ɲy
to
ill
ɛr-
ɪst
nt
ɪle
to
ⱨe
leɔ
il-
v.

West's F.S.A. § 768.76.—Measom v. Rainbow Connection Preschool, Inc., 568 So.2d 123.
   **Fla.App. 5 Dist. 1985.** Collateral source statute [West's F.S.A. § 627.7372] expressing policy of state that injured person may not recover from tort-feasor such amounts as injured party has received from collateral sources is constitutional. —Amica Mut. Ins. Co. v. Gifford, 473 So.2d 220.
   **Fla.App. 5 Dist. 1983.** Amica Mut. Ins. Co. v. Gifford, 434 So.2d 1015, appeal after remand 473 So.2d 220.

⬚⟿**60. Benefits incident to injury.**
   **Fla.App. 1 Dist. 1985.** Social security benefits and state retirement disability benefits to which plaintiff was entitled prior to injuries incurred in automobile accident, but which plaintiff first received following accident and which compensated plaintiff for damages not sustained or claimed in the accident, were not collateral to award of damages for injuries incurred in automobile accident, and thus, such benefits could not be deducted from damage award. West's F.S.A. § 627.7372. —Jenkins v. West, 463 So.2d 581.
   **Fla.App. 4 Dist. 1983.** Robert E. Owen & Asso-

**Figure 3.3.** Tracing a Decision

To find a case that may be relevant to your own, there are five steps you need to follow. They are detailed above and on the following page.

West Publishing Company materials reprinted with the permission of West Publishing Company.

> **5** The citation for the case tells you the statute involved (Florida statute 627.7372); the name of the case (Jenkins v. West); and where to find the decision (Volume 463 of the *Southern Reporter*, Second Series, page 581).

rce
ich
rty,
ven
ab
in
of

any
to
fill
ber-
ost
unt
ble
to
the
tle-
hil-

state that injured person may not recover from tort-feasor such amounts as injured party has received from collateral sources is constitutional. —Amica Mut. Ins. Co. v. Gifford, 473 So.2d 220.

**Fla.App. 5 Dist. 1983.** Amica Mut. Ins. Co. v. Gifford, 434 So.2d 1015, appeal after remand 473 So.2d 220.

**⬅60. Benefits incident to injury.**

**Fla.App. 1 Dist. 1985.** Social security benefits and state retirement disability benefits to which plaintiff was entitled prior to injuries incurred in automobile accident, but which plaintiff first received following accident and which compensated plaintiff for damages not sustained or claimed in the accident, were not collateral to award of damages for injuries incurred in automobile accident, and thus, such benefits could not be deducted from damage award. West's F.S.A. § 627.7372. —Jenkins v. West, 463 So.2d 581.

Case: Jenkins v. West
Volume 463
Southern Reporter
Second Series
Page 581
Florida Statute 627.7372

## USING THE LIBRARY

Before you attempt to use a law library, be aware of the relationship between some of the books we have just described. To show this relationship, we will research a hypothetical case. To do this, and with the permission of West Publishing, we have reprinted (with our own annotations) several sections taken from Florida law books.

Sally Jenkins was injured in an auto accident. Although liability was conceded by the defendant, the issue of damages was brought to trial. At the time of the accident, Sally was entitled to receive social security and disability benefits (totally unrelated to the accident that was the subject of the damage claim). In addition to Sally's claim, her husband, who had lost a degree of consortium (love and affection) from his wife, claimed compensation for that loss.

The case went to a jury trial and the judge erred in his treatment of Sally's benefit income. The Jenkinses appealed. The appellate court ruled in the Jenkinses' favor and established a precedent. The appellate judge, in his opinion, cites the trial judge's interpretation of the statute known as 627.7372, "Collateral Sources of Indemnity." If you were involved in a similar situation, this is how you would trace the decision and the law.

Looking at Figure 3.3, you can see that you would go to a *Digest* and look up the subject. Finding the key number, you would then go to the volume containing that section (the section on damages), and look for the key number.

Once you find the case and have reviewed the synopsis, if the facts seem to fit your situation, then review the statute (or statutes) that the case and the synopsis relied on. In this instance, you would turn to Statute 627.7372 in the *Annotated Statutes for the State of Florida* (see Figure 3.4).

To understand how the statute was applied and to review the details of the case that you are planning to cite in support of your own case, look at the actual record of the court case in the appropriate *Reporter* that was cited in the *Digest* and the *Annotated Statutes* (see Figure 3.5).

If you know the plaintiff's name, you can find a particular case in the *Digest* by simply looking up the name in the alphabetical listing. (See Figure 3.6.)

## SHEPARDIZING

In the practice of law, statutes, reported cases, court rules, opinions of the attorney general, and reported state court decisions are called "authorities." Examples of such authorities are the following:

- State and federal constitutions.
- State and federal statutes.
- State and federal reported cases.
- State and federal court rules.
- Municipal ordinances and charters.
- Opinions of the state and federal attorney generals.
- Certain federal administration decisions: Securities and Exchange Commission, Federal Administrative Regulations/Code of Federal Regulations.
- Federal labor law and administrative decisions.
- Patent, trademark, copyright citations and decisions.
- Treaties and other international agreements.
- Law reviews.

To make a legal case for your point of view by citing authorities, you must find authorities that deal with facts as closely related to your set of facts (the circumstances of your case) and in jurisdictions as close to your jurisdiction as possible. Then, using the correct method of citing the authority, the information can be quoted to make your point.

INSURANCE                                                    § 627.7372

627.7372.  Collateral sources of indemnity

*[See main volume for text of (1) and (2)]*

(3) Notwithstanding any other provision of this section, benefits received under Medicare or any other federal program providing for a federal government lien on the plaintiff's recovery, the Workers' Compensation Law or the Medicaid program of Title XIX of the Social Security Act,[1] or from any medical services program administered by the Department of Health and Rehabilitative Services shall not be considered a collateral source.

Amended by Laws 1986, c. 86–220, § 70, eff. Oct. 1, 1986; Laws 1989, c. 89–203, § 1, eff. Oct. 1, 1989.

[1] 42 U.S.C.A. § 1396 et seq.

### Historical and Statutory Notes

Laws 1985, c. 85–320, § 2, quoted the text of this section without making an amendment.

Laws 1986, c. 86–220, § 70, eff. Oct. 1, 1986, inserted in subsec. (3) "Medicaid program of Title XIX of the Social Security Act, or from any medical services program administered by the Department of Health and Rehabilitative Services".

Laws 1989, c. 89–203, § 1, eff. Oct. 1, 1989, in subsec. (3), provided that benefits received under Medicare or any other federal programs providing for federal government liens on plaintiff's recovery would not be considered a collateral source.

### Law Review Commentaries

Florida's new collateral source rule. William A. Kebler and Steven L. Robbins, 64 Fla.B.J. 25 (Dec.1990).

No Fault Systems. Josephine Y. King (Winter 1984) 4 Pace L.Rev. 297.

### Notes of Decisions

Compromise and settlement  6
Employee benefit plan  12
Future benefits  13
Insurance covering health, sickness, or income
    disability  2.5
Preemption  1.6
Products liability  9
Purpose  1.5
Recovery from tortfeasor  14
Ships and shipping  10
Social security  11
Subrogation right of insurer  7

42 F.S.A.—5
1992 P P

Wrongful death  8

_____

### 1.  Validity

In truck driver's action against tire manufacturer for breach of implied warranty of mer-

### 2.  Construction and application

Evidence of collateral source payments is allowed in motor vehicle injury cases only to establish set-off for damages awarded for same expenses under Florida law; thus, as long as plaintiffs do not seek recovery for expenses already covered by collateral source payments, evidence of those past payments is irrelevant to any issue before court. Shessel v. Murphy, C.A. 11 (Fla.)1991, 920 F.2d 784.

Under this section, evidence of disability payments to be received by personal injury plaintiff in future was not admissible. Shessel v. Murphy, C.A. 11 (Fla.)1991, 920 F.2d 784.

Defendant in personal injury suit arising from motor vehicle accident was properly precluded from introducing collateral source payments

Amount received by injured motorcyclist from insurers for past medical expenses could only be deducted against portion of verdict representing same item of damages, not against total verdict. Ganley v. U.S., C.A. 11 (Fla.)1989, 878 F.2d 1351.

Social security benefits and state retirement disability benefits to which plaintiff was entitled prior to injuries incurred in automobile accident, but which plaintiff first received following accident and which compensated plaintiff for damages not sustained or claimed in the accident, were not collateral to award of damages for injuries incurred in automobile accident, and thus, such benefits could not be deducted from damage award. Jenkins v. West, App. 1 Dist., 463 So.2d 581 (1985).

179

**Figure 3.4.**  Using an Annotated Statutes Volume.

Annotated Statutes volumes reprint statutes together with copies of relevant court decisions, law review commentaries, and other references. The case of Jenkins v. West is among a number of annotations given for Florida Statute 627.7372.

West Publishing Company materials reprinted with the permission of West Publishing Company.

JENKINS v. WEST                                    Fla.  **581**

Cite as 463 So.2d 581 (Fla.App. 1 Dist. 1985)

maintain life insurance for the benefit of his minor child.

Under the facts of this case and in light of the above authorities, we find that appellant is entitled to the insurance proceeds in question. The trial judge erred in refusing to impose a constructive trust as to those funds.

REVERSED.

WENTWORTH and THOMPSON, JJ., concur.

**Plaintiff** — Sally Clayton JENKINS, joined by her husband, Taylor Jenkins, Appellants,

v.

**Defendant** — Charles Ray WEST, Frances Elaine West, and Atlanta Casualty Company, Appellees.

**Case Number** — No. AX–405.

District Court of Appeal of Florida, First District.

**Court**

Feb. 19, 1985.

**Date of Opinion**

Wife brought action for injuries suffered in automobile accident, and husband sought damages for loss of consortium. Liability was conceded by defendant. The Circuit Court, Gulf County, N. Russell Bower, J., entered judgment on jury verdict awarding wife damages, and husband and wife appealed. The District Court of Appeal held that: (1) social security benefits and state retirement disability benefits to which wife was entitled prior to injuries incurred in automobile accident, but which wife first received following accident and which compensated wife for damages not sustained or claimed in the accident, were not collateral to award of damages for injuries incurred in automobile accident, and thus, such benefits could not be de-

ducted from damage award, and (2) husband was entitled to at least nominal damages, since husband offered substantial, undisputed evidence of loss of consortium, and since liability was conceded.

Reversed and remanded.

**1. Damages ⬥60**

Social security benefits and state retirement disability benefits to which plaintiff was entitled prior to injuries incurred in automobile accident, but which plaintiff first received following accident and which compensated plaintiff for damages not sustained or claimed in the accident, were not collateral to award of damages for injuries incurred in automobile accident, and thus, such benefits could not be deducted from damage award. West's F.S.A. § 627.7372.

**2. Damages ⬥11**

Husband, whose wife was injured in automobile accident, was entitled to at least nominal damages, since husband offered substantial, undisputed evidence of loss of consortium, and since liability was conceded.

Cecil G. Costin, Port St. Joe, for appellants.

Jack G. Williams of Bryant, Higby & Williams, Panama City, for appellees.

PER CURIAM.

On September 2, 1982, plaintiff Sally Jenkins was injured in an automobile accident for which defendant conceded liability. The issue of damages was tried to a jury. Loss of income, past or future, was not claimed.

Prior to this accident, plaintiff was under the care of an orthopedic surgeon for a previous disability. Her left kneecap was removed, and, pursuant to her doctor's advice, she retired from her employment. Plaintiff was totally disabled prior to the September 2, 1982 accident. Plaintiff began drawing social security in 1981 and applied for disability under the State retire-

**Figure 3.5.**   Using a Reporter.

Reporters provide the actual records of court cases. The record of Jenkins v. West, found on page 581 of Volume 463 of West's *Southern Reporter*, Second Series, allows you to review the details of the case. Reading the

ment program prior to the accident, but received her first payment in April of 1983, subsequent to the accident.

At trial, the court instructed the jury that any social security payments and State retirement program disability payments received by the plaintiff were collateral source payments which should be deducted from their overall verdict. The instruction was based on Section 627.7372, Florida Statutes (1981). We do not construe that statute to allow deduction for social security benefits and disability payments which preexisted the instant accident. Indeed, an interpretation which would allow such a deduction could render the statute subject to challenge on constitutional grounds.[1]

[1] We hold that social security benefits and state retirement disability benefits to which plaintiff is entitled prior to the instant injury which compensate plaintiff for damages not sustained or claimed in the instant injury, are not collateral to an award of damages for the instant injury. *See Transit Homes, Inc. v. Bellamy,* 671 S.W.2d 153 (Arkansas 1984).[2] The jury instruction was error; therefore, the award is reversed.

[2] As to the second point on appeal, we agree that the plaintiff Taylor Jenkins offered substantial, undisputed evidence of loss of consortium. *Hagens v. Hilston,* 388 So.2d 1379 (Fla. 2d DCA 1980); *Albritton v. State Farm Mutual Insurance Company,* 382 So.2d 1267 (Fla. 2d DCA 1980); *Webber v. Jordan,* 366 So.2d 51 (Fla. 2d DCA 1978); *Shaw v. Peterson,* 376 So.2d 433 (Fla. 1st DCA 1979). Therefore, since liability was conceded, he is entitled to at least nominal damages. A zero verdict cannot stand.

For the foregoing reasons, the case is reversed and cause remanded for a new

trial on all damages consistent with this opinion.

BOOTH and SHIVERS, JJ., and TILLMAN PEARSON (Ret.), Associate Judge, concur.

> Earlier court decision (precedent) the judges may have relied on. Precedent affirmed.

> This court's holding (the decision).

1. Constitutional vulnerability on this or any other ground is not at issue in this appeal.

2. In *Transit Homes, Inc. v. Bellamy,* 671 S.W.2d 153 at 160 (Ark.1984), the Arkansas Supreme Court explained:
   We do not think the court erred in allowing appellants credit for the $1,257 which the

record of the case, one finds that the appellate court reversed the lower court's decision, citing the precedent of *Transit Homes v. Bellamy.*

West Publishing Company materials reprinted with the permission of West Publishing Company.

Jenkins v. Wainwright, CA11 (Fla), 763
F2d 1390.—Crim Law 394.1(3); Jury
33(2.1); Witn 198(1), 372(1).
Jenkins v. Wainwright, CAFla, 488 F2d
136, cert den 94 SCt 2620, 417 US 917,
41 LEd2d 222.—Hab Corp 45.2(4).
Jenkins v. Wainwright, Fla, 322 So2d
477.—Courts 207.1, 475(1); Crim Law
1210(4); Hab Corp 44.
Jenkins v. Wainwright, Fla, 285 So2d
5.—Crim Law 1216(2).
Jenkins v. West, FlaApp 1 Dist, 463
So2d 581.—Damag 11, 60.
Jenkins v. Wilson, FlaApp, 397 So2d
773.—Work Comp 1565.
Jenkins, State ex rel., v. Maginnis, Fla-
App, 254 So2d 11. See State ex rel.
Jenkins v. Maginnis.
Jenkins Trucking, Inc. v. Emmons, Fla,
207 So2d 278.—App & E 483.

Jennings v. State, FlaApp, 106 So2d 99.
—Crim Law 518(1), 531(3).
Jennings v. State, FlaApp 2 Dist, 419
So2d 750.—Crim Law 394.4(3).
Jennings v. State, FlaApp 3 Dist, 457
So2d 587.—Crim Law 867.
Jennings v. Stewart, FlaApp, 308 So2d
611.—App & E 204(7).
Jennings v. U. S., CAFla, 391 F2d 512,
cert den 89 SCt 154, 393 US 868, 21
LEd2d 136.—Arrest 68(1); Crim Law
317, 412.1(2).
Jennings v. Wainwright, CAFla, 486
F2d 1041, cert den 94 SCt 2614, 417
US 913, 41 LEd2d 218.—Hab Corp 85.-
4(1).
Jennings Const. Corp. v. C. H. V. Inv.
Corp., FlaApp, 386 So2d 290.—Judges
32.
Jennings Const. Corp. v. Grossman

JEPSCO Bldg. M:
stwick Steel Lat
BR 122. See JEF
Inc. In re.
Jepsen v. Florida
Fla, 754 F2d 924.
46(12).
Jepsen v. Florida
Fla, 610 F2d 13
Fed Civ Proc 160
J. E. R. v. State, Fl
Infants 212.
Jerabek v. Heckler,
—Social S 140.20,
Jerabek v. U. S., C.
Embez 44(1).
Jergens v. C.I.R., U
US 784, 88 LEd
F2d 497.
Jergens v. Gallon

**Figure 3.6.** Using a Digest's Index

If you know the name of the plaintiff in a case in which you are interested, you can locate the Digest listing for the case by looking up the plaintiff's name in the alphabetical listing.

West Publishing Company materials reprinted with the permission of West Publishing Company.

The law, however, is fluid, with decisions and interpretations continually changing as new cases are brought before the courts. In order to be sure that the case or cases you have found are the current renditions of the law and reflective of the decisions being made, it is necessary to check the status of your research. (Cases may be reviewed and changed, affirmed, or reversed by higher courts.) *Shepard's Citations* is available for that task. The many volumes of *Shepard's Citations* contain tables of cases and references to when any activity on the same subject has taken place within the court systems. Using Shepard will permit you to shepardize, or review the current status of, your research (see Figure 3.7). These books are also useful for finding similar cases to the one you are shepardizing.

## How to Shepardize

1. Locate the correct set of *Shepard's Citations* for the type of authority you are working with: United States Supreme Court decisions, *Federal Reporter, Federal Supplements, Regional Reports*, or *State Decisions.*

2. Be sure you have the correct volume numbers, as many of Shepard's books have more than one volume: Statute volumes for statutes, case volumes for cases, and so on. Also, be sure you have the correct volume for the date of your case—more than one volume may be needed depending on the date of the authority you are shepardizing.

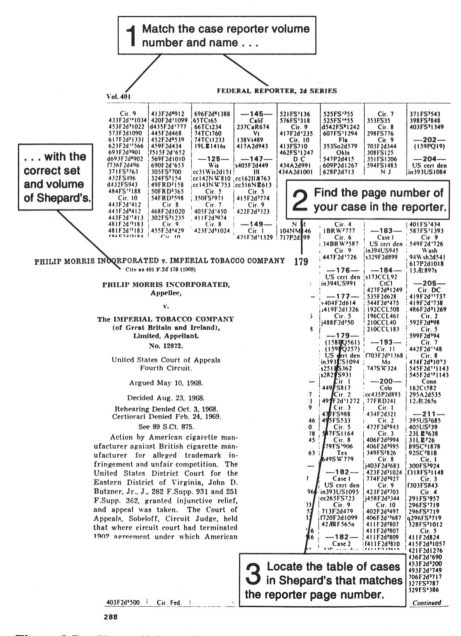

**Figure 3.7.** Shepardizing a Case.

To find out whether the decision you plan to cite was subsequently changed, affirmed, or reversed, follow the steps detailed above.

3. Use the correct table of citations. You must use the correct series (reports of cases are sometimes in several different series). If the case you are working with does not appear in the table, you might have the wrong series.

4. To conduct a thorough research job, you must shepardize in the tables for all parallel citations, as well as in the principal citation. For example, for *Wisconsin Reports, 2nd Series*, the parallel reporter is *Northwestern Reporter, 2nd Series* (Wisconsin Cases).

5. Once you have found the correct table of citations, look for the volume number you are sheparizing (see example).

6. Once you have found the correct volume(s) and the correct page(s) containing the volume number of the case reporter that has your case, find in the table the page number of your case. Then review the citations listed under it. Citations in parentheses indicate parallel cases. It's important to check the abbreviations listed in the front of each Shepard volume to completely understand the citations. For instance, raised letters refer to headnotes in the case you are reviewing, which means a particular point of law can be found in a case with the same headnote. When attempting to shepardize a particular point of law, this is exceedingly helpful.

The basic form for a citation contains the following information: the name of the case; published sources, if any; a notation that indicates the court; year or date of decision; subsequent history, if any.

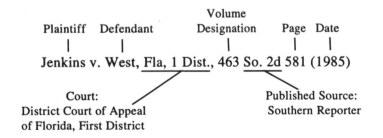

One important caveat: Courts may overrule parts of cases or entire cases. Don't rely totally on Shepard; instead, retrieve and read the authority cited. There are many nuances in the law that may or may not apply to your case, and cryptic numbered codes cannot transmit them.

# Some Common
# Legal Abbreviations

*Law books contain not only a vast amount of information, but a large and specialized collection of abbreviations as well. To do legal research effectively, you should become acquainted with some of the more commonly used abbreviations you will find.*

| | | | |
|---|---|---|---|
| Administrat(ive,ion) . . . . . . . . Admin. | Federal . . . . . . . . . . . . . F.,Fed |
| Appellate . . . . . . . . . . . . . . . . . . App. | House of Rep . . . . . . . . . H.R. |
| Associate . . . . . . . . . . . . . . . . Assoc. | Institute . . . . . . . . . . . . . Inst. |
| Association . . . . . . . . . . . . . . . Ass'n | International . . . . . . . . . . . Int'l |
| Board . . . . . . . . . . . . . . . . . . . . . . Bd. | Law Journal . . . . . . . . . . . L.J. |
| Circuit Court (state) . . . . . . . . . Cir.Ct. | Law Review . . . . . . . . . L.Rev. |
| Circuit Court of Appeals. . Cir.Ct.App. | Municipal . . . . . . . . . . . Mun. |
| Commission . . . . . . . . . . . . . Comm'n | North(ern) . . . . . . . . . . . . . N. |
| Commissioner . . . . . . . . . . . . Comm'r | Securit(y,ies) . . . . . . . . . . Sec. |
| Department. . . . . . . . . . . . . . . . Dep't | Senate . . . . . . . . . . . . . . . S. |
| District . . . . . . . . . . . . . . . . . . . Dist. | South(ern) . . . . . . . . . . . . S. |
| District Court (fed) . . . . . . . . . . . . D. | Statute(fed.) . . . . . . . . . U.S.C. |
| District Court (state) . . . . . . . . Dist. Ct. | West(ern). . . . . . . . . . . . . . W. |
| East(ern). . . . . . . . . . . . . . . . . . . . . E. | |

Examples of Published Sources
Supreme Court Reporter . . . . . . . S.Ct.
Federal Reporter . . . . . . . . . . . . . . F.2d
Federal Supplement. . . . . . . . F.Supp.

## COMPUTERIZED RESEARCH

The computer age has now impacted legal research. Two databases are available for legal research via computer: Lexis and West Law. Most large law firms subscribe to one or both of these electronic information systems, and some law libraries, particularly at universities, have access to them. Your research is greatly enhanced and streamlined with these services, although the cost is high.

## LEGAL HISTORY

Legal research is not just slogging through indexes and digests. You just might come across some fascinating stories. *Success in Court*, originally published in 1941, contains a collection of essays by nine prominent American trial lawyers. (See Chapter 19 for other books of interest.) One essay was by Frederic R. Coudert concerning international law. Coudert tells about an American, Mr. Underhill, who had a contract to operate the waterworks in a Venezuelan city. Faced with political upheaval in the country, Underhill prepared to abandon his contract and return to the United States. However, a Venezuelan general named Hernandez "gently impos[ed] the military hand upon him . . . insist[ing] that [Mr. Underhill] continue to operate, which he did for some time under the gentle persuasion." Shortly thereafter, Underhill returned to his native Brooklyn.

A few years later General Hernandez came to the United States in triumph. Observing that this "villain" was now in the country, Underhill obtained a writ from a New York State court and had the general arrested right in the middle of his ticker-tape parade and celebration, "in connection with false imprisonment, assault and battery." Unfortunately for Underhill, his charges did not stick, although the case did become an important precedent in American law. In *Underhill v. Hernandez* (168 U.S. 250) the court held that the general could not be tried: "the immunity of individuals from suits brought in foreign tribunals for acts done within their own states, in the exercise of governmental authority, whether as civil officers or as military commanders, must necessarily extend to the agents of governments. . . ."

As Coudert explains, "the case represents the settled law today on that subject. Underhill on the witness stand spoke of Hernandez as 'the Great Mogul.' On cross examination the phrase proved fatal, for the jury rightly concluded that Hernandez was acting as Government [agent], not as a mere individual."

The volumes of a law library have among them thousands of such interesting stories, many of which would put to shame the contrived stories of fiction writers.

# CHAPTER 4
# Proceeding Pro Se

*To resort to power one need not be violent, and to speak to conscience one need not be meek.*

—Barbara Deming

One of my first pro se cases was a suit against Sears, Roebuck & Company for what I believed was a breach of warranty. Wearing a suit and tie (not my usual attire in the music business) and clutching a legal-size manila file and a yellow legal pad, I assaulted the marble steps of the Somerset County, New Jersey courthouse. The building was one of those ornate structures with a large rotunda, with grand staircases and corridors leading off in almost every direction and courtrooms that seemed as though they were hidden chambers. As I entered the grand portal, I was totally confused, and I had a swarm of butterflies in my stomach. (Probably most citizens feel this way on their first contact with the judicial system.)

I was all set to execute an about-face and give up when an officer of the court approached me and asked in a soft but authoritative voice, "Counselor, may I help you?" That was just what I needed—I felt the officer was accepting me as one of the courthouse regulars. The butterflies settled a bit, and I felt a surge of self-confidence. With the court officer's directions to the small claims courtroom and a renewed sense of purpose, I was ready to present my case.

Having spent two years in drama school, I shouldn't have been surprised by the court officer's mistake. After all, I had the right costume (suit and tie), the right props (legal pad and folder), and the right setting (courthouse). Playing the part will help you increase your comfort level in this unfamiliar arena. A working knowledge of the judicial system will also contribute to your confidence. This book is designed to put you at ease with the system and its center—the courthouse.

In many jurisdictions, the courthouse is also the depository of public records that could be important to you at some point in your life. Most traditional courthouses contain the following offices:

- Courtrooms and judges' chambers.
- Court filing rooms.
- Court clerk's office.
- District attorney's office.
- Public defender's office.
- Land records.
- Probate.
- Property tax office.
- License bureaus.

Your best sources of information and help are the courthouse staff, the people who spend their lives administering the many departments, sections, bureaus, and courts. Don't be shy or vain about asking for help if you need it; on any critical matter, ask more than one source. This is very important, as there are so many details that must be handled and a bit of wrong information can jeopardize your rights in a matter. Depending on the size of the courthouse and the court clerk's office, there could be different individuals handling motion calendars, court dockets, appeal dockets, appeal filings, and the interim filings of the various pleadings. Wander through the courthouse finding which parties handle the various functions of the justice system.

## COURT CLERK

In Florida, the court clerk's office is the keeper of the paperwork monster. (The Broward County courts churn out over 55,000 new files each month.) In addition to collecting fines, fees, and forfeitures and seeing that documents are stored reliably, this office must assist the public in the proper filing of lawsuits and related documents. What the clerk's office must not do, according to Florida statutes, is provide legal advice to the layperson. Thus, the clerk's office staff (and this applies to such offices around the country) must walk a fine line between the duty to assist and the legal responsibility to refrain from giving legal advice.

The highly trained staff solves this dilemma by giving well-thought-out answers that can lead you to the right source or right procedure without crossing the delicate line between help and advice. In the Broward County Court Clerk's office, for instance, the deputy clerks will provide you with a set of small claims forms and even a list of the methods to collect a judgment if the claim is won. But the staff will not get involved in your decision as to whether to spend the nearly $100 in costs to file an action. The staff will help you prepare the documents for a collection effort, but you must choose the method of collection from a preprinted list. And so it goes throughout the court system—clerks assisting where possible and suggesting the use of attorneys when either a statute mandates it (such as probate) or a question requires advice instead of procedure. In the words of one Broward County deputy clerk, it becomes clear as to the kind of help you can expect from the typical courthouse personnel:

> By law and by statute we're just deputy clerks, clericals if you will. However, in the appeals division we'd be glad to furnish you a fill-in-the-blanks notice of appeal, we could certainly advise you of the filing fees, and get the thing [notice of appeal] filed for you and then we could refer you to the proper rule book and rule number in the law library to do research. . . . Any one of them welcome pro se individuals to do law research.

## CUSTOMS AND TRADITIONS/DRESS

When you appear in a courthouse pro se, think of yourself as a substitute attorney. Just as you would not expect to see a substitute teacher, bus driver, or police officer out of uniform, so do judges, court officers, and court personnel feel about how an individual appears in their presence. Therefore, never appear at court proceedings wearing anything other than a suit and tie for men, or a suit or conservative dress for women.

Learn the customs and traditions of court procedure. This will help eliminate much of the anxiety that you will feel as a stranger to the proceedings. Visit the courthouse before you are scheduled to appear and watch some of the proceedings. The human dramas played out daily are usually interesting and, by observing such things as procedures, formalities, and general decorum, you will become more comfortable in the court setting. If you have the opportunity to sit in on a procedure similar to the one you are contemplating, watch how the attorneys address the judge, the order of events, how the hearing is conducted, who starts the argument, how much argument the court allows, and what limitations appear to be imposed upon the arguing parties. You won't need permission to observe open court proceedings; however, if you want to observe hearings that might be in the judge's chambers, such as motion calendar or short hearings, speak to the judge's secretary or assistant and obtain advance permission.

Just as important as addressing the court in the correct verbal manner (see Stage Presence and Courtroom Style, page 61) is addressing the court (and other parties) in the correct written form. Many court documents will appear similar at first glance; only upon close examination do the differences become apparent. Court rules mandate paper size, and in some jurisdictions "bluebacks" are still used. These are preprinted backings or bindings for the documents being filed in a lawsuit or action. The case number and parties involved are typed on the blue paper in the space provided for that information; the actual documents are stapled inside.

## THE PUBLIC BUSINESS IS ALSO YOUR BUSINESS

Since court business is public, the files of other cases are usually open to all, and these case files can provide a ready source of form and style (descriptions of plaintiff and defendant) to use as examples. Reviewing cases in different stages of development can help you determine the proper format (and maybe some strategy) for any of the similar actions necessary in your case. Another source of information is the judge's secretary, particularly with questions relating to the judge's procedure and paperwork format. The court rule book will tell you the size of the paper you must use, the spacing requirements, the typing layout, and the borders required on documents to be filed with the court. (West Publishing Company publishes such books for thirty-seven of the fifty states.) However, you should ask someone these key questions:

1.  Where should the name of the court be placed on the paper?
2.  Where should the names of the plaintiff and defendant be placed?
3.  Where should the case number be placed?
4.  Is there any other identifying information that must be on the face of the pleading? Where should it be placed?

The top half of the first page of the pleading or court document is often referred to as the style of the case; this sets forth the names of the parties involved, the case number, and the name of the court in which the case has been filed. If you are involved in a divorce matter, looking through a few divorce files will provide information on format and procedure. If your subject is mortgage foreclosure, review mortgage foreclosure files.

# Stage Presence and Courtroom Style

As Art of Advocacy *(New York: Times Mirror Books, 1989)* states, *"The trial of a case may be described as a theatrical production: the artistic combination of the facts in consort with the law, highlighted by the back-drop—the scenery and props of the set. The end product is a moving, real drama that tells a story of truth and justice."*

*In any theatrical production, the player's stage presence—that unspoken combination of demeanor and mannerisms, that magical something that articulates the aura of being special—is important to capturing the audience's respect and attention.*

*In the theater of the courtroom, presence adds to the jurors' respect for you and indirectly benefits your case. Being comfortable in your environment, self-assurance, and belief in your case all contribute to presence. Here are some things you can do to increase your presence.*

- *Always be courteous—it signals your comfort.*
- *Stand when you are introduced to the jury.*
- *Always stand when you address the court.*
- *Stand when responding to the court, and use the words "Yes, your honor."*
- *Always demonstrate, by word and by deed, complete respect for the judge.*
- *Insist on your rights and the correctness of your position, but do it courteously.*
- *When addressing the jurors, always begin with, "May it please the court."*
- *Always begin any address to the court with "Your honor."*
- *Always end each exchange with the court with, "Thank you, your honor," even when a ruling goes against you. (Swallow hard.)*
- *Some courts require you to ask permission to move about (toward the jury, to the witness box, to an easel, etc.). Always say, "May I . . . your honor?"*
- *When requesting a sidebar conference, say, "May we approach the bench, your honor?" (You must request that the court reporter attend the sidebar if you want the discussion recorded. This may be important for an appeal.)*

- *Wait your turn. Bite your lip if you must, for interrupting conversation may turn people against you.*
- *Be the first to ask your witnesses not to nod "yes" or "no," but to speak up so the answer can be recorded by the court reporter.*
- *Be a professional at all times. Be neat and organized. Don't speak until you have decided what to say, and don't talk just to fill silence. Start questions with ideas, and don't stammer.*

*Presence cannot be acquired by watching movies or emulating courtroom "stars"; it must come from within. If you are uneasy about what will happen at your trial, you might benefit from talking to the deputy clerk assigned to your courtroom or judge. This person will certainly know the proper moves to make on the courtroom stage.*

## ASSIGNMENT OF CASE NUMBERS AND JUDGES

When a new suit is filed, the clerk usually stamps it with a sequential number. Each case is usually assigned to a judge randomly, using a "blind" system. This helps to assure that the judge assigned to your case will have been chosen by an impartial method. However, if you have reason to believe that the judge who will be hearing your case will not be impartial, you can file a motion requesting that the judge recuse himself (remove himself from the case). You can't do this on a whim: You must state why you believe the judge may be less than impartial. A judge may recuse herself if she becomes aware of the fact that she knows one or more of the parties involved, is affiliated in any way with someone who is involved in the case, or has a special interest in the outcome of the case.

## OTHER TIME AND RULE CONSIDERATIONS

The following are examples of some circumstances when time considerations may be important in determining strategy or compliance (again depending on jurisdiction):

- Does one judge handle a case from start to finish, or is the case split (hearings and motions by one judge, trial by another)?

- Time limit for filing initial response to the complaint.
- Time limit for response to notices for despositions and discovery.
- Strategy based on taking advantage of a particular rule.

An example of a strategy based on taking advantage of a rule would be, in Florida, if you propound certain discovery along with the initial summons and complaint, the rules allow forty-five days from the date of service for the reply. However, if your request is propounded at a later time, the required response time is only thirty days from the date of the request. Serving the discovery with your initial complaint creates greater initial pressure on your opponent and may result in winning points early in the game, even if your opponent has an extra fifteen days to reply.

In probate matters, there may be several time limits to consider. Some to check are the following:

- How soon after the death of an individual must the initial probate pleadings be filed?
- Are there time limits for filing documents such as inventory of property?
- Is there a time limit on placing a public notice in local papers?
- What are the time limits and procedures for handling claims of creditors?
- What is the overall time limit before needing a court extension of time?
- What tax questions must be addressed?
- Does the size of the estate determine the procedure, and what are the limits and guidelines?

*Always check the rules* for the motion you are contemplating. Many do not require a specific response time or, for that matter, any response at all. Many notices of hearing do not need to be delivered by a certain time prior to the hearing. However, if you receive a hearing notice less than five days before the hearing date, especially in a complex matter, and you are not prepared to be heard, you might seek court protection with regard to that hearing date. To accomplish this, you would move the court (make a motion) for a protective order; that is, ask that the court intervene and suspend the hearing until you have been given reasonable time to prepare.

It's not always necessary, however, to run to the court for protection—most of us still think this is a civilized world. More often than not, you can call the opposing attorney and say, "I have these problems with this hearing date." Notwithstanding the adversarial nature of the process, if your dealings with the other side have been reasonable, courtesy should be given, if possible, in changing the hearing date. This is especially true when no material loss will occur by waiting a few more days or weeks before that particular hearing. If the other party feels that a loss will occur, however, be prepared to ask the court to intervene.

All dates and time frames are important. However, there are certain situations in which you must take special care.

## SUMMARY JUDGMENT

A motion and notice of hearing involving a request for summary judgment is one such situation. (A summary judgment is a determination by the court that there is no question of fact or law to be decided in the case, therefore entitling one party to an immediate favorable finding.) For example, a minimum of twenty days' notice might be required by the rules prior to a summary judgment hearing. Say you file your notice of hearing along with the original motion, providing the required twenty days' notice, but you are either delayed in filing an appropriate affidavit or you later seek to amend or further supplement your original motion for summary judgment. You may then have to renotice the hearing, since you may have to provide at least twenty days' prior notice from the filing of all papers on which the motion for summary judgment relies.

## POST-TRIAL MOTIONS AND REQUESTS TO BE REHEARD

Many jurisdictions require that these motions be filed within a particular period of time; for example, within ten days following the rendering of an adverse judgment. If a motion to request a rehearing or a motion to set aside a judgment is timely filed, you must then determine whether or not that tolls (holds in abeyance) your time requirement in which to file an appeal (assuming you are contemplating such an appeal). The filing of a motion stops the clock until a ruling by the court is made. The clock then picks up after the court's ruling at the point where the tolling occurred.

Let's assume, for example, the time for filing an appeal is tolled and the judge rules against your motion at a later date. You must then determine what time is still available in which to file the appeal. Very often, appeals must be filed within ten, twenty, or thirty days following the final judgment.

## DIVISIONS OF THE COURT SYSTEM

Most court systems are divided into units representing the type of cases with which they deal. A typical breakdown within a state might be as follows:

1. Traffic Court.
2. Small Claims Court.
3. Lower Trial Court.
4. Upper Trial Court.
5. Family Court.
6. Criminal Court.
7. Probate Court.
8. Appeals Courts.
9. State Supreme Court.


## Traffic Court

This is probably the court that the most people know. Every minor traffic infraction; contested summons, license, or registration infraction; and other traffic or automobile violation passes before its judge. (A lawsuit involving damages that occurred as a result of a traffic accident will usually be heard in a higher court where appropriate money damages can be awarded.) The atmosphere is generally relaxed and the rules are on the informal side. Acting pro se in this arena can be beneficial, especially when the arresting officer doesn't show for your trial or can't remember the conditions on the day you were ticketed. Also, by studying the rule book and statutes, you may find a mistake, loophole, or piece of information that will give you a chance to win your case. One person I know did some research and found that the particular statute the officer cited concerned pedestrians. She explained this to the judge and won her case instantly.

I was once ticketed for driving through a yellow light that was turning red. I pled not guilty. On the day of the trial, I went to the scene and timed the length of the yellow light with a stopwatch. Then I went to several other intersections in the same area and timed the lights there. The light I went through seemed to be on the short side. (Yellow lights in Florida must be at least 4.5 seconds long, and the light in question was half a second under the standard.) When I presented my findings to the judge, he asked me one question: "Did you use a stopwatch?" I answered, "Yes, your honor," and he found me not guilty of the offense. He then actually thanked me for providing the information to the community, and indicated that he planned to reprimand the traffic department for their negligence. The lesson is that if you plan to act pro se in traffic court, as in any judicial process, know what you are talking about.

## Small Claims Court

Another court with relaxed rules and a user-friendly philosophy in most jurisdictions is the small claims court or its equivalent. This court provides access to the justice system for matters concerning amounts that range from under $1,000 to about $5,000. Many rules are either waived or shortcut; for example, extensive and often expensive discovery procedures are generally not allowed, except as requested by motion and approved by the judge. At its discretion, the court can allow the use of either part of or all of the rules of civil procedure.

## Lower Trial Court

Next in the court system is the lower trial court. Adhering to the rules of civil procedure, many of these courts have a monetary jurisdiction not exceeding $5,000, or $15,000. Matters are handled more expeditiously in this court than in its bigger cousin, the upper trial court. This court (in Florida at least) handles evictions, lower-level criminal cases (usually designated misdemeanors), and traffic matters that are beyond the scope of traffic court.

## Upper Trial Court

The upper trial court generally has a jurisdictional amount of $10,000 or $15,000 and up. This court usually also takes responsibility for equity cases. The court operates more formally than the lower trial court, and the full rules of civil procedure apply. Divisions of this court might handle family matters, upper-level criminal matters (felonies), and probate. Operating pro se in the upper trial court is certainly feasible, but exacting attention to the rules is a must; you should also expect less help from the judicial staff.

## Appeals Court

The structure and organization of the appellate courts is much more formal than in trial courts. Appellate courts operate with anywhere from a single judge to a panel of three or more. Cases are presented by filing a written brief or reply brief. Oral argument is permitted only when the court authorizes it and deems it beneficial to justice. (The appeals process is discussed in Chapter 17.) It is extremely difficult, though not impossible, for a pro se litigant to navigate the appellate system.

In general, each level or division of the various courts will have its own pace, flavor, attitude, and presence, which you must perceive and contemplate before venturing into the arena. For instance, divorce matters may fall into one of the trial courts or into family court, depending on the jurisdiction. Within any particular court there may be arbitrators, general masters, mediators, or the like assigned to certain types of cases, and/or particular judges handling certain matters. Again, each type of case is handled in its proper court division, and the documentation used may vary from division to division. One jurisdiction may require that financial affidavits be filed either with or shortly after the initial filing of a lawsuit for dissolution of marriage (and it is a lawsuit!), whereas others may not.

## COURTHOUSE SAVVY

Courthouse savvy is that edge which goes beyond knowing the rules and regulations, statutes and ordinances. The law, of course, is important, but knowing what's going on in the courtroom can place you ahead of the pack. Seeing the subtle nuances of activity taking place around you, and your own reactions to them, often gives you that edge. The following, which I call the "piano case," is an example of what can happen if you do not do this.

The trial was in full swing before a judge in downtown Pittsburgh. The plaintiffs: Two former partners and would-be music producers and their attorneys. The defendants: Myself as a corporate officer of Gateway Records, represented by our attorneys. Gateway was being sued by the partners for the price of a used Steinway baby grand piano.

Keep in mind that, under Pennsylvania rules, once a defendant admits indebtedness of any amount, it no longer makes any difference what the plaintiff has said, including a denial that the debt even existed—the case must be found in favor of the plaintiff.

The two would-be producers had just contradicted each other's testimony on the stand, substantially undermining their case. In fact, for all intents and purposes, the case was over. The plaintiff's lawyer, Popovitch, was standing in the back of the courtroom wishing he could disappear into the woodwork. The plaintiff rested, and my attorney, Stewart Barman, lawbook in hand, began to speak to the judge: "Your Honor, while we do admit some indebtedness...." The judge interrupted: "Counselor, would you first like to consult with your client?" My attorney continued, "Your Honor, we admit some indebtedness, but...." Again the judge interrupted, trying to save the day for the defendant whom, he had just learned, was a victim of the two squabbling partners: "Counselor, would it not be advisable to first speak to your client before continuing?" Now I was the one looking for a place to hide, while Popovitch moved forward with a grin from ear to ear.

My attorney, however, was deaf to the judge's broad hints. When he finally finished his dissertation, the judge said his piece: "I find in favor of the plaintiff; the law gives me no other choice." I paid the judgment for a piano I had already paid for in a trade for time and materials.

My attorney missed the partners' contradictory testimony. He also missed their attorney's reaction to the ruined case, and the not-so-subtle attempt by the judge to help him recognize what everyone else understood was happening. A little courtroom savvy might have saved a difficult judgment to pay.


## KNOW YOUR JUDGE

Over time, most attorneys come to know the judges with whom they deal. This gives the attorney an intangible edge. The attorney is addressing the judge on a more friendly basis than you will be when you act pro se. Notwithstanding the judge's fairness and impartiality, the intangible edge may still exist. Therefore, not only do you need to know the law, statutes, ordinances, and rules and procedures; not only must you develop a perception of what is going on around you; you should also learn about the judge (or arbitrators) assigned to your case. However, since in most jurisdictions you don't have the luxury of picking who your judge will be (you may have the opportunity of vetoing an arbitrator), how can you find out about the person who will hear your case?

Once you know who will be hearing the case, ask attorneys and court personnel about the judge—the pros do. What is the judge's reputation regarding promptness and appearance? If, for instance, the judge is a stickler for promptness, subtly make your promptness and any lack thereof on your opponent's part known to the judge. Be outspoken, courteous, and friendly. Initiate introductions of yourself and the parties with you, and say "good morning" or "good afternoon" to the judge. Every courtesy may affect the judge's basic attitude toward you. Don't come before the bench with a chip on your shoulder, as this attitude neither wins friends nor influences judges. If you have an axe to grind or are going to show that you can beat the system or the judge, you will probably wind up being shown the door.

Finally, remember the importance of the calendar. Study the rules and note on your own calendar the deadlines for each function of your case: Each filing deadline, hearing date, response time, discovery deadline, motion, and trial. Proceeding pro se makes you responsible to yourself and the parties with whom you are involved. You, after all, are in the role of attorney.

## COURT JURISDICTION

The subject of jurisdiction is a prerequisite to other topics of law. To anyone involved in litigation, and especially to those in business, the jurisdiction that a lawsuit is brought in is extremely important. First, the expense of defending (or prosecuting) a legal action away from one's home turf will double or triple the already high cost of legal activity. If the venue is away from your home, in another part of your state, or elsewhere in the country, then you may have to engage counsel in that area who would be familiar with the statutes and rules there. Mail, telephone, fax, and transportation costs must then be factored into every legal move, whereas such costs may be minimal or even part of your existing overhead when the action is local. Second, the venue chosen may provide the opposition with a court that has a history of sympathetic precedent, monetary and subject matter jurisdiction, and set of procedures that your opponent's counsel perceives to be beneficial to your opponent's case.

The practice of looking for an advantageous court in which to file a lawsuit is known as forum shopping. It is perfectly legal, save when the bounds of propriety are pushed out by the shopper and successfully challenged by the defendant. (If this happens, the plaintiff has to move the venue and bear the costs of doing so.) Here's an example of forum shopping on an international scale.

For over five years, my record company represented the BBC exclusively in the United States for the sale of records and cassettes, manufacturing here in the United States from the BBC's tapes and artwork. In addition to the specialty and folk recordings we deemed suitable for the American market, we released such titles as "Dr. Who," "Monty Python," "Fawlty Towers," and even themes from famous BBC-TV programming. The recordings were designed to follow closely the BBC television fare offered on many of America's PBS stations, providing a built-in vehicle to promote the recordings. In fact, we sold BBC records and cassettes to many stations for use as premiums in fund drives.

Being even a small part of the world's largest broadcasting and creative operation was prestigious. Our relationship with the BBC was wonderfully exciting and profitable. For instance, when the actor/comedian Peter Sellers died, it took only a telex to my counterpart in London to apprise the BBC of the fact that there was a market in America for the comedian's work on record and cassette. Shortly thereafter, we received tapes and photographs of Sellers' great performances, and used them to produce a memorial album.

Unfortunately, the relationship soured when politics changed in London, and our contract was not renewed. Warner Audio, the short-lived audio/book arm of Warner Brothers, had convinced the new management of BBC Records to provide them with the American rights. To use the vernacular, we were left holding the bag: Tens of thousands of dollars' worth of inventory, master tapes, hard work, and the like. After attempts to negotiate a solution, the BBC bureaucracy took exception to the way my company was phasing out the sale of their product and decided to sue for alleged copyright violations. They chose to do this in U.S. federal court, despite this statement in our contract: "This Agreement shall be construed and given effect to according to the Laws of England and the High Court of Justice in England shall be the Court of Jurisdiction."

The parties made their contract in Fort Lauderdale, Florida; the BBC had shipped merchandise there; BBC officials had visited and negotiated the agreement there; and BBC executives had even attended a yearly party in their honor there. Pursuant to the contract, the parties agreed to operate under the laws of England. Now the BBC, in its infinite wisdom, decided to use a New York law firm to sue a Florida company in New York. Since the action was a federal copyright matter, the BBC's legal counsel claimed that, since my corporation had some sales contacts and had contracted for manufacturing to be done on Long Island, New York, they could avail themselves of the federal district court in New York to file suit. (This court, incidentally, was convenient to the BBC's New York office and its New York attorney.)

About this matter, the United States Service Code (USCS) Section 1391(c) states:

> A corporation may be sued in any judicial district in which it is incorporated or licensed to do business or is doing business, and such judicial district shall be regarded as the residence of such corporation for venue purposes.

The key words *doing business* are ambiguous, and so permit venue shopping. Precedent is important in determining the legal definition of this phrase.

Two years after the case was filed, the jurisdictional question of whether the suit should be heard in New York or in Florida or even England was still before the New York court. The success of this particular instance of forum shopping may not be known for some time. As you can see, the interpretation of rules and statutes is an ongoing problem. You will have to sift through apparently contradictory rules at many stages of the game, especially if the matter concerns international commerce.

There are fifty-two judicial systems in the United States, including each state system, the federal system, and the system for Washington, D.C. In addition, laws and statutes promulgated by individual state legislatures may give you multiple choices as to which court to file a lawsuit. For instance,

Broward County has a main courthouse and three satellites around the county. There is substantial driving time between each location. You could choose any of the locations to file your suit, thereby bringing all parties involved to the particular part of the county that you deem is best for you.

So where should you file your lawsuit? If the case is of a federal nature, the final judgment will be recognized and enforced in all other federal jurisdictions without reexamination of the case's merits. In state matters, the Constitution requires that the several states give "full faith and credit" to the findings and judgments of the courts of other states. It may be necessary to "localize" a judgment from one jurisdiction to another, but this is generally a matter of procedure, and the defendant has little ability to alter the original court's findings. Any attack on the judgment is limited to that which could have been raised in the original proceedings; no new matter will be considered by the court that is contemplating the localization of the original judgment.

When you are deciding which of the fifty-two systems to file in, your choice might rest on something much more important than convenience or the preference of your lawyer. For example, limits on damage assessments vary from state to state, as does the propensity of certain higher courts to authorize certain formulas for the calculation of those damages. One successful instance of venue shopping concerned an accident that took place in Kansas on a machine made in Wisconsin (*Schruber v. Allis Chalmers Corp.*, 611 F.2d 790 [CA10, 1979]). Since the defendant was authorized to do business in Mississippi, the plaintiff got around the expired statutes of limitations in Kansas and Wisconsin by using Mississippi's six-year statute of limitations, which applied in the case as brought in federal court. On appeal, the appellate court ruled that the case should be tried in federal court in Kansas, but that Mississippi's six-year limit would apply.

The plaintiff is obviously in a better position to choose the forum than is the defendant. Robert Casad, in *Jurisdiction and Forum Selection* (Wilmette, IL: Callaghan, 1988) states, "It is often said that the plaintiff is given the right to choose from among the alternative courts that could hear the action as compensation for the fact that the plaintiff must bear the burden of proof." So the plaintiff chooses the ballpark, and if one court offers advantages that may help the plaintiff's case, so be it.

On the other hand, the defendant's choices are quite limited. If the defendant can establish that the court chosen by the plaintiff lacks proper jurisdiction, then the defendant may be able to have the action transferred to a more favorable court or even dismissed. Also, based on obligations placed on attorneys by the 1983 amendment to Rule 11 of the Federal Rules of Civil Procedure, "*Attorneys now have a special obligation to investigate the legal and factual support for every paper they file in connection with a lawsuit,* including those filed in choosing the court in which action is to proceed" (Casad, *Jurisdiction and Forum Selection*, Chapter 1, page 6; emphasis added). This helps to prevent frivolous lawsuits.

One other remedy that a defendant may be able to use is the doctrine of *forum non conveniens*, in which the chosen court is found to be legally "incorrect" because witnesses, evidence, and parties are located primarily in another jurisdiction. However, the defendant will have to demonstrate to the court the inconvenience of the particular venue. In cases brought in federal court, it may be possible for an out-of-state defendant to have the case removed to the federal court in the defendant's home state.

Except for these circumstances, the defendant has little hope of moving the case unless there is a contractual agreement that provides for a particular court. Yet even then, as the BBC case shows, one party may try to circumvent the agreement by attempting to distinguish or interpret the facts that are the basis for their argument establishing jurisdiction.

On the state level, especially in states that do not operate under the standardized Federal Rules of Civil Procedure, you may be able to find a more favorable venue. Here is a list of procedural subjects to examine relative to your case when considering one forum over another:

- Differences in pleading systems.
- Rules relating to discovery.
- Rules of evidence.
- Witness availability.
- Jury-related concerns.
- Reputation and quality of judges.
- Court docket (waiting time).

Another consideration has to do with compulsory process—requiring a witness to appear involuntarily. If you must bring a witness to court this way, shopping for a state that provides for compulsory appearance may be beneficial. But regardless of your concerns, the court you choose must be legally able to exercise jurisdiction over the individual and subject matter of the action.

## JURISDICTION OVER THE INDIVIDUAL OR ENTITY

Remember playing tag as a child? Someone was "it," and became the focus of everyone else's attention until someone else became "it." Becoming subject to a court jurisdiction is quite similar to this childhood game, except it's real-life and very serious.

The most common form of becoming "it," of being brought under the control of a court, is when you or an entity you represent is served with papers by a court-authorized process server, sheriff, or representative. Although the server didn't touch you and say, "You're it," the result is the same, as you are now "tagged"—involved in the legal game. Your body is now subject to the jurisdiction of the court.

Being "it" in the legal game may mean you're a defendant, a respondent, a witness, or even a potential juror. Fortunately, the serving must be accomplished according to the law of the jurisdiction in which the court is located. In addition, you can challenge the authenticity or correctness of the service.

The procedures necessary to obtain control over an individual or entity may vary from one jurisdiction to another; if out-of-state or multiple locations are involved, securing service that will withstand the test of law may be complicated. Thus, "tagging" someone may be more difficult than you may first assume.

The Fourteenth Amendment to the Constitution guarantees citizens due process. Therefore, in order for a court to obtain jurisdiction over an individual or entity, two things must happen: Basis and process. Basis means that there must be a connection between the state (from which the court has obtained its authority) and the defendant; the defendant must be a citizen of the state, a company must be authorized to do business in the state, and so on. Process requires that the court must take formal steps to bring a particular individual under its authority by issuing a subpoena or a writ served by an authorized court appointee.

Normally, the court issues a subpoena or document because a lawsuit has been instigated by one or more parties. However, in many jurisdictions the court may take a neutral position and alert the party being served as to their rights to a proper venue. In Florida, for example, proper venue is spelled out on certain county court forms in this way:

1. Where the contract was entered into.

2. Where a note is signed or where maker resides (unsecured promissory note).

3. Where the property is located (recovery of property or foreclosure).

4. Where the event giving rise to the suit occurred.

5. Where any one or more of the defendants reside.

6. Any location regarding venue agreed to in a contract.

Since the plaintiff initially chooses the venue, these conditions of course apply to the defendant. The defendant can petition the court to transfer (or dismiss) the case, as previously discussed, by arguing improper venue or forum non conveniens.

Interestingly, the U.S. Supreme Court has found that for a state to recognize a "foreign" (out-of-state) judgment, that judgment must meet the federal basis requirements implicit in the full faith and credit clause of the Constitution. However, the Supreme Court did not specify what those requirements are. Justice William Johnson made this eloquent statement on jurisdiction: "There are certain eternal principles of justice which never ought to be dispensed with. . . . one of those is, that jurisdiction cannot be justly exercised by a state over property not within the reach of its process, or over persons not owing them allegiance or not subjected to their jurisdiction by being found within their limits" (*Mills v. Duryee*, 11 U.S. 481, 3 L.Ed. 411 [1813]).

With so many possible constitutional issues involved, and so many possible sets of facts, the question of jurisdiction over an individual or entity will always be in flux. Precedent will play a major role in the individual decisions made, unless, of course, the Supreme Court makes another major shift, as it did in *International Shoe Company v. State of Washington* (326 U.S. 310, 316), which changed the criteria and set a whole new precedent. In this case, the Supreme Court determined:

> . . . due process requires only that in order to subject a defendant to a judgment in personam, if he be not present within the territory of the forum he have certain minimum contacts with it such that the maintenance of the suit does not offend traditional notions of fair play and substantial justice.

Note that the language of this decision could have prompted the interpretations and actions of the BBC's lawyers in the case discussed previously.

## REACHING ACROSS STATE BOUNDARIES

In legal terms, it's called "extraterritorial jurisdiction." To the average person, it's the "long-arm statute," but both mean the ability to gain jurisdiction over an individual who may reside or otherwise be in another state. Virtually every state has a long-arm statute, but almost every state differs in the criteria that must be met for the stretch to be effectively used. (All fifty states permit jurisdiction over out-of-state motorists who have caused or been involved in an automobile accident.) The California statute, for instance, makes it possible to gain jurisdiction "when the defendant has the necessary minimum contacts with the state and jurisdiction would not be contrary to the Constitution or Laws of the United States" (Mary Kay Kane, *Civil Procedure in a Nutshell*, St. Paul, MN: West Publishing, 1985, page 34). This definition is intentionally vague, allowing the court to interpret jurisdiction in an expanded ability to reach beyond its borders.

In contrast, some states precisely specify the types of activities that will permit the use of the long-arm statute. It's common for such a statute to permit jurisdiction when (1) business has been transacted in the state, (2) goods or services have been supplied to the state, (3) a crime has been committed in the state, (4) acts outside the state that cause injury in the state have taken place along with business activity in the state, and (5) real property is owned or used in the state.

Federal courts are bound by the long-arm statutes of the states. The federal system (with congressional consent) has never established its own jurisdictional rules. Federal courts look to the individual state statutes. An exception occurs where a specific federal cause of action, statute, or law addresses the question of jurisdiction, such as the interstate transportation act. Another exception is the right of federal courts to obtain jurisdiction within 100 miles of their seat, regardless of state boundaries, to require a person to attend court proceedings for discovery or trial. Notwithstanding these exceptions, if the facts of a case do not fit within the state statute, or no state statute exists, then even the federal court in a particular location cannot gain jurisdiction over the individual or entity.

The bottom line is that obtaining jurisdiction of an out-of-state individual is strictly a matter of statute. You must examine your state's long-arm law and the circumstances of your case to see if they fit within the criteria for stretching out beyond your state's borders.

## JURISDICTION OVER SUBJECT MATTER

Nowhere in our Constitution is it made so clear as in the area of subject matter jurisdiction that great pains have been taken to organize the judicial branch consistent with the principles of civil liberty that played such an important role in the founding of our country. To understand subject matter jurisdiction, you must first understand the judicial relationship between the federal government and the individual states as provided for in the Constitution.

### Federal Jurisdiction

Despite the enormous power the federal government seems to have, it is actually a government of limited powers—that is, limited by the powers given to the individual states and therefore not in the hands of the national government. In the judicial branch, this proposition is reflected in that all federal courts are courts of limited jurisdiction. (Federal courts in the District of Columbia and U.S. territories are excepted; in addition to their federal powers, they function as state courts do.) Also, the power or subject matter jurisdiction of the federal courts is limited by the Constitution and by acts of Congress. This leaves the balance of subject matters not enumerated in Article III, Section 2 of the Constitution within the province of the individual states and their court systems.

The Constitution also limits the power of the federal judiciary by defining (and thereby restricting) the power of the U.S. Supreme Court. The Constitution specifies that the Supreme Court shall have original jurisdiction in certain matters, and that in other matters within the federal area, it shall have only appellate jurisdiction (with such exceptions and under regulations that Congress makes). Unlike the Supreme Court, the inferior federal courts gain their power directly from Congress, receiving their subject matter jurisdictions from the statutes by which Congress ordains and establishes those courts.

Generally, the federal court system gains jurisdiction when a case involves diversity of citizenship (parties to the case live in different states) and in matters that have been legislated by Congress—copyright, trademark, patent, federal tax, interstate commerce, and the like. (A typical jurisdictional allegation in a federal complaint might be, "Jurisdiction in this case is based on a diversity of citizenship of the parties and the amount in controversy. Plaintiff is a citizen of the State of X. Defendant is a citizen of the State of Y.") The total dollar amount of a case may also allow or limit the use of the federal court system.

Two terms, which one judge described as having an iceberg quality (more below the surface than above), actually create an extreme limitation on the subject matter jurisdiction of federal courts. These terms are *cases* and *controversies*. In a nutshell, cases and controversies limitations prevent the federal courts from encroaching on areas reserved to the executive and legislative branches, and confine "the actions of the federal courts to matters they can deal with effectively through their institutionalized processes" (Casad, *Jurisdiction and Forum Selection*, Chapter 3, page 8). The limitation of cases arising under federal law and controversies between citizens of different states is sometimes referred to as *justiciability*, or the ability of a case to meet the criteria for review by the court.

The concept of justiciability restrains the federal courts from abusing their power of judicial review in cases where they must render decisions on the constitutionality of acts of Congress, the executive branch, a federal agency, or a state government. Another limit occurs in cases involving political questions, or matters that would place a court in a policy-making role. The court cannot give an advisory opinion in such cases— there must be a concrete issue of law upon which to act. A political question does not constitute the type of controversy that is contemplated as justiciable under the Constitution.

Another aspect of the cases and controversies requirement is standing, which requires that only a party who has something to gain or lose will be regarded as an appropriate party in federal litigation. This is extremely important when you consider the possibility of a court being asked to review an act of a government agency or a state. The doctrine prevents bringing an action against the government for political or academic purposes, in which case the standing of the petitioning party will not be recognized: "If a person is challenging a governmental act because it violates a right belonging to that person, then that person can claim injury sufficient for 'standing'" (*Tennessee Electric Power Co. v. Tennessee Valley Authority*, 306 U.S. 118, 83L, Ed. 543, 59 Sct. 366 [1939]).

Interestingly, even if Congress passes a law that is blatantly unconstitutional, unless a party can claim "sufficient injury" to meet the requirements of standing, a federal court cannot assume jurisdiction of the case:

> We have no power per se to review and annul acts of Congress on the ground that they are unconstitutional. . . . the Party who invokes the power must be able to show, not only that the statute is invalid, but that he has sustained or is immediately in danger of sustaining some direct injury as a result of its enforcement and not merely that he suffers in some indefinite way in common with people generally (262 U.S. 447, 488).

Standing serves another purpose. An individual or party that has something to gain or lose will be a particularly effective advocate for that position, protecting the court from frivolous cases.

The Eleventh Amendment provides further limitations on federal court subject matter jurisdiction with wording that limits Article III. It prohibits federal courts from entertaining suits against a state by a citizen of another state or of a foreign country. This strengthens the doctrine of sovereign immunity, which was accepted prior to the formation of the Union (Casad, *Jurisdiction and Forum Selection*). After the Civil War, the state governments were brought under federal control in ways not previously thought possible. States were prohibited from denying citizens within their borders life, liberty, or property without due process, and from denying their citizens equal protection under the law. Congress even went so far as to enact remedies, available in federal court, for parties whose federal rights were violated by state actions, further defining subject matter jurisdiction of the federal courts. (This area of constitutional law is quite interesting, though complex. The Eleventh and Fourteenth amendments are actually at odds with one another in certain instances.)

## State Jurisdiction

Understanding the operation of the federal court system provides an insight into the operation of the parallel state systems.

In most states, the state constitution or the legislature defines what types of cases a particular court may hear. Some state courts may be given limited or specialized jurisdiction, whereas others may be given general jurisdiction. Regardless of the makeup, there is at least one court in every state empowered to hear "original cases of every kind" (except those assigned exclusively to a court of specialized jurisdiction). The name for the general jurisdiction court may vary from state to state; some are called "circuit courts," others "superior courts." In New York, the general court is named the "Supreme Court." In some states, if the court you are pleading to is one of these general courts, it is presumed that you will not have to allege facts substantiating subject matter jurisdiction. However, you may have to recite such facts in your pleadings if your case is in a limited jurisdiction court. Limits on various state courts include the following:

- Family law.
- Decedent's estate (probate).
- Geographical location.
- Dollar value of the case.
- Cases not involving land titles.
- Cases not including equitable remedies.
- Traffic matters.

In addition to the specialized and general courts, most states have appellate systems with the power of review. The appellate level will usually have additional powers, such as the power to entertain extraordinary writs such as habeas corpus, mandamus, prohibition, certiorari, and quo warranto.

Table 4.1 shows a typical state court system and its area of subject matter jurisdiction.

**Table 4.1**  Typical State Court System

| |
|---|
| Supreme Court—Highest appellate court<br>  Limited jurisdiction |
| Appellate Courts—Mid-level appellate courts<br>  Limited original jurisdiction<br>  Limited direct access |
| Trial Courts—Courts of original jurisdiction<br>  Small claims courts (upper and lower courts based on dollar<br>    amounts)<br>  Traffic court<br>  Criminal courts (misdemeanor/felony divisions)<br>  Probate<br>  Family<br>  Juvenile<br>  Equity divisions or jurisdictions |

The word *jurisdiction* has a number of meanings, depending on the context. We have attempted to provide you with a working knowledge of jurisdiction, an extremely complex subject. As you progress through the following pages, you may want to refer to this section. You should anticipate revisiting jurisdiction tactically at most stages of planning and reviewing your legal involvements.

## JURISDICTIONAL QUIZ

*Case 1:* A business maintains its corporate headquarters in Atlanta, Georgia, and branch offices under various names in several other states. You live in the same state as one of the offices, and you use its services. A dispute ensues and you find it necessary to file a lawsuit. What do you do to obtain jurisdiction over the company in your area?

*Solution:* Prepare and file a lawsuit (complaint) against the entity you did business with in your state, and have the authorized process server hand-deliver the summons and complaint to the defendant's authorized agent.

*Case 2:* You have conducted business in your state with an individual who lives in your town. That person owes you money. One day you discover that the person has moved to another state. What do you do to obtain jurisdiction over that person in your state's court system?

*Solution:* If your state's long-arm statute provides jurisdiction over individuals who have done business in your state, then jurisdiction may be obtained over that individual in another state by causing an authorized process server to hand-deliver the summons and complaint and provide you with the appropriate documents according to your state's long-arm statute affecting service.

*Case 3:* Your marriage is on the verge of breaking up. Your spouse picks up and moves out of state and cannot be located. You want to settle the question of assets and get on with your life. Can you obtain jurisdiction over your spouse?

*Solution:* Yes and no. Many jurisdictions have statutes that permit service by publishing newspaper advertisements along with affidavits reflecting that the party sought cannot be found. This procedure, depending on the jurisdiction, may or may not permit certain remedies. For example, the basic divorce decree may be granted under these conditions, but monetary or property relief could be another story. If a judgment is entered and executed and the disappearing party suddenly shows up, the entire legal proceeding might be challenged on the basis of whether proper service was obtained.

# CHAPTER 5
# Stopping the Clock

*A man can do half a dozen jobs if he has proper control of time.*

—Arthur T. Vanderbilt

One of the best things to do for yourself pro se is to buy yourself time. You may have just been served in a legal action, and haven't chosen a lawyer yet. Or perhaps you feel the need to sue someone, and you need to get the process started quickly. Using time as a strategy can be very effective.

Whether you are the defendant or the plaintiff makes a difference as to how you would proceed. First, we'll look at the plaintiff's point of view. If you are bringing an action against someone, the strategy is limited. You may need to stop the clock when the statute of limitations is about to expire and to do this you must file a lawsuit under the rules of the court system. You file the case in order to preserve your right to prepare and conduct discovery. (See Chapter 7.)

If you are the defendant, time is really on your side. Use it. Life is fluid; anger subsides; companies move, change management, or close; and people pass on or change relationships. The first blush of anger is a double-edged sword. Often a lawsuit filed in a burst of anger, with determination to collect and zeal to get even, wears thin as time marches on. I once had a business arrangement where cartons of recorded cassettes arrived at a warehouse, were inventoried and stored, and then shipped out. My company was charged a certain handling fee for each full box of thirty cassettes, and another fee for counting loose stock as it arrived from the factory. (A factory-sealed carton is presumed to contain the proper quantity in most businesses.)

One day I made an unexpected visit to the warehouse and noticed that my company's factory-sealed cartons were being systematically opened, counted, and then sealed again—an excessive expenditure of time and money. I asked the owner of the warehouse, a former vice president of CBS and RCA Records, why this was being done. He said, "I have to make money some way."

I immediately objected to my company's current and past warehouse bills based on the unnecessary work I had seen. The warehouse, having been caught red-handed in a scam to create billing, promptly took the offensive and sued my company for nonpayment of the bills and threw in a count for commissions they thought a third party owed them as a result of our business relationship. I was now the defendant. The legal activity flew hot and heavy for a while, but time began to take its toll. My opponent's legal expenses were mounting and the case dragged on and on. Then one day my attorney received a call: "Would you agree to settle?" The settlement was a set of mutual releases; it was all over.

You can gain time by placing legal roadblocks in front of your opponent, by simply using the system while accomplishing a purpose that is entirely consistent with the law. (Any attorney would do this to protect your every and ultimate interest.) This creates work and frustration and additional legal expenses for your opponent. A thorough review of the documents, statutes, applicable defenses, venues, and jurisdiction is essential to making this work.

Let's take a hypothetical defendant, Harriet, who has just been sued and received, via a sheriff's deputy, a summons and complaint. The first thing Harriet has to do is read the summons, the complaint, and all attachments. In most cases, these will indicate the amount of time allowed to file an answer. In Florida, Harriet would have twenty days; this will vary in other states. Since Harriet has not had time to shop for an attorney, she is going to buy time and stop the legal clock by acting pro se.

In many states, motion practice may be available, and Harriet should determine if any of her rights would be protected by filing a motion. Issues of venue and jurisdiction, and the basic question of whether or not the form of the complaint is correct, are possible grounds for a motion. Perhaps Harriet's opponent hired an attorney who filed the lawsuit in a particular county or area more convenient to the attorney rather than a venue where Harriet could require the case to be filed. For instance, in a commercial dispute, there may be a statement in a contract or promissory note that says jurisdiction is allowable in a particular court within a particular county or area of the state. If Harriet lived within that jurisdiction, she would have no argument. However, if the lawsuit were filed upstate and Harriet lived downstate, and the only basis for filing upstate was the attorney's convenience, Harriet could, by proper motion, request the court to transfer the case to the proper venue—where she resides. Her chances of success with this kind of motion would be good.

Jurisdiction is an important concept when stopping the clock. Harriet might be able to raise questions as to whether an action has been filed in the appropriate court. For example, is the value of the suit in excess of the maximum for the court? Should the case have been filed in a court having an appropriate monetary or equitable jurisdiction? Harriet should examine the lawsuit with the many nuances and meanings of jurisdiction in mind. This kind of defense may not dispose of the action; instead, it allows the case to be dismissed and transferred to an appropriate court, where the process must begin again. If Harriet is successful, she will have gained precious time and protected her interests.

Often a complaint is drawn in such a way that it does not clearly state a proper cause of action, or even that the statute on which it is based or case law does not permit the relief sought. If Harriet can spot this kind of defect, a motion to the court could be made, using appropriate language: "The case stated in the complaint is so improperly drawn that it should be dismissed." (This is called a motion to dismiss.) The court may actually find that Harriet is correct and dismiss the case, but most often the opposing party will be allowed to research, redraft, and refile an amended complaint or amended pleading within a specific time. Still, time is working for Harriet.

Presenting a properly drawn motion to the court is essential for defensive strategy. The following are some motions that she might use at the beginning of the case—prior to filing her answer to the original complaint:

- Motion to dismiss for improper venue.
- Motion to recuse (for change of judge).
- Motion for enlargement of time or continuance (for more time).
- Motion for injunctive relief (for court-ordered action).

## DRAFTING AND FILING A MOTION

Let's look at what it takes to draft and file a motion. First and foremost, check the rules of practice in your jurisdiction, or obtain a form and work from that. Here are some questions you'll need to ask:

- Where is the original version of the motion to be filed?
- Where is the court clerk's office?
- How many copies are needed?
- What size paper should be used?
- Which parties receive a copy?

- What, if any, certification should be given above the signature, setting out the date the motion is being filed?
- Are there any time limits in which the motion must be filed?

The original motion filed with the court must have your signature, the date you filed, and your address and phone number if you are acting pro se (or the name and address of your attorney or law firm).

It's imperative to check the correct place to file the original of your motion or pleadings—the proper court clerk's office in the appropriate courthouse, the judge's chambers, or somewhere else. Different jurisdictions and different courts may require a different number of copies; likewise for the use of legal- or letter-size paper. Check with the court clerk. The rules of court will indicate the parties to be served and the method, but generally speaking, each party named in the suit will receive one copy, with the original filed with the court. Here is an example of a typical certification that would be used at the end of a motion:

> I HEREBY CERTIFY that a true and correct copy of the foregoing
> was mailed this _____ day of _____ 19____ ;
> to _____

Appearance is important. Have your motion typed in a professional manner.

In regard to time limits, check your local rules for instructions. In many jurisdictions you may be able to receive a stamped or "clocked in" copy of your motion from the court clerk, proving the date and time the court received it. This provides you with proof that the document was timely filed. Make sure you have checked the rules carefully. If you leave something out of your initial motion that should be raised at that point, filing your motion may preclude you from raising that matter later. Filing an appropriate motion may, however, preclude other activity until it is heard and decided. For instance, if you do not raise the issue of venue in your initial pleading, you may lose the right to raise the issue at a later point, notwithstanding that you may have since retained an attorney who has pointed out what could or should have been filed along with your original motion. By filing the motion you have effectively obtained a period of time in which adverse action is minimized and you have retained the opportunity for greater time to prepare. It is probably better to take the time and effort to file whatever motions you can reasonably determine are feasible before filing your answer. (See Chapter 6.) The answer will eventually raise the legal arguments, denials, rebuttals, counterclaims, and statements that will be the basis of your defense.

*Note:* In some areas, filing a motion will stop the clock and allow you additional time to answer a summons and complaint. However, in other jurisdictions, the clock may continue to run, putting you in jeopardy of a default judgment being entered against you. Therefore, carefully check what the court requires regarding filing a full and complete response to a summons and complaint—whether you may present a motion to the court or whether you must first file an answer to the complaint.

Our hypothetical case against Harriet was filed by another individual. However, suppose you as the plaintiff or defendant are not an individual, but represent a legally recognized entity such as a corporation, trust, estate, minor, incompetent, or other party. Most states don't allow a non-attorney to represent a corporation (see Table 1.2, page 17), and you may be accused of acting improperly if you try to do so. Even though in the eyes of the corporate officers and directors you are the person to take charge, in the eyes of the court you may be committing a crime and/or subjecting yourself to the liability of acting as an attorney. In this case, taking charge means doing only enough to gain the breathing space to obtain counsel.

Now, assuming that Harriet is going forward with her case, has studied the rules and procedures of her jurisdiction, has prepared the proper motions, has filed them correctly, and has provided the proper parties (including opposing counsel) with their respective copies, the next step is to cause the appropriate hearing to occur.

## SCHEDULING A HEARING

Each court has its own rules and procedures for scheduling a hearing. Some localities have special hearing times for less involved or quickly heard matters. The time reserved for these hearings, usually at the start of a court session, is called a motion calendar in some jurisdictions. Other jurisdictions might require you to forward a copy of the motion and the notice of hearing to the judge's secretary or assistant; in some court systems, this may be accomplished by the person in the court clerk's office responsible for setting hearing dates for motions.

A typical notice of hearing looks like this:

> YOU WILL PLEASE TAKE NOTICE that the undersigned will call up for hearing on ___, the ___ day of _____, 19_ at [ time ], before the Honorable Judge Joseph Smith, at the Broward County Courthouse, 201 S.E. 6th Street, Room _, Ft. Lauderdale, Florida 33301 the following motion(s):

<Motion for Extension of Time to File Answer>

PLEASE GOVERN YOURSELF ACCORDINGLY.

I HEREBY CERTIFY that a true and correct copy of the above was mailed this 18th day of August, 1992, to Thomas W. Brown, Esq., Attorney for Plaintiff, 73 West Flagler Street, Miami, Florida 33130.

Very often the judge's secretary or assistant can tell you the appropriate procedure for getting a hearing date. For instance, if the motion is more involved or requires a longer time for the argument than is normally allowed on a quick hearing calendar, then the judge's secretary or assistant could guide you in obtaining a special setting for your motion. In all probability you will be asked how much time you need for your argument. You will normally be granted the time you request unless the court feels you are overstating the time needed for the type of motion, in which case a compromise will be made. The court will also advise you whether you are responsible for preparing and forwarding the appropriate notice of hearing to the court and all appropriate parties.

When the hearing date is arranged, note it in your diary! If you forget to do this, you may forget the hearing. Even the best memory gets distracted by a busy business schedule and personal involvements. Even with a trained legal secretary as an assistant, I have missed several of my own hearings. The penalty for missing a deadline may range from losing certain rights, or the motion at hand, to losing your case entirely.

Once your hearing date has been assigned, and you have marked the date on your calendar, allot enough time in your schedule so that you can arrive at the courthouse early and prepare yourself for your appearance before the judge. Before the hearing, check with the court to find out what you need to bring to the hearing. Should you bring a courtesy copy of your paperwork to give to the judge at the hearing? Should you have a court reporter in attendance? Court reporters are skilled individuals who are trained to take down testimony verbatim. They should be scheduled well in advance. (See The Origin of Modern Court Reporting, page 87.)

Court reporters are certified by the state and, like attorneys, are officers of the court. It's the court reporter's responsibility to transcribe every word spoken during a hearing, trial, or judicial proceeding. The reporter is also charged with the responsibility of transcribing the words spoken at depositions that occur outside of the courthouse, such as in an attorney's office or even in a hotel room, a hospital room, or a place of business.

# The Origin of Modern Court Reporting

*English court reports published in the late thirteenth century were called yearbooks. Later reports of court activity published by private entrepreneurs were examples of early attempts to chronicle the events of the justice system. It was not until just after the Civil War era that court reporting of verbatim testimony took place.*

*Philander Deeming, a newspaper reporter in Albany, New York, and protege of Henry Richmond (founder of The New York Times) was attending a trial in 1866. Suddenly the proceedings erupted into argument as to what a witness had said. Deeming, who had studied the science of phonology (shorthand) to aid in his work, offered to provide the testimony. He was immediately challenged to prove his claim that he could copy the testimony verbatim. A test was set up and he accomplished the feat and instantly became the nation's first court reporter. In 1879, he became the nation's foremost reporter when his training manual for court reporters was published, effectively changing the court system in the United States.*

It's important to remember that court reporters are only transcribing words; they make no mention of a person's grimaces, eye twitches, tears, or rate of respiration. Only the words will be available for later reference, and the subtext (as opposed to the text) will remain only in the minds of those who were in the courtroom. Thus, it would be impossible to use the transcript at a later time to convince an appellate judge that "everyone in the courtroom could see the fellow was lying." Only the words will survive; only the words are available to review, study, and base a judgment on.

## POST-HEARING PROCEDURE

Now that Harriet has been granted a hearing date, all parties have been notified, and her paperwork is filed in the court clerk's office, she must be concerned with post-hearing procedure—the judge's order. The judge's decision, or "order of judgment," is reduced to a written order. On simple or quick motions, the order citing the ruling will usually be prepared in advance, allowing the judge a place to insert *granted* or *denied*, or possibly adding a few handwritten additions or instructions if the matter is a little more complicated. Often in a quick hearing, the individual seeking the hearing will be required to bring a prepared order. In more complex matters, the judge might provide instructions as to which party should draft the proposed order and submit it to the court for review and signature, as well as providing copies to the opposition.

Where a motion is used to stop the clock, clarify an issue, change the venue, or challenge jurisdiction in response to the original complaint, a ruling must be made. Once the court's order is signed, the next step on the road to adjudication of the issue in question is the filing of the answer.

Our hypothetical hero Harriet, having successfully negotiated her motion through the initial stages, and having been granted an extension of time, now has twenty additional days in which to file her answer to the complaint.

# CHAPTER 6
# The Kickoff

*One may fall, at the beginning of the charge . . . but in no other way can he reach the rewards of victory.*

—Oliver Wendell Holmes

An answer, your reply to a summons and complaint (the kickoff of a legal action), is tantamount to the runback of a kickoff in a football game. A strong kickoff returner can set the tone for the game, as you can set the tone of the case with a properly drawn answer. With its potential supplements (affirmative defenses and counterclaims), it can provide you, the defendant, with your best chance for a successful outcome.

A complaint sets forth certain allegations of fact. Until the case is adjudicated, these are allegations only. An answer admits or denies the specific allegations contained in the complaint. The admission or denial of the complaint's allegations may be followed by affirmative defenses and counterclaims against the complainant as applicable.

If you intend to act pro se, you must know your rights and obligations at the outset of an action. Taking the time at the start of litigation will protect your rights and save a great deal of aggravation later. As we have stated before, you must (1) know the rules of procedure of your local or state jurisdiction, (2) use the correct forms throughout the course of your lawsuit, and (3) determine local procedures that may guide you through your lawsuit.

*Note:* If you fail to follow the rules and procedures that protect your rights, paying for an attorney to try to undo your mistakes at a later date will be more costly than hiring one at the start!

If you find you need more time to prepare your answer properly, file the appropriate documents requesting the court's permission for additional time.

Many jurisdictions allow this, and a motion for enlargement of time may be all that is needed. With an affirmative nod from the court, you have some additional time to complete your work.

## ANSWERING ALLEGATIONS

The first part of your answer will admit or deny each specific allegation in the complaint. If an allegation is made and you do not address it in a timely fashion in your answer, the rules usually provide that the allegation will be deemed admitted. In other words, an allegation not denied will be found in favor of the plaintiff—effectively against you.

In this section of the answer you indicate, for instance, "Yes, I live in the State of Wisconsin," or "No, the Ace Trucking Company is not my corporation." Whether or not your answers are true and whether or not the complainant's allegations are true is a matter of discovery, trial, and decision by a judge and/or jury. At this point, your answer is not questioned.

## RAISING AFFIRMATIVE DEFENSES

The second section of your answer includes what are called "affirmative defenses." These are new matters (your side of the story) raised as allegations against your opponent, and act as a defense to the action brought against you. Only certain defenses can be used as affirmative defenses. (This will be discussed in Chapter 8.) Also, the specific court rules may vary as to which affirmative defenses may properly be raised. In fact, if affirmative defenses are not timely filed, it may be impossible to bring in those subjects at a later date without the court's permission.

I once traded some of my company's recording studio time and materials for a Steinway baby grand piano owned by a music teacher-turned-record producer. The main street of downtown Pittsburgh was blocked off and a rented crane lifted the instrument through a window in my studio that had been removed by a union carpenter, all at great expense. The instrument functioned beautifully, but the music composed on it by the would-be producer was a total disaster. After three pop recordings flopped miserably, I said, "Our dues are paid," and ended the relationship. The producer disagreed with my decision and filed suit for the price of a used Steinway piano.

My recording business was affiliated at the time with a company that retained the services of a hotshot Pittsburgh attorney. He prepared a form answer, a denial of the claim by the would-be producer, without consulting with his client. When new counsel was selected (after the business was sold), it was discovered that my rights had not been protected. A counterclaim for our studio time and manufactured phonograph records, which would have exceeded the value of the piano, had not been filed, and it was now too late to file the counterclaim. Our rights to add that fact in a counterclaim to the answer had expired.

The case went to trial; the unfortunate (for my company) outcome was described in Chapter 4. What is important to remember is that once certain rights are lost, they are lost forever (unless you retain a superstar appeals attorney). You must be precise in meeting the deadlines and adhering to the rules of procedure in filing your answer.

A friend told me recently about a complaint that had been served upon him. After he sold a boat, the purchaser accused him of not fulfilling his obligations to repair the craft. My friend answered the specific allegations in the complaint, which were a litany of problems with the vessel and its engine. In addition, he had a copy of the bill of sale, which clearly stated that the boat was sold "as is." His affirmative defense was clear: Regardless of the specific allegations made, no warranty could be implied if the purchase terms were "as is." A timely answer and production of the bill of sale should end his legal involvement with the dissatisfied boater. (Note: "As is" is not as absolute as it seems. Statutes limit certain "as is" contracts. For example, in the sale of real estate, hidden defects must be disclosed if known by the seller and not readily observable to the buyer.)

Another example of an affirmative defense is the statute of limitations. If the amount of time the law allows has passed without action being taken, action at a later date is prohibited. Remember, however, that you must raise the statute of limitations claim in a timely manner; if you don't, your opponent's claim may proceed because it has become too late to block it this way.

Following are other matters that are normally raised as affirmative defenses:

*Accord and satisfaction.* This means exactly what it says. The existence of a settlement to which both parties agree when performed bars all other actions. In other words, if you caused a fender-bender, and the other party accepted payment on the spot from you and acknowledged same in writing, that would be the end of the matter. The individual with the damaged vehicle could not, at a later date, ask for an additional sum.

*Arbitration and award.* If a legal proceeding and/or arbitration has taken place on some matter previously and the matter has been judicially settled, there can be no additional claim for the same matter at a later date.

*Assumption of risk.* This states a legal principle that no recovery is possible for an injury when an individual agrees to something, knowing beforehand that it is dangerous, and then proceeds with the dangerous condition present. For instance, say there is a barricade across a private road indicating that a flood has washed away a section of the road. As you approach the barricade, a police officer steps out and warns you not to travel on the road. You decide not to heed the warning and proceed down the road. Your car falls into a gully and the axle breaks. Even though the road is a private one, you generally would have no case against the owner under the principle of "assumption of risk."

*Contributory negligence.* This is conduct by a plaintiff below the standard to which she is legally required to conform for her own good and which is a contributing cause in causing the plaintiff to be harmed. In other words, if it takes two to tango and one breaks a leg, each has contributed to the accident. (Be aware, however, of proportionate liability, which has crept into certain areas of the law.)

*Discharge in bankruptcy.* If a matter has been brought before bankruptcy court, adjudicated, and discharged, it cannot be brought up again in any action outside of that bankruptcy proceeding.

*Duress.* Duress includes exposure or illegal imprisonment, threats of bodily harm, mental stress, or any other means of coercion actually inducing an individual to perform an act contrary to the person's free will.

*Estoppel.* This is not a member of a Latin dance team, but actually a complicated legal principle that, if the circumstances fit, can be used as a defense. Estoppel can best be explained by the following examples:

- *Acts and declarations:* Where the acts and declarations of an individual induce another individual to alter his position to his detriment.
- *Estoppel by deed:* The grantor of a warranty deed who does not have title at the time of the conveyance, but who subsequently acquires title, is estopped from denying that she had title at the time of the transfer and such, after acquired title, ensures to the benefit of the grantor or her successors.
- *Estoppel by judgment:* When a fact has been agreed to or decided on in a court of law, neither of the parties shall be allowed to call it into question so long as that judgment or decree is not reversed.
- *Estoppel certificate:* A signed statement by a party, such as a tenant, certifying for the benefit of another party that a certain statement of fact is correct as of the date of the statement. For instance, suppose a landlord engages the services of a manager to collect rent. A document, or certifi-

cate, from the landlord to the tenant indicating that the rent is up-to-date as of the date the manager takes over would later prevent the manager from attempting to collect back rent from the tenant.

- *Estoppel en pais:* This is a legal doctrine by which a person may be precluded by his act, conduct, or silence, when it is his duty to speak, from asserting a right which he otherwise would have had. For instance, if a landlord continually allows the rent to be thirty days late without complaining, the landlord may be precluded from later enforcing the provision of the lease concerning timely payments.

*Failure of consideration.* This implies that a consideration, originally contemplated to exist and to be of good standing, has since become worthless or has ceased to exist partially or entirely. For instance, you might agree to deliver a case of lobster tails to a restaurant that has paid you in advance. Your truck takes longer to deliver the precious tails and, by the time they reach the restaurant, they have spoiled. The restaurant would have a valid claim for the return of its payment because you have failed to provide proper consideration (a usable product). This tale of failure of consideration would be clear to anyone in close proximity to the spoiled fish.

*Fraud.* This is an intentional perversion of truth for the purposes of inducing an individual or entity to rely upon it for the purpose of parting with some valuable thing belonging to the party or entity or to surrender a legal right. The elements of fraud include false representation of a past or present fact, action in reliance thereon, and damage resulting from such misrepresentation. In other words, it is a deceitful act with intent to deprive another of his right or property or to cause some injury. Fraud, as distinguished from negligence, is always positive and intentional.

*Illegality.* An act that is contrary to the principles of law. If an individual had to break the law in order to comply with a contract, then an affirmative defense would be illegality.

*Injury by fellow servant.* We might create an eleventh commandment, "Thou shalt not injure a fellow servant," because if one employee is partially or wholly responsible for an injury to a fellow employee or employees, then the boss has a reduced or extinguished degree of liability.

*Laches.* This is a complicated and important legal principle known as the "doctrine of laches." It is based upon the maxim that "equity aids the vigilant and not those who slumber on their rights." In other words, if an individual or entity fails to assert her right or claim, together with a lapse of time and other circumstances causing prejudice to the (potential defendant) adverse party, the individual or entity is then barred from pursuing the claim. If you neglect to do or omit doing what you should do, it may be deemed that you have abandoned the right or claim. This is generally interpreted to be unconscionable, inexcusable, unexplainable, or unreasonable delays in the assertion of rights. Knowledge, unreasonable delay, and change of position are essential elements of the doctrine of laches. An example of this doctrine is if an individual received a loan of $350 from an elderly neighbor, who later became senile and then passed away. The estate might want to recover from the debtor, believing that the statute of limitations had not run out and that the statute of fraud was not involved (the amount is under $500). However, the debtor might claim laches, in that too much time had transpired for the estate to now make a claim.

*License.* In its most simple terms, license means permission by a proper authority to do an act that, without such permission, would be illegal; in other words, a permit granted by an arm of the government, generally for a consideration, to a person, firm, or entity, to pursue some occupation or to carry out some business activity. If you were licensed by the local government as a garbage collector and you were in the act of collecting garbage when accused of trespassing, your defense would be "license."

*Payment.* Payment is the fulfillment of a promise or the performance of an agreement; a discharge of an obligation or debt. Obviously, a defense to a claim for payment is the proof of payment in part or in whole. Payment need not be money, but whatever it is must be placed beyond the dominion and control of the individual or entity making the payment.

*Release.* This is the relinquishing or giving up of a right, claim, or privilege by an individual or entity in whom it exists to the person or entity against whom it might have been demanded or enforced. The release may be gratuitous or for a consideration. Proper evidence of a release becomes an affirmative defense for an action brought against the person or entity holding the release for the same claim.

*Res judicata.* As mentioned earlier, if a court of competent jurisdiction has passed judgment on a matter, then it cannot be brought again before another court.

*Statute of frauds.* This is not to be confused with fraud as described above. The statute of frauds is a principle adopted by the English in 1677 and which is, in its modified form, found in nearly the entire United States. It's a fairly simple principle. In certain classes of contracts or engagements between individuals and/or entities, unless there is a note, document, or memorandum in writing and signed by the parties involved or their authorized agents, no legal action may be taken in the matter. The Uniform Commercial Code of the United States (see Chapter 18) provides that a contract for the sale of goods in the amount of $500 or more is enforceable only if there is some written instrument that indicates that a contract has been made between the parties. This statute was originally enacted to end numerous frauds and perjuries that were taking place under the guise of an oral contract, hence the name "statute of frauds."

*Statute of limitations.* Most laws and statutes have a prescribed time limit during which they may be enforced. Once that time has expired, no legal action under that law or statute may be undertaken.

*Waiver.* A waiver of rights takes place when an individual or entity possesses full knowledge of the material facts and intentionally or voluntarily relinquishes a known right. In other words, the repudiating, abandoning, renouncing, or surrendering of some right, claim, or privilege constitutes a waiver. This is a doctrine of equitable principle that many courts of law will recognize.

The preceding legal or affirmative defenses to an action are applicable in the state of Florida, and may not be the same as those available elsewhere. (This list is not necessarily all-inclusive.) Therefore, it is important to review the rules of court in your particular state or location before you actually use one of these defenses. You should be able to consult the rules of court for your state; West Publishing (St. Paul, MN) publishes them for all but thirteen of the states. The rules in these books are clearly stated and easy to follow.

Once you have determined the allowable affirmative defenses in your court or jurisdiction, examine the facts of your case and see how they might fit each of the defenses. Keep in mind that depending upon the particular rules under which you are operating, unless these issues are raised in a timely manner, they may be barred later regardless of the rights you may have to them.

For pro se individuals, there is some flexibility and compassion in the court system, as the following quotation from the Florida Rules of Court indicates: "When a party has mistakenly designated a defense as a counterclaim or a counterclaim as a defense, the court, on terms if justice so requires, shall treat the pleading as if there had been a proper designation."

## MAKING COUNTERCLAIMS

Once you are satisfied that you have used all the affirmative defenses that fit the circumstances of your case, you have to determine if you have any valid counterclaims, or setoffs, against the plaintiff. Apply this question: "Do I have any claims against the plaintiff that would result in an adverse ruling against the plaintiff in an independent lawsuit?"

If you decide that you do have such claims, examine each one from two perspectives. If the claim arises from the same general set of facts involved in the plaintiff's lawsuit against you, then you must raise the matter in your answer in order to protect your right to raise the issue. By not doing so, you may cause yourself to lose your right to raise it by having failed to set forth the claim in a timely manner (in your answer).

However, if your claim, based on the facts, is totally separate from the suit at hand and distinct from the plaintiff's claim, then you may raise your claim as a counterclaim or in a separate suit, if you so desire. Either way, if you prevail in the process of adjudication, a judgment in your favor based upon your claim could result.

Your counterclaim might read something like this:

> Yes, I owe the manufacturer $100,000 for 100,000 widgets. However, on a previous transaction, I was supposed to receive credit for $11,250 for defective merchandise which I returned to your company. I have never received the credit and therefore your company, as my supplier of widgets, owes me the sum of $11,250.

This is an oversimplified example, but it does illustrate a typical counterclaim.

Adding a counterclaim to your answer and affirmative defenses may be a useful move if you can prove your claim to the judge or jury. If your claim is sustained, it will either nullify or partially nullify any adverse ruling against you; or, if you prevail in the counterclaim and it exceeds the plaintiff's claim, you would receive damages equal to the difference.

Following the preparation of the answer, appropriate affirmative defenses, counterclaims, and third party claims, you will enter a phase of the litigation that involves close scrutiny of the attitudes and tenacity of your opponent. Expect additional motions and then discovery—the stage that allows each side to obtain information, documents, materials, exhibits, and the like to help determine the facts from each side's point of view.

# CHAPTER 7
# Discovery

*A patient pursuit of facts and cautious combination and comparison of them, is the drudgery to which man is subjected.*
—Thomas Jefferson

"Your motion for discovery is granted. You will have the full subpoena power of this court." Those were the words of a Florida small claims court judge who granted me the right to use discovery in a lawsuit I had filed. As I left the courtroom, the judge's words resounded in my head. Although I had used discovery procedures in the past, and had been involved in many cases where I had to give testimony or provide documents under the rules of discovery, never before had I really understood what it meant to be personally granted full subpoena power.

In small claims court, a layperson proceeding pro se under a valid lawsuit may be granted the ability to do discovery; this ability is usually automatic in higher courts in most jurisdictions. Subpoena power is incident to the discovery procedure, which is used to learn, investigate, obtain, and develop the facts of a case from your opponent, other parties, or nonparties. To understand the immensity of this power, let's examine exactly what "full subpoena power of the court" entails.

A *subpoena* is a command to appear and testify; a *subpoena duces tecum* is a command to appear and to produce certain documents or papers that may be pertinent to the issues at hand. Subpoenas are instruments of the court and carry with them the full weight and authority of the judicial system and the particular court where the action has been filed.

Subpoenas are enforceable by the court either at the request of the party deprived of information because of noncompliance with the subpoena or at the request of the court itself. Enforcement can range from a reprimand to a finding of contempt of court, which could result in fines and/or incarceration. Therefore, if a subpoena is issued and served in the process of discovery, and if the recipient does not comply with that subpoena, it could ultimately mean contempt of court and possibly jail for the noncomplying party. Since most of us do not want to risk the wrath of an angry judge, we comply with the discovery process regardless of our reluctance to disclose information. (If done in a timely fashion and if the basis is legally correct, a party can object to requested discovery.) Still, with the "full subpoena power of the court" available to you acting pro se, you have a powerful tool to fight the system.

There are four elements of discovery open to the litigant in most jurisdictions:

- Request for admissions.
- Interrogatories.
- Notice to produce.
- Depositions.

A *request for admissions* may be served by one party on another party involved in the litigation. It is a *written* request for the admission of truth on any matter within the scope of the lawsuit. Copies of any documents referred to must be provided with the set of questions (requests) unless they have been provided with other paperwork in the same action. Each matter of which an admission is requested is to be set forth separately. The matter is deemed admitted unless an answer to the contrary is provided timely. Be aware that the answer to requests for admissions *must* be filed on time. If the party served cannot either admit or deny the matter, then she must state why. A request for admissions is used in an attempt to narrow the issues in dispute. It's basically a set of questions that one might consider answering true or false and usually not in any greater detail.

*Interrogatories* may be served by a plaintiff at the time the complaint is served, and on any party to the litigation after an action has commenced. Interrogatories are questions to be answered by the recipient, and should not exceed a prescribed number of questions in most jurisdictions. Questions are to be answered separately and fully (and possibly under oath) and within a prescribed length of time. Interrogatories are particularly useful, along with the production of documents, in preparing for depositions.

A *notice to produce* is used to obtain documents or things that a party believes are related to the lawsuit and will be beneficial to discovery. Depending on the nature of the document or thing, you might end up examining it at a specified time and place. This might entail going to the opposing party's office or place of business to observe a large item or a set of documents and to copy the documents, make notes, or photograph the particular documents or things as needed. The documents or things might be used as a basis for further interrogatories or an oral deposition, or may simply be used as evidence at trial. If there is a basis to object, then an appropriate objection in proper form should be filed before the end of the prescribed time period to produce. It is up to the court to decide whether or not a proper objection has been filed and whether or not the production should proceed under the court's further direction.

A *deposition* is the "big daddy" of discovery—an oral examination before a court reporter of any party or person (with proper notice). If the notice of deposition is entitled *duces tecum*, then the party being deposed must bring to the deposition the documents and items named in the notice or subpoena.

A good illustration of the scope of discovery is given in the Florida rules for depositions, which state that the material sought in discovery must be "relevant to the subject matter of the pending action." Questions that "appear reasonably calculated to lead to the discovery of admissible evidence" are allowed. Over the years, courts have tended to expand the scope of discovery prior to trial to minimize surprises during trial and to allow a more informed decision by the judge or jury when all the facts are laid before the court (see Basic Goals of Discovery, page 100). It is also logical that disputes can more often be settled when professionals, trained at evaluating evidence, can present the "big picture" to a client and discuss settlement possibilities. (This is an example of how all-encompassing the discovery process can be.) In Florida, you can even subpoena the opposing attorney's trial preparation materials if you can show "the need of the materials in the preparation of the case and that you are unable, without undue hardship, to obtain the substantial equivalent of the materials." Of course, privileged communications between attorney and client are exempt, but the power of discovery can be quite awesome.

Although the rules differ from state to state and from jurisdiction to jurisdiction, there are twelve basic elements of a deposition:

1. Witnesses are under oath.

2. Witnesses are examined and cross-examined (as in a trial).

3. Testimony is recorded.

4. The party requesting a transcript usually pays the cost of transcription.

5. Any objection made as to the manner of taking the deposition, evidence, conduct, statements of parties, or any other objection, usually must be noted in the record.

# Basic Goals of Discovery

*Discovery is an important stage of litigation that allows each side to obtain information, documents, and other materials to help them determine and prepare their cases for presentation. It is important to keep in mind some of the basic goals of this process, which are:*

- *To acquire information that might lead to admissible evidence;*
- *To obtain relevant, admissible evidence, such as documents, admissions, testimony, and physical evidence;*
- *To understand the factual and legal bases of the opposition;*
- *To identify the opposition's lay and expert witnesses, and determine what their testimony will be;*
- *To find out what documents or other tangible evidence the opposition will use;*
- *To familiarize yourself with your opponent's style, techniques, and character;*
- *To attempt to weaken your opponent's witnesses by securing admissions or demonstrating lack of real competence to testify to the facts (for lay witnesses) or expert opinion (for expert witnesses).*

6. When an objection is made, the testimony is then taken subject to the objection.

7. Written questions may be used, with oral answers recorded.

8. Courts may limit the scope of questioning or the length of time in which the deposition is taken; or they may assess the cost of the deposition or transcription under special circumstances; and the court may require the deposition to be taken in front of the judge under other circumstances.

9. Witnesses have the right to review their testimony and note whether they believe there should be corrections to the transcript. Additions or deletions must be noted by a court officer (reporter), along with a statement by the witness as to the reason for the change.

10. If the transcript is not signed by the witness, or the right to sign is waived, then the officer of the court signs it.

11. Documents and items provided during examination are marked for identification and annexed to the deposition.
12. Depositions are not usually filed with the court unless the court needs to consider their contents or needs the materials to reach a decision.

Discovery is usually limited to a prescribed length of time that, depending upon the jurisdiction, may begin thirty days after a lawsuit has been served and end ten days before the start of the trial or final hearing, or when the plaintiff announces readiness for trial.

The product of discovery, answers to interrogatories, documents, and transcripts, do not usually become part of the court file. If it becomes necessary to file the answers to interrogatories or one party or another desires to have the answers to interrogatories or transcripts of depositions made part of the court file, appropriate arrangements can usually be made. However, it may take a motion and an order; check local rules for the particulars.

During discovery, the procedures—admissions, interrogatories, production, and depositions—are your tools; the subpoena is your muscle and power. However, the planning and thought you give to their use will be a major factor in how productive they are.

## TAKING A DEPOSITION

Taking a deposition is analogous to the excitement and trepidation of a treasure hunt through a constantly shifting maze. The treasure hunt involves unearthing the facts and other information as the drama in which you are taking part unfolds. Possibly some or all of the new information uncovered by your probing questions may lead you down unexpected paths and into new revelations. You may even discern information that will necessitate several new depositions to fully explore these paths.

The feeling of being in a maze results from certain questions leading to dead ends and others opening up to a whole new set of questions. Since this is a process of discovery, you will want to pursue these new avenues of interest; however, you must be sure to make your way back to your main line of questioning. Once a digression is completed and you've hit its dead end, you must be able to pick up where you left off and follow your original plan of questioning through to its conclusion.

Being prepared for a deposition is like having a list of the clues for the treasure hunt well in advance. Having the chance to plan your moves should give you a distinct advantage over the other players. So proper preparation for a deposition, with questions laid out carefully and thoughtfully and your thoughts noted on paper, should enable you to move ahead quickly and efficiently. Otherwise, you'll spend more time and effort on a longer deposition; and since the cost of typing or transcribing the deposition is based on its number of pages, your costs will go up, too.

There are a few tactics that might help you when you are taking a deposition. For example, you might want to use the complaint as a guide, asking your questions based on each allegation in sequence, then moving to questions relating to the response to the allegations, and then to questions relating to the answer and/or affirmative defenses and counterclaims that might be involved in your case. You might also do some legal research before taking the deposition so that you can direct your questions at particular concepts of law and possibly elicit responses that would support your theory and the concept of law under which you are proceeding.

When you are taking a deposition, be prepared to object to certain matters that you feel should not be part of the record. Such objections may play a part in determining whether or not certain materials and/or statements brought up will be taken from the deposition for use at trial. Some jurisdictions may just require a simple objection, and others may require you to indicate the reason for your objection. Before starting the process, check the rules on depositions in your jurisdiction to learn how to handle not only an objection, but a refusal to answer, as well.

The deposition is an extension of the courtroom, so the rules of propriety and court rules of civil procedure apply as if you were sitting in the courtroom before a judge and jury. Keep in mind that the judge (and possibly the jury) may read the transcript at some future time (see Chapter 10). Although you may at times find it difficult, maintain a high level of decorum. Keep your cool, regardless of what may be happening or what may be said. The purpose of the deposition is discovery in a civilized fashion; thus, you should consider an overbearing attitude on the part of an attorney (or party) and the use of heavy-handed methods to be cause for objection. There is no place in the deposition for the repetitious or abusive questioning that sometimes occurs when individuals or attorneys are trying to make a point.

Besides developing information, facts, and documents that may be used as evidence at a hearing or a trial, discovery can also be used to impeach the testimony of a witness. The following story shows how this might be done.

The sailboat on which I was living was taken into custody under a writ of execution in a financial dispute between my corporation, which owned the vessel, and one of its creditors. Without warning, the vessel was seized, inventoried, and locked up—notwithstanding my personal possessions inside the boat.

Through negotiation, I was allowed to enter the ship (my home) accompanied by a sheriff's deputy to retrieve some clothes and medicine. Upon entering the vessel, I discovered in the deputy's presence that a diamond ring was missing from a locked cabinet. What remained in the cabinet was a miniature gold record inscribed *Aerobic Dancing*, which commemorated the production of the first aerobic dancing instruction record to be placed on the market. (It sold over 1 million copies in 1982.)

The box containing the ring was gone, but the gold record was in its original place. The deputy, who had conducted the inventory when the vessel was seized a week earlier, claimed he never saw a ring or any jewelry on the vessel.

The local police refused to get involved, so I made a report to the Internal Affairs Office of the Sheriff's Department. Internal Affairs investigated and, in what I believe to be a total whitewash, pronounced the deputy (hence, the Sheriff's Department) free of complicity in the missing ring and of any negligence in the matter. My only recourse was a lawsuit. I couldn't find a lawyer who was willing to represent me in a suit against the Sheriff of Broward County, so I went pro se.

Part of my discovery process for the suit was deposing the two Internal Affairs officers, a sergeant and a detective, who made their own investigation and search of the vessel, and the deputy who made the original seizure and inventory. All three depositions were taken at separate times, so none of the individuals knew what the others had said.

The thief was not exposed in the discovery process, but the deputy's statements were sufficiently impeached by his fellow officers to call his credibility into serious question. First, the person who did the original inventory of the property on the vessel, a deputy sheriff, was deposed:

*Q.* Okay, did you inventory any jewelry?

*A.* It does not appear on the inventory sheet, either one or two.

*Q.* Did you not? Did you see any jewelry on the boat?

*A.* No, I didn't notice any jewelry on the boat.

*Q.* Did you see any rings?

*A.* I don't recall any jewelry or rings.

*Q.* So you saw no jewelry of any kind on the boat?

*A.* At this time, I can't recall if I ever did.

*Q.* If you had, would it have been on the inventory?

*A.* Yes.

*Q.* Is it your practice to normally put jewelry on the inventory if it's on something that you have seized?

*A*. Yes.

*Q*. That would apply to a ring, a watch, or a bracelet, or a necklace, or anything that would appear to have value?

*A*. Yes.

Next to be deposed was the detective, a member of the Internal Affairs team that had concluded the deputy was innocent. Her hostility is evident, even in this small section of transcript:

*Q*. Did you see other personal items such as paper, pens, reading material?

*A*. There was an awful lot of stuff on that boat, Mr. Schachner. I don't remember—I remember a lot of clothes, a lot of fancy equipment. That's it.

*Q*. Did you see any jewelry on the vessel?

*A*. Not while I was there, sir.

*Q*. I'm going to ask you again, in your opinion, did it appear that someone was residing in the vessel?

*A*. Certify the question, Mr. Schachner, through a judge. [See Certifying a Question, page 105.]

*Q*. Okay. At any time when you first reviewed the inventory of the items on the vessel, did you find any jewelry on it or did you notice whether there was any jewelry reported on the inventory?

*A*. To the best of my memory, I don't recall any jewelry listed on the inventory when I first received it, no sir.

*Q*. Did you think anything unusual about the fact that although clothes and personal items and keys and flashlights were on the inventory that there wasn't a single piece of jewelry? Did you find that unusual?

*A*. No, sir.

Finally, the deposition of the sergeant, the second member of the Internal Affairs team, was taken. Without an axe to grind, he told it like it was:

*Q*. Okay. And did you or the detective find any jewelry whatsoever on that boat during that search?

*A*. I believe we did find a few items of jewelry, but not the items we were looking for. There were some items.

*Q*. Do you recall in among those items of jewelry finding a gold record, a small piece of jewelry resembling a record about two inches around and in a black jewelry box?

*A.* Could you describe it further, the size of the record?

*Q.* About two inches in diameter, gold in color, a loop on the top of it so that it could be hung around someone's neck if they chose to, on a chain and it was in a small black jeweler's case, not an expensive case?

*A.* I have some recollection of seeing something like that but, as far as where it was found and who exactly found it or—I couldn't say.

*Q.* Okay. The last question, sir, is just to reiterate, you do remember seeing some items of jewelry on the boat?

*A.* Yes.

After reviewing these depositions, it was clear that someone either wasn't telling the truth or had a poor memory. As a final witness, a friend and reporter for the *Miami Herald* testified in a deposition that he saw the diamond ring on the vessel the evening before the vessel was taken into custody. The depositions provided sufficient verification of the evidence to schedule the case for trial, and on the trial date, the judge assigned the case to an arbitrator. Upon review of the evidence, the arbitrator awarded me 50 percent of the claim. Counsel for the defendant (the Sheriff's Department), at the suggestion of the arbitrator, indicated the bonding company for the deputy would be informed and the case would be made a permanent part of his personnel record.

## Certifying a Question

In her deposition, the detective asked me to certify a question through a judge. If a deponent refuses to answer a question, regardless of whether or not there is an objection made for the record, a motion to compel answer to certified question can be filed with the court (with copies to all appropriate parties). A hearing can then be held on the question of whether or not the witness should be required to answer the question. If the judge decides that the question should be answered, it will be so ordered. If the witness still refuses to answer, he or she is flirting with contempt of court.

## PROTECTIVE ORDERS

If during discovery, you believe that the intended action or procedure sought by your adversary (such as a scheduled deposition) is either improper, inconvenient, or contrary to the rules of the court, you can make a motion for a protective order. If granted, this order will stop or limit your adversary's action or procedure.

Florida's rules state that protective orders can be requested through a motion by a party to an action or by the individual from whom discovery is sought. In most jurisdictions, you may request a protective order on any of the following grounds:

- Annoyance.
- Embarrassment.
- Oppression.
- Undue burden.
- Undue expense.

Once a motion for a protective order has been made, the judge has, under the rules, the following options in managing the case:

- Not hold the deposition at all.
- Allow the deposition to be taken under certain terms and conditions.
- Hold the deposition in a manner designated by the court.
- Limit the subject matter of the deposition.
- Limit those present at the deposition.
- Seal the deposition's transcript, opening it only by court order.
- Protect trade secrets and other confidential matters.
- Require parties to simultaneously file information in sealed envelopes, to be opened only as directed by the court.

These options give judges at the trial court level wide latitude or discretion. (In other areas of case management, judges are bound by statutes or rules to make certain rulings.) Thus, if the judge decides that a hearing you want blocked should be held, don't begin to plan your appeal. Keep in mind that relatively few cases are appealed; the game is usually won or lost at the trial level whether or not the judge was right or wrong on a particular point of law or procedure. It's up to you to deal with adverse rulings, and to present your case in such a manner that you will win despite such rulings.

## USING DEPOSITIONS AT TRIAL

Once a person is served as a witness, he or she might under certain circumstances provide testimony in the form of a deposition. All states allow the use of depositions at trial under some conditions (see Impeachment of Testimony,

Chapter 16), and more than half the states allow the use of depositions as outlined in Federal Rule of Civil Procedure 32. Providing the court finds the conditions in Rule 32 to be relevant, the depositions can be used for any purpose:

> (A) that the witness is dead; or (B) that the witness is at a greater distance than 100 miles from the place of trial or hearing, or is out of the United States, unless it appears that the absence of the witness was procured by the party offering the deposition; or (C) that the witness is unable to attend or testify because of age, illness, infirmity, or imprisonment; or (D) that the party offering the deposition has been unable to procure the attendance of the witness by subpoena; or (E) upon application and notice, that such exceptional circumstances exist as to make it desirable, in the interest of justice and with due regard to the importance of presenting the testimony of witnesses orally in open court, to allow the deposition to be used.

Whether you are contemplating a request for admissions, interrogatories, a notice to produce, or a full-blown deposition with a court reporter and opposing counsel, remember that discovery is a potent tool for developing the information necessary to pursue or defend a lawsuit.

# CHAPTER 8
# Defensive Strategy

*Before we do that let's agree on the theory of the reply . . . that you
had to have an idea before you expressed it.*

—Felix Frankfurter

In discussing the dangers of trying a case in his courtroom, Judge Paul
Marko III of the Florida Circuit Court said, "You have to know the rules.
It's [winning] got nothing to do with your case being right." The judge
was talking about losing a litigation without even getting to the main issue
of the case. In other words, the judge was concerned about rules, technicalities, and even laws and statutes themselves being used to thwart the enforcement of an otherwise legitimate claim.

But such is life in the courtroom. The plaintiff, even one who has a
legitimate claim, can lose a case because of the defendant's sophisticated use
of the legal process. (This would not usually be true in small claims court).
There is little room for moral, ethical, or personal considerations when
formulating a defensive posture, save an acknowledgment that your position
may be in the legal right or wrong. Assess your position in regard to the
statutes, case law decisions, and rules in order to locate the deficiencies in
your opponent's claim, procedure, or format. The correctness of your position
may have only passing or even no influence on the outcome of your case.
Winning may depend solely on your ability to use the system to block your
opponent's advance.

The defensive strategies that you may use will depend on the area of the
law and the nature of the case in which you are involved, and what your
objectives are. However, the outcome of any defensive posture is limited to
the following:

- Outright win: The plaintiff loses, and is assessed costs, punitive damages, and/or penalties.
- Outright win: The plaintiff loses, and is assessed costs.
- Partial win: The court allows some portion of the plaintiff's claim to stand.
- Outright loss: The plaintiff's claims are sustained against you.
- Outright loss: Costs, penalties, and/or punitive damages are assessed against you.
- Settlement: This may occur before, during, or after the trial or judge/jury's decision.

The process leading up to the resolution of the claim against you as described above can be as simple as choosing not to defend the claim at all and allowing a judgment. (This may be considered when an individual or entity is judgment-proof—has no apparent assets that can be levied or seized pursuant to the court's judgment.) It might be as technical as working to improve your settlement posture through various responses and procedures. It might be as involved as launching a full-blown counterclaim. Or it might involve a combination of these strategies. Before we discuss strategies aimed at prevailing with these procedures, let's look at the management of a typical (though hypothetical) lawsuit—the case of Jim and Nicole Anderson. This case will provide a model with which we will demonstrate and apply some defensive moves.

Three years ago, Jim and Nicole Anderson bought an expensive car when Jim's company promoted him. Unfortunately for the Andersons, Jim's company later lost a large part of its market share and had to reduce its executive staff. Jim was fired.

Nicole and Jim reviewed the family budget and decided that the car had to go in favor of a more economical model. Jim called the finance company that had lent them the money to buy the expensive auto. The sympathetic loan officer suggested that Jim turn the car in along with his payment book, and that everything would be okay. As far as the Andersons were concerned, the matter was closed. They were willing to swallow the loss of the plush car in favor of lower overhead for the family.

However, almost a year later, after the paperwork had worked its way through the finance company, its attorney's office, and the court clerk's office (the finance company having instituted a lawsuit), a process server knocked at the Andersons' door late one afternoon when only the Andersons' fourteen-year-old son was at home. The server left the summons and complaint with the youngster, and instructed him to give the papers to his parents when they got home. The lad promptly went out to play with his friends, and he left the suit papers on a pile of other papers lying on the kitchen counter.

Being concerned with other matters, Jim and Nicole did not look for, and find, the wayward complaint in the kitchen until they received a default judgment in the mail. The finance company had sold their expensive car at auction, and had received less than the amount the Andersons still owed, leaving a deficiency. According to the promissory note and security agreement the Andersons had signed when they bought the car, the Andersons were responsible for any and all deficiencies following such a sale, along with attorneys' fees and collection costs. With the haunting realization that they might have to pay a judgment of several thousand dollars, a major blow to their much-reduced budget, a black cloud settled over the family. Their son even assumed guilt for forgetting to tell his parents about the delivery of the court papers that unfortunate afternoon. The crowning blow was a call from the finance company's attorney demanding full payment of the default judgment in ten days, or else.

Now, let's look at some of the issues raised in this case. The Andersons' first concern would be to determine how the default was obtained. The manner in which papers are served on a defendant is extremely important. If the papers are not served upon a proper party in a proper way, then the default and/or judgment should be set aside. Remember that the Andersons' fourteen-year-old son received the court papers. In most jurisdictions, such a person is too young to receive papers; if that is the case where the Andersons live, the finance company—the plaintiff—did not obtain proper jurisdiction over the Andersons—the defendants. (Had the original court papers been served on Jim or Nicole personally, there would be no basis for claiming improper service, and the Andersons would have had the responsibility to answer the summons and complaint within the allowed time.) The Andersons could go to court and, after presenting proper sworn testimony or a sworn affidavit along with the motion, have the default and judgment set aside. This would provide them with an opportunity to be heard with regard to any defenses they might have to the finance company's claim and with their reason for not timely filing their answer.

It is not usually sufficient just to demonstrate that service has been defective; you must also show the court that a valid defense exists. If no valid defense exists, then it doesn't matter when the judgment was obtained, and any delay would just be a waste of time. However, the Andersons can demonstrate, at least at this early stage of litigation, a defense based on their claim they were misled by the finance company's employee into believing that the physical return of the vehicle and payment book and its acceptance by the finance company constituted a release and waiver. This ultimately may or may not prove to be valid, but it is a starting place.

Let's assume the judge, upon a hearing, had granted the Andersons twenty days to file their answer to the complaint, ruling that service was not properly made and that a defense may exist. The next thing that Nicole and Jim must do is review the papers that were served on them, noting each particular item that is claimed. They would be looking for some technical error or deficiency that might exist in the drafting, preparation, or handling of the original complaint that would give them the basis for a motion for a more definite statement, a motion to strike, or a motion to dismiss. For instance, there might be a recitation in the complaint that exhibits are attached to the complaint, when no exhibits are attached. They are entitled to those exhibits. The Andersons could use the fact that they are missing as a basis for a motion for more definite statement or a motion to dismiss and, through such motion, ask the court to require that all documents that are alleged in the complaint be attached. If the complaint talks about agreements that were made, and does not state that the agreements are attached, there is the similar likelihood that those agreements are required as attachments or exhibits to the complaint. If they are not attached, the Andersons would have the basis to file either of these two motions.

Going one step further, if the complaint talks about agreements but fails to state whether these agreements are oral or written, the Andersons would be entitled to know which type of agreement is alleged. They are, of course, entitled to obtain copies of any written agreements. If there is an oral agreement, they would then want to look to see whether or not the complaint alleges what the terms and conditions of that oral agreement are in sufficient detail. If the complaint simply states there was an oral agreement but does not state the terms and conditions of the agreement, then the Andersons would ask the court for relief in an appropriate motion.

These are the kinds of procedures that give you the time to sit back and reflect upon the case against you. You also gain an opportunity to make the other side show some of its hand at an earlier stage than they would like to.

When examining the complaint, look carefully at the claim or claims against you. If the language used is so imprecise or so legal that it doesn't really say what the claim is, then you should bring this to the court's attention. Explain in your motion that you simply cannot decipher what the plaintiff is alleging, or even why there is a complaint against you. A motion for a more definite statement is something that the court may then determine. If that's the case, the court would direct the plaintiff to rewrite its complaint so that not only the defendant, but the court would understand what the claims are.

As we have emphasized before, response time is critical in the legal arena. To protect your rights, note any deadlines on your personal calendar. Once you have noted the date, and understand when the clock starts and stops ticking, you can seize control of time and possibly use it to your benefit. For instance, the response time to a summons and complaint might be twenty days in your jurisdiction. Unless there is a compelling reason to make some kind of responsive filing almost immediately (a "time is of the essence" case), file on or near the last day of the period. Taking the maximum time allows you to prepare yourself for procedures, review the facts, make an outline of your defenses, consider and determine your claims, review the rules, and draft and redraft your response (whether you have an actual answer or choose to use one or more of the motions already described). Your opponent will just have to wait the allotted time before reading your response and proceeding with the case.

Another aspect of time that can work for you is the statute of limitations. Most claims may be filed only within a certain period of time, the average being about three to four years from the date of the incident involved in the claim. If a claim against you is based upon an occurrence that long ago, you should definitely check your jurisdiction's statutes on time limitations. Certain kinds of claims must be filed in a shorter period of time, such as (in Florida) lawsuits regarding professional liability (medical, legal, and accounting). Areas involving fraud, oral contracts, auto accidents, and negligence may each have a different time limit for filing claims. If you determine that the statute of limitations in your particular situation is three years, and you have been served well into the fourth year, then you must timely raise the statute of limitations defense in your answer's affirmative defense section. (You would allege that the particular claim against you is barred by the statute of limitations.) The court would then have sufficient basis to find in your favor and stop the action upon proper motion and hearing.

Keep in mind, however, that there are always exceptions and differing interpretations of the same laws and statutes. The complaint might be ambiguous as to whether it is dealing with an agreement or with fraud, and the particular claims may fall under different statutes with different time limitations. Thus, you may find yourself avoiding one claim but defending another.

Other ambiguities may come up. The agreement that brought you to court, and which you perceived as an oral agreement, may be interpreted by the judge as a written agreement because there exists a written memorandum that was previously overlooked. The memo, which substantially recites the terms and conditions of what was previously just an oral agreement, would then be the basis for the allegations in the plaintiff's complaint and the judge's ruling. A case with a set of ambiguous facts such as these is a living, fluid situation in which the parameters can change simply on the presentation and perception of evidence.

Another gray area occurs in professional liability cases. It may be difficult to determine when the statute of limitations takes effect. Lawmakers have recognized the fact that an individual may not be able to recognize that a violation or damaging action has occurred until many months or years later, when a circumstance arises that brings attention to the professional mistake. Say that upon selling your home, you agreed to hold the mortgage for the buyer. You had an attorney prepare a mortgage document that included certain sanctions for nonpayment. You had no reason to enforce these clauses in the document until five years later, when payments were not timely made and you had to go to court to foreclose to protect your interests. Suddenly, you learn that you cannot foreclose because the document was incorrectly drawn and your attorney was the culprit. You might be able to get a finding that the statute of limitations clock started ticking only at the the time you learned the document was not properly drawn.

Now back to the Andersons. Nicole and Jim have solved the initial default crisis, and have gained some breathing room to contemplate their strategy and legal position. First, they need to review thoroughly all documents pertinent to their case. They must calculate the interest rate they were charged for the loan in relation to the jurisdiction's usury statutes. (Perhaps a mistake was made and they were charged a rate in excess of what was allowable.) The Andersons must review the language of the note and security agreement for possible defects and/or inconsistencies with the jurisdiction's statutes that control finance agreements and security interests. Jim and Nicole also have to decide whether or not to add a third-party defendant in the suit. It might be found that the dealership was involved in the same or related improper acts as the finance company, and vice versa. This may bring the sales contract, which was the original basis for the obligation, under consideration. It too should be carefully examined for possible errors. The names of the parties, their capacities, whether a party may be an improper party, or whether a party is competent to enter into the transaction are all factors that must be examined.

I had personal experience with discovery after the fact that a party (me) was not competent to enter into a transaction. As a young wholesale record distributor representing forty record labels in the Midwest in 1961, I found I needed a more suitable car for my lengthy road trips. I found a sporty red MG at a typical used-car dealer. My bank account was not flush, since I was just starting out in business, but the dealer was so anxious to unload the good-looking car that he arranged not only the primary financing, but also a second loan with a small local finance company. I was off and motoring, and my first road trip was through the mountains of Maryland—a real treat with a peppy little sports car. Sales were good, the ride was fun, but the car was burning a quart of oil per tank of gas—a sign of major motor problems to come.

I went back to the dealer and asked him to fix the engine. I was still enjoying the car and hoped to have it repaired quickly. The dealer said, "I can't do anything for you—it's your car now."

Fortunately, before I returned to the dealer, someone had tipped me off to an obscure Pennsylvania law requiring that a vehicle be taken back (the transaction rescinded), with a full refund, at any time if it could be established that the purchaser was under 21 at the time of the sale. I was not yet 21, and although I didn't know it when I bought the car, I was not a competent buyer. Thus, I replied to the dealer, "No sir. Since you won't fix the car, it's yours—I'm not yet 21 years old." I produced my driver's license as evidence, and within moments my old car was placed in front of me and I was abruptly asked to leave. Someone else got stuck with that good-looking, oil-burning lemon.

In Jim and Nicole's case, the dealership might not have given proper value as contemplated. Was the vehicle delivered to the Andersons as represented or valued in the sales contract, or was the car overvalued by the dealership? (This occurs most frequently with a car that is financed.) An investigation into the facts of a case such as this would extend to whether or not the dealer and lender are properly licensed to run or own a dealership and a lending institution.

The next step is for the Andersons to review the jurisdiction's list of possible affirmative defenses. Just looking at this list might raise issues that were vague concerns for the Andersons following the repossession: Was there full and proper consideration? Was the auction sale an arm's-length transaction? Were there misrepresentations or elements of fraud perpetrated by the finance company by virtue of the sale and disposal of the vehicle? Did the finance company use an auction sale at a price that didn't reflect the so-called loan value of the car? Did they intend to get sufficient value to cover the outstanding loan amount?

The Andersons should give special consideration to attacking the loss the finance company suffered in auctioning the car. If the car was sold at auction, it is likely that the finance company represented to the Andersons that it checked certain publications to determine the value of the vehicle at the time of the sale in order to determine the retail, wholesale, and loan values of the car. However, when the Andersons bought the car, the finance company required sufficient value for the purpose of protecting its interest (the amount of the loan). The finance company effectively indicated to the Andersons, by approving the loan, that the value they placed on the car would be sufficient. Yet, notwithstanding the representations of value made when the Andersons bought the car, the Andersons now find that the sales price at auction is uniformly very low. The Andersons had every right to expect, based on representations made to them by the dealer and the finance company, that the lender's interests were covered in the event of a sale.

There is an interesting parallel to this concerning real estate foreclosures. Following the sale on the courthouse steps, fair market value would be given to the borrower even when the bid amount is less than the amount of the judgment, or if the fair market value is less than the amount lent. Thus, the auction price is usually enough to cover the first mortgage. For automobiles, however, in some jurisdictions there is no law establishing a value of the property consistent with its appraised or fair market value. And in the Andersons' case, the values of the autos in the auction were established well below their market values.

Jim's lender had to be aware that the price obtained at the so-called auto auction did not reflect the car's blue book loan value, even after depreciation. The dealer also had to be aware of this at the time of the original sale to the Andersons, but effectively misrepresented and defrauded the Andersons by allowing them to believe that the value of the vehicle would be sufficient to cover the amount of the loan, after the deposit and monthly payments. The Andersons were therefore misled and misdirected in returning the vehicle without fear of a deficiency, and in anticipating that the vehicle's value would be sufficient to cover the outstanding loan amount.

This theory generates certain defenses related to fraud. Such a defense occurs often, but is unusual in cases like the Andersons'. However, at any time, new theories may come into vogue. By looking at the standard defenses set forth in the jurisdiction's rules and by applying their set of facts, the Andersons can determine whether they have a potentially unique application.

Now that Nicole and Jim have looked at some of the factors that can go into a defense, they are ready to file their answer, along with any appropriate affirmative defenses, counterclaims, or third-party claims. The Andersons must go through each paragraph of the complaint and review each allegation of fact for correctness. They will then admit or deny each paragraph unless they use a general denial for all the allegations in the complaint. (In many jurisdictions it is possible to file an answer that simply denies the entire set of allegations as opposed to specifically denying each allegation used to establish a case against you.) In effect, they are saying that the allegations are not true, and are requiring the plaintiff to present evidence, appropriate testimony, documentation, exhibits, and the like to the point where a preponderance of the evidence is in favor of the plaintiff in the mind of the trier of fact (judge or jury).

It is usually pretty difficult to deny allegations such as that you are a certain age, that you are you, and that you are a resident of a certain jurisdiction. However, you may deny allegations that you were involved in the contract, that you were obligated pursuant to the contract, that a set of facts occurred that you believe did not occur, and the like. For example, in a mortgage foreclosure, if there is an allegation that you are the owner of a property, and you are the owner, you would admit that allegation. However, you must look at the allegation from several viewpoints. If the suit is against you as an individual, but you are one of two persons who own the property with a right of survivorship and in your jurisdiction such joint ownership is treated as a separate entity from you as an individual, then you could properly deny the allegation of ownership.

What about the Andersons' counterclaims? Careful consideration of the facts in the case may reveal counterclaims or third-party claims. For instance, if the Andersons had purchased an extended warranty and service contract through the dealership and that contract terminated when the car left the Andersons' control, there might be a refund due for unused premiums. If the dealership did not make this refund, a counterclaim for that amount would be proper. In this case, however, the Andersons did not buy the warranty and service contract; there was no transaction whereby the dealership and/or lending institution obligated themselves to the Andersons. After reviewing the balance of the facts, no other counterclaims came to light.

The Andersons then chose a unique approach to their defense: They drew a parallel between how their over-appraised car had been sold at auction and what happens when over-appraised real estate is sold at auction, leaving the lender with a deficiency. This is a creative defensive strategy; so creative that, if carried through the appeals process with an affirmative decision, it might set a precedent.

Some defenses may be tried and true; others may be creative. Don't expect always to find a new legal path to solution, but always be on the lookout for one.

Finding a new way to attack an old problem can bring a separate set of difficulties. One difficulty is how to find a means, as a layperson, to test a theory. Lawyers engage in shoptalk with each other, often exploring untested theories. A layperson who is not constrained by convention may develop fresh ideas, but will need to test or discuss these new approaches with a professional to check their validity. Using an innovative defense also makes the case more complex, and deciding whether to request a jury or to stay with the decision of the judge becomes more difficult.

Jim and Nicole must now decide whether or not to ask for a jury. They know that choosing a jury trial will add some wrinkles to their strategy. Since a jury's deliberations are based on the material placed before it, they would have to be concerned—from the answer all the way through the taking and presentation of evidence—with the thought that a group of laypeople (guided by the judge) will determine the case's outcome.

Another consideration is what type of person the judge is, based on observations and experience. The Andersons are testing new legal ground with their defense. Will the judge be willing to rule adversely to the continuing interests of banks, established auto dealerships, or any other well-entrenched businesses or organizations that may be affected, and all of which may be represented by prestigious law firms? Lawyers with these firms associate with the various judges, and may know their personal habits, attitudes, and manners, their professional and business relationships, their prior decisions on similar or parallel issues, and their courtroom demeanor. Even though the judge may be a learned person with great integrity, the situation may call for a jury to balance the judge.

Jim and Nicole decide not to ask for a jury trial simply because for them to attempt a full jury trial would create too much of a burden on their limited knowledge and resources. Also, they feel that their case would be best tried by a judge alone, who will give them a professional hearing on a complicated issue.

Next, the Andersons have a waiting game—waiting to be hit with the various motions that a plaintiff will so often use to try to overcome the defendant. They should expect a motion to strike, a motion for judgment on the pleadings, and possibly a motion for summary judgment. The plaintiff will certainly try to shortcut the Andersons' unique defense and press the case more quickly than Jim and Nicole can respond. If this happens, the Andersons should approach the court by proper motion and ask for a continuance (additional time) to properly respond to the plaintiff's allegations. This may entail time to complete discovery or certain phases of discovery in order to gain information that will buttress their defensive claims.

The amount of time granted will depend on the jurisdiction in which the case is being heard, along with the position the court takes regarding the plaintiff's motions—whether they are stayed or continued (postponed). If Jim and Nicole do not take this immediate defensive position and ask the court for the time necessary to use the discovery process, the plaintiff may hit them with a volume of pleadings that is too great for the Andersons to respond to, or with a notice to set the trial that will move the case ahead too quickly, preventing complete discovery.

For the court to accept affirmative defenses, and for these defenses to prevail, they need to be carefully expressed, in a particular form and based on the rules and practice in the jurisdiction. Also, the plaintiff will try to have the affirmative defenses knocked out quickly. Jim and Nicole are aware that they may be faced with an untimely hearing on their case relative to the affirmative defenses. If this happens, they plan to respond with a request for time in which to file an amended answer, with a sharper focus on their affirmative defenses. However, by doing this, they are using up important leverage. The court may allow two or even three opportunities to amend, but there will be a point where the court will finally not allow any changes to the pleadings, especially defenses that are not well-drafted or are unreasonable in terms of what the court finds to be the requisite format for these defenses. For instance, an affirmative defense that does nothing more than state that the defendant was defrauded at the time of the transaction will not be accepted, for the court will want to see reasonable and specific allegations of what constituted the fraud.

Another look at the real estate arena will illustrate this. If a defendant who has not made mortgage payments for six months to two years now attempts to raise defenses, a simple denial of the basic allegations of the complaint will not likely forestall a properly drafted motion for summary judgment. Just a claim that "the mortgageholder defrauded the defendant at the time the mortgage was established" won't be sufficient. The court will want to see reasonably specific allegations of what is claimed to constitute fraud. However, if the claim is that the loan was written in such a way that negative amortization resulted (the loan amount is actually increasing, and the monthly payments will not cover the principal and interest in the time specified in the mortgage), and this was not reasonably disclosed to the borrower at the closing of the loan, basic elements of a potential fraud on the part of the lender exist. Once the affirmative defense is asserted and the allegation of fraud by the lender is made, the defendant would need to prove the factual basis for that claim and then provide the court sufficient research or law to show a basis for the affirmative defense of fraud.

Discovery may be necessary to develop the facts of a case. Once the facts are known, research can begin to apply the facts to varying principles of law. In other words, research is necessary to find the legal doctrine permitting the application of the discovered facts. These legal principles, or doctrines, can then form the basis of an artfully drafted affirmative defense that encompasses the facts of the case within the framework of an acceptable legal theory. Therefore, after discovery has been completed, it may be necessary to amend the affirmative defenses based on the facts discovered.

Fortunately, at their first appearance before the judge, the Andersons kept their presence of mind and related the difficulties they foresaw in obtaining the information necessary to prove their affirmative defenses. They asked for, and received, sufficient time to take the depositions of the original lending officer, representatives of the dealership, sales personnel, and other representatives of the lending institution. Also, they indicated to the judge that they might use expert testimony from a person in the automotive field that they felt would corroborate the true value of the car at the time they returned it and at the time it was auctioned. The Andersons hope to show that the value was substantially less at the auction than what was shown in the industry blue book, which every dealer and lender has and normally uses.

The Andersons' plan is to have some pieces of discovery (evidence) to present to the court in support of their contention of fraud. They will also use the information gained in discovery to amend their affirmative defenses.

The defense of a motion for summary judgment, a judgment on the pleadings, or a motion to strike affirmative defensives will require not only the presentation of issues of fact to the court, but also the presentation of some elements of law or precedent that, when applied to the facts of the instant case, will create a question of law for the court to decide. When your affirmative defenses are unique and you can't find a decision exactly on point, one way around this dilemma would be to look to another area of law for a reasonable parallel. Jim and Nicole are relying on the courthouse foreclosure sale as their parallel. They have successfully beaten back their opponent's challenges with discovery information and enough legal research to convince the judge that a parallel might indeed exist and need to be adjudicated in a trial where all the evidence and all the law can be presented by both sides.

With the completion of pretrial motions; amended complaints, answers, and affirmative defenses; and discovery, the case is ready for trial. In most jurisdictions, there are heavy burdens on the judicial system and it may be necessary to wait quite a while before receiving the trial notice. During this period, Jim and Nicole will have a chance to reflect on their legal position and the evidence discovered, and prepare for their presentation to the judge. No doubt, just as the legal issues, facts, and emotions of the case begin to fade from their minds, they will receive their notice of trial.

## ADDITIONAL DEFENSIVE STRATEGIES

A well-known maxim is, "The best defense is a strong offense." You may not always be able to find an angle for a counterclaim, but when one exists or appears to be viable, you should use it to your every advantage.

### Counterclaims

My record company once used a single manufacturer to do everything involved in producing our records. This included making the master record and metal parts for molding, creating the art and design for the jacket, and printing and fabricating the jacket as well as pressing the finished record. The manufacturer did all this in what was then a state-of-the-art facility for making phonograph records. (Its enormous capability was demonstrated when I produced 40,000 record albums there in less than a week for comedian Dick Gregory.)

Unfortunately, our relationship with the factory turned sour when its eccentric owner (my mentor in the music business) demanded full payment on the outstanding account—without warning and with no compromise. Nothing was going to be shipped out of the factory unless the sum was paid in full.

There I was at 22 with a $30,000 lawsuit. As a defensive posture began to take shape in my mind, I started to add up the value of the materials in the factory (and not in my possession) that my company had either paid for or for which my company had been billed. My attorney and I developed a counterclaim for the value of these goods and services, including inventories of finished records and the parts used to produce them. Our claim was more than double the factory's claim. The factory never contacted us again, and probably disposed of any inventory in a manner they saw fit.

## Compulsory Counterclaims

One of the two types of counterclaims is a compulsory counterclaim. It must be filed at the time the answer is filed, and it relates directly to matters on which the plaintiff has sued. Say a plaintiff sold you a large quantity of widgets for which you still owe a certain sum of money. You then determine that the widgets were in some way defective; you are getting a large number of returns, plus a quantity of bad product is still out in the field. Not only are you having to issue credit for the returned widgets, but you may also face damages from third parties because your product was represented to your customers as being in good condition. Since the defective widgets created damages in excess of the simple value of the product itself (your profits), you now have a counterclaim that exceeds the value of the goods. This is a compulsory counterclaim, and must be filed at the time you file your answer to protect your right to make the claim.

## Permissive Counterclaims

An alternative situation might develop that provides you with the second type of counterclaim, a permissive counterclaim. For example, you may find that your supplier provided certain materials, which you used to manufacture a product that you then sold to customers. Because the plaintiff had need for your product, he arranged to buy it from you. When he failed to pay you, it became an overdue account. This would be a separate transaction on your accounts receivable ledger that was never previously pursued for collection.

At a later date, the plaintiff—your supplier and customer—files a suit against your company and, although you don't have a counterclaim arising out of his suit, your claim for the past indebtedness from the plaintiff is an appropriate setoff or permissive counterclaim because this claim could have been pursued by your company independently either before or after and separate from the supplier's action. This is contrasted with a simple setoff for a credit or return, which is usually a bookkeeping question and handled as an affirmative defense against the amount of the obligation being claimed against you.

Keep in mind that just because you have (or believe you have) a counterclaim or a setoff against the plaintiff, that does not mean you have no ultimate obligation. In fact, your obligation to the other party may be increased by virtue of attorneys' fees, costs, and interest, which may be assessed against you if the court finds against you on the plaintiff's primary case. This potential liability is especially treacherous when your claim is not a clear and obvious setoff that generates an obvious reason to hold back money. Unless you happen to be judgment-proof, a small obligation might be turned into a monumental one by allowing a legal battle to ensue, creating costs and exposing you (or your company) to attorneys' fees, costs, and interest if you lose. And it is not often correct to hold back payment when it is clearly due pursuant to a written document. For example, rent is not usually properly held back where required by a written lease. An adverse claim in a leasehold situation does not usually void the need to pay rent on a timely basis, unless a situation exists for placing the rent in trust with the court.

In addition to counterclaims, let's look at other defensive strategies that an astute attorney or layperson might use. (These designations are my own.)

## Testing a New Theory

I have always believed that the practice of law can be creative. One important area of creativity is the development of a new theory as a useful defense or offense. Carefully crafted and researched, the new defense can be incorporated in the first pleading (the answer) in a case brought before a court. If the theory doesn't fly in the opinion of the judge, nothing will be lost. In the early stages of a failed defense, the court will probably instruct you to correct or amend your answer. In doing so, the court will either impose a time limit for filing the amended or corrected answer; more simply, it will allow the time set forth in the rules for correcting a pleading. If your theory is actually accepted by the court, not only have you successfully tested a new theory, but your approach to your defense will probably throw your opponent well off stride.

However, even if the court allows your new theory to stand, you will need to prove its validity in relation to the facts of the case, which is probably no small task. But at the very least, you have gained time and seized the initiative.

## The Tortoise Versus the Hare

Why drag out the settlement process if the outcome seems inevitable? One compelling reason, especially if your case appears to be a losing one, is that you may have very little defensive strategy otherwise, but you may not wish to throw in the towel. Therefore, you press on, taking advantage of the slowness of the system, hoping that circumstances will change to your benefit. Looking for a slip-up by your opponent, you dutifully file your responses and go through discovery, perhaps even nitpicking your way to a trial date. Then it happens—the inevitable is overturned, and you win against all odds. Here's an actual case of this happening.

A nationally known freight company sued a record manufacturer for some past-due freight bills. At the deposition of the record company executive, the freight company's attorney pointed out that the faxed copies of the alleged open invoices were unreadable. A second attempt to fax the invoices from the freight company's headquarters again produced unreadable copies. A settlement was then proposed and appeared to be accepted by both parties. However, the record company, having fallen on hard times because cassette tapes and compact discs were eliminating sales of phonograph records, could not consummate the deal. The freight company sued the manufacturer, a trial date was set, and the trial should have resulted in a judgment for the plaintiff.

At the trial, the plaintiff's attorney offered to provide the court with affidavits from the freight company attesting to the invoices they claimed to be due. The lawyer even provided the court with readable copies. The record company's attorney objected to the affidavits as opposed to the presentation of live testimony.

There was no witness present for the plaintiff, for their attorney was so sure of winning that she had not made arrangements to secure a witness. You cannot cross-examine an affidavit. The case ended with a decision in favor of the defendant, with prejudice (see Glossary). The hare had stumbled, and the tortoise moved ahead to victory.

## Examination for Defects and Flaws

Life can be very complicated, especially life in business. To paraphrase William Shakespeare, the best-laid plans of corporate counselors and businesspeople often go astray. I've seen David slay Goliath because David had better vision. Goliath was so consumed by his objective that he didn't see the missile that shot him down until it was too late.

You can use your opponent's oversight, ineptness, or laxness to your benefit. But to take advantage of this strategy, you have to know the rules and the ins and outs of the particular subject better than your opponent does. Many practicing attorneys believe they know the law and the rules involving a given action or set of actions. Because they think they know, they do not research, study, examine, and contemplate the words in the rule book or statute book for each case they handle. A layperson acting pro se must do this, for she has no previous knowledge on which to rely. Her examination of the rules and statutes makes her an expert on the subject at that time. Therein lies her advantage. The layperson acting pro se or an astute attorney will look at the whole transaction as if it were under a microscope, searching for flaws and defects, and then use any inadequacies to construct a defense. Sometimes, every word in every paragraph of the supporting documents in a case must be examined in relation to the laws and statutes that control the subject matter.

In this chapter, we have tried to provide you with the means for an effective defense regardless of the facts of your case. There is always the possibility that you will win your case because you are right and your opponent is wrong. However, as Judge Marko said, winning may not have anything to do with who is right. Thus, whether you have all the evidence on your side or not, use the strategies in this chapter to their fullest extent.

# CHAPTER 9

# Safeguarding Your Claim: Documentation

*We do not brag about our plans in advance. We do something, then we tell everything.*

—A Russian Scientist

C ollecting and objectively evaluating evidence is, of course, paramount in successful litigation. You may have a strong desire to pursue an injustice after your first blush fades, but the availability of evidence may be the determining factor as to whether a claim, however just, can be pursued. The availability of evidence can run the gamut from being so restricted that the cost of obtaining it outweighs any possible benefits of prevailing in a lawsuit, to complete accessibility.

From 1961 through 1965, I produced, with the support of the Aluminum Company of America, a recording entitled *Year in Review*. This was an audio-news digest with the actual voices and sound of the news linked to a commentary—a yearbook on record. The series, on the Gateway Record label, had such actualities (recorded voice and sound news clips) as Martin Luther King, Jr.'s speech at the 1965 Washington civil rights rally; Joan Baez singing "We Shall Overcome" at the same rally; Adlai Stevenson's angry United Nations speech to the Soviets in which he said, "I will wait 'til hell freezes over for your answer"; and most of the other noteworthy utterances of presidents and kings, scientists and victims, and politicians and private individuals caught in circumstances that projected them into the world's headlines. Even Collier's Encyclopedia used the recordings as an adjunct to their yearly encyclopedia supplement. Alcoa advertised the recordings in their plants and offices, and Gateway Records placed ads in scholarly publications. (See Figure 9.1, an ad from *Library Journal*, October 1963, page 359.)

**Figure 9.1.** An advertisement from *Library Journal*.

In January 1964, an ad concerning a 1963 recording produced by RCA appeared in *Billboard* (January 25, 1964, page 15), the recording industry trade paper. This recording copied our *Year in Review* concept exactly. Chet Huntley and David Brinkley had their own version of "my" product. I was stunned and hurt—not because an idea had been copied, not because this popular news duo chose to release a competitive product, but because the ad read, "The only record to cover the entire momentous year 1963." They might have said, "the best," "the greatest," "the most complete," "the only one with Huntley/Brinkley"; instead, they chose "the only."

There was no hunt for evidence in this instance; no expensive discovery to pursue, no depositions to be taken. The evidence was right there in a published advertisement. The magnitude of RCA's error was reflected in that, after they were placed on legal notice, the giant corporation chose to have their chief counsel answer our attorney's letter.

In a commercial dispute, documentation is usually the primary source of evidence to prove or disprove a contention of fact. It's not always as easy as clipping an advertisement out of a newspaper, and may require chasing an extensive paper trail to find the facts of what took place. Think about the class action suit against A. H. Robins for the defective and dangerous Dalkon Shield contraceptive device. (There are over 200,000 claimants.) It took numerous trips by special U.S. magistrates and one trip by federal judge Miles Lord from his home base in Minneapolis to the offices of the manufacturer in Virginia to amass the documents necessary for the case. The litigation lasted thirteen years.

If you have original documents in your possession, you should copy and carefully review them with discovery procedures in mind. If the documents are in your opponent's possession, a notice to produce can be served or a deposition (with a subpoena duces tecum) could be held in an attempt to gain possession of a copy and/or additional information from the documents. If you have original documentation, do not give it up at any time, including at depositions and pursuant to notices to produce. You can make and deliver copies in accordance with the terms of the discovery process in your jurisdiction.

The paper chase (or treasure hunt, if you like) for evidence can be complicated. You must look under every stone, pebble, and grain of sand for evidence that might sustain your position. Very often your transaction, the one that is the subject of the litigation, or evidence of it will end up being part of or recorded indirectly in other documents:

- Federal income tax returns.
- State sales returns.
- State tax returns.
- Accounting ledgers.
- Financial reports.
- Applications to banks and other lending institutions (including factors).

All of these documents may have references that could directly or indirectly tie into the transaction under contention. Some other items to look for that may become part of your discovery process are documents related to your transaction, memoranda (internal or external), diaries, calendars, and third-party documents.

Here's an example of the result of a not-so-thorough search. Three years after losing a zoning case in a small New Jersey town regarding an application for a nonconforming use expansion of a dog kennel, I happened across the original survey of the property that was filed in the township records. The plan indicated that the building that was the subject of the contested expansion had previously been used as a dog kennel, my intended use, and was in fact listed in the township records as such. This single piece of evidence, located in the very halls of justice where the hearings were conducted three years earlier, would have been enough to prove my case and force the zoning board to remove its restrictions upon the use of the building. Obviously, this loss can only be attributed to some sloppy legal work done by the lawyer who handled the zoning application and hearing. Your search for evidence must be extremely thorough.

As you collect evidence, you must index and file it. The more extensive the case and the more complicated the issue, the more paper will be generated. Organization for fast and efficient referral and retrieval of documents and information is essential to effective case management for both the seasoned attorney and the individual acting pro se.

If a transaction involves damage to goods, materials, or equipment, additional steps should be taken to safeguard a possible claim. It may be an old adage, but a picture is worth a thousand words and may save, avoid, or supplement considerably more expensive discovery. Taking pictures is also a simple and effective way to preserve evidence. (In the courtroom, pictures should have backup testimony from the person who took them, along with testimony as to the date, time, place, and circumstances under which the pictures were taken.) Using experts to make an independent evaluation or a testing laboratory to make a report (written or verbal) is another option that you might use if circumstances warrant.

It's common for most of us to have at one time or another sustained damage by workers, retailers, manufacturers, or technicians, but it's not always easy to prove the complaint, or ineptness or negligence on the part of the offending party. A little foresight and clear thinking can help in situations that you feel might be heading toward a legal confrontation. Here's an example.

Living on a sailboat, as I once did, presents a unique set of maintenance problems. I didn't have to mow the lawn or fix the roof; instead, I had to deal with things like maintaining the auxiliary diesel electric generator. Since its workings are beyond my mechanical expertise, I hired what I thought was a competent technician to maintain and repair that very sophisticated piece of equipment. After several general maintenance calls, which built my confidence in the individual, the mechanic informed me that the starter had to be replaced. A few months later, he informed me that the job had to be done again, that it was not his fault, that something else had gone wrong in the machine to burn out the starter a second time. This time I decided to do some independent checking.

When the mechanic completed the work, I asked him for all the parts that were replaced. Carefully packaging them up, I sent them to the Onan Corporation, the manufacturer. I asked Onan for an evaluation of the damage to the parts in light of the repairs I was forced to make a second time. Their report stated, in part: "The starter solenoid could have failed as a result of: (1) incorrect adjustment of the linkage, causing damage."

I now had documented evidence that the "qualified" mechanic was, in fact, incompetent (in my judgment). Since other problems ensued with the machine during the months it took to secure the report from Onan, I believed I was justified in taking my evidence in hand and, with the help of my attorney, filing a lawsuit against the mechanic. The fact that the mechanic made his living from Florida's boating community ensured his continued availability until the matter could be adjudicated.

Unfortunately, there are all too many instances of defendants being elusive or of final judgments being uncollectable. Defendants may also hide behind the protection of a corporation. Rarely is it possible to "pierce the corporate veil" and hold an officer or director personally responsible for the corporation's actions. (Two exceptions: The Internal Revenue Service and U.S. trademark and copyright law hold corporate officers and board members liable for a corporation's actions.) Doing this usually entails proving fraud or intentional deceit. If there is any question as to the availability or validity of a possible defendant, plunging headlong into costly litigation would be foolish without first establishing the culpability and financial soundness of your potential adversary. Here's a case in point.

In the late 1960s, I built a phonograph record manufacturing plant on a farm in Pennsylvania. It was with great excitement and heart-pounding anticipation that my crew and I started up the plant late one summer evening. Unfortunately, one record after another came out of the press with what appeared to be foreign matter embedded in the plastic, rendering them useless. The delicate metal stampers used to press the records were also being ruined. These stampers cost about $50 per set and had to be made 400 miles away in New York. I tried everything! Our engineer tried everything! Then one record came out of the press with a half-inch triangular piece of foreign material that resembled a lead fishing sinker embedded in its surface. Not only did the substance damage the stamper, but it cracked the die that held the stamper, resulting in several thousand dollars of damage.

Believing that our supply of plastic contained foreign material, we scrapped the plant's entire stock and brought in fresh plastic from another manufacturer. The press began to make perfect, high-quality records each time it closed on the extruded material.

Some time later, after examining bags of the original plastic and not finding any foreign material in it, we thought that perhaps the plastic itself was defective. We sent samples to a laboratory that examined the plastic and reported that under extreme heat and temperature (like those used in manufacturing records), the plastic would congeal into a "metallic-like substance." The culprit was found, but only after we had almost been put out of business. I immediately went to a lawyer, who checked out the source of the supply. Unfortunately, the vendor of the plastic had filed for bankruptcy. Our valid claim, with documented evidence, was useless. Our clear-cut damage and our ability to prove it did us little good against a company that had already thrown in the towel.

There are many steps you can take during the normal course of business to secure your position. You can take an individual's affidavit or ask for a written memorandum at any time to begin building a file. You can also generate your own memos for the file, noting pertinent facts and pieces of information that you feel might be important later. If you have employees, add documents and memoranda from them to the file. Even if a piece of evidence is later thrown out, the information that it contains may provide a basis for testimony at the time of trial. Months and even years may pass between the time the transaction took place to when you may be in court contesting the matter. So much time may have elapsed that even an expert would need a set of notes in order to render an opinion on a given topic. Building a file of evidence early, even if there is doubt as to whether or not litigation will ensue, can mean the difference in proving your claim if and when the matter is contested.

In nonbusiness matters, such as auto accidents, neighborhood disputes, domestic disputes, and the like, it's also important to build your evidence file as early as possible. For example, if you are in an auto accident, take the following steps (provided that you are not hurt). Immediately document what just happened in your own words. Get a copy of any official report that might have been made, but recognize that such a report may view the accident from another perspective, one that may not be favorable to you. To protect your claim—your side of what may be a controversy later—follow these steps:

1. Take your own notes.
2. Take pictures if you happen to have a camera with you: The location of trees, street signs, light poles, bushes, curbing, center islands, the vehicles, and the like.
3. Interview witnesses and get names, addresses, and phone numbers.
4. Check the attitude of witnesses; that is, are they sympathetic to or opposed to your view, and what is their degree of willingness to help?

5. Get pertinent information, including insurance company names, policy numbers, and driver's license numbers from all those involved in the accident.

6. Organize all material into a file, and add the police report when available.

7. Get independent appraisals of any damage.

8. Add any expert reports to the file, such as medical or hospital reports and/or specialists' reports.

Whether it's a business situation or an accident or other nonbusiness situation, the sooner you collect evidence, the more likely you will be able to put together a successful case, even if success is only containing the damages against you.

In the immediate aftermath of a situation you believe may be eventually heading to court, ask yourself what documentation, what facts, what physical evidence would be helpful to prove your side of the story. Picture yourself explaining your case to a judge and think of what you might need to convince him or her of the truth of your story. When you have answered these questions and are building your evidentiary record, keep in mind the major types of evidence allowed under the rules in a courtroom (for more details on evidence, see Chapter 10):

- *Testimony:* Witnesses, either at the time of trial or sworn at deposition. An affidavit is not usually allowed unless the person who made the affidavit is present to testify about it. (See Chapter 10 for exceptions to the exclusion of the use of affidavits with live testimony.)

- *Documentary evidence:* All written forms of documents, printed materials, photostat copies (see Chapter 10), photographs, and mechanical or electronic recordings. (See Rules of Best Evidence for certain provisions and limitations.)

- *Demonstrative evidence:* Things that have a connection to the case.

Divide your quest for evidence into lists representing the above. We will not now discuss how to present your evidence in court, or its effect on a case (see Chapter 10), but the search for pieces of evidence must be well thought out and conducted with diligence and tenacity to provide you the best chance of successful litigation or settlement.

Building an evidentiary record can be as simple as clipping a newspaper ad (as already shown) or as complex as having thousands of documents cross-referenced and indexed for a case that may take years to adjudicate.

For instance, one of the longest trials in history was the McMartin preschool child molestation case, which cost the taxpayers of California over $15 million and had 124 witnesses, 917 exhibits, and 63,000 pages of testimony.

An awareness of the evidence needed at trial will help you have the documents and things you might need to use in court on hand at the outset of a situation, even before any need for action arises. This will help you in your quest to gather evidence, and at the trial itself. The following are some tips on how to conduct your affairs in order to safeguard any claim that may occur:

- Try to pay financial obligations with checks in order to keep a record of all payments. This will also give you a record of the payee's bank account (through the endorsement on the back of the check).
- Note disputes or special conditions of the transaction on both sides of the check, if appropriate.
- Put any complaints in writing at the earliest possible date and document delivery to the recipient (i.e., certified mail, return receipt requested; Federal Express receipt; or other bill of lading or delivery notice).
- Take notes of all occurrences for your own recollection—names and dates of conversations and the like.
- Try to obtain copies of your adversary's documents whenever possible.
- Take a witness along if you anticipate a problem in a meeting, situation, or confrontation. The more independent the witness, the less likely that the relationship between you and the witness will be challenged.
- For protection of creative written works, send a copy to yourself or to a trusted third party via certified mail, and do not open the envelope until before a judge if the matter is actually contested. This procedure will give you a date certain that you created the work in lieu of a copyright or other registration.
- Document direct expenses, costs, consequential damages (damages that do not flow from the damaging act or party, but only from the consequences of the act), and even your feelings and emotions at the time of the incident.
- Review all damages allowable under the law—punitive, exemplary, treble, contractual, statutory, and common law.

The various forms of discovery, expert cross-examination of witnesses, and a well-planned legal offense are all important to a successful claim or settlement, but a well-documented case is, as we have said, paramount for ultimately successful litigation and the safeguarding of your claim. There are other things you can do in your normal dealings to safeguard your rights before they are challenged. By carefully following normal procedure, future claims and disputes can be avoided or mitigated. Deeds are recorded with physical descriptions of real property; mortgages, notes, and judgments are recorded with such terms as interest and payment indicated; fictitious names ("doing business as," or d/b/a) are advertised and then recorded (in most jurisdictions) to protect the owner's interest in the name (and to provide creditors with d/b/a information); corporations are incorporated by the state to register the name, thereby protecting the shareholders' and creditors' interests in the entity. States that have adopted the Uniform Commercial Code (UCC; see Chapter 18) can provide their citizens with a means of registering or filing a claim to or interest in personal property (such as machinery, equipment, or inventory) as a means of securing the owner's claim of ownership to the item or items. Vehicles are registered by the state, a form of protection for the owners and those who have a security interest in the vehicle. Boats are also registered by the state and can be registered by the United States Coast Guard as documented vessels, affording a measure of protection in international waters relative to ownership. Even many purebred animals can be registered in appropriate clubs or societies to safeguard their owners' interests and authenticity of their lineage.

When my ex-wife and I were raising and selling purebred Puli (Hungarian sheepdog) pups, we easily won a lawsuit filed by a customer who thought his dog, after it was grown, was not a purebred. Because we had always adhered to American Kennel Club (AKC) regulations for registration, the AKC investigated and backed our position, and far be it for a New Jersey judge to challenge the hierarchy of the AKC. Our claim of authenticity was sustained.

Authors concerned about plagiarism or claims regarding their original material can gain protection from the Writers' Guild of America before ownership is challenged. Other proprietary works can be safeguarded. These fall into three categories: Creative works, inventions, and trademarks.

## CREATIVE WORKS

Many creative works can be protected through U.S. government copyright, which establishes the creator's interest in the work as of a specific date. The United States Copyright Office will copyright the following:

- Literary works.
- Musical works, including any accompanying words.
- Dramatic works, including any accompanying music.

- Pantomimes and choreographic works.
- Pictorial, graphic, and sculptural works.
- Motion pictures and other audiovisual works.
- Sound recordings.

In the language of the copyright law:

> Copyright protection subsists, in accordance with this title, in original works of authorship fixed in any tangible medium of expression, now known or later developed, from which they can be perceived, reproduced, or otherwise communicated, either directly or with the aid of a machine or device.

However, the Copyright Act also states: "In no case does copyright protection for an original work of authorship extend to any idea, procedure, process, system, method of operation, concept, principle, or discovery, regardless of the form in which it is described, explained, illustrated, or embodied in such work."

## INVENTION

United States patent law defines invention as "the finding out—the contriving, the creating of something which did not exist, and was not known before, and which can be made useful and advantageous in the pursuits of life, or which can add to the enjoyment of mankind." Not every improvement is invention; but in order to be entitled to protection, it must be the product of some exercise of the inventive faculties and must involve something more than what is obvious to persons skilled in the art to which it relates. "Mere adaptation of known processes to clearly analogous use is not invention" (*Firestone Tire & Rubber Company v. U.S. Rubber Company*, CCA Ohio, 79 F.2d 948, 952, 953). The United States Patent Office, in an effort to safeguard the claims of individuals who have truly invented new things, can grant patents in the categories of process, machine, manufacture, and composition of matter.

## TRADEMARK PROTECTION

This includes any word, name, symbol, or device, or any combination thereof, adopted and used by a manufacturer or merchant to identify his or her goods and distinguish them from those manufactured or sold by others (15 U.S.C.A 1127). Such protection can be granted as the following:

- Trademarks.
- Service marks, used in the sale or advertising of services of one person as distinguished from the services of others.
- Collective marks, used by members of a cooperative association or other group or organization, including unions.
- Certification marks, used in connection with the products or services of one or more persons other than the original owner of the mark. (This mark can certify regional or other origin, material, mode of manufacture, quality, accuracy, or other characteristics of goods and services of the work or labor on goods and services as performed by members of a union or other organization.)

Even with copyrights, patents, and trademarks, there is no guarantee that you will not be challenged at some point as to your right to your creative work, invention, or mark. The principles outlined in this chapter for safe-guarding your claim also apply to these claims. By obtaining the proper governmental registration of your creative work, patent, or mark, you will begin the process of building a file that is necessary to establish your rights in what you believe is yours.

# CHAPTER 10
# Evidence

*The mind in doubt ever turns to tangible objects.*
—Scientillae Juris (1877)

When Lord Coke said in 1622, "It is no satisfaction for a witness to say that he thinketh, or that he perswadeth himself about a matter," little did he know how much influence his remarks would have on the criteria for the presentation of evidence in a modern courtroom. For instance, the personal knowledge requirement, affecting the use of evidence in court, is one of Lord Coke's legacies. This rule excludes testimony that could be considered inference and conclusion by witnesses who had *no personal knowledge* of the facts. Witnesses must testify as to "facts" within their personal knowledge or observation, excluding inferences, conclusions, and opinions, even though the latter may be based upon personally observed data. There are hundreds more: The hearsay rule, the adverse witness rule, the original document rule, and on and on, all designed to insure what Lord Coke was addressing and what John Adams said in a provision of the Commonwealth of Massachusetts Constitution more than a hundred years later, in 1784:

> Every subject of the Commonwealth ought to find a certain Remedy by having recourse to the laws, for all injuries or wrongs which he may receive in his person, property or character. He ought to obtain Right and Justice freely, and without being obliged to purchase it, completely and without denial; promptly and without delay.

Every rule of evidence must be tested against the principles and "rights of man," as stated above, and all other constitutionally mandated guarantees and protections. Whether the rule itself or its operative effect in an actual trial situation, its effect must be related to the policy or principles to which it owes its origin and must stand in concert with our basic freedoms.

## CATEGORIES OF EVIDENCE

The preceding notwithstanding, the rules of evidence, like their larger mirror image, the laws and statutes society has agreed to live by, must constantly be in a fluid state, refined and reviewed as society and technology metamorphose. The end result is (using Florida as an example) a four-volume looseleaf set just on the subject of evidence, its definition, scope, application, and review in relationship to the Evidence Code as enacted by the state's legislature. Not even a practicing trial lawyer would likely know *all* the rules of evidence of all the jurisdictions, but certain principles form a common basis for various rules of evidence and are expressed in the following terms:

- *Testimonial evidence:* Information relative to the case that comes from the oral statements of sworn witnesses, either through deposition or in open court, and could qualify as evidence to be considered by the trier of fact.
- *Documentary evidence:* Evidence "set down by handwriting, typewriting, printing, photostating, photography, magnetic impulse, mechanical or electronic recording, or other form of data compilation, upon paper, wood, stone, record tape, or other materials."
- *Real or demonstrative evidence:* Objects or tangible items that become evidence in a proceeding because of their value or connection to a case, such as a tire with a nail embedded in its tread.

The next two classifications have as their root the nature and origin of the information:

- *Direct evidence:* Material that instantly becomes evidentiary in nature without the need for supportive facts or other evidence to sustain its connection to the case. For example, a promissory note between parties that clearly states the terms and conditions of the obligation.
- *Circumstantial evidence:* Evidence that may support the inference or proof of some intermediate fact that legitimately leads to the reasonable conclusion that the fact(s) in dispute actually exists. I learned the meaning of this concept when a witness reported seeing record albums that were missing from my warehouse on the shelves of a local Fort Lauderdale retailer. I

thought I had the scoundrel dead to rights, and then learned the observation was circumstantial.

Two other classifications have as their basis whether the piece of evidence is cast in positive or negative terms:

- *Positive evidence:* Evidence that involves proof that an issue of fact does exist or actually has taken place.
- *Negative evidence:* Evidence that develops when witnesses claim that they did not receive any sensory impression of a claimed fact, such as not hearing any signal from an approaching train.

The following terms deal with procedural consequences when evidence is offered:

- *Prima facie evidence:* Evidence that is evident on its face— deemed in law sufficient to support a finding that an issue of fact may exist. If unexplained or uncontradicted, this evidence is sufficient to sustain a judgment in favor of the issue that it supports.
- *Conclusive evidence:* The relatively rare instance when evidence proves a fact that will be deemed in law to be equal to rendering the presumed fact conclusive and irrebuttable.
- *Judicial notice:* Facts that are determinable by the judge and are usually based on facts of common or general knowledge, such as the chemical makeup of water.

A triumvirate of quality controls helps guide or establish the nature and flow of evidence at trial. Whether the evidence is circumstantial, prima facie, testimonial, documentary, or conclusive, in order to provide a meaningful guide to the trier of fact, it must meet the following tests.

1. *Competency* (reliability): This shields the judge and jury from inherently unreliable information.
2. *Relevancy* (probative): This allows the judge and jury to consider all the evidence having some probative value; that is, the evidence must logically tend to prove what it is offered to prove.
3. *Materiality* (pertinency): This protects the judge and jury from the inefficient, time-wasting, and misleading presentation of facts and details that are not at issue.

The classification of evidence, the quality controls, and other rules are applied at trial in a mix based on the type of case being adjudicated. These cases fall into four categories: (1) Commercial, (2) accident or negligence, (3) divorce and family, and (4) criminal. Putting aside the differences in applications of the rules in each category (consult the rules of evidence for each jurisdiction), let's look at how some of the more important rules can affect your ability to obtain and present evidence at trial.

## RULES ON OBTAINING EVIDENCE AT TRIAL

One of the primary sources of evidence is the testimony of a witness under oath. Despite some of the antics seen on television, attorneys must follow certain rules as to conduct, demeanor, and behavior when examining or cross-examining a witness. First, Federal Rule of Evidence 611 provides that the judge shall exercise "reasonable control over mode and order of interrogating witnesses." (See Table 10.1 for a list of the applicable Federal Rules of Evidence.) The rule also provides that the judge should do the following:

- Ensure that the interrogation and presentation are effective for the ascertainment of the truth.
- Avoid a waste of time.
- Protect witnesses from harassment and undue embarrassment.

The all-encompassing Rule 611 goes on to direct the scope and demeanor of questioning:

- The scope of cross-examination should be limited to the subject matter of the direct line of questioning, and also matters affecting the credibility of the witness. (The judge has the discretion to permit additional areas of inquiry on direct examination.)
- Leading questions shall not be used on direct examination except as may be necessary to develop the witness' testimony. (A leading question is an instructional question that informs the witness of the expected answer.) Normally, leading questions are permitted on cross-examination or for a hostile witness, an adverse party, or a witness identified with an adverse party.

Remember, a judge may interpret the hostile witness exemption in a broad sense, such as seeing an individual as a partner to the defendant.

**Table 10.1.** Federal Rules of Evidence (as amended through November 1, 1988).

---

Article I. General Provisions
  Rule 101. Scope
  Rule 102. Purpose and construction
  Rule 103. Rulings on evidence
  Rule 104. Preliminary questions
  Rule 105. Limited admissibility
  Rule 106. Remainder of or related writings on recorded statements

---

Article II. Judicial Notice
  Rule 201. Judicial notice of adjudicative facts

---

Article III. Presumptions in Civil Actions and Proceedings
  Rule 301. Presumptions in general civil actions and proceedings
  Rule 302. Applicability of state law in civil actions and proceedings

---

Article IV. Relevancy and Its Limits
  Rule 401. Definition of "relevant evidence"
  Rule 402. Relevant evidence generally admissible; irrelevant evidence inadmissible
  Rule 403. Exclusion of relevant evidence on grounds of prejudice, confusion, or waste of time
  Rule 404. Character evidence not admissible to prove conduct; exceptions; other crimes
  Rule 405. Methods of providing character
  Rule 406. Habit; routine practice
  Rule 407. Subsequent remedial measures
  Rule 408. Compromise and offers to compromise
  Rule 409. Inadmissibility of pleas, offers of pleas, and related plea statements
  Rule 410. Payment of medical and similar expenses
  Rule 411. Liability insurance
  Rule 412. Rape cases; relevance of victim's past behavior

---

Article V. Privileges
  Rule 501. General rule

---

Article VI. Opinions and Expert Testimony
  Rule 701. Testimony by lay witnesses
  Rule 702. Testimony by experts

## CROSS-EXAMINATION

Cross-examination follows the adverse party's direct examination of a witness, and even seasoned attorneys don't agree as to the scope of cross-examination. There are two views to consider:

- *Restrictive view*, or American Rule (a term used by Joseph Pellicciotti in *Handbook on Basic Trial Evidence*, Lanham, MD: University Press of America, 1988), cross-examination is restricted to the issues first brought out in direct examination. Any other information the witness has about the case cannot be brought out until further direct examination.
- *Wide open view*, or English Rule (see Pellicciotti), considers cross-examination to have unlimited scope.

Federal Rule of Evidence 611(b) applies the restrictive view to cross-examination, but gives the judge discretion to open up areas of cross-examination. The use of this discretion will vary from jurisdiction to jurisdiction; check local rules unless the federal rules apply to your case.

Federal Rule 614 continues the traditional practice of allowing the judge to call and interrogate witnesses. Rule 615, which is what people are usually referring to when they say they are "invoking the rule," allows a party to a case, under most conditions, to exclude witnesses from the courtroom so that they will not hear the testimony of other witnesses. (There are exemptions to this, which are enumerated in Rule 615.) This sequestering of witnesses and the right of a party to remain in the courtroom create due process and right of confrontation issues, respectively, that are left to the judge to decide in any given trial.

## JOGGING THE WITNESS' MEMORY

The subject of memory is another area covered by the rules of evidence. A witness with a failing memory cannot just enter the witness box and start testifying from written notes and documents. There are two ways to provide memory recollection: One is called past recollection reviewed; the other is past recollection recorded.

Past recollection reviewed is a process that refreshes a witness' memory by using something in writing. For example, a sales slip can be used to help the witness remember the date of a purchase or an activity, but the sales slip itself cannot be admitted into evidence. After the witness has looked at the slip, it must be taken from the witness, who must then speak to the occurrence unaided.

Past recollection recorded (diaries, memoranda, or notes made by witnesses concerning the issue) is allowed if the "writing" (data set down in words and figures) refreshes the witness' recollection of the past. If the writing meets certain standards, it might be admitted as evidence, providing the facts were clear to the witness when the writing was made, that the witness made the writing within a reasonable time after the occurrence and not in preparation for litigation, and that the witness can establish and attest to the accuracy of the writing when it was first made.

## IMPEACHMENT

You have certainly heard the term impeachment, and you may have heard it associated with a witness, but you probably don't know that there are more than five different federal rules of evidence dealing with the subject. The definition of impeachment is "the process of establishing that a witness' testimony is not worthy of weight and credibility." (See Pellicciotti.) Since the judge and jury must decide how much weight to give to a witness' testimony, the impeachment process in cross-examination can be quite important. Here are several ways that a witness' testimony can be impeached.

- Demonstrating untruthfulness via character evidence. (Crimes that can be used for impeachment, covered in Federal Rule 609, may vary from jurisdiction to jurisdiction.)
- Evidencing a prior inconsistent statement.
- Attacking credibility via a third party.

Once you attack a witness' credibility, the other party will try to rehabilitate that credibility. To accomplish this, it is necessary to restore the judge's and jury's confidence in the witness' testimony. The method used to rehabilitate usually depends on the method used to impeach. For example, if a statement is inconsistent, the other party may seek to explain the circumstances of the inconsistency. If character evidence is used for impeachment, then evidence of truthfulness may be presented.

Certain individuals may be exempt from testifying, as covered in Federal Rule 501. Especially in civil actions, the federal rules (except as required by the Constitution or an act of Congress) specify that state law shall control the decision as to who may be privileged. Parties involved in any one of the following relationships can generally invoke a privilege:

- Patient privilege (psychotherapists, doctors).
- Client privilege (attorneys).
- Spousal privilege.
- Penitent privilege (priests).
- Governmental privilege (state secrets, ongoing investigatory files, government informants, executive privilege, qualified privilege).
- Privilege against self-incrimination (it has been held that fingerprints, photographs, measurements, demonstrations of voice and handwriting, and the requirement to stand in a police lineup for identification do not violate this privilege, as these are considered examinations or tests for identification purposes only).

The Miranda warning ("You have the right to remain silent. . . .") which has become so well known through television police dramas, is a form of privilege. In the landmark Supreme Court decision *Miranda v. Arizona* (384 U.S. 436 [1966]), the majority stated: "The prosecution may not use statements, whether exculpatory or inculpatory, stemming from custodial interrogation of the defendant unless it demonstrates the use of procedural safeguards effective to secure the privilege against self-incrimination. . . ."

In order to follow the Supreme Court's mandate of procedural safeguards, in criminal cases the Miranda warning provides additional privileges:

- The right to remain silent.
- The right to have an attorney present before any questions are asked or answered.
- The right to have an attorney appointed if the accused cannot afford one, before any questions are asked or answered.

Remember that to protect a privilege, do not make a disclosure to a third party. Any such disclosure may jeopardize or nullify the claimed privilege. Also, you must carefully check the rules of the jurisdiction, because certain other privileges have been recognized in varying forms, and these change from state to state and jurisdiction to jurisdiction.

Privilege is usually considered personal, and is held by the party or parties whom the law seeks to protect. Therefore, a privilege may be waived by the holder or holders, allowing the disclosure of information at a trial.

There are three areas relating to the rules of evidence that are important for you to know about: (1) Best Evidence Rule, (2) Opinion and Expert Testimony, and (3) Hearsay.

## BEST EVIDENCE RULE

When you seek to prove the contents of a writing, such as in a deed, will, negotiable instrument, or contract, the Best Evidence Rule requires that the original instrument be used "unless its production is not feasible for some reason other than the serious fault of the proponent." The preference for the original is supported by logic and a large body of judicial experience, as in the prevention of fraud. However, aside from deliberate tampering, there exists the hazard of innocent mistransmission of the writing's contents and the risk of imprecision if witnesses or other secondary evidence (of the writing) are used to establish its existence and contents. This philosophy stems from the early common law concept that the proponent of a fact at issue must produce direct and conclusive evidence of the contention. This translates, in the case of writings, into the forced production of the original as evidence; any lesser degree of proof would be unacceptable and inadmissible in court. The failure (except with certain mitigating circumstances and recognized exceptions, such as the business records rule) to produce the original will cause the judge and jury to draw a negative inference and find against the party unwilling or unable to produce the original document or to testify conclusively as to its whereabouts.

Modern technology has forced the expansion of the Best Evidence Rule; in addition to writings, it now covers recordings and photographs. (Federal Rule 1001 defines writings, recordings, and photographs to which the requirement of the original apply.) Some jurisdictions may also include inscribed objects, not usually found in the definition of writings, as being applicable to the Best Evidence Rule, such as:

- Numbering on police badges.
- Legends on buttons, banners, and billboards.
- Carved initials on rings.
- Identifying numbers on automobiles and guns.
- Laundry marks.
- Names on whiskey bottles and tombstones.

Logic allows for the exclusion of an item too costly or difficult to bring into the courtroom; the judge may then allow secondary evidence to be presented to substantiate the proponent's contention.

Obviously, precision is necessary in the proof of the terms of a writing. The slightest error or change in a word or figure in a writing might jeopardize the rights of one or another of the parties. Therefore, secondary testimony usually will not ensure a high enough degree of safety. There are, however, some exceptions where the writing is a mere memorial of a happening. For instance, an individual may testify to the fact of his or her marriage or birth without being forced to produce or account for the lack of availability of a marriage or birth certificate. Proof of payment for property without the availability of the instrument that contains the price and even facts contained in private records can be offered in court without stepping on the Best Evidence Rule's foul line.

In the absence of the original or "best" evidence, there seems to be controversy as to when the court should admit other proof of the existence of a written contract and its terms. Excused nonproduction of the original seems, in many jurisdictions, to depend upon the following:

- How important the writing is to the litigation.
- How important precision is in the presentation of the writing's terms to the judge and jury.
- How much risk of mistransmission or fraud there may be if nonproduction of the original is allowed.

The next question to arise, in our world of carbon copies, photocopies, NCR forms, and the like, is: What is the original, and what is the duplicate? The Federal Rules define original this way:

1. The original of a writing or recording means the writing or recording itself, or any counterpart intended to have the same effect by a person executing or issuing it.
2. An original of a photograph includes the negative or any print therefrom.
3. The original of data stored in a computer or similar device is the printout, or other output readable by sight and shown to reflect the data accurately.

The next question is which documents are counterpart originals and which are merely counterpart duplicates. Under current rules, the distinction is made this way:

1. Counterparts of writings or recordings will be accorded original status under the Best Evidence Rule when such counterparts are fully executed and intended to be of equal legal force as embodying the terms of the transaction.
2. Counterparts that fail to achieve original status in their own right (as above) may be classified as duplicates. By definition, a duplicate is a counterpart produced by the same impression as the original, or from the same matrix, or by means of photography or by mechanical or electronic reading, or by chemical reproduction—or by other equivalent techniques that accurately reproduce the original.

It's clear under the law that what is a counterpart original and a counterpart duplicate is a matter of the intent of the issuing parties. Counterpart originals are intended to be of equal legal force as originals, whereas counterpart duplicates are not. However, counterpart duplicates may be admissible, depending upon the rules of the jurisdiction. For instance, Rule 90.953 of the

Florida Evidence Code tells us that duplicates may be admissible to the same extent as originals unless the following circumstances exist:

- The document or writing is a negotiable instrument or any other writing that evidences a right to the payment of money, and is itself not a security agreement or lease, and is of a type that is transferred by delivery in the ordinary course of business with any necessary endorsement or assignment.
- A genuine question is raised about the authenticity of the original of any other document or writing.
- It is unfair under the circumstances to admit the duplicate in lieu of the original.

Obviously, at least in Florida, duplicates are not accorded complete equality with originals. There may be a situation in which the duplicate covers only a portion of the original, and the remainder would need to be substantiated under cross-examination or by qualifying information. This raises competency and reliability concerns. Since the intent of the law is to "promote the ends of justice, and guard against fraud or imposition," the Best Evidence Rule is applied in those situations.

## SECONDARY EVIDENCE

When it can be shown that the best evidence is unobtainable, then secondary evidence becomes admissible. In this situation, the rule must be put aside in accordance with the maxim *cessante ratione legis cessat ipsa rex* ("the reason for the law ceasing, the law itself also ceases"). Copies of original documents that do not meet the criteria of counterpart originals or counterpart duplicates are considered secondary evidence. Despite improvements in technology, the feeling that anything but the original deserves reduced status stems from the unreliability of older methods used to make copies. Hand copies, letter press, and so on were subject to human error. (See Using Photocopies in the Legal System, page 150.)

The law in Florida (90.951[4]) has addressed itself to the subject of executed (signed) carbon copies:

> An executed carbon copy, not intended by the parties to be an original, will be considered a counterpart duplicate and thus conditionally admissible in court in the same manner as the original.
>
> Regarding public records, under the Federal Rules of Civil Procedure, a properly authenticated photocopy of these documents

# Using Photocopies in the Legal System

*In this age of copiers and fax machines, it is important to know when copies or duplicate documents can be used in pleadings, evidence, and appellate briefs.*

Pleadings. *The rules of many courts will permit clean copies of professional quality to be used for service. However, most trial courts (lower courts) want to have typed originals (or printed copies) to be used for filing with the court clerk. This may vary from state to state.*

Evidence. *The Federal government, through Act 28 U.S.C.A. Section 1732 (as amended August 28, 1951), permits all U.S. courts to accept into evidence a photocopy made in the regular course of business, whether or not the original is still in existence. This act (the Uniform Photographic Copies of Business and Public Records as Evidence Act) is recognized by at least thirty-three states.*

Briefs. *When it comes to using photocopies in the appellate courts, you must check the court rules of each jurisdiction. Copies of the record and briefs are often typewritten originals, and carbon copies are acceptable for filing. Many jurisdictions will permit you to use quality photocopies, although you should always check the rules.*

*The U.S. Supreme Court and many state appellate courts will not accept a typewritten brief—printing or high-quality duplicating is required. Even the style of the document may vary from state to state; check this in each jurisdiction.*

are admissible in Federal courts as best evidence, as are official records, if published in official U.S. government publications.

The bottom line is that the Best Evidence Rule is preferential rather than exclusionary. To support an offer of secondary evidence, a foundation must be laid to show a clear-cut, excusable nonproduction of the original, such as loss. The court will have to decide, under its rules of evidence, whether there is sufficient reason to move to secondary evidence. The same rule charges the jury with the responsibility of deciding whether the asserted writing ever existed; or whether another writing, recording, or photograph produced at trial is the original; or whether the other evidence of contents correctly reflects the contents of the original.

This obviously places a heavy burden on the jury, who will ultimately decide, if a judge allows the question to be heard at all, the validity of the evidence. Unless the judge finds favorably for the proponent on the point of excusable loss, the secondary evidence of the original's contents will not be allowed as evidence, and the jury will not have the opportunity to entertain the question.

The law even covers the claim that the original was destroyed. If it can be shown through testimony that the destruction was not due to the bad faith of the custodian or proponent, secondary evidence of the contents may be used. But failing such proof of "innocent destruction," secondary evidence will not be admissible. In the case of loss, which may be more difficult to establish than destruction, clear proof of a diligent search for the missing item must be presented.

In cases where an original is not obtainable, such as its being out of state and not subject to the control of the jurisdiction hearing the case, secondary evidence of its contents will be admissible. Likewise, if your opponent possesses a document and does not tender it even after a notice to produce, then the absence of the response to the notice will provide a basis for the admissibility of secondary evidence.

In most instances, it is the original that offers the best evidence available of the contents of a writing. As shown, there are exceptions, and these may vary from jurisdiction to jurisdiction. So again, you must check your local rules for your jurisdiction's Best Evidence Rule.

## OPINION AND EXPERT TESTIMONY

The "personal knowledge" concept discussed at the beginning of this chapter required that witnesses speak only what they knew for certain and testify only to what they saw or heard. This requirement has gradually taken on a more strict interpretation: The acceptance of testimony as to facts within personal knowledge or observation of a participant witness, with inferences, conclusions, and opinions excluded, even if the opinions are based on personal observations. This doctrine has become known as the Opinion Rule. Simply, it states that no opinions are allowed.

However, well-recognized exceptions, based on real and compelling necessities, developed. Under controlled conditions, the rule now allows opinion into the body of testimony. The safeguards are many, though, the regulations complicated, the requirements stringent; all are designed to protect the search for truth. Before you can fit within the exception of allowing expert, scientific, or lay opinion testimony, you must conclusively demonstrate the following:

- The facts are not of a kind that can be placed before the judge and understood without expert testimony, and the witness' opinion or inference is based on facts, not opinion.
- The facts are such that the jurors are not qualified to understand the subject and form an opinion, and the expert's testimony and opinion would not be redundant and time-consuming and of no practical benefit to the trial.

The admissibility of opinion testimony is then subject two primary trial situations:

- Trials concerning such matters that would not permit the judge to deduce the ultimate truth from the factual detail. Under these circumstances, the lay witness may testify as to opinion or conclusion.
- Trials concerning subjects distinctly related to some science, profession, business, occupation, or area of interest so as to be beyond the range of understanding of the ordinary judge, or material so specialized that the jury would not be competent to review the matter.

To quote from the Florida Evidence Manual, "Expert opinion is admissible only when the facts to be determined are so observed that they can be made clear to the fact-finder [judge or jury] only by and through opinions of persons skilled in relation to the subject matter under investigation." (Kenneth Hughes, *Florida Evidence Manual*, Clearwater, FL: D&S Publishers, 1982.) Thus, the law provides a basis for the admissibility of expert testimony: The trial judge needs to be satisfied that the opinion is so completely related to a specialized field as to put the subject beyond the unaided understanding of the judge and jury. In other words, would the judge or jury be able to determine the issues without the enlightenment from those having expertise on the subject? Does the subject matter fall outside the "ordinary experience of men moving in the ordinary walks of life"? These tests or questions must be considered before the Opinion Rule can be set aside to allow opinion to enter the courtroom, regardless of how learned the expert may be.

(Certain sciences have been accepted in most jurisdictions: Ballistics, fingerprint, palm print, identifications, alcohol tests, and so on. Others have not been accepted by certain jurisdictions: Lie detector tests, hypnosis as a truth propellant, and the like. Check your local rules of evidence to find out what is admissible in your jurisdiction.)

In addition, expert opinion testimony must be subject to the same quality controls that apply to all evidence. The testimony must be applicable to the evidence at the trial in order to be relevant. Federal Rule 702 sustains the need for materiality of expert testimony:

> If scientific, technical, or other specialized knowledge will assist the trier of fact [judge or jury] to understand the evidence, or to determine a fact in issue, a witness qualified as an expert by knowledge, skill, experience, training, or education, may testify thereto in the form of opinion or otherwise.

The court must be satisfied of the competency (qualifications) of the witness presented as an expert; that the witness has the requisite expertise with regard to the subject of interest or inquiry—based upon skill, knowledge, or experience.

With so many forms of human activity and so many cause-and-effect relationships out of reach of the average individual, our reliance on information and understanding of exotic concepts must turn on the use of expert opinion. Likewise, with so many experts and specialists in our society, it becomes the trial court's responsibility to determine the qualifications of a proposed expert witness, as well as the range of subjects on which the individual will be permitted to offer opinion. (The courts have held that this decision is almost sacredly the province of the trial judge, and the trial judge's ruling will not be reversed except in cases of clear-cut abuse.)

From a tactical standpoint, the more questions the expert is asked in the qualifying process, the better it is for the expert's proponent, for the degree of respect for the expert's credentials will rise in the mind of the judge and jury. Care should be taken to show the range of the expert's experience and also the manner in which the experience relates to the opinion he or she may be expected to render from the facts.

There are generally considered to be two classes of expert witnesses. The difference lies in the manner in which they acquire the evidential data upon which their statements will be based.

- *Percipient witness:* The word *percipient* means one who obtains information by the use of the physical senses. Such a witness is a person who is expert in the subject under discussion, and who has first-hand knowledge of the facts drawn from his or her own observations and experience with the area under investigation.

- *Nonpercipient witness:* A person with no first-hand experience or involvement with the subject matter under discussion and who has made no independent study of the facts.

The determination of classes of expert witnesses is made to direct the type of questions and answers to be allowed and entered into evidence. For instance, the witness with no first-hand information will not be able to testify as to factual details. Such a witness may, however, be questioned with a factual predicate or hypothetical question.

There are several acceptable sources of facts and data on which expert opinion can be based:

- First-hand observation of the percipient expert witness, such as the testing physician. No hypothetical question is necessary, but one may be used based on personally observed facts only.
- Facts or data made known to the expert at or before the trial. The expert's opinion will then be based on (1) courtroom testimony the expert has heard, and (2) facts used as the basis for a hypothetical question.
- Facts that experts in the subject would reasonably use to support the opinion now being expressed. For example, a testing physician would also rely on the findings of others, such as lab reports. (Some jurisdictions require the expert to validate the use of extrajudicial materials such as lab reports.)

The degree of exposition of underlying facts required or allowed of an expert witness rests with the class of the witness. This area of the law is fuzzy and may vary from jurisdiction to jurisdiction. The opinion of a layperson, however, will be received as evidence only as necessity dictates. When the facts that are the subject of the lay witness' testimony are incapable of precise delineation, opinion may be offered in such areas as age, speed, size, color, mental state, handwriting, and so on. Under Florida law, for instance, factual testimony must precede any such lay opinion. In addition, asking a lay witness a hypothetical question is strictly forbidden when that witness is offering opinion testimony.

In general, much care is taken in most jurisdictions to protect against the abuse of testimony expounded by so-called experts. Florida's Rule of Evidence 90.705(2) states: "Prior to the witness giving his opinion, a party against whom the opinion or inference is offered may conduct a voir dire examination of the expert witness. . . ." (*Voir dire* means "to speak the truth." This is the preliminary examination the court may make of a person presented as a witness—or a juror—when there is an objection about that person's competency or interest in the matter.) This provision may seem cumbersome and disruptive; indeed, it is not included in Federal Rule 705. However, many jurisdictions offer this protection to establish the integrity of a so-called expert.

Another area for careful review in your jurisdiction is the use of hypothetical questions with experts. The rules vary considerably, and in some jurisdictions are extremely complicated.

## HEARSAY

In layperson's terms, hearsay evidence includes statements made by a witness about things that the witness was told by another individual. Thus, the facts in these statements are not personal knowledge. In the legal context, the definition of hearsay evidence is far more complicated.

Here is what Federal Rule 801, which forms the basis of local rules in many jurisdictions, says about hearsay evidence:

a. Statement—a statement is (1) an oral or written assertion or (2) nonverbal conduct of a person, if it is intended by him as an assertion.
b. Declarant—a "declarant" is a person who makes a statement.
c. Hearsay—"hearsay" is a statement, other than one made by the declarant while testifying at the trial or hearing, offered in evidence to prove the truth of the matter asserted.
d. Statements which are not hearsay—A statement is not hearsay if it is a/an
   1. Prior statement by witnesses—the declarant testifies at the trial or hearing and is subject to cross-examination concerning the statement, and the statement is:
      a. Inconsistent with his testimony and was given under oath subject to the penalty of perjury at a trial, hearing, or other proceeding or in a deposition; or
      b. Consistent with his testimony and is offered to rebut an express or implied charge against him of recent fabrication or improper influence or motive; or
   2. Admission by party opponent—the statement is offered against a party and is:
      a. His own statement, in either his individual or a representative capacity; or

b.  A statement of which he has manifested his adoption or belief in its truth; or
c.  A statement by a person authorized by him to make a statement concerning the subject. . . .
d.  A statement by his agent or servant concerning a matter within the scope of his agency or employment, made during the existence of the relationship; or
e.  A statement by a co-conspirator of a party during the course and in furtherance of the conspiracy.

Some legal scholars believe the term *hearsay* is actually meaningless unless the particular kind of information offered is taken into account and the circumstances that surround its attempted use in the courtroom are also considered. However, the rule exists because hearsay tends to lack trustworthiness; that is, the statement not made under oath is also made with no fear of perjury or prosecution. In addition, the declarant makes the statement outside the trial setting, where his or her demeanor cannot be observed by the judge and jury. Also, without the opportunity for cross-examination, with its inherent attempt to impeach, the witness may restate the words incorrectly. With these dangers inherent in hearsay, and its lack of reliability, the rule is needed.

Courts recognize that there are some forms of hearsay that are more reliable than others, and so exceptions have developed— in fact, there are at least forty exceptions. Many of them center on using information from the public record or even the absence of an entry in the public record. Dying declarations, statements of personal or family history (pedigree), reputation as to character, statement of memory or belief concerning a will, and excited utterances are known in the law as *res jestae*, and are just some of the exceptions to the hearsay rule that have been accepted in many jurisdictions. Some of the law books that cover this subject indicate that it is tactically important for an attorney to try to mold and frame the use of certain testimony in such a way as to take advantage of one of these many exceptions to accomplish the admission of testimony that might otherwise be inadmissible under the hearsay rule.

Let's look at a few of the more important exceptions to the hearsay rule that could help you to successfully use or thwart the use of certain testimony.

• *Excited utterance:* Most courts recognize spontaneity as a predicate for truth. This exemption deals with an individual who has been placed in a state of excitement. Statements "relating to" the startling event or "condition" spoken while the individual was excited are exempted from the hearsay rule.

- *Present sense impression:* Closeness in time replaces excitement in this exception. Thus, statements made close to the occurrence are given credence.

- *Then-existing mental, emotional, or physical condition:* The courts will allow witnesses to state their present (not past) state of mind or physical condition.

- *Statement for purposes of medical diagnosis and treatment:* The basis for this exception is that individuals will usually tell the truth when speaking to medical personnel about their medical histories or ailments.

- *Past recollection recorded:* Logically, a set of notes made or adopted by the witness while the matter was fresh in his memory should be an exception to the rule.

- *Record of regularly conducted activity:* Books of original entry (as I was taught in business to call them) have a special significance, providing information that otherwise might be lost in the search for the truth. Hence, they are given an exception to the hearsay rule. For the records to qualify, (1) they must be kept in the course of a regularly conducted business activity, (2) it must be the regular practice of that business activity to make those records, and (3) the records must be made at or near the time of the occurrence by or from information transmitted by a person with knowledge. A person with no personal knowledge may under this exception present the relevant business records in court. This is because the "business," not any individual, made the records. Taking this exception a step further, the absence of information in business records that may establish the nonexistence of something is a permissible expansion of this exception.

- *Public record and reports:* Public records, reports, and records of vital statistics, along with the absence of public records or entry are exceptions to the hearsay rule, since it would be a burden to call every public official to the courthouse to testify. It is presumed that public officials act properly.

- *Regularly kept records of religious organizations:* Records of births, marriages, deaths, legitimacy, ancestry, family history, and relationships by bond or marriage kept by religious organizations along with factual statements made in marriage, baptismal, and similar certificates form the basis for this exception.

- *Family records:* Entries into Bibles, tombstones, and the like comprise another example of this common law exception.

- *Records of documents affecting an interest in property:* This (and its sister exemption, statements in documents affecting an interest in property) provides a means for public records, such as deeds, to be admitted into evidence as proof of the content of the original recorded document.

- *Statements in ancient documents:* Any document that is twenty or more years old and can be authenticated as such is exempted. Letters, maps, and newspaper articles fall into this category.

- *Market reports, commercial publications, and learned treatises:* Reports and publications generally used and relied upon by the public or by persons in a particular occupation are exempt on the basis that public reliance translates into trustworthiness.

- *Reputation concerning personal or family history:* Reputation evidence (meaning commonly accepted knowledge) concerning a person's birth, adoption, marriage, divorce, death, legitimacy, and relationship by blood, ancestry, or other random fact of personal or family history is exempted.

- *Reputation concerning boundaries or general history:* This exemption allows for the use of community reputation in land boundary disputes and to establish information on events of general history.

- *Reputation as to character:* Character evidence is subject to the specific regulations of Rule 404, but representation as to character is an exception to the hearsay rule when reputation is an issue in the case.

- *Judgments (legal):* Judgments as to personal, family, general history, or boundaries, as documented in civil court judgments, qualify as exceptions to the extent that such information would be provable by evidence of reputation.

- *Judgment of previous conviction:* This exception provides for the limited use of a final judgment of prison conviction to prove a fact in a current case.

This great catch-all exists in the subdivision on exceptions: "The general purpose of these rules and the interests of justice will be best served by admission of the statement into evidence." (Joseph M. Pellicciotti, *Handbook on Basic Trial Evidence*. Second Edition. Lanham, MD: University Press of America, 1988, page 122.) This gives the judge carte blanche to expand the hearsay rule in the interests of justice to admit into evidence what he or she feels will add to the search for the truth.

Rule 804 provides for some additional exceptions:

- Former testimony (taken under oath in another proceeding or deposition).
- Statement under belief of impending death (must deal with "cause or circumstances" of what the person believes to be imminent death).

- Statement against interest (made by a nonparty and "so far contrary to the individual's interests that a reasonable man, in his position, would not have made the statement unless he believed it to be true").
- Statements of personal or family history (a person's own family history, or where the witness is likely to have accurate information because of intimate association).

Rule 805.25 concerns hearsay within hearsay: "Hearsay included within hearsay is not excluded under the hearsay rule if each part of the combined statement conforms with an exception to the hearsay rule provided in these rules." Suppose a passenger in an automobile involved in an accident, in his excitement, made a statement to a police officer (excited utterance) and the officer placed the statement in her official report (public records and reports); then the hearsay (passenger's statement) in the hearsay (officer's written report) is permissible as evidence.

## ETHICAL CONSIDERATIONS

Attorneys are officers of the court. This affiliation invokes an extraordinary responsibility for ethical behavior in the presentation of evidence (and other court matters). The attorney's education includes training in the collection and presentation of evidence. The local bar organization, to which lawyers must belong, also provides a means of ethical control and discipline for the errant attorney if the need arises. However, the individual acting pro se has only the judge and jury to monitor and discipline his or her actions in court. Crossing the ethical or even evidentiary boundaries is a big mistake. The majority of judges I have interviewed would just as soon not deal with a pro se situation if they had a choice, and their overwhelming concern is that the rules not be bent. This applies, of course, to evidence as well as procedure. It would be reasonable to assume that ethical considerations will not be compromised for the layperson. Ignorance of such considerations, procedure, or the law will generally not be tolerated in the courtroom.

Just as proper dress and decorum will help you to present a professional appearance, so will your use of ethical practices in presenting evidence. Here are a few suggestions (the source for this list is the Florida Bar Code):

- Do not ask any questions that you have no reasonable basis to believe are relevant to the case.
- Do not deliberately ask a question intended to degrade an individual.

- Do not assert your personal knowledge of the facts unless you are testifying.
- Do not assert your personal opinion as to the justice of a cause, the credibility of a witness, or the guilt or innocence of an accused. You may, however, argue an analysis of evidence in a case with respect to credibility, culpability, or guilt or innocence of a witness.
- Do not intentionally violate any established rule of procedure or evidence.

The procedures of discovery are designed to prevent or avoid the courtroom surprises so often seen in Perry Mason or other dramatic shows. The presentation of evidence is a methodical process designed to inform and convince the judge and jury as to the correctness of the legal and factual position offered by the proponent. Bob Hope used to ask his audience, "Is sex dirty?" and then answer, "Yes, if it's done right." You might ask, "Should a trial have surprises?" The answer is, "No, not if it's done right."

# CHAPTER 11
# Offensive Action

*In law, it is good policy to never plead what you need not, lest you
oblige yourself to prove what you can not.*

—Abraham Lincoln

T he strategy for aggressive, offensive legal action begins before you file
a complaint. Some localities may require you to file a preliminary claim
or notice with an agency of the government or public institution before
you file an actual complaint against it. In Florida, for instance, if you want
to sue the local board of education, you must give six months' notice
(effectively giving the board six months to attempt settlement). If such a
preliminary claim is required, give it the same care that you would give the
actual complaint. Recognize that parties and/or theories left out of the
preliminary claim may be barred from your actual complaint, restricting your
ultimate goal and chances of success. Check with your local court clerk's
office for information regarding the preliminary claims; at the same time, you
can ascertain the filing fees for your complaint.

## STATUTE OF LIMITATIONS

Another consideration in the pre-filing process is the statute of limitations.
Liability under many laws and statutes may be enforceable for only a specific
period of time from the date of the occurrence. In medical malpractice cases,
for instance, many jurisdictions have a two-year statute of limitations from
when the event took place, or two years from when the individual found out
or should have found out that malpractice had occurred. Therefore, if a
surgical instrument was left inside a person and that person found out three

years later when an x-ray for an unrelated ailment was taken, the clock would start ticking at the time the x-ray results were made known to the patient, not when the instrument was left inside.

Here's another example of a statute of limitation case. In 1979, the revenue room at the New York City subway system headquarters was burglarized of $600,000. New York police pursued every clue for ten years. In 1989, the statute of limitations expired. (The thieves were thought to be city employees; if they had been private citizens, the statute of limitations would have been five years.) The thieves could have come forth and announced their guilt on national television and been safe from prosecution because their liability under the statute had expired. A third type is the Federal Tort Claims Act (a *tort* is a civil wrong or injury other than breach of contract), which has a particularly short, two-year statute of limitations. Conversely, there are statutes that allow you to file documents that will actually "stop the clock" on the statute of limitations, but this must be checked carefully from jurisdiction to jurisdiction.

## NAMING DEFENDANTS

The question of who the defendant will ultimately be is extremely important in your overall strategy, but it does not necessarily have to be fully answered on the day you file your complaint. However, it becomes more difficult to add defendants at a later date. A popular method of naming defendants, sometimes referred to as "shotgunning," is to list every possible defendant (consistent with a reasonable interpretation of the law), even those on the periphery of liability. This can accomplish two goals: You can protect yourself (the plaintiff) by involving all possible defendants from the start of the case, and you can apply pressure on the primary defendant or defendants by involving associates. (Associates may also be third parties who are involved only by virtue of a particular transaction or claim.) But one consideration when shotgunning is whether a potential defendant is a friend. Your suit might ruin the friendship, or you may lose that individual as a witness who would have otherwise been beneficial to your case.

Here are some other considerations when choosing defendants:

- The more defendants, the broader (and more costly) the discovery.
- The impact of a person's statement as a nonparty witness may be different than the impact of the statement if the individual is a defendant.
- You might waste resources when involving fringe defendants and there is little to gain.

- Joining additional defendants can affect the admissibility of evidence.
- There may be consequences arising from interfering with the business or professional relationship between the possible defendant and yourself.

Adding or omitting a defendant may also affect the venue; if so, this should certainly weigh on your decision as to whom you will name. Another consideration is how a jury (if one is used) will view a single plaintiff battling an array of defendants. Another angle is the charisma that any one of the litigants might have, and how that might influence a prospective jury. All of these judgments must be factored into your initial decision-making.

Whatever your strategy regarding multiple defendants, at least one opponent must be accessible to be served with the complaint. Give careful thought to the assets owned or controlled by the defendant, because a judgment against a judgment-proof or penniless individual or bankrupt corporation leaves you with only a piece of paper suitable for framing.

## DRAFTING YOUR COMPLAINT

With the questions of accessibility and collectability answered in the affirmative, your next step in filing a lawsuit is to establish the "cause" or "causes of action" that constitute the suit. You may feel you have myriad reasons to file a lawsuit, but for the court to recognize your lawsuit's validity, you must have one or more legal reasons or causes.

*Black's Law Dictionary* defines a cause of action as "the fact or facts which give a person a right to judicial relief; the legal effect of an occurrence in terms of redress to a party to the occurrence." Therefore, for your lawsuit to survive what may be attempts to discredit it on its form (rather than on its substance), its cause must be clearly defined in legal terms. To do this, your complaint must outline a set of facts that, taken together, constitute something that is actionable. In 90 percent of all situations that lend themselves to a lawsuit, you should be able to spot valid legal causes of action very quickly.

Although these causes can be found in form books, cause of action books, and specific court documents, the trick is to define the cause carefully and then, using an approved standard form, state that cause in the form of a complaint. Figure 11.1 shows what a complaint heading might look like. (Cause of action books include *Shepard's Cause of Action*, published by Shepard's/McGraw-Hill, 1986; and *Actions and Remedies*, published by Callaghon & Company, 1985.) Your complaint must contain enough facts and legal theory to clearly establish your legal right to redress. Basically, the complaint must state the following:

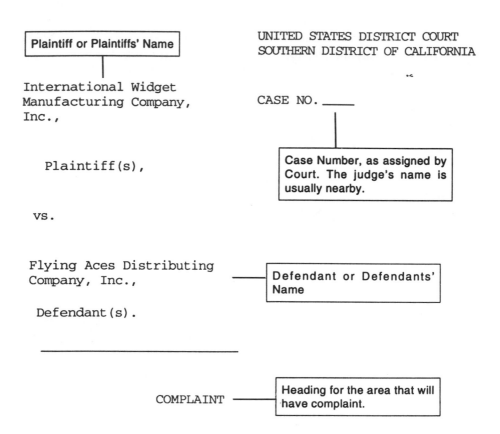

**Figure 11.1.** Sample Complaint Heading.

- When you may sue (depends on a careful review of the statute of limitations and the documents involved in the case).
- Where you may sue (depends on a careful review of the parties involved and where the facts indicate the occurrence involved in your potential lawsuit took place).
- Why you are suing (depends on a careful review of what your opponent did that gives you legal reason or cause of action).
- Whom you are suing (depends on a careful review of the considerations enumerated under Naming Defendants, and also the specific statutes or

laws under which you can expect a redress of the wrong you feel has been suffered).

For complaints in federal court, the rules are quite flexible and require a minimum of initial commitment to information; plus, you have a liberal right to amend. The basic elements of a federal complaint are the following:

1. Basis of the court's jurisdiction.
2. Name, address, and state of citizenship of plaintiff and defendants.
3. Date and place of the event.
4. A brief account of the event.
5. Prayer (demand) for relief.

Many states' rules of civil procedure provide not only the correct form for a complaint on a given subject or cause of action, but also specific form complaints for the most common areas of offensive action. Here are some common causes of action:

- *Account stated:* Money owed for a particular bill.
- *Breach of bond:* Failure to comply with terms of bond agreement.
- *Breach of contract:* Failure to perform terms and conditions of contract.
- *Breach of warranty:* Failure to comply with terms of specific warranty.
- *Civil theft:* Using the civil court system to enforce an obligation where the property was taken "criminally."
- *Declaratory action:* Seeking an interpretation, clarification, direction, or guidance—to obtain the court order to "declare"—as to an ambiguous contract, transaction, or situation.
- *Dissolution of marriage:* Termination of a marriage (divorce), involuntary division of property, custody of minor children, support, change of alimony and other equity issues involved in the extrication of two parties from one another.
- *Ejection:* Removal of a party from a property based upon contract.
- *Equity:* Actions capable of obtaining relief where a specific law, statute, or other legal remedy may not exist.
- *Eviction, residential:* Removal of a tenant from a rental residence.
- *Forcible entry and detention:* Breaking in and detaining an individual.
- *Goods sold:* Merchandise purchased and not paid for.
- *Implied warranty:* Enforcing a "warranty" obligation, where goods may be

defective and where the warranty flows from common law and not a written statement.

- *Intentional tort:* Injury occurring through an intentional act.
- *Money lent:* Money borrowed and not repaid.
- *Mortgage foreclosure:* Default of terms and conditions of mortgage.
- *Negligence:* Damages due generally through a breach of duty or care negligent action. For example, injury due to a "slip and fall" where an improper and dangerous condition was instrumental in causing a fall.
- *Negligence, motor vehicle:* Damages caused by the negligent operation of a motor vehicle.
- *Open account:* Money owed for purchases on account.
- *Pleading in equity:* Seeking a special remedy; that is, a restraining order, an accounting, or requiring performance.
- *Pleading in statutory cause of action:* Violation of specific state statute resulting in damages to a party.
- *Unjust enrichment:* Where a party receives a definable benefit for which compensation should reasonably be paid, but the obligation did not result from a clearly documented transaction.
- *Promissory note:* Failure to make payment of obligation as required under the terms of a written agreement that is characterized by a promissory note.
- *Specific performance:* Equitable remedy to complete requirements of an agreement.
- *Tenant eviction:* Removal of tenant pursuant to terms of lease agreement.
- *Usury:* Statutory damages and/or other remedies for charging interest in an amount greater than allowed by a particular statute.

In the event of a unique situation with an unusual set of facts that does not fall under one of the more standard causes of action, you will need to research the subject. (For an obscure situation, you must do legal research to determine whether the occurrence, taken together with the facts, constitutes a legal reason or cause of action.) For instance, if a merchant took your credit card from you on instructions from the credit card company, which in turn canceled your account because of information from a credit report (without notifying you that it requested the report), you actually would have a cause of action against the credit card company. You, the debtor, can sue the creditor under Section 1681 of the United States Code, which requires that consumers be notified of the name and address of the consumer reporting agency when the agency's information is used regarding the consumer. If you think you have been wronged, research the problem. Finding a unique cause of action is something very special in the creative application of the law.

In order to better understand the process of finding a cause of action, let's look at some everyday circumstances that may occur in your business or personal life and find the possible causes of action.

*Example 1:* You are holding a note on a loan to a business associate. Until three months ago, you received payments as agreed upon in the terms of the note. Then the monthly payments stopped. You have already spent an additional month discussing with the debtor his broken promises to make the required payment. Then the debtor becomes unavailable on the phone, refusing to even discuss the situation; now your letters are getting no response. What are your causes of action? *Money lent or monies owed pursuant to a promissory note.*

*Example 2:* You sold merchandise to a retailer who is a new customer. The retailer receives the product you sent her. The retailer contacts you and returns a small portion of the merchandise (claiming overstock), for which you give her a credit. Your terms are a 2-percent discount if paid within ten days. You do not receive payment within ten days. The balance is due at thirty days, but you do not receive payment then. At forty-five days, your bookkeeper calls the customer and is told that the check is in the mail. You ask your bookkeeper whether or not you have the appropriate credit application on file, and you find that the credit application form was overlooked. Now you are getting upset. At fifty days, you personally contact the customer and determine that she is having financial difficulties. The amount of the bill is $2,200, which is less than the small claims limit in your jurisdiction. You now make a beeline to the small claims court and pick up the appropriate forms. What are your causes of action? *Open account, account stated, merchandise sold and delivered, unjust enrichment.*

*Example 3:* You are the landlord of an apartment house with a tenant who has not paid rent for two months. For the past two years the tenant has paid his rent in a timely fashion and has twice renewed an annual lease. You have checked your file and you have a fully signed renewal lease. Your rental manager contacts the tenant and determines that the tenant has lost his job, is actively seeking new employment, and is short on funds. Your manager takes half a month's rent and informs you of the difficulty. You tell your manager to keep in contact with the tenant on a weekly basis and attempt to obtain weekly payments of rent. After three weeks of not receiving any more rent, you make the decision to put the tenant on notice that he will be evicted and owes the balance of rent based upon a defaulted lease. You must now follow the appropriate format for providing notice to the tenant of imminent eviction and that a continuing obligation for rent which may be due pursuant to the lease is his responsibility. You go to your courthouse and pick up the appropriate form complaints regarding the eviction of a tenant. (You may or may not have available from the court the appropriate forms seeking money damages for the rent due, depending on the laws of the area in which you live.) What are your causes of action? *Eviction, monies due from a tenant, monies due pursuant to a written lease.*

*Example 4:* You live in a neighborhood where there are lots of children of all ages. Three months ago, a teenager who lives two blocks away was playing in front of your house with other neighborhood kids. A rock was thrown through the picture window in your living room by one of the children. You spoke with the teenager's parents, and they initially agreed to be responsible; however, your calls are no longer being returned and you are getting nowhere with written notices and letters to the parents demanding payment. What are your causes of action? *Negligent actions of the teenager causing damage to your property.*

*Example 5:* You have an independent contracting business and you have been working for a company over the past ten months installing plumbing. Initially you received payment for services rendered within a week of submitting your bill. In the past two months, however, your bills have not been paid for at least two or three weeks from the date submitted, and now you find yourself waiting indefinitely for payment of the outstanding bill for services rendered. Through the grapevine you learn that other contractors are having similar problems, despite everyone having written at least two or three times to the company's comptroller asking, and then demanding, payment. What are your causes of action? *Damages due pursuant to monies owed on a contractual obligation, monies owed pursuant to services rendered, account stated, open account, unjust enrichment.*

*Example 6:* You have a personal relationship with an employee and, during the course of that relationship, you lend the individual an automobile, some money, and several pieces of stereo equipment. You retain the title to the auto, indicate the word loan on the check for the money, and make it clear verbally that the equipment, which matches your own stereo, is a loan. The individual leaves your employment and moves away with the aforementioned items. What are your causes of action? *Civil theft, money lent, replevin—the recovery of goods wrongfully taken.*

*Example 7:* You are a car phone manufacturer's sales representative. To obtain greater coverage in your territory, you hire several sales reps, one of whom arranges to go to your supplier and pick up several car phones. Under your arrangement, he is responsible for leaving a check with the supplier for the wholesale cost of the car phones. The rep writes out the check and hands it to the appropriate person behind the counter. When that person goes to package the phones, the rep reaches behind the counter and takes his check back. The phones are delivered and later installed in the rep's customers' cars, and you contact the rep for payment. He denies owing anything for the phones. What are your causes of action? *Fraud, civil theft.*

Finding a cause of action may turn out to be the easiest part of prevailing in a lawsuit. A case in point occurred when Jane Fonda made her workout album. The physical fitness record market, of which my Gateway Records had previously been a leader, became a star market. Suddenly the tens of thousands of recordings of the Bill Rogers' Runner's Workout, as well as those by the President's Council on Physical Fitness, D. Kylene (Miss America 1979), and others, began coming back from the retailers, who were now getting requests for the star product only. This caused a number of defaults by our customers on payments that were due for purchases of records and cassettes, the largest being $350,000 from the Handleman Company.

Handleman Company, one of the nation's largest distributors of recorded music, serviced the K mart chain almost exclusively. When K mart wants to place a major advertisement in American newspapers (at tremendous cost), they contact their suppliers and suggest that a certain amount of space has been allotted for "co-op" advertising for their product. What this actually means, at least in the music business, is that K mart finds a certain number of suppliers to pay the cost of advertising, then K mart "cooperates" by giving them the space at a price sufficient to cover the cost of the ad space allotted. Handleman passes along this cost to vendors who supply the goods by taking an agreed sum off the bill to pay for the vendor's share of the ad. In other words, a discount on the cost to Handleman, or an advertising allowance as it's sometimes called, actually pays for the ad, if the merchandise sells. But what if it doesn't sell?

As I walked into the lobby of the Century Plaza Hotel in Los Angeles for the 1982 National Association of Recording Merchandiser's Convention, I was greeted by the suave, cigar-smoking, diamond-ringed vice president of purchasing for Handleman. He indicated that K mart was planning a national ad in May and asked if I wanted to participate. I replied, "Of course, count us in." He replied, "I can buy $60,000 each of four titles, or a total of $240,000 in merchandise. I want a $48,000 advertising credit." I agreed and the deal was struck right there in the lobby.

Despite the financial strain for Gateway, the deal was done; the merchandise was delivered and distributed by Handleman to K mart stores throughout the country. By the beginning of June, it was apparent that Fonda (and also

Richard Simmons, to a lesser degree) were taking all the sales, and our product failed to "sell through" to any major degree—at least according to Handleman. For us, the ad was obviously not very successful. What K mart obtained with the extensive national newspaper coverage was of no consequence to my company at the time—our product did not fare well, and we had to consider the possibility of a large return.

But a return is not a default on payment; at least, it shouldn't be. Our company's sales policy, which had previously been delivered to Handleman via Federal Express with a copy of the bill of lading to prove delivery (usable evidence), stated that our customers could have a 100-percent exchange on goods purchased (no returns for credit).

The cause of action was clear—account stated; goods delivered and invoiced, but not paid for. That would seem a simple and straightforward basis for suit. Handleman didn't see it that way. Although their orders were either telephoned in to Gateway Records or given verbally, they always followed up with a confirming written purchase order. In light, small type on the reverse side of this document, Handleman claimed the right to a 100-percent return of unsold goods for a period of five years after the date of delivery. So the complicating factor was, whose terms applied? Gateway's tendered sales policy (via Federal Express) or Handleman's written purchase order (after the verbal order was placed and the goods shipped on that verbal order)?

The case wound up in federal court with Gateway asking for $350,000 and Handleman denying any indebtedness. During the discovery process, several interesting things came to light. The aforementioned purchasing vice president, who had since retired from the company, happened to be visiting in Handleman's offices on the day we were there taking depositions. He agreed to be deposed and his comments on K mart's advertising policy confirmed our suspicions. Handleman used us to help satisfy the demands K mart made for vendors to come up with advertising dollars to support large, expensive national newspaper ads:

*Q:* Sir, do you have any personal knowledge of the advertising program with K mart, which involved GEMCOM [Gateway] merchandise, and Handleman's transactions with K mart?

*A:* . . . I have some of the knowledge.

*Q:* Are you personally informed as to how the dollars were computed, which GEMCOM [Gateway] was requested to pay for participation in an ad with K mart?

*A:* We would receive the size of the ad and the dollar amount that it would cost for the total ad, and then make a decision on how many suppliers [record companies] and how many releases [recordings] would be included in the ad, and then divide each proportionally for the total dollars, for the amount of space allotted per supplier.

*Q:* Then you determined how much space should be allowed to GEMCOM [Gateway] in such an ad; is that right?

*A:* . . . We would possibly call GEMCOM [Gateway] . . . and tell them what the cost per inch or per item would be.

*Q:* Did you do that before the ad was run, or did you tell them after the ad had been run?

*A:* Before it was run.

*Q:* Did you . . . provide any documentation to GEMCOM [Gateway] in advance of the ad being run, as to what their advertising obligation would be . . . ?

*A:* . . . The ad was not charged for until we were charged by K mart. . . .

*Q:* Did Handleman ever share in the cost of that ad with the suppliers, such as GEMCOM [Gateway]?

*A:* I don't—I can't answer that. I don't know.

*Q:* Did you get an invoice from K mart in advance, or a projection from K mart . . . ?

*A:* . . . our purchasing department received it from our sales department who, in turn, received the cost from K mart.

*Q:* Then is it true that Handleman is the one who determined how much GEMCOM's share would be in that ad, and not K mart?

*A:* No.

*Q:* Are you saying, then, that K mart determined how much GEMCOM's [Gateway's] cost would be?

*A:* K mart would advise our sales department who, in turn, advised us.

*Q:* Did K mart know in advance how many releases of GEMCOM's [Gateway's] merchandise would appear in the ad?

*A:* No.

*Q:* Who made that decision?

*A:* We made that decision with the—our sales department when we were informed of the date, the size, and all the information about the ad.

*Q:* What was the factor which determined how much money would be paid per item in the ad?

*A:* The amount of space that K mart requested from our sales department, and the cost of that space.

Another interesting sidelight was that the federal judge hearing the case, Charles Levin, came to the bench from our attorney's law firm and had previously helped to make the small amount of law on the subject of modification of previously agreed terms in the case of *American Parts Co., Inc. v. American Arbitration Association and Derring Milliken, Inc.* In that case, brought before the appellate court, it was found that "a written confirmation of oral agreement is of no force and effect whatsoever unless agreed to by the other party." This ruling was in our favor, and on this single precedent we pinned our hopes of winning the present case.

Unfortunately, the cost of the suit was draining Gateway's resources; so when Handleman offered a settlement of $75,000 and the promise to attempt to sell off the excess inventory, we accepted. After our attorney's fee of $20,000, the balance was available for producing new recordings in fields other than physical fitness.

To this day, I believe that if I had known at the time how to act pro se, I would never have accepted the settlement. We felt we were entitled to the payment of $350,000 before any records or cassettes were exchanged for other product. Handleman's failure to pay for goods ordered was, in my opinion, part of a scheme to accumulate advertising dollars at the manufacturer's expense simply to satisfy pressure from their customer, K mart, for ad space.

Once all the determinations of when, where, why, and who have been made, then a complaint can be drawn that will state, with enough facts and legal theory, a clearly established legal right to redress, or cause of action. Here's an example of what does and does not constitute a complaint, and what meets the criteria for a cause of action, in our version of when Harry met Sally.

When Harry met Sally, Harry (who knew Sally was in love with him), asked Sally for a loan that, unfortunately, Harry failed to pay back. If Sally were to file a lawsuit against Harry and state simply, "Harry owes me money and didn't pay it back," this would not be sufficient under the law to sustain a valid lawsuit. However, if Sally stated that "Harry owed me X dollars and borrowed it on such and such a date, and promised to pay it back under terms that were clearly agreed to, which included a certain date," then Sally would have asserted sufficient facts, along with the fact that she had made written demand for return of the loan, to constitute a legal cause of action. She could then expect the court to sustain her suit at least through the point at which the other side attempts to discredit her evidence.

In essence, the pleadings (complaint and associated court documents) are your argument presented to the court and your opponent. The language of your complaint should be as broad as possible, because the laws, statutes, and remedies are constantly changing. Between the time you make the complaint and the time your case gets before a judge and jury, the law under which you have made your claim may become subject to a new interpretation. If your claim is worded broadly, you have room for expansion or contraction to fit the new interpretation. Another ploy is to frame your complaint using alternative theories of law (causes of action). This strengthens your legal argument and makes it harder for your opponent to succeed with a motion to dismiss, a motion for summary judgment, or an attack on the specificity of your complaint.

Obviously, there are many elements to deal with before you can hope to prevail in a lawsuit. The first step is to successfully prevent any challenge to the form of the complaint. Here are some common pitfalls to avoid in drafting your complaint:

- Failure to list all proper and necessary parties as defendants.
- Failure to state the exact name(s) of the defendant(s).
- Failure to state the proper name of the court in which the action is filed.
- Failure to use correct form, such as typing layout.
- Failure to properly designate "competence" of each party (to be competent, a party must be over 18 or a corporation, not in the armed forces, and not under legal disability—guardianship, trust, or estate).
- Mistakes in elements of jurisdiction, dollar amount, correct division of court system, and so on.
- Mistake in recitation and determination of proper venue.
- Failure to set forth one cause of action per count.
- Lack of recitation of proper background factual allegations.
- Failure to recite ultimate facts constituting the cause of action.
- Failure to recite resulting damages.
- Mistake in proper recapitulation in "prayer for relief"; that is, lack of a wherefore clause clearly setting forth all the elements of issues and damages for which you are requesting relief.
- Missing court-required attachments or special pages, such as cover sheets, backings, designated forms, and so on.

If none of these flaws exists in your complaint after you have carefully checked and rechecked the facts, your suit is ready to be filed. Be it pro se or with attorney, you should feel confident that, at least as to form, your complaint will survive its challenges—motions to dismiss and motions to strike. Fighting such challenges will require defending the causes of action as stated in your complaint. You should be able to tell the judge the theory of your complaint and outline quickly the elements of the cause of action contained in your complaint.

## MANAGING THE CASE

The use of discovery by the defense has been explained in Chapter 7. When viewed from an offensive standpoint, the process must be seen as a prospecting expedition with all possible sources mined for information. The more carefully formed the questions, the more succinct and probing the direction, the better the chance to receive substantive answers that will help in the discovery process.

The defense will attempt to gain time by stonewalling or otherwise delaying, hoping that the additional costs will cause the offense to lose interest in prosecuting the case. Thus, it is incumbent upon you, as the offense, to manage the case effectively. To do otherwise is equivalent to aiding and abetting the opposition. This means you will have to move the case along within the framework provided by your jurisdiction's court system; keeping track of deadlines, completing discovery quickly and efficiently, and then docketing the case for trial.

Aggressive and vigorous action includes using as many procedures as quickly as possible within the framework of the rules in an attempt to keep your opponent unsettled, unsure, and on the defensive. For example, file for extensive discovery with your complaint instead of at a later date, and include notices of depositions and any appropriate hearings. Discovery could include interrogatories, request for production of documents and specific items (subpoena duces tecum), and request for admissions, all of which are designed to overwhelm your opponent.

One method of case management is to prepare an outline at the outset of your legal action and to make it part of your case file. Here's a suggested outline of action:

1. Type of case: _____

2. Opposing parties and lawyers:_____

_____

_____

3. Case objectives:_____

_____

4. Rationale—why pursue this case? _____

_____

_____

5. What documents, exhibits, and witnesses need to be developed in preparation?_____

_____

_____

6. What information do I need and how am I to get it?_____

_____

_____

7. What are the legal issues of my case? _____

_____

_____

8. What factual allegations are necessary to properly state my case?____

_____

_____

9. What research is needed?_____

_____

_____

10. What is my overall strategy?_____

_____

_____

11. What is my time frame?_____

_____

12. What resources will I need?

People:_____

Materials:_____

Financial: _____

13. Whom can I count on for help?_____

_____

_____

14. What outside consultants or experts do I need?_____

   _____

   _____

15. What are the important legal issues of this case? _____

   _____

   _____

   _____

16. Which legal issues, if any, would set precedent?_____

   _____

   _____

17. What are my opponent's claims?_____

   _____

   _____

18. What are my claims?_____

   _____

   _____

19. Do any third parties have liability?_____

   _____

   _____

20. Expense budget (court reporters, transcripts, fees):_____

   _____

   _____

21. Plan of action:_____

   _____

   _____

22. Goals:_____

   _____

   _____

Once you are involved in litigation, whether with counsel or pro se, keeping track of paperwork becomes a major undertaking. The following is a recommended system for organizing your case file (all of which should be kept in chronological order within the suggested breakdown):

- Correspondence.
- Pleadings.
- Legal research.
- Discovery.
- Witness list and information.
- Documentation or evidence (See Chapter 15 for organizing and marking evidence for the court trial.)

When the time arrives that you don't anticipate any further need for discovery—when you have obtained all the information you believe you are likely to obtain from your opposition, experts, or third parties—then you inform the court, with the appropriate notices, that you wish the case to be placed on the court's trial docket.

# CHAPTER 12
# Damages

*If he has shattered a gentleman's limb, one shall shatter his limb.*

—Hammurabi's Code

Whether we like to admit it or not, the basic law of Western society is still, at least figuratively, "an eye for an eye." The concept of cutting off a thief's hand is now repugnant to our culture, although the ancient Code of Hammurabi set forth this doctrine in "The Laws of Recompense" and other teachings that form the basis of our present-day law of damages (Howard Oleck, *Damages to Persons and Property*, Brooklyn, NY: Central Book Company, 1961). These excerpts from Hammurabi's code illustrate the doctrine.

*Laws as to Bodily Injuries:*
*Rule 196.* If one destroys the eye of a free-born man, his eye one shall destroy.
*Rule 202.* If anyone has injured the strength of a man who is high above him, he shall publicly be struck with sixty strokes of a cowhide whip.
*Rule 203.* If he has injured the strength of a man who is his equal, he shall pay one mina of silver. . . .

*Laws Concerning Physicians:*
*Rule 220.* If he has opened his tumor with a bronze lancet and has ruined his eye, he shall pay the half of his price in money. . . .

*Laws Concerning Builders (of houses):*
*Rule 229.* If a builder has built a house for someone and has not made his

work firm, and if the house he built has fallen and has killed the owner of the house, that builder shall be put to death.

## Laws Concerning Shipbuilding:

*Rule 235.* If a boatman has cauled a boat for a man, and has not made firm his work, if in that year that ship is put into use and it suffers an injury, the boatman shall alter that boat and shall make it firm out of his own funds; and he shall give the strengthened boat to the owner of the boat. [For the loss of a boat or if a boat sank after a collision, a boat was to be paid; for the loss of a cargo, a similar cargo was to be paid.]

## Laws Concerning Bailments and Conversion:

*Rule 244.* If anyone has hired an ox or an ass, and if in the field a lion has killed it, the loss is its master's.

*Rule 245.* If anyone has hired an ox and has caused it to die through ill-treatment or blows, he shall return an ox for an ox to the owner of the ox.

*Rule 259.* If anyone has hired an ox and God [act of God] has struck him and he has died, he who hired the ox shall swear by the name of God and be guiltless. . . .

As the exchange of money replaced the exchange of goods as the basis of our economy, damages evolved to be fundamentally money compensation or indemnity. Thus the court's definition of the word damage is "the compensation granted by the law, to an injured person in order to repair an injury suffered by him" (*Hartzell v. Myall*, 115 Calif. App.2d 670, 252 P.2d 676; *Hanna v. Martin*, 49 S.2d 585 [Fla.]; see Carroll Daniels, "Measure of Damages in Personal Injury Cases," *Miami Law Quarterly*, Vol. 7, 1953, p. 171).

Another way of describing damages, as noted in *Delehanty v. Walzer* (59 N.W.S.2d 777, revd. on other grounds, 271 A.D. 886, 67 N.Y.S.2d 25, affd., 298 N.W. 820, 83 N.E.2d 863) is recompense, reparation, or satisfaction in money, given in order to make good for a loss or injury sustained. In another court decision, the basic principle of the law of damages is eloquently stated: "(O)ne who negligently or wrongfully does or omits an act, and thereby causes injury to another should be held liable for the damage he thus caused" (*Lane v. Southern R. Co.*, 192 No.Car. 287, 134 S.E. 855, 51 A.L.R. 1114; 15 Am.Jr., Damages, Sec. 3).

Therefore, in order for damages to exist, some legal right of the injured party must be violated before any cause of action arises for that party (*Sloan v. Hart*, 150 No.Car. 269, 63 S.E. 1037, 21 L.R.A. [N.S.] 239). No cause of action for damages exists if there is a wrong without damage or a damage without wrong. (1 Am.Jr., Actions, Sec. 28.) Assuming there is a wrong and damage can be proven, then the cost of recovery must be factored into a realistic assessment of the value of the case. (In some states costs incurred in obtaining a judgment for damages is deemed to be part of the judgment.) So regardless of how upset you are about a legal involvement, expect an attorney to first evaluate the economics of the case before making the decision to represent you. Even with the different financial parameters of self-representation, you should conduct the same cost/benefit review before commencing legal action.

This is a well-established mode of operation. Even as far back as 1303, concerns were more about the cash value of a case than about retribution. In that year, Henry De Bodreugam was accosted by several thugs who took a child who had been placed in De Bodreugam's care. (We know about this case because English cases from the reign of Edward I [1272–1307] through the reign of Henry VIII [1509–1547] were transcribed by the chief scribes of the courts and were published annually in volumes called *Yearbooks*.) De Bodreugam filed charges against Thomas Le Arcedekne, one of his attackers, and was awarded damages of 100 marks. In those days, the victim had a great deal to say about the incarceration of the perpetrator, and Henry allowed Thomas to be bonded (bailed) out. When questioned about the wisdom of possibly allowing Thomas to get away from the court's jurisdiction, Henry, wise to the law, said he would be able to collect the same amount of damages if Thomas were to attack him again. The compensation was obviously more important to Henry than seeing Thomas rot in jail, which considering the circumstances of the day, he would certainly have done.

Even though the decision as to whether or not a defendant who is judged guilty goes to jail is not in the hands of modern-day plaintiffs, your decision to litigate or not must be considered in light of what tangible results you can obtain if an award is tendered by the court. However, even before dreams of victory creep into your mind, you must realistically assess the damages, or economic loss you have suffered.

Before we look at methods of calculating damages, we must clarify some of the legal principles controlling the application of the law to actual circumstances and facts of a given infringement of a person's rights, creating damages:

All private injury or loss through the acts of others arise either from the invasion of some recognized legal right, as a right of property, a right secured by contract, or a personal right, or from the neglect of some duty resulting in damage (Arthur Sedewick, *The Law of Damages*, 2nd ed., Boston: Little, Brown, 1909, p. 16).

The law of damages is a matter of rights. These rights are enforceable against particular persons when a contract exists, and against all the world when the matter concerns property or personal rights (in the case of negligent actions where someone's rights are invaded). Civil law consists of the rights and duties between members of society. Consequently, it is the legal duty of each individual not to damage another by ignoring the amount of care required by circumstances. Conversely, it is everyone's right not to be damaged. (This includes damage through deceit, which by its use creates fraud.)

Going back even before De Bodreugam's 1303 damage claim, the law has recognized certain types of damages, and has disregarded those of no consequence under the law. In a general sense, these situations may exist:

- Damages without any legal injury or right to recover.
- Legal injury but without damage.
- Actual damages with legal injury (or the infringement of right) with money damages provided.
- Damages sustained by the neglect (act or omission) of a duty that, if not for the loss, would be a matter of indifference to the law.
- Damage that alone will give the right to action even though there has been no breach of legal duty.

These divisions are but guideposts in applying the law to actual circumstances resulting in a loss. When it comes to the discussion of the extent or worth of the loss, then the fundamental rule is less esoteric: *The remedy shall be commensurate with the injury sustained.* The amount of damages is determined by rules of law that neither judge nor jury are at liberty to disregard; and the damages must be certain both in nature and in cause. Hypothetical damages are not recoverable, and neither are damages that do not result in a loss.

When an act that would normally damage a party turns out to be beneficial, most jurisdictions will not allow the so-called damaged party to be compensated. For instance, in Connecticut, a railroad was planned, to run over a plot of land that had a canal. The canal had to be filled, which actually increased the value of the land. As a result, that portion of the land that was left after the railroad took the space it needed was worth more than the entire lot before the railroad condemned the land. This case set the precedent in Connecticut that where an owner has a claim for damages for land taken, and has received benefits equal to the value of that land, these benefits shall offset the damages and the damaged party shall be allowed nothing (*Whitman v. Boston, etc.*, R. Co., 3 Allen, 133). The law is so sensitive to certainty that when proof of damages under this principle is sustained but the degree of damage is questionable, the law will revert to estimating the damages that are the most definite and certain (per J. Seldon, in *Griffin v. Colver*, 16 N.Y. 489, 495).

As a precedent to the actual calculation of damages, there are seven generally accepted "measures of recovery":

1.  Loss suffered.
2.  Gain prevented.
3.  The value of the use of the thing.
4.  Interest.
5.  Difference between actual and contract value.
6.  Value of a bargain, less such expenses as plaintiff must incur to obtain it.
7.  Difference between the thing as it is and as it would have been had the warranty been true.

The facts and circumstances of a case are, of course, paramount as to which if any of these measures of recovery apply.

Like so many other things in life that have become more complicated, refined, and defined over the ages, the law of damages has been expanded and divided into various categories or types of damage:

*Accumulative damages (enhanced):* Damages guaranteed to the plaintiff by statute over and above those available by common law.

*Actual damages:* Real or compensatory damages that may also consist of general and special damages.

*Added damages:* Punitive or exemplary damages added on to a purely compensatory award.

*Civil damages:* Good only under liquor sale laws. A parent, guardian, relative, or employer of a person who was injured as a result of improper sale of alcholic beverages may have a claim against the beverage seller.

*Compensatory damages:* Compensation for the actual damage of the injured party that simply makes good or replaces the loss caused by the act in question.

*Consequential damages:* Damages or losses that do not flow directly from the act in question, but stem from some of the consequences or results of the damaging act and may include fairly remote consequences of the wrong.

*Continuing damages:* Damages that accrue from the same loss or from a repetition of similar acts during a specified period of time or continuing injury.

*Damages ultra:* Damages claimed by plaintiff over and above those already awarded (or posted as deposited with the court by the defendant) based on the belief that the award is inadequate.

*Direct damages:* Damages that stem from a breach of contract and can in the ordinary course of human experience be expected to result from that breach.

*Double damages:* Damages doubled by judge or jury, in special cases of willful or reckless negligence, pursuant to express statutory authority.

*Exemplary damages:* Damages awarded on an increased scale to the plaintiff over and above what will justly compensate for property loss. Generally used where the wrongful act was aggravated by circumstances of violence, oppression, malice, fraud, or wanton and wicked conduct on the part of the defendant. These damages are intended to aid the plaintiff for mental anguish, shame, degradation, or other conditions arising out of the the original act.

*Expectancy damages:* Damages generally awarded in actions for nonperformance of contracts and intended to put the injured party in the position he would have been had the contract been performed.

*Fair damages:* Damages that are more than a nominal award that balances out most of the elements of injury, both tangible and intangible.

*General damages:* Damages that are the natural, necessary, and usual result of the wrongful or negligent act in question.

*Inadequate damages:* Damages that, when recovered, do not compensate the injured party and place her in the postion she was formerly in.

*Incidental damages:* Damages that include any commercially reasonable charge, expense, or commission incurred in stopping delivery, transportation, care, or custody of goods after the buyer's breach in connection with the return or resale of the goods made necessary from the resulting breach. This also includes expenses reasonably incurred in inspection, receipt, transportation, care, and custody of goods rightfully rejected and any other reasonable expenses surrounding the delay or breach.

*Indeterminate damages:* Damages that cannot be determined accurately in monetary terms.

*Intervening damages:* Damages occurring to plaintiff during the time the case is held off by bond, appeal, or review.

*Irreparable damages:* Irretrievable rights and lost opportunities are typical of damages not easily ascertainable; those for which no money standard exists for measurement. Damages can be estimated only by conjecture.

*Land damages:* Damages awarded to the owner of land in condemnation proceedings.

*Limitation of damages:* Contract provision by which parties agree in advance to limit the amount of damages for a breach.

*Liquidated damages:* Damages that parties to a contract agree to pay if one of the parties breaks some promise as specified in the contract.

*Nominal damages:* A trifling sum awarded to a plaintiff in an action where there is no substantial loss or injury for which to be compensated. However, the law still recognizes an invasion of rights or a breach of the defendant's obligations, and in a situation where the plaintiff has failed to show the amount of damages incurred, nominal damages may be awarded.

*Nonpecuniary damages:* Damages for pain and suffering, mental anguish, fright, loss of reputation, impairment of senses or faculties that are not measurable in monetary terms.

*Ordinary damages:* Fair or reasonable damages.

*Pecuniary damages:* Damages that can be calculated to a reasonable certainty, always measured in monetary terms.

*Prospective damages:* Damages that are expected but have not yet occurred. It is assumed that in the nature of things, these damages most probably will result from the act complained of.

*Proximate damages:* Damages that are the immediate and direct result of the act complained of.

*Punitive damages:* Damages used for punishing the defendant or setting an example for society, and generally used in cases where it is proven that a defendant has acted willfully, maliciously, or fraudulently. Punitive damages are generally used to punish outrageous conduct.

*Remote damages:* Damages immediately attributable to an intervening cause, such as events that are one of the links in an unbroken chain of causation. Damages that would not have taken place if the original act or event did not take place.

*Rescissory damages:* Damages contemplating a return of the injured party to her situation before she was induced by wrongful conduct to enter into a particular transaction. If the return of property is not possible, then the damages would be the monetary equivalent of that property.

*Special damages:* Damages that are the natural, but not necessary and inevitable, result of the occurrence.

*Speculative damages:* Anticipated damages that stem from the same act or occurrence that constitutes the present cause of action. They depend on future developments that are contingent, conjectural, and possibly improbable.

*Statutory damages:* Damages that are set by statute, as opposed to damages assessed at common law.

*Stipulated damages:* Damages as specified in a contract or liquidated damages as specified by an agreement.

*Substantial damages:* Damages of a considerable amount, as distinguished from nominal damages.

*Temporary damages:* Damages allowed for an occasional wrong or intermittent period. Their cause is usually removable.

*Treble (triple) damages:* Damages provided for in certain statutes or laws that triple the amount of damages originally found by the judge or jury for the particular occurrence. Copyright and antitrust are two areas that provide for such damages.

The law of damages differs greatly from jurisdiction to jurisdiction, with each state placing its thumbprint on the types of damages and the claims that can be awarded under its laws and attitudes, perceptions, and experiences of judges within a given venue. Litigation attorneys practicing in a particular county or state will generally know what type of claim a particular judge will rule in favor of and how high the award of damages may be. One court may allow liberal claims for recovery of profits while another may take a stricter position and rarely allow such claims. Consult a knowledgeable professional before making a damage claim either pro se or through an attorney.

Once a right can be shown to have been violated, the law will presume that some loss or damage has occurred. Even if the amount is nominal, it is presumed that enough of a loss has been sustained to support a cause of action or lawsuit. The calculation of damages and proof thereof is the next step, if not already prescribed by contract or by statute.

An assessment of the possible damages in a particular case first requires a look at the measures of recovery (Chapter 18) and the types of damages that a particular jurisdiction, statute, and court may allow as a remedy. In the event the damage results from a breach of contract, the damaged party must first look to provisions of the contract that may limit or set the parameters of a claim. In cases where the statute controls the allowable claim, you must review the specifics of the statute before computing a possible prayer for damages. For instance, U.S. copyright law provides for specific damages, including treble damages under certain conditions. You have only to study the statute to know what may be a possible recovery. Many real estate contracts state that if a sale does not take place, the amount of damages is limited to the amount held in escrow, or alternately, the party seeking to enforce the transaction is given the right of specific performance. (Attorneys' fees, costs, and interest may also be awarded, depending on the contract provisions and the statutes of the jurisdiction.)

A promissory note is a form of contract. For instance, if the terms call for $10,000 at an annual interest rate of 10 percent with the full sum of $11,000 ($10,000 principal plus $1,000 interest) payable at the end of one year, damages for nonpayment would be those stipulated in the contract ($11,000), plus attorneys' fees, service of process, and other usual or reasonable costs involved with regard to the collection of the damage and continuing interest.

Here is a slightly more complex situation: A company making and distributing widgets uses a component in the production that is supplied by the Axon Corporation. There exists a contract for delivery of this component with specific delivery dates. An Axon ship has an accident at sea and is unable to deliver the needed component. In the absence of insurance, and with widgets back-ordered across the country, an element of damages may be lost profits from the sale of the widgets, provided the widget company can establish a history of profitability from its normal operations. The accident may make Axon responsible for a proportionate share of the widget company's lost profits. A key factor here is whether or not Axon had knowledge that the materials were being used in a product that was then commercially offered for sale, as distinguished from a product being placed in storage by a wholesaler for possible sale at a later date. Also, the court would examine how difficult it would have been for the widget company to find an alternative source of supply. If the proof offered sustains that Axon's component of the widget is unique and not readily replaceable, then damages for the widget company's lost profits might ensue.

The starting point in calculating damages is finding definable or certain values. With the promissory note, the terms of the note provide the needed certainty. The definable value is found in the calculation of damages, which becomes a matter of arithmetic based upon the conditions set forth in the note. The widget example, however, requires more complex calculations, and such factors as the level of selling price (cost versus retail) enter into them. Providing a factual basis so that the judge and jury can be assured or convinced of your claim is paramount for having a claim sustained.

Damages related to negligence are more difficult to value. Intangible factors enter the picture, such as pain and suffering, loss of consortium, the value of human life or some of a person's senses (if such a value can be calculated), and economic loss. The computation of damages is further complicated when figuring an individual's future needs. This happens frequently in claims involving automobile accidents, malpractice, and slip-and-fall cases, where a particular set of injuries will need X number of dollars for immediate care and Y dollars amortized through annuities over a long time. Medical expenses, living expenses, and general expenses related to pain and suffering must be taken into consideration. This is how negligence cases result in the huge awards so often reported in the media.

Sometimes the statute itself can protect the damaged party. One summer afternoon a young musician who had recorded for my company came to see me. He was carrying several record albums that I had produced in the early 1960s. He was so proud to have found these albums in a local record store and wanted to show his admiration by letting me know that he had purchased the albums and that they would become part of his jazz collection. But what resulted from this incident was the discovery that a former employee had stolen those albums, and many others, from our warehouse to open his record shop. A visit to his store revealed walls lined with recordings that my company exclusively manufactured and distributed in the years the store-owner worked for us.

We made all the proper police reports, and the Fort Lauderdale and Davie police departments agreed to raid the record shop. Unfortunately, before the raid occurred, the young musician went back to the owner of the shop and told him how upset I was that he had these products on display. That tipped off the thief, and he removed most of the merchandise. The raid produced only three of the stolen recordings. A civil claim was all that was left.

Our attorney reviewed the statutes, and found that Florida's law protects employers with treble damages from thefts by employees. The damage claim and resulting judgment came to $27,000, which included treble damages, attorneys' fees, costs, and interest.

## PUNITIVE DAMAGES

When a defendant has transgressed the bounds of legal propriety with conduct considered malicious, oppressive, violent, reckless, or wanton, exemplary damages may be called for by statute or assessed by the court or jury. Punitive damages, as they are often called, have evolved as a form of punishment for the guilty and a deterrent for the bystander.

Some jurisdictions do not recognize the doctrine of punitive damages except as they are called for in a statute, but most jurisdictions and federal law accept it as a matter of public policy. Some jurists believe punitive damages have a healthy effect upon society, especially when the injured party is unlikely to press criminal charges or lacks the legal right to a more severe form of punishment. Since some jurisdictions will allow these damages with no prerequisite showing of actual damages, and others grant punitive damages only after actual damages have been proven, it is important to check your state law when considering a claim for these "vindictive" or "smart money" damages.

Before adding a claim of punitive damages to your complaint, you should review several things. First, if you have a strong case to begin with, will seeking punitive damages actually bolster your position, or will it complicate the case and your ability to prove it? Second, will a claim for punitive damages enhance or impede the chances of settlement? Third, will the defendant, if found guilty, actually have the assets to make a large judgment collectible?

In your anger and frustration over a legal matter, you may desire to "go for the jugular"—to punish by way of punitive damages—but before you do, consider all the options.

## COMPUTING DAMAGE

Economic loss in an accident case where injury has been sustained might be determined using the following elements of damage, and calculating their corresponding values (keeping appropriate state laws and decisions in mind).

*Elements of Damage*

1. Loss in wages

   Present                                                                              _____

   Future                                                                               _____

   Total                                                                                _____

2. Loss in fringe benefits (health insurance, pensions, etc.)

   Present                                                                              _____

   Future                                                                               _____

   Total                                                                                _____

3. Medical costs

   Supplies/special devices                                                 _____

   Therapy                                                                            _____

   Medical visits                                                                   _____

   Future operations                                                             _____

   Recuperation time                                                            _____

   Total                                                                                _____

4. Housekeeper or nurse                                                      _____

5. Household services now being performed by others        _____

6. Institutionalization (if necessary)                                    _____

7. Special housing or housing modifications (factor

in state laws and decisions regarding
discounting, inflation, productivity, and taxes)           _____

Total                                                     _____

Added to the actual economic loss (and costs) is an evaluation of pain, suffering, and loss of consortium. This is where the knowledge of local awards for similar cases comes into play. These elements are difficult to view objectively and often depend on the jurisdiction's precedent.

## DETERMINING NEED

No matter how painful or disruptive an accident, life goes on after it. This means the plaintiff's (and family's) needs must be considered in calculating damages sought. In addition, whereas elements of damages are usually based on work life, needs must be calculated for the person's total life expectancy, and in the case of death, the lives of the remaining family members. Since the assessment of needs shows actual expected outlays over time, it is subject to much less interference by state law.

*Needs Assessment*

1.  Expenses through the date of expected settlement

    Unreimbursed medical expenses                      _____

    Worker's compensation                              _____

    Medical insurance payments                         _____

    Loans payable                                      _____

    Special devices (wheelchairs, specially designed
        home, etc.)                                    _____

    Costs of litigation                                _____

    Miscellaneous (unexpected items, plus some amount
        of money to enjoy)                             _____

2.  Future expenses

    Special operations                                 _____

    Appliances or devices                              _____

    Special vehicles                                   _____

| | |
|---|---|
| Sales taxes | _____ |
| Maintenance of living standard (cost of lifestyle before injury) | _____ |
| Housekeeper services | _____ |
| Therapy | _____ |
| Institutional care | _____ |
| Educational costs | _____ |
| Rehabilitation | _____ |
| Special schooling | _____ |
| Schooling at primary or high school level for children | _____ |
| College education for children | _____ |
| Total | _____ |

It is sometimes difficult to document damages, and it is sometimes even harder to believe you will actually need to take steps to protect your legal position. One such case was the treatment I received from ABC Records and pop vocalist Bobby Vinton.

In 1966, I did some location recording for Vinton (who sold 50 million records between 1962 and 1972). By coincidence, in the early 1970s my secretary had been Vinton's private secretary and confidante. At the time of this particular incident, the former teenage idol had recently been dropped by CBS's Epic Records and was at a low point—for the first time in his career, Vinton was between recording contracts. Yet few industry executives were aware of his availability.

Being heavily involved in selling Polish polka music at the time, I was interested in getting a Polish recording from Vinton (who was sometimes called the "Polish prince") on my DYNO record label. My secretary arranged an appointment with Vinton at his Waldorf-Astoria suite. I wore one of our DYNO promotional buttons that read "Kiss Me, I'm Polish," and Vinton was so eager to have one that he practically ripped it off my lapel. I outlined my plans for his career revival centered on a Polish radio campaign and hopefully a hit polka recording that would be crossed over to pop audiences. Vinton indicated that he liked the concept and then auditioned a song that was perfect for the plan. Although he made no commitment at the time, he did disclose that a rumored deal with Capitol Records had not been consummated, and that he was still a free agent.

I could hardly wait until 9:00 A.M. California time to call my friend Leonard Korobkin, then vice president of business affairs for ABC Records. He was utterly surprised to hear that Vinton was free. I proposed a deal: He would sign Vinton to ABC Records, give me the Polish recording, and ABC would have a Vinton Christmas recording (which Korobkin had previously said he wanted) plus future recordings. I waited for a reply.

Just a few weeks later, Vinton had a Polish hit on the charts—"Melody of Love"—on ABC Records. The recording was one of his biggest hits ever; it reached number three on the *Billboard* chart and remained there for seventeen weeks. It was responsible for the resurgence of Vinton's sagging career. I was dumbfounded and damaged in legal terms. Vinton and Korobkin had concluded a deal, the Polish recording I had suggested was on ABC Records, and my label was excluded.

I called Korobkin for an explanation. His comment was, "Well, all I can say is Vinton owes you a favor." No discussion of the proper finder's fee or of compensation of any kind was ever mentioned.

Some years later, backstage at a performance, I said to Vinton, "Bobby, I have a message for you from Leonard Korobkin." When he looked at me, I said, "Len says you owe me a favor." Vinton simply turned away, and never spoke to me again. No recognition, financially or otherwise for the ABC contract was ever provided.

What were my damages? None. There was no documentation to establish and protect my claim. Had I followed the advice in this book, I could have safeguarded my claim.

## SAMPLE DAMAGE CLAIMS

The cases that follow exemplify various damage claims and their outcomes. The law may vary from jurisdiction to jurisdiction, and these *examples* should be used only as starting points, for laws and practices change over time.

*Contract default—profits recoverable:* A contractor agrees to furnish marble from K&M's Quarry to erect a building for a stipulated price. The marble is delivered for some time until the contract is broken by a refusal to receive any more. The profits that would have been made are recoverable.

*Service default—profits recoverable:* A railroad company wrongfully refuses to furnish a shipper with transportation for stove wood. The measure of damages may include profits that would have been made on a contract with a third person for the sale of the wood.

*Contract default—profits not recoverable, compensatory damages:* The contract is for having silicate of soda manufactured; there is no market value. The seller's measure of damages is the difference between the contract price and the cost of production.

*Service default—profits recoverable, compensatory damages:* The action is for breach of a contract for employment of a general manager of an insurance company at a salary based on a percentage of new and renewed insurance secured. The plaintiff may recover for expenditures and also anticipated profits based on actual new business proved or estimates by actuaries as to renewals.

*Tenant lease/contract—profits recoverable:* A tenant is wrongfully ejected by the landlord from premises where she was established as a jeweler; she is entitled to recover for loss of profits.

*Tenant lease/contract—profits recoverable:* A landlord, by cutting off steam power, destroys the tenant's business. The landlord is responsible in damages for loss of profits. Evidence of the extent of the business and profits previously made is admissible.

*Contract services/commission—profits recoverable:* The contract makes A exclusive selling agent of 85 percent of B's catch of fish on commission for a definite term. On breach by B, evidence of sales by B through its agents subsequent to the breach and during the contract term is admissible as showing gains prevented.

*Negligent or intentional act—profits not recoverable:* H sues C for overflowing his land and preventing its cultivation. His measure of damages is the fair rental value of the land, not the value of the crops that might have been grown (less the cost of producing and marketing them).

*Product warranty/defective product—only determinable net costs recoverable:* Seed sold is warranted good, but does not produce a crop. The expected profits are entirely speculative, and the measure of damages is the cost of the seed, the value of the labor in preparing the ground less any benefit to the land resulting from such labor, together with interest.

*Product warranty/defective product—determinable profits recoverable:* Seed sold is of inferior quality, and produces an inferior crop. The uncertainty of the quantity of the crop, dependent upon the weather and season, is removed, and the measure of damages is the difference between the value of the crop raised and the value of the crop as it should have been.

*Use of property contract/lease—only determinable net costs recoverable:* The cause of action is A's breach of a contract with B to furnish a hall for performances of a theatrical company, for which A was to receive half of the gross receipts. The measure of recovery is not conjectured profits, but the expenses of preparation for the performances.

*Contract for services—only cost of service recoverable:* A telegraph company negligently delays the transmission of a message directing the purchase of property. As a consequence, no timely purchase is made by the addressee, and with the price advancing, he does not purchase at all. There is no proof that the sender gave the order in expectation of profits on an immediate resale, or that she could have resold at any subsequent time. She cannot recover for lost profits and her measure of damages is the cost of transmitting the message.

*Delaying delivery—only fair market value of use recoverable:* In an action for the price of an engine, the plaintiff claims damages by showing nondelivery at the time agreed. The engine was to have been used in a mill, and through the delay the vendee loses the use of certain machinery. The measure of damages is not the possible profits, but the fair value of the use during the period of delay.

*Delayed use of product due to defects—profits not recoverable:* In an action for the price of a steamboat, the vendee claims the right to deduct from the contract price loss of profit on trips that might have been made but for construction defects. Such damages are not recoverable.

*Breach of contract/nonpayment—only costs of repairs and use recoverable:* A and B enter into a contract. A is to deliver a product to B. The product is delivered on schedule and B fails to pay per the terms of the contract. A anticipated using the funds from B in a new venture. The cause of action is breach of contract for nonpayment of money. Profits that might have been made by employing the money are speculative, and cannot be recovered. The damages likely will include interest on money not timely paid.

*Negligent or intentional act—only costs of repairs and use recoverable:* M, a fisherman, sues W for damage to a fishing net. It would have required ten days to restore the net, but this was not done. The plaintiff can recover the cost of repairing and resetting the net, and the value of its use for the ten days, but not such prospective profits as might have been made during that period.

*Contract/sale of patent—nominal damages only where profits not proved:* L buys W's interest in a patented article, and agrees to put it on the market and pay W $5,000 from the net profits. L breaches the contract. Plaintiff W cannot recover profits that might probably have been made; if no profits are proved, only nominal damages are recovered.

*Negligent or intentional act—conjectural profits not recoverable:* Action is by a florist against the owner of pipes from which gas has escaped and injured her plants. A claim for damages based on injury to plaintiff's business reputation on account of sales of damaged plants is conjectural and cannot be allowed.

# CHAPTER 13

# Settlement Strategy

*In presiding over lawsuits, I'm as good as any man. The thing is to aim so that there should be no lawsuits.*

—Confucius

A breach of contract took place between Radio Press International (RPI) and a partnership consisting of the Aluminum Company of America and Gateway Records, which was called Audio Press, Inc. (API). RPI, a voice news agency similar to the Associated Press, had breached its agreement to supply API with what is known in our business as "actualities" (bits of voice news). These actualities were intended to be used in a recording entitled *The Year in Review*, sold as a premium to *Collier's Encyclopedia Yearbook.*

RPI should have been a successful venture. Unfortunately, Straus Communications Company, the parent company of RPI, decided to close the financially unsuccessful RPI after only three years of operation, without deference to the five-year contract Gateway Records held with RPI (see page 126).

The dispute was scheduled for trial when the court in Pittsburgh sent a notice requesting a settlement conference. Holding a settlement conference is but one of the many ways to end a dispute between parties without a costly trial.

## THE CONTRACT—THE FIRST LINE OF DEFENSE IN A SETTLEMENT

Preparing for a settlement conference can begin even before a breach or a dispute takes place. In fact, it can begin with the drafting of the written instrument that embodies the original agreement. This can be a lease, mortgage, note, letter of agreement, insurance policy, or even deposit receipt. All of these documents delineate the terms of an agreement between parties.

Agreements that legally bind are known as contracts. They create rights and duties that are recognized by courts of law and that are enforceable by the civil justice system. Providing the contract or agreement has (1) an offer (proposal to enter into a contract), (2) an acceptance (showing a willingness to agree to the terms offered), and (3) consideration, the document becomes binding upon the parties.

The first line of defense or offense in a dispute is a well-conceived, well-drawn, fully executed contract, defined by William F. Elliot in 1913 as "an agreement such as is enforceable at law, between two or more persons, whereby a right is acquired by at least one of them to an act or acts or to forbearance on the part of the others." In other words, a contract is a transaction in which each of the parties comes under an obligation to the other, and each in turn acquires a right to what is promised by the other. Elliot continues, "Agreement in the legal sense . . . is the union of two or more persons in a common expression of will either by words or conduct or both, affecting their legal relations." (William Elliott, *Commentaries on the Law of Contracts*, Indianapolis: Bobbs-Merrill, 1913.) Agreement, therefore, becomes an essential element of every contract. The object of a contract is to create some obligation between the parties who have come to an agreement.

The written word or oral agreement is what the court will address, not what one of the parties may say he intended or thought he intended to agree to. However, the law of contracts may take into account an individual's state of mind when the contract was executed in regard to the meaning of his words and his conduct, regardless of any hidden intent.

Here are the essential elements of a contract:

1. The parties to a contract must be capable of making the contract.

2. There must be consideration of a nature that the law recognizes, such as money, forbearance, or property.

3. The subject matter or property that the contract is about must be legal.

4. There must be an offer and acceptance, or a meeting of the minds by the parties as to their legal relation.

In most jurisdictions there can be no contract if any one of these elements is lacking. Thus, you can see the reason for a properly drawn and documented agreement.

Little attention is given in uncivilized societies to enforcing promises, but since the protection of life and property is a primary consideration of our society, so is the enforcement of promises. This task has become so monumental that it has created a huge body of law known as contract law. A legal scholar described this kind of law "as including nearly all the law which regulates the relations of human life . . . the basics of human society . . . for out of contracts, express or implied, declared or understood, grow all rights, all duties, all obligations, and all the law . . . the whole procedure of human life . . . is the continued fulfillment of contracts." (Theophilus Parsons, *The Law of Contracts*, Vol. 1, Boston: Little, Brown, 1883.)

But what happens if the promises so earnestly made at the time they were embodied in the contract are not kept? Aside from walking away and giving up your right, acquiescing, or complaining to a regulatory body, you have three choices: (1) Negotiate, (2) arbitrate, and (3) use the civil justice system to resolve the dispute.

First, negotiation. (The other options will be covered in Chapters 14 and 15.) Filing a lawsuit could be considered a step in the negotiation process if attempts to work out differences between the parties fail in the normal course of business. More than 90 percent of all lawsuits filed in the United States are settled out of court, for several good reasons. First, many litigants gradually realize that attorneys' fees and other costs are enormous. Second, the passage of time has a mellowing effect on an individual's expectations. Life goes on, and changing needs and desires sometimes give a lawsuit and its underlying dispute a much lower priority than they had originally. Third, the discovery process may turn up something that makes a party want to settle. Perhaps a party finds that a bill is virtually uncollectible, that the law was not broken as previously thought, or that there is other evidence mitigating, reducing, or wiping out the basis for legal action. The truth, if it is revealed through discovery, can temper the desire to litigate, and give impetus to the desire to settle. Some of the forces behind such desires are the following:

- Personal principles.
- Strong convictions.
- Ego.
- Animosity.
- Changing economic conditions.
- Abhorrence of the trial process.
- Future business.
- Personal relationships.

These and other factors can dissipate or change in the stark light of discovered facts that support or destroy one's case.

## NEGOTIATING A SETTLEMENT

The legal process provides many opportunities for formal and informal settlement talks. To secure a position of strength in these talks, you should become adept at language games. We are not suggesting deception to the point of losing your integrity, but bluffing and banter are common elements of negotiation. (See Psychology in Negotiation, page 199.) You have to watch what you say, for making concessions when there is no equal concession from the other party will be detrimental to your ultimate outcome. Likewise, disclosing information at the wrong time may have a deleterious effect on your settlement possibilities.

Each trip to the courthouse for motions, settlement conferences, and calendar calls (also called docket calls or docket reviews, and not to be confused with status conferences, used in some areas to prompt settlement), and each contact during the discovery process gives you an opportunity to sound out the other side regarding a possible route to settlement. For this process to work for you, observe some basic rules:

- Don't show weakness.
- Use impending deadlines to generate pressure to settle.
- Take advantage of your opponent's (or her attorney's) lack of preparation.
- Prepare properly for each step in the movement of a case.
- Assess the impact of such factors as a busy court calendar, trial delays, and timeliness of your opponent's responses to deadlines.
- Review problems in trial preparation.
- Based on knowledge gained from discovery, assess expense in continuing the action and the cost of trial preparation in light of the possible outcome.
- Review availability or unavailability of proof, such as documents, witnesses, and the like.
- Consider the effect of publicity on both sides.
- Examine collectibility of an award if you were to prevail.
- Assess bankruptcy potential on both sides.
- Assess the individual desire on the part of one or more of the parties to settle.

As you proceed into actual negotiations, follow these additional guidelines:

- The best results occur when an agreement is beneficial to all parties concerned. One-sided agreements may not be honored.

# Psychology in Negotiation

*To improve your chances of gaining the upper hand in any negotiation, you must recognize your opponent's psychological makeup and your personal reaction to different types of personalities. The following information comes from psychologist Stephen P. Schachner, Ph.D.*

*Effective negotiators present a variety of character traits at different times in a negotiation. By doing this, they control the flow of the talks, as well as the feelings of the opponent. For example, good negotiators will be argumentative, headstrong, and demanding. They will act as if their opponent is behaving inappropriately or ignorantly by questioning their position. This posture may later switch to one of generosity, support, and understanding, as the negotiator rides on to victory, throwing a few bones to the vanquished foe.*

*When you enter negotiations, you must be willing to go always one step further in your argument, to be unreasonable, and to carry a lance of pointed complaints. Those unfortunate "knights of ethical behavior," whose lances are composed of cooperativeness, trust, and gentle demeanor, will fall in the heated battle of negotiation.*

*Different situations require different strategies, depending on your opponent's strengths and weaknesses, and your purposes for engaging in the battle. To best your opponent, you will have to withstand strong, irritating tactics from expressive fighters to hold your view and win what you feel is your due.*

- An opening demand should be as high as can be reasonably justified; an opening offer should be correspondingly low. This will leave room for reciprocal concessions.
- A series of demands, offers, counter-offers, and counter-demands are normal prior to reaching a settlement.
- Offers or demands can be made not only in dollar amounts, but also in terms of payment, rate of interest, security, or in a manner where there is a tax advantage for one party or the other.

- Experience has proven that even after "take it or leave it" offers or demands, there is usually room for more negotiation.

Remember that negotiation is a form of salesmanship. Any good salesperson will tell you that product knowledge and thorough preparation for a sales call is part of the formula for success. Likewise, preparation in a lawsuit—discovery, retention of expert witnesses, and other steps that show a sincere intent to try the case—is an important aspect of the litigation and settlement process. Preparation includes thorough knowledge of the law on which the case is based, learning as much about the opposition as possible, and understanding who has negotiating authority. Any appraisal of the opponent should also include as much understanding as possible of the financial condition of the parties involved. Failing to identify the opposition's points of weakness, or failing to zero in on them during negotiations, may allow your opponent an unnecessary advantage.

## NEGOTIATION TACTICS

*Good Guy/Bad Guy Approach:* I once knew a team of brothers who had been working together for so long that they would instinctively fall into this routine in any negotiation. Howard, Jason, and Sam built one of the country's premier record store chains, National Record Mart, based in Pittsburgh. No one, be it a lowly salesman or corporate entertainment vice president, could ever win a negotiation with these three astute businessmen, who had the good guy/bad guy approach down to a science. Once the discussion began, the dialogue would go something like this:

*Good Guy (Jason):* Gentlemen, we need to talk about getting a lower price for your product, a longer payment period, and an increase in the payment discount allowed.
*Record Company Executive:* Our company gives you our lowest price for the category your stores are in.
*Instigator (Howard):* So you do have a lower price to offer!
*Bad Guy (Sam):* I knew it, I knew it! You've been shafting us all along!
*Good Guy:* Now Sam, let him explain.
*Executive:* As I said, you've got the very lowest price in your category and we have been looking the other way regarding your payment history. Ninety to 120 days, with trade acceptances extended another 60 days, what do you expect?
*Instigator:* We're not talking about payment terms, no one asked you for a further extension of the terms . . . .

*Executive:* We have gone as far as we can go in accommodating your company.

*Bad Guy:* Accommodating, ha! You manufacturers are robbing the retailers blind. Maybe you should get your damn records out of our stores and see what the hell you will sell in this part of the country without us.

*Good Guy:* Now Sam, don't get so worked up.

*Instigator:* (grunt) They clearly have a lower price category.

*Bad Guy:* No, I say get his product out of the store—now! We can live without his bullshit or his product.

*Executive:* Gentlemen, gentlemen, we've been working together for years now. We have given you chart hits constantly, generous payment terms, return allowances, defective allowances, advertising credit, and even accepted your 2-percent discount for payment. What do you want?

*Bad Guy:* Throw the son of a bitch out!

*Instigator:* Get us the lowest price level based on . . .

*Executive:* On what?

*Instigator:* . . . based on, on . . .

*Executive:* There is no legal or moral justification to put you in a lower price category!

*Bad Guy:* Throw the son of a bitch out!

*Instigator:* . . . on, on, on . . .

*Good Guy:* Now look, we are all adults just trying to make a living here. Let's compromise. Sam, take it easy. Howie, just think about this.

*Executive:* I don't know what I can do.

*Good Guy:* Give us an additional 5-percent advertising allowance with tearsheets supplied—and I think I can convince Howie to give you the fall stocking order for the seventy stores he's been working on for the last month.

*Bad Guy:* I don't know, Jas—I think we can live without him. The Beatles are hot, Presley's hot . . .

*Instigator:* (grunt)

*Executive (looking at Jason):* Okay—you've got a deal!

This strategy doesn't need three people to work. Any negotiating team can create the approach—lawyer and client, husband and wife, corporate president and treasurer, corporate officer and stockholder, employee and employer. Just make sure that you have planned it all out in advance.

*One-Upmanship:* One way to show strength is to obtain or utilize such legal items as a preliminary injunction, writ of attachment, *lis pendens* (notice of claim), or the like, which provides your side with a "one-up" position of power. Your being one step ahead tends to give your opponent additional incentive to settle. Another incentive may be to present a final offer in the form of a check or certified check, rather than just the mere promise of payment. Conversely, threatening to withdraw an offer may be just what is needed for the other side to accept it.

If a deadlock occurs, you might react by setting reasonable time limits for some action, initiating discovery, or changing your demeanor (displaying irritation or anger) in a credible way. (See The Origin of a Radical Settlement Strategy, page 203.) Even if your prospects are bleak and it is obvious to you that the case should not be tried, you must project a willingness to go to trial right up to the point of trial. It is far better that your opponent believe your decision to settle was a reluctant one than to show weakness or intimidation regarding the case.

In reality, the critical point in the negotiating process is near the time of trial. A trial takes an enormous effort, in both preparation and execution. Your opponent knows this. Waiting for the moment just before time and resources are fully committed to a trial may produce results that could not otherwise be obtained.

Regardless of which settlement stance you take, it is generally considered that a face-to-face conference can provide you the opportunity to (1) better evaluate the other party's attitudes, (2) begin developing a relationship (however hostile), and sometimes (3) show or explain certain evidence that may bring the other side to agree with your position. Here are some points to consider for the negotiating table:

- Tackle major points first; the smaller points will fall into place.
- Keep hostility to a minimum.
- Watch out for deal-killers; that is, attorneys, other professionals, other parties, or technical points that can unravel an agreement.
- Don't nitpick if you don't have to; it can be a deal-killer.
- Hold something in reserve as ammunition for later concessions.
- Don't appear to be under pressure. Don't show time or scheduling concerns.
- If one party is represented by an attorney and one party isn't, insist on a paragraph in the agreement substantially like the following:

   All parties were advised to retain an attorney and _____ refused to do so, although the opportunity was provided. All parties concur with this statement. (initials)

# The Origin of a Radical Settlement Strategy

*The year was 1880; the place was Ireland. Desperate farmers who had suffered a poor harvest pleaded with the Third Earl of Eire to lower their rents so they could survive. Their pleas fell on deaf ears, so the farmers began to withhold their payments. Enraged, Eire sent his agent to collect the past-due rents. However, the agent didn't collect any rents; in fact, the tenant farmers wouldn't even talk to him. They shunned him completely, even when he tried to evict them for nonpayment. The agent was forced to hire outside help to bring in the harvest under military guard. The infamous agent, Charles Cunningham Boycott, gave his name to the boycott— now an accepted means of pressure to accomplish social change.*

- Consider stating in the finished agreement sanctions for noncompliance, such as attorneys' fees, court costs, injunctive relief, liquidated damages, and excusing performance by the nonbreaching party.
- Attach to the final agreement exhibits such as escrow instructions, promissory note, deeds, side agreements, and other forms intended for use of performance consistent with the agreement.
- Document any agreement reached.
- Review the deal before signing. Discuss it with knowledgeable associates and professionals.
- Beware of undue delays in the signing of the final agreement.

## USING BUSINESS MANEUVERS TO FORCE AGREEMENT

Before you can get to the negotiating table, the parties must desire agreement. It is not always necessary to use the threat of litigation to bring the parties to the table. Occasionally, it is possible to use a business maneuver to force discussions and a settlement.

When the Human Beinz had the number-eight record in the United States—

"Nobody But Me"—for three weeks (*Billboard*, February 3, 1968), Gateway Records had in its tape vault four selections that the group had recorded a year earlier. I contacted Capitol Records and offered to sell them the four selections, with the suggestion that they either use them in a long-play recording or buy them to keep them off the market. (The songs were not really representative of what the group was doing at the time it was hot.) Capitol's artist and repertoire vice president would not budge—no deal!

A number-eight record is nothing to sneeze at, and I knew our tapes had to have some value. So Gateway recorded six songs by a group, invented for the occasion, called the Mammals. One of the songs recorded was the Human Beinz' "Nobody But Me," which was used for the title of the Gateway album. (Capitol's album was also called "Nobody But Me," but titles cannot be copyrighted.) The six selections were connected (or "coupled," in music business terminology) with the four from the Human Beinz, and an album was rushed onto the market, subtitled "The Human Beinz Meet the Mammals." Advance distribution was made to the music industry on a Friday evening with special-delivery envelopes sent to all Gateway retailers and wholesalers. By Monday afternoon the legal department of Capitol Records was on the phone. "Get it off the market or else!" said a young Capitol lawyer.

I knew the law and my rights, and I knew I was on solid ground, so I told the young attorney "no." Here were the opposing positions:

*Capitol's position:*

1. The selections released by Gateway distorted the current image of the Human Beinz.

2. The recordings were included in an LP release without the group's consent.

3. The graphics (cover) were misleading.

*Gateway's position:*

1. The recordings were by the Human Beinz regardless of the genre.

2. The Human Beinz had no contractual interest over the recordings and how they were used. The masters were produced without restrictions.

3. The cover of the album was not misleading, except in the eyes of the beholder—Capitol Records.

The so-called negotiations that followed ended by the weekend, when an agreement was reached. Capitol would allow us to sell our inventory manu-factured (approximately 5,000 LPs) and would pay us $5,000 for the master tapes (a fair sum of money in 1968).

The final agreement was embodied in a settlement contract establishing a framework for the consummation of the deal. The terms of the agreement provided for the delivery to Capitol of the master tapes and matrix in exchange for a certified check. This was done at a Capitol branch office after the agreements had been reviewed by attorneys for both parties.

Obtaining a negotiated settlement can be complicated, and may sometimes require a thorough knowledge or study of the applicable law involved. Here's another example of positioning for an enhanced negotiation posture.

In 1980, I took several steps to insulate my life from the cash-flow gyrations of the record industry. One step was to operate with the lowest possible overhead. I turned a wing of my home—a rambling brick ranch in Davie, Florida—into the company's executive offices, with warehousing facilities provided by our vendors.

The office wing consisted of an outer office accommodating two secretar-ies and the telex, a bookkeeping office, and my office, a study with its floor-to-ceiling shelves and library ladder. It was a compact, comfortable working space for the staff, and it kept overhead to a minimum.

I closed our high-rent recording studio on East 52nd Street in Manhattan and moved it to new facilities built in an orange grove adjacent to my house in Davie. I could walk from the office, through the neighbor's squeaky gate and past the barn and lake, past a plant nursery, and up to the rear door of the studio control room. What a pleasant way to live and work—that is, until the City of Davie zoning officer showed up.

The officer's eyes fixed upon the two desks and the telex, and he declared the premises an "office" and threatened to fine us $500 a day if it wasn't cleared out. Our beautiful low-overhead world in the orange grove was about to be squashed by a zoning officer acting on complaints from the neighbors, who objected to the number of cars parked on the property.

Almost by reflex, I called our attorney, who contacted the city, which reiterated what the zoning officer had originally said—the suite was indeed an office and should be subject to the fine unless it was abolished. Again by reflex, I asked our attorney to find an expert on zoning.

The expert he found—Don McClosky—turned out to be the individual who almost singlehandedly undermined the Florida zoning law that protected what little pristine oceanfront property was left for the public's enjoyment. Florida had enacted the Coastal Construction and Evacuation Regulation, which was intended to "prohibit construction within fifty feet of the line of mean high water at any . . . coastal location . . . fronting the Atlantic Coast." McClosky was the lawyer for a group of builders challenging this regulation. His prowess in zoning matters is best described by the *Miami Herald*, which wrote, "The builders  easily won what could have been their most difficult development permit when Governor Bob Graham and the Cabinet unanimously agreed to allow significant parts of the project to be built seaward of the state's coastal construction control line."

As it turned out, McClosky was not only a brilliant tactician and attorney, but was compassionate with my pocketbook (or knew I could not afford his services). He gave me a peek into his secret world of accomplishing change within the system. His quickie course in do-it-yourself zoning politics was offered in lieu of ongoing services—a gesture of friendship to my attorney.

McClosky suggested as Plan A personal appeals from me to the five commissioners who had the power to okay an exception to the township ordinance and permit my two secretaries and bookkeeper to work in my house. However, he anticipated that the council, or a majority, would not be swayed in my favor. So we drew up Plan B: First, I was to obtain a copy of the township code and study the zoning of the area in question. Then I was to find the most objectionable legal thing that could be done with property and appear to proceed to use the property for that purpose. At a propitious time, I would trade not doing that objectionable activity for a compromise allowing what I really wanted to do— the lesser-of-two-evils approach.

The City of Davie has five commissioners, one of whom is the mayor. I needed three yes votes to obtain my special ordinance permitting my office to exist. I picked out the most likely positive votes, which did not include the mayor, and worked on those commissioners. Much to the mayor's chagrin, the special ordinance was passed by a three-to-two majority. The crisis was resolved, or so I thought.

The mayor was furious; his boisterous constituents defeated and rebellious. Who was this outsider who challenged and upset the mayor's authority? The mayor went into action and scheduled a recall of the special ordinance at the next regular township meeting. All of my work was about to go down the tubes because, it was said, the mayor was applying pressure to one of the commissioners—the one vote needed to reverse the original decision. It was time to put Plan B into operation.

My house was in an area that was zoned A-1, an agricultural district. The Davie Code indicates "the following regulations shall apply in all A-1 districts":

Uses permitted:

(a) One-family detached dwelling, which must be ancillary to an agricultural, conservation or other permitted nonresidential use of the property.

(b) Grove, produce farm, truck garden, horticultural farming, botanical garden, floriculture, nursery, sod farm, crop raising, hydroponic garden, greenhouse, slat house, forestry, beekeeping.

(c) Research park, for investigation and experimentation in fields of inquiry such as medical, biological, chemical, agricultural and others of a similar nature, not including any manufacturing or sales on the premises.

(d) Cattle or stock grazing, dairy farm, not including hog raising.

(e) Dude ranch, riding stable, livery stable, boarding stable. . . .

The Code also permits (in A-1 districts) wayside stands, flood-control facilities, storage and sale of earth materials, radio or television antennas, fish hatcheries, and keeping sheep, goats, and poultry for commercial purposes.

I chose the botanical garden (for reasons that will become obvious). The first step was to apply for an occupational license (which, according to the Code, the town had to permit). Then I asked my art director to draw up the most garish-looking sign he could conceive of for the Gemcom Botanical Gardens, conforming to the proper size and shape as permitted by the township Code. Next was a presentation to the city of the plans for the sign, for a permit, which again according to the Code, the town had to issue, however reluctantly.

There was one more detail. What did a botanical garden have to do with the music business? Well, it just so happens that a Buffalo, New York music distributor produced in the late 1970s an album called *Music to Grow Plants By*. After a few phone calls, I had this album leased to me for sale and use by the botanical garden. All the elements were now in place, including extensive newspaper coverage about the new enterprise experimenting in horticulture to music. I set up a meeting with the township manager, a transplanted New Yorker and former manager in that city's Lindsay administration, and someone with whom I thought I could talk seriously. I walked into his office, closed the door, rolled the sign out on his desk, presented him with my occupational license and my sign permit, and said, "Irv, I'll do an old-fashioned horse trade. Allow the special ordinance to stay on the books, giving my two secretaries and bookkeeper the right to stay in my home and work, and I will discontinue my plans for the botanical garden, the sign, and the commercial enterprise that would ensue." Irv looked at the sign and then at me, and said, "I think I can persuade the mayor to leave the ordinance on the books." In the spirit of compromise, I agreed to keep the cars to a minimum and not add any more employees.

## SETTLEMENT LAW

Settlement agreements are viewed as contracts and are, therefore, subject "to the rules governing the formation, performance, and enforcement of contracts" (Gerald Williams, *Legal Negotiation and Settlement*, West Publishing, 1983). A growing body of law exists on the subject, consistent with the judicial system's policy of encouraging mediation and affirming settlements because of "an overriding public interest in settling and quieting litigation" (*Van Brankhorst v. Safeco Corp.*, 529 S.2d 943, 950 [9th Cir. 1976]). Reducing litigants' expenses and saving precious time for overtaxed court systems are the two motivating factors for the trend toward out-of-court dispute resolution. This trend is reinforced by the greater powers legislators are giving the courts to enforce mediation procedures on those doing battle within the judicial system.

Enforcement of settlement agreements (paramount for the success of the whole process) depends upon at which stage of the dispute the settlement has been reached. If litigation has begun, documenting a settlement gains paramount importance. This can be accomplished by a settlement agreement that leads to two possibilities: (1) The agreement may be such that the parties can simply dismiss or terminate the existing litigation; or (2) the agreement may be such that one or more of the parties would seek a court order resulting in an enforceable judgment that embodies the agreed-upon settlement terms. If the second route is taken and a judgment is issued by the court, enforcement, reconsideration, or appeal would require the same process as any court-ordered judgment.

In situations where a settlement takes place within the context of a trial, or even during the preparations for trial, it is likely that the judge may ask to have the settlement made part of the record. This is a process whereby the litigants are asked under oath if they agree to the settlement terms and a court reporter documents the proceedings. If this process is used to affirm a settlement, the litigants may very well find the court vigorously backing the terms in any future disagreement regarding the settlement.

Although settlement agreements are contracts, we need not discuss contract law any further; however, it is still important to discuss good-faith bargaining, the absence of which might cause a settlement to be overturned by the courts. "Good faith" excludes "bad faith" by definition and practice. Conduct that "violates community standards of decency, fairness, or reasonableness" (Sec. 205, UCC, V.L.Rev., 1968) is bad faith, and therefore must be excluded from conduct considered to be good faith. Another definition of good faith is "honesty in fact in the conduct or transaction concerned" (general contract law and the sales provision of the UCC). Therefore, in cases where a settlement has been achieved using bad faith or in settlements that run contrary to the public opinion, there is the danger that the courts may overturn the settlement. (In *Middlesex Concrete v. Carteret Industrial*, the New Jersey Supreme Court held that taxpayers or their representatives properly exercised their rights in interfering in a proposed settlement. Although the municipality and the contractor had settled, the taxpayers were left with too large a bill.)

Whether the matter be a new contract delineating an agreement between two or more parties to the negotiation or the settlement process of a dispute, good faith conduct requires the exclusion of conduct that may give the opposition an actionable reason or excuse to breach the contract or to allow them to ask the court to set aside the settlement agreement. Any one or more of the following acts may or may not affect the legal situation, depending on the context and facts surrounding their use, but they are clearly acts of bad faith:

- Making up a pretended dispute.
- Asserting an interpretation different from one's own understanding.
- Falsifying facts and/or documents.
- Extorting a modification of a contract by taking advantage of another party's circumstances.
- Making overbearing demands for assurances of performance.
- Rejecting performance for unstated reasons.
- Willfully failing to mitigate damages.
- Abusing power to force compliance or to terminate a contract.
- Issuing a threat if the threat is an illegal act, crime, or a tort.
- Issuing a threat of criminal prosecution to achieve a civil goal.
- Issuing a threat if it will cause a breach of the duty under the terms of a contract with the recipient.
- Issuing a threat of harm to the recipient, but one that would not benefit the party making the threat.
- Issuing a threat or using one's power for illegitimate ends.

Whether a settlement takes place in court or out of court, with or without attorneys, you should consider using a release. A release is a legal document that represents an agreement between the parties that extinguishes or ends a cause of action in return for some consideration. The signing of a release with one party may or may not release other parties in the action; local laws and jurisdictions vary on this point. For instance, New York's release (or covenant not to sue) statute, Section 15-108, specifically provides the following:

> A release or covenant not to sue or not to enforce a judgment is given to one of two or more persons liable or claimed to be liable . . . for the same injury, or the same wrongful death, it does not discharge any of the other(s) . . . from liability for the injury or wrongful death unless its terms expressly so provide, but it does reduce the claim of the releasor against the other(s) to the extent to any amount stipulated by the release or the covenant, or in the amount of the consideration paid for it, or in the amount of the released (parties') equitable share of the damages under Article 14 of the Civil Practice Law and Rules whichever is greatest.

The law continues at some length and is a prime example of the need to review local laws before agreeing to a release.

In the event the settlement process breaks down and you cannot reach accord, you may be able to turn to mediation or arbitration—two other forms of dispute resolution.

# CHAPTER 14

# Mediation and Arbitration

*An ill agreement is better than a good judgment.*

—George Herbert

// The settlement of civil dispute in a satisfactory manner is a necessary part of economic life of all civilized communities. The procedure for the settlement of disputes can no more remain static than any other branch of the life of the community but must be adapted or altered from time to time to meet changing conditions." (London Chamber of Commerce report, "Expense of Litigation," 1930, p. 1.)

This process in the United States began when Congress and some progressive states, particularly Massachusetts and New York, began to authorize the use of mediation to help resolve disagreements and often violent conflicts between labor and management. The federal government began to fear anarchy if peace was not brought to the industrial community. Gradually, the use of these nonjudicial forms of dispute resolution were used in nonlabor matters. By 1923, Cleveland, Minneapolis, New York City, Milwaukee, and the state of North Dakota had "conciliation" programs related in some fashion to the court system—and the practice was beginning to spread. (Addresses on conciliation, ABA J 746-751 [1923], in Nancy Rogers and Craig McEwen, *Mediation, Law, Policy, Practice*, Rochester, NY: Lawyers Cooperative Publishing, 1989.) The cost effectiveness of the mediation process for all involved was a prime factor in its growing use.

Mediation offered parties honorable compromise, a way to be involved in controlling their own legal destiny (rather than attorneys having total control), and the traditional values of speed, cost, response, and fairness, and so it was seen as an attractive alternative to the courtroom. Rising divorce rates in the

1940s and 1950s and the civil rights struggle of the 1960s also contributed to the legal system's policy of expanding out of formal proceedings to handle court disputes. Legislative awareness of the effectiveness of arbitration and mediation was reflected in the statutes that were being written to address some of society's social problems. And the inclusion of arbitration clauses in labor contracts, providing a means of resolution outside the courthouse, became commonplace.

Because of a continuing trend toward litigiousness in our society, the courts began to experience tremendous case loads. Chief Justice Warren Burger eloquently expressed the frustration of the average litigant, "People with problems like people with pains, want relief and they want it as quickly and inexpensively as possible" ("Our Vicious Legal Spiral," 16 Judges J., Fall 1977, pp. 22, 49).

In 1925 Congress passed the U.S. Arbitration Act (codified July 30, 1947 and amended September 3, 1954 [68 Stat. 1233]; Chapter 2 was added July 31, 1970 [84 Stat. 692]), establishing a pattern for the individual states to follow as out-of-court dispute settlement spread. As of 1992, all fifty states had one or more of the following forms of *alternative dispute resolution (ADR)*:

- *Conciliation:* Settlement of a dispute in a friendly manner; used by courts in the hope of avoiding trial, and in labor disputes prior to arbitration.
- *Mediation:* Imposition of a neutral third party as a link between the disagreeing parties.
- *Voluntary arbitration:* Submission of a controversy to arbitration by agreement or by prior contract.
- *Compulsory arbitration:* One or more of the parties to a dispute are forced to use arbitration (by court order or by statute).

Many jurisdictions have attached mediation and/or arbitration programs to the court system or community programs aimed at citizen involvement in ADR. Judge William Cannon, of Clinton, Michigan, is the only judicial official for Mount Clemens, a Michigan community of almost 100,000 citizens. He began an arbitration program in 1978 out of a desperate need to free court time for cases that were either too complex for mediation/arbitration or not suitable for the out-of-court process. In Judge Cannon's words, "the help that [arbitration] has been to me is inestimable. . . . If I had to have all of those cases . . . my job would be extremely more difficult. This has freed me up to do research to . . . try civil matters of a more profound nature . . . more time for my criminal docket. It has just done wonders."

Since informal alternatives to court also appeal to those who advocate avoiding lawyers, we must sound a note of caution: There is often no clear-cut distinction between mediation and arbitration. The terms should be used in the context of the rules and statutes in a particular jurisdiction. If you are attempting pro se representation, you should understand the rules in your jurisdiction before making any of the following assumptions:

- If I don't like the outcome, an automatic appeal is possible.
- The outcome is final, and I can have the immediate support of the judicial system to collect my award.
- Once I agree to the terms, I can always change my mind later.

Here are general rules of thumb to follow:

- If it's mediation, in or out of the court environment, the decision can be rejected and/or appealed to a court or settled in some other manner.
- If it's mediation/arbitration under the auspices of a judge in the context of a court proceeding, the outcome is appealable within the court system.
- If it's arbitration under the rules promulgated by the U.S. Arbitration Act or on a state act patterned on the federal version, the grounds for appeal (described later in this chapter) are extremely narrow.

In jurisdictions where a court-arbitrated award provides an automatic right to appeal, you can represent your own cause and be secure that the outcome does not have to be final—you can still obtain an attorney's help for an appeal. (The term appeal may allow for a full rehearing in this context, as opposed to an appeal limited to appealable issues after a court trial.) However, in the appeal, the original decision may be given more weight by the judge and jury. (Although in some states, like Pennsylvania, where arbitration is mandated for any case worth $20,000 or less [$25,000 for motor vehicles], the loser may automatically appeal and a jury trial may be held.) However, any decision to go pro se in arbitration must be made just as carefully as in a lawsuit. The terms associated with ADR—conciliation, mediation, and arbitration—tend to be confusing and often inadvertently misused, even among professionals in the field.

## CONCILIATION

Conciliation is a dispute resolution procedure that uses a neutral party to clarify the issues in a disagreement and then guide the parties in a discussion of the issues. Hopefully, this discussion, and the presence of a neutral third party, will lead to a mutually acceptable resolution of the argument.

As early as the seventeenth century in Japan, the preferred method to settle a controversy was conciliation. In the United States, the Taft-Hartley Act provides for conciliation, especially in industries involved in interstate commerce, through the Federal Mediation and Conciliation Service. Many international treaties also provide for conciliation (with the consent of the parties) prior to invoking arbitration.

## MEDIATION

Mediation can take place only when the parties to a dispute voluntarily agree to submit their claims to a mediator. Usually the mediator is chosen through an agreement between the parties. The American Arbitration Association (AAA) claims that "in most cases mediation results in a settlement." If mediation fails, the parties have the option of arbitration with a decision that is binding, or litigation.

The AAA suggests using the following sentence when parties to a disagreement desire to use mediation: "The parties hereby submit the following dispute to mediation under the Commercial Mediation Rules of the American Arbitration Association. . . ." This sentence may also include the qualifications of the mediator(s), method of payment, location of meetings, and any other items of concern to the parties.

Oklahoma's dispute resolution statute (Sec. 1801) is typical of many programs set up by the state legislatures to meet the demand for nonlitigation mechanisms to deal with the increasing need for out-of-court settlement procedures: "It is therefore the purpose of this act to provide to all citizens of this State convenient access to dispute resolution proceedings which are fair, effective, inexpensive, and expeditious." The Oklahoma act even provides a form entitled "Agreement to Mediate" (Figure 14.1) and another form to record the termination of proceedings (Figure 14.2). Table 14.1 is a directory of most mediation programs as mandated by each state's laws (as of 1989). The table indicates the area of concern (labor, automobile, family, and so on), and the applicable statute or code number of the particular mediation law.

## VOLUNTARY ARBITRATION

Arbitration can be provided for in two ways: (1) In the original contract covering an agreement between parties, and (2) by agreement to arbitrate after

## AGREEMENT TO MEDIATE

_____           Case No: _____

Initiating Party

_____           Date: _____

Responding Party

We, the undersigned, as disputing parties consent to the commencement of a dispute resolution proceeding in an attempt to resolve our dispute through mediation and agree to participate in the mediation process. The method by which we shall attempt to resolve the issues of our dispute is as follows:

a. Both of us shall appear before a mediator in an out-of-court setting.

b. The mediator will examine the facts of the dispute by allowing each of us to present our individual positions.

c. The mediator will assist us and facilitate our resolution of the dispute.

Our rights pursuant to the Dispute Resolution Act, 12 O.S.Supp. 1985, Section 1801 et seq., and the Rules and Procedures for the Dispute Resolution Act promulgated thereunder are as follows:

a. To participate in an informal, private proceeding, no part of which is a matter of public record.

b. To attempt to resolve our dispute with the assistance of a mediator.

Our obligations under the Act and the Rules are as follows:

a. To cooperate with each other and the mediator in working toward a mutually acceptable resolution of our dispute.

b. To accept personal responsibility for any legal proceedings which are pending or are needed to protect our individual rights or property.

We understand that any information received by a mediator or a person employed to assist a mediator is privileged and confidential and that a mediator must disclose information brought to his/her attention that an elderly or handicapped person or a child under the age of eighteen (18) has been physically abused or neglected.

We acknowledge that we have read and understand this Agreement, and we hereby agree to abide by its terms.

Initiating Party: _____   Date: _____
                (Signature)

Responding Party: _____   Date: _____
                (Signature)

Adopted April 8, 1986. Revised April 20, 1989.

**Figure 14.1**  Oklahoma Agreement to Mediate Form

RECORD OF TERMINATION

_____          Case No:_____

Initiating Party

_____          Date: _____

Responding Party

Starting Time: _____          Ending Time:_____

If a mediation session was not held, indicate whose absence was responsible: (a) Initiating party, (b) responding party, or (c) both parties.

_____

If a mediation session was held, please complete the remainder of this record.

1.  Nature of Dispute (briefly describe).

_____

2.  Relationship of Parties (briefly describe).

_____

3.  Persons, other than the parties, present at mediation (name, address, telephone, relationship).

_____

4.  Indicate at what stage the mediation session terminated:

_____          Introduction                    _____          Negotiations

_____          Information Exchange             _____          Agreement

5.  Comments:

_____

6.  If there is a referral to another agency, indicate which party was referred and to what agency.

_____

7.  Describe follow-up plan.

_____

8.  Recommendations and Remarks.

_____

                                        _____

                                        Mediator

Adopted April 8, 1986. Revised April 20, 1989.

**Figure 14.2**   Oklahoma Record of Termination Form

**Table 14.1** States That Apply Arbitration and/or Mediation (and the Applicable Statute or Code)

| State | Kind of Dispute | Statute/Code |
|---|---|---|
| Alabama (Code) | Labor | 25-7-4 |
| Alaska (Statutes) | Labor | 42.40.840 |
| | | 23.40.190 |
| | Family | 25.20.080 |
| | | 25.24.080 |
| | Automobile Warranty | 45.45.355 |
| Arizona (Statutes) | Family | 25-381.01 to 25-381.24 |
| | Automobile Warranty | 44-1265 |
| Arkansas (Statutes) | Labor | 11-2-201 to 11-2-206 |
| California (Code) | Labor | 65, 66, 3518 |
| | Family | 5180 to 5183 |
| | | 4351.5, 4607 |
| | Education | 48260.6, 48263, |
| | | 48263.5 (truancy) |
| | | 56503 (special education) |
| | Government | 53066.1(n)(1) |
| | | (cable TV franchise) |
| | Food and Agriculture | 13127(c)(1) |
| | | (pesticides and environ- |
| | | mental regulation) |
| | Business and Professional | 465 to 471.5 |
| | | (community dispute) |
| | Water | 1219 (water rights) |
| | Welfare and Institutional | 601.3 (truancy) |
| Colorado (Statutes) | Labor | 8-3-113 |
| | Family | 14-10-129.5 |
| | Agricultural Debt | 6-9-101 to 6-9-106 |
| | Dispute Resolution | 13-22-301 to 13-22-310 |
| | Mobile Homes | 38-12-216 |
| Connecticut (Statutes) | Labor | 31-91 to 31-100 |
| | | 5-276, 5-276a |
| | Family | 46b-59a |
| | | Public Act 87-316 |
| | | Sec. 8 (1987) |
| | | 42-182 |

| State | Kind of Dispute | Statute/Code |
|---|---|---|
| Connecticut (continued) | Criminal | 54-56m |
| Delaware (Code) | Labor | tit. 14 Sec. 4002<br>Sec. 4014<br>tit. 19 Sec. 110<br>Sec. 113<br>tit. 19 Sec. 1614 |
| | Automobile Warranty | tit. 6 Sec. 5007 |
| Florida (Statutes) | Labor | 448.06<br>681.110(4)(d) |
| | Family | 44.101, 61.183<br>39.42, 39.427 to 39.429,<br>39.436, 39.44, 39.442 |
| | Automobile Warranty | 681.108, 681.111 |
| | Any Civil Action | 44.301, 44.302, 44.305,<br>44.306 |
| | Mobile Home | 723.037, 723.038 |
| | Citizen Dispute Settlement Centers | 44.201 |
| | Juvenile Delinquency | 39.04 |
| | Regional Planning Council and Local Governments | 186.509 |
| Georgia (code) | Labor | 34-2-6(5), 25-5-1 to<br>25-5-14, 45-19-32,<br>45-19-36 |
| | Public Employee Grievances Unlawful Practices | 45-19-36 |
| Hawaii (Statutes) | Labor | 371-10<br>98-11(b)(1)(d)<br>89-12(a), (b)(13)(6)<br>380-8, 377-3 |
| | Automobile Warranty | 490:2-313.1 |
| | Geothermal Resources | 205-5.1 |
| | Medical Conciliation | 671-11 to 671-20 |
| | Design Professional Conciliation | 672-1 to 672-14 |
| | International | 1988 Haw. Sess. Laws,<br>Ch 186, Sec. 1 to 9 |
| Idaho (Code) | Labor | 44-106 |

| State | Kind of Dispute | Statute/Code |
|---|---|---|
| Illinois (Statutes) | Labor | Ch. 48, para. 1612, 1706, 1712, 1713(b) Ch. 10, para. 26 |
| | Family | Ch. 40, para. 602.1 607.1 |
| | Automobile Warranty | Ch. 121 1/2, para. 1204, Sec. 4 |
| | Public Utilities Service Board | Ch. 11 2/3, para. 702.12a |
| | Nonprofit Community Dispute Resolution Centers | Ch. 37, para. 851.1 to 856 |
| Indiana (Code) | Labor | 5-14-1.5-6.5(2) 22-1-1-8(d) 22-6-1-7 20-7.5-1-9 to 20-7.5-1-13 |
| | Family | 31-1-24-1 to 31-1-24-9 31-1-23-5 to 31-1-23-9 (domestic counseling) |
| | Automobile Warranty | 24-5-13-19 |
| | Civil Rights | 22-9-1-6 |
| | Consumer Protection | 4-6-9-4(a)(4) |
| | Water Rights | 13-2-1-6(2) |
| Iowa (Code) | Labor | 20.19 to 20.20 679B.1 to 679B.27 |
| | Family | 598.16 598.41(2) |
| | Agricultural Debt | 654a.1 to 654a.14 |
| | Civil Rights | 601A.15(3)(c) |
| | Informal Dispute Resolution | 679.1 to 679.14 |
| Kansas (Statutes) | Labor | 44-817, 44-819(j), 44-820(c), 44-826, 44-828, 72-5413(h), 72-5427; 72-5429, 72-5430(b)(7), 72-5430(c)(7), 75-4322, 75-4323, 75-4332, 75-4333 |
| | Family | 23-601 to 23-607, 23-701 |
| | Automobile Warranty | 50-645(e) |
| | Civil Rights | 44-1001, 44-1004, 44-1005 |

| State | Kind of Dispute | Statute/Code |
|-------|-----------------|--------------|
| Kansas, continued | Barbershop Business | 65-1824(4) |
| Kentucky (Statutes) | Labor | 337.425, 345.080, 336.010, 336.020, 336.140, 336.151 to 336.156 |
| | Family | 403.140(b), 403.170 |
| | Automobile Warranty | 367.860 to 367.880 |
| | Civil Rights | 344.190 to 344.290 337.425 |
| | Education | 165A.350, 165A.360 |
| | Production and Distribution of Agricultural Products | 260.020.030(e), 260.020.040(1) |
| | Community Agency Funding | 273.451 |
| Louisiana (Statutes) | Labor | tit. 23, Sec. 6 |
| | Family | tit. 9, Sec. 351 to 356 |
| | Automobile Warranty | tit. 23, Sec. 1944 |
| | Civil Rights (housing) | tit. 40, Sec. 597 |
| | Barbershop | tit. 37, Sec. 381 |
| | Medical Review Panel | tit. 40, Sec. 1299-47 |
| Maine (Statutes) | Labor | tit. 26, Sec. 1026, 965, 931 to 936, 979-D, 1281 to 1282, 1285 |
| | Family | tit. 4, Sec. 18 (1 to 5) tit. 19, Sec. 214, 1, 4 tit. 19, Sec. 518, 1, 2, 4 tit. 19, Sec. 656, 665 tit. 19, Sec. 752(4), 581 |
| | Automobile Warranty | tit. 10, Sec. 1165 |
| | Professional Negligence Claims | tit. 24, Sec. 2851 to 2589 |
| | Production and Distribution of Agricultural Products | tit. 13, Sec. 1956 to 1959 |
| Maryland (Code) | Labor | Art. 6, Sec. 408(d) Art. 89, Sec. 3, 9, 11 |
| | Employment Agency | Art. 56, Sec. 169 |

| State | Kind of Dispute | Statute/Code |
|-------|-----------------|--------------|
| Massachusetts (General Law) | Labor | Ch. 150, Sec. 1 to 3, 9 to 10A Ch. 23C, Sec. 1 to 4 |
| | Community Mediation | Ch. 218, Sec. 43E |
| | Cable Television | Ch. 166A, Sec. 16 |
| Michigan (Compiled Laws) | Labor | 423.1, 423.9 to 423.9c, 423.25, 423.207 |
| | Family | 552.64, 552.505, 552.513 to 552.527, 552.531 |
| | Automobile Warranty | 257.1327 (service) |
| | Tort Actions | 600.4951 to 600.4969 |
| | Long-term Health Care and Medical Training | 400.586g(3)(h)(vi) |
| | Medical Malpractice | 600.4901 to 600.4923, 600.4951 to 600.4969 |
| | Small Claims Conciliation | 730.147 to 730.155 |
| | Production and Distribution of Agricultural Products | 290-714 |
| Minnesota (Statutes) | Labor | 179.01, 179.03, 179.04, 179.06, 179.14, 179.15 179.02 to 179.09 |
| | Family | 518.167, 518.619 |
| | Automobile Warranty | 325F.665 |
| | Agricultural Debt | 583.20 to 583.32 |
| | Civil Rights | 63.01, 63.04, 63.05, 63.06 |
| | Conciliation Courts | 487.30 |
| | Civil Mediation | 572.31 to 572.40 |
| | Debtor-Creditor Mediation | 572.41 |
| | Worker's Compensation | 176.351(2a) |
| | Environmental | 40.22, 40.23(3), 40.242, 40.244 221.035F, 221.036(9), 116.072(l), 116.072(6) to 116.072(8) |
| | Environmental Waste Management | 115A.29(2)(a), 115A.38(2) |
| | Producer-Distributor Agricultural Bargaining | 17.692, 17.695, 17.697 to 17.701 |

| State | Kind of Dispute | Statute/Code |
|-------|-----------------|--------------|
| Minnesota, continued | Civil Litigation | 484.74 |
| | Nonprofit Regional Programs | 480.24 |
| | Community Dispute Resolution Programs | 494.01 to 494.04 |
| Mississippi (Code) | Automobile Warranty | 63-17-159, 63-17-163 |
| | Agricultural Debt | 69-2-43 to 69-43-51 |
| Missouri (Statutes) | Labor | 290.400, 290.420, 290.430, 295.030 to 290.190, 105.525 |
| | Civil Rights | 213.010(1), 213.020, 213.075 |
| Montana (Code) | Labor | 39-31-307 |
| | Family | 26-1-811 40-3-111 to 40-3-127 |
| | Agricultural Debt | 80-13-191, 80-13-201 to 80-13-214 |
| | Civil Rights | 49-2-501(1), 49-2-504 to 49-2-506, 49-2-601 |
| | Worker's Compensation | 39-71-2401 to 39-71-2411 |
| | Special Education | 20-7-462(4) |
| | Medical Malpractice Panel | 27-6-101 to 27-6-704 |
| | Production and Distribution of Agricultural Products | 80-1-101, 80-11-103(9) |
| Nebraska (Statutes) | Family | 42-801 to 42-823 42-360 |
| | Agricultural Debt | 2-4801 to 2-4816 |
| | Civil Rights | 20-113.01, 20-114(1)(2) |
| | Medical Review Panel | 44-2840 to 44-2847 |
| Nevada (Statutes) | Labor | 288.190, 288.200, 288.205, 288.215, 288.220, 288.270, 614.010, 614.020 |
| | Automobile Warranty | 598.761 |
| | Civil Rights | 233.020 to 233.210 244.161 |
| | Education | 394.11 |
| | Consumer Credit, Civil Rights | 598B.150 |

| State | Kind of Dispute | Statute/Code |
|---|---|---|
| Nevada, continued | Mobile Home | 118B.024, 118B.025, 118B.260 |
| New Hampshire (Statutes) | Labor | 273-A:1, 273-A:12, 273.215, 273.220, 273.270, 614.010, 614.020 |
| | Automobile Warranty | 357.0:4 |
| New Jersey (Statutes) | Labor | 34-13A-4 to 34-13A-16 34-13A-15, 34-13A-16 |
| | Civil Rights | 52:27D-315 |
| | Alternative Dispute Resolution Program | 2A:23A-1 to 2A:23A-19 |
| | Developmentally Disabled | 52:27E-40, 52:27E-41 |
| | Home Warranty | 46:3 B-9 |
| | Radioactive Waste | 32:31-5 |
| New Mexico | Family | 40-12-1 to 40-12-6 40-4-9.1(B), (J)(5) |
| | Automobile Warranty | 57-16A-6 |
| | Small Claims, Specified Criminal Complaints | 34-8A-10 |
| New York (Law) | Labor | Sec. 205, 209 (civil service) Sec. 750 to 760 (labor) |
| | Family | Sec. 911 to 926 (judicial law) |
| | Automobile Warranty | Sec. 198-a (general business) |
| | Criminal | Sec. 170.55(4) (criminal proceeding law) |
| | Tax | Sec. 170 (3a) (tax law) |
| | Community Dispute Resolution Program | Sec. 849-a to 849-g (judicial law) |
| North Carolina (Statutes) | Labor | 95-32 to 95-36 |
| | Automobile Warranty | 20-351.7 |
| | Civil Rights | 143-422.3 (unemployment) 41A-6(6), 41A-7(a), 41A-8 (housing) |

| State | Kind of Dispute | Statute/Code |
|-------|-----------------|--------------|
| North Dakota (Code) | Family | 14-09.1-01 to 14-09.1-08 27-05.1-01 to 27-05.1-18 |
| | Automobile Warranty | 51-07-18(3) |
| | Agricultural Debt | 6-09.10-01 to 6-09.10-09 |
| | Debtor/Creditor | 11-26-01 to 11-26-08 |
| Ohio (Code) | Labor | 4117.02(A), 4117.02(E) to 4117.02(H)(7), 4117.02(N) 4117.14 (A), 4117.14(C) |
| | Family | 3117.01 to 3117.08 3105.091 |
| | Automobile Warranty | 1345.75, 1345.77 |
| | Civil Rights | 1901.331 (housing) |
| | Mental Disability Ombudsman | 5123.601 to 5123.603 |
| Oklahoma (Statutes) | Automobile Warranty | tit. 15, Sec. 901(f) |
| | Civil Rights | tit. 25, Sec. 1505, 1704, 1705 |
| | Dispute Resolution Programs | tit. 12, Sec. 1801 to 1813 |
| Oregon (Statutes) | Labor | 662.405 to 662.455 662.705(4), 662.715, 662.785 243.650 et seq. |
| | Family | 107.510 to 107.615 107.755 to 107.795 107.179(4) |
| Pennsylvania (Statutes) | Labor | tit. 43, Sec. 211.31 to 211.39, tit. 43 Sec. 213.13 (public utilities) tit. 43, Sec. 1101, .801, .802, tit. 43, Sec. 217.3 |
| | Automobile Warranty | tit. 73, Sec. 1959 |
| | Civil Rights | tit. 43, Sec. 957(i) (unemployment) tit. 43, Sec. 959(a) to 959(c) (employment) |

| State | Kind of Dispute | Statute/Code |
|---|---|---|
| Pennsylvania, continued | Eminent Domain | tit. 52, Sec. 1406.15 |
| Rhode Island (General Laws) | Labor | 28-10-1, 28-9.4-10, 28-9.4-17, 28-7-10 |
| | Consumer | 42-42-5 to 42-42-7 |
| South Carolina (Code) | Labor | 41-10-70 (wage mediation) 41-17-10 |
| | Civil Rights | 1-13-70, 1-13-90 (employment) |
| | Consumer | 37-6-117 |
| | Employment Grievances | 8-17-360, 8-17-370 |
| South Dakota (Codified Laws) | Labor | 60-10-1 to 60-10-3 |
| Tennessee (Code) | Bank Patron | 45-1-301 to 45-1-309 |
| Texas (Code) | Labor | Art. 5154c-1, Sec. 9 |
| | ADR Procedures | Art. 4590f-1 tit. 7, 154.001 to 154.073 Sec. 3.07(d) |
| | Low-level Radioactive Waste | Sec. 152.001 to 152.004 |
| Utah (Code) | Family | 30-3-16.2 to 30-3-17.1 30-3-4.1, 30-3-4.3 |
| | Automobile Warranty | 13-20-7 |
| | Medical Malpractice | 78-14-1, 78-14-2, 78-14-12 to 78-14-16 |
| Vermont (Code) | Labor | tit. 21, 924 to 925 tit. 3, 8.25 tit. 21, 521 to 554 |
| | Special Education | tit. 16, Sec. 2941, 2959 |
| Virginia (Code) | Labor | 40.1-70 to 40.1-75 |
| | Family | 16.1-69.35, 16.1-289.1 |
| | Automobile Warranty | 59.1-207.15 |
| | Civil Mediation Programs | 16.1-69.35(d) |
| | Local Government Dispute Mediation | 15.1-945.1 to 15.1-945.3(G) 15.1-945.3(H)(4), 15.1-945.6 |

| State | Kind of Dispute | Statute/Code |
|---|---|---|
| Washington (Code) | Labor | 49.08.010, 41.56.430, 41.56.440, 41.56.450, 41.59.120 |
| | Family | 26.09.015 |
| | Automobile Warranty | 19.118.150 |
| | Civil Rights | 49.60.130 |
| | Dispute Resolution Centers | 7.75.010 to 7.75.100 |
| West Virginia (Code) | Labor | 21-1A-1 |
| | Automobile Warranty | 46A-6A-8, 46A-6A-9 |
| Wisconsin (Statutes) | Labor | 101.24, 111.11, 111.39, 111.53, 111.54, 111.55, 111.56, 111.70, 111.77 |
| | Family | 753.016 (conciliation) 767.081 to 767.082 767.001(3), 767.001(4) 767.11, 767.327(1)(2) |
| | Automobile Warranty | 218.015(3) to 218.015(7) |
| | Agricultural Debt | 15.13 to 15.135 |
| | Civil Rights | 118.20 (employment) 230.85 (employment) 1419 (governor and mediation) |
| | Environmental Waste Disposal | 16.08(11) |
| | Medical Malpractice | 655.42 to 655.68 |
| Wyoming (Statutes) | Automobile Warranty | 40-17-101(a), 40-17-101(f) |
| | Agricultural Debt | 11-41-101 to 11-41-110 |
| | Environmental | 35-11-701(a) to 35-11-701(c) |
| District of Columbia | Judicial Pretrial Conciliation | 16-3906 |
| Puerto Rico (Laws) | Informal Dispute Resolution | Ch. 44, Sec. 532 to 532e |
| United States (Code) | Labor | 29 USCS Sec. 172 et seq. 45 USCS Sec. 155 et seq. |
| | Agricultural Debt | 7 USCS Sec. 5101 to 5106 12 USCS Sec. 2202e |
| | Civil Rights | 42 USCS Sec. 2000e-5 42 USCS Sec. 2000g-1 42 USCS Sec. 3608(d) |

the disagreement has surfaced. If you are drawing up a contract and all parties agree to arbitrate any conflict that arises, insert a clause similar to the following in the contract or document:

> Any controversy or claim arising out of or relating to this contract, or the breach thereof, shall be settled by arbitration in accordance with the commercial arbitration rules of the American Arbitration Association, and judgment upon the award rendered by the arbitrator(s) may be entered in any court having jurisdiction thereof.

Including this clause allows one party to force arbitration if a dispute arises by simply filing a demand for arbitration with the AAA's regional office.

Courts have held that when language is ambiguous or unclear, any doubts about the use of arbitration should be resolved in favor of arbitration. In addition, courts have held that the phrase "relating to" is broader than the phrase "arising out of." This may seem like a great subtlety, but deleting either phrase may produce a somewhat different interpretation by a court of the responsibility of the parties to arbitrate than does including both phrases.

If a dispute surfaces, there is no prior agreement to arbitrate, and both parties agree to arbitration, the following suggested statement should be signed by all parties.

> We, the undersigned parties, hereby agree to submit to arbitration under the commercial arbitration rules of the American Arbitration Association the following controversy: [Cite briefly]. We further agree that the above controversy be submitted to one [or three] arbitrator[s] selected from the panels of arbitrators of the American Arbitration Association. We further agree that we will faithfully observe this agreement and the rules that we will abide by and perform any award rendered by the arbitrator[s] and that a judgment of the court having jurisdiction may be entered upon the award.

If arbitration under the auspices of the AAA occurs, the association assigns a tribunal administrator who will follow the case through to its conclusion. The following steps then occur, as outlined by the AAA (reprinted with permission of the AAA):

1.   Other parties named in the demand are notified and replies are requested.

2.   The tribunal administrator reviews panel (arbitrator) qualifications and

selects individuals suitable for the particular case. Information on AAA panelists is maintained on a computer.

3.  The list of names is sent to the parties, each of whom numbers (in order of preference) the names that it finds acceptable.

4.  An arbitrator is selected by the administrator according to the mutual desires of the parties. If the parties are unable to agree, the AAA may appoint an arbitrator.

5.  The administrator arranges a hearing date and location convenient to the parties and to the arbitrator.

6.  At the hearing, testimony and documents are submitted to the arbitrator, and witnesses are questioned and cross-examined.

7.  The arbitrator then issues a binding award, copies of which are sent to the parties by the tribunal administrator.

The rules at a commercial arbitration hearing are similar to those used in a courtroom, though a little less formal. (The AAA maintains separate sets of rules for certain industries, such as construction and securities, and for labor-management disputes.) The parties and their attorneys sit on opposite sides of a conference table while presenting their evidence to the arbitrator. The arbitrator expects to hear all pertinent evidence and will usually permit evidence that a judge might not allow in an effort to ascertain all the facts. Arbitrators are not required to follow the various evidentiary rules that exist in the court system, but that is the price of using an informal process. Obviously, the arbitrator will decide how much weight to give each piece of evidence.

Once the wheels of arbitration are set in motion, you should prepare just as thoroughly as you would if the case was going to be heard by a judge and jury. You should take these nine steps before walking into your hearing:

1.  Assemble all documents, papers, and notes you will need at the hearing. If you believe the other party has documents or records you may need, ask that they be brought to the hearing. (Under some states' laws, arbitrators may have the power to subpoena documents and witnesses.)

2.  Make a checklist of your documents and exhibits and prepare copies of those items for the arbitrator and your opponent.

3.  Interview all prospective witnesses. Coordinate the presentation of their testimony so a complete picture of your case will unfold.

4.  Prepare your witnesses for your opponent's likely cross-examination.

5. Review what you expect each witness to prove and make a checklist so you won't leave anything out.

6. Look at the case from your opponent's point of view and be prepared to answer or rebut your opponent's evidence.

7. Prepare in advance for any on-site visits, such as to warehouses, offices, or manufacturing plants. Both parties should be accompanied by the arbitrator during these visits.

8. If the case warrants the expense, or you are concerned about later court appeals or involvement with the courts (see section on the limited rights of appeal of arbitration decisions), engage the services of a court reporter to record your hearing. Average costs are $45 an hour, plus a transcription cost of approximately $3.25 a page.

9. In large, complicated cases, a prehearing may be called by the arbitrator to arrange for the orderly presentation of witnesses and documents and to set future schedules.

The arbitrator will hear the evidence and review the documents (and probably keep a set of documents for further study). At the end of the hearing, the parties will be asked to sum up their positions. The arbitrator will most likely reserve a decision pending further study of notes and the evidence presented. Once the arbitrator's decision is made, it is binding. Under AAA rules, arbitrators are not required to state the reasons for their decisions, and their decisions cannot be negotiated.

## COMPULSORY ARBITRATION

The process and rules of compulsory arbitration are identical to those described for voluntary arbitration, except that the parties are forced to the arbitration table by statute or court order. Sometimes the term binding arbitration is confused with compulsory arbitration; by definition, arbitration is binding, except in the narrowest matters.

## COLLECTING A JUDGMENT

If you are on the winning side of an award and have received written notice of the decision, your next step is to attempt collection. If your opponent does not respond to the obligation as awarded to you, you should proceed to court in one of two ways.

- *State Court:* (1) File an action in state court to have the arbitration award affirmed by the court system within the state your arbitration took place (within one year of receipt of award); or (2) upon receipt of a court affirmation, commence collection procedures as in any valid judgment under that jurisdiction's rules. (See Chapter 18 regarding collection.)
- *Federal Court:* When the arbitration is a federal matter, or one that is suitable to move from state to federal jurisdiction, you would file an action in the appropriate federal district court.

## VACATING AN AWARD

Vacating an award occurs when a court with higher authority than the AAA nullifies an award made by the arbitrator. There is solid precedent in court decisions making it difficult to overturn an arbitrator's award, except in the most narrow set of circumstances. In 1875, the New York Court of Appeals held, "The courts in this State have adhered with great steadiness to the general rule that awards will not be opened for errors of fact on the part of the arbitrator" (*Fudickar v. Guardian Life Insurance Co.*, 62 N.Y. 392, 400 [1875]).

Even before that decision, an 1854 United States Supreme Court decision held, "If the award is within the submission, and contains the honest decision of the arbitrator, after full and fair hearing of the parties, a court of equity will not set it aside for error, either in law or fact." (*Burchell v. Marsh*, 58 U.S. 344, 349 [1854].)

More recently, in *United Paperworkers International Union, AFL-CIO v. Misco, Inc.* (56 U.S.L.W. 4011 [U.S. December 1, 1987]), the United States Supreme Court held, "absent fraud or dishonesty, the merits of an arbitration award may not be reviewed by courts for errors of fact or alleged contract misrepresentations." The Fifth Circuit Court had found that the award ran counter to public policy, and the Supreme Court determined that "judicial review for any other reason would undermine the federal policy of private settling [disputes through arbitration] without governmental interference."

As stated in the Uniform Arbitration Act of the United States and the United States Arbitration Act, the courts will entertain the vacatur (rescinding) of an arbitration award only under the following circumstances:

- There was an undisclosed relationship between arbitrator and a party or his counsel affecting the arbitrator's impartiality or appearance of impartiality.
- An arbitrator was corrupt.
- The arbitrator did not schedule or conduct a hearing in a fair and judicious manner.

• The arbitrator granted relief that he or she was not authorized to grant under the contract pursuant to which the arbitration was held.

Unless the arbitrator clearly exceeded his or her power, the courts will not vacate the decision, even on grounds such as the discovery of new evidence, for preserving the arbitration system requires strict adherence to the arbitrator's decision. If arbitrators did not have the complete backing of the courts, then the very reasons for having an arbitration system—saving the court's time and the litigants' money—would be for naught, since many awards would be challenged by the losers.

Given all this, you may feel it is necessary to make an application to the court to vacate or modify an arbitration award. You must file an action within the appropriate court that will allow you to continue. The action must conform to the rules of court in the jurisdiction where it is being filed. Thus, the procedure may vary from jurisdiction to jurisdiction.

If you are unhappy with the arbitrator's award, even if you won, you must make application to an appropriate court asking that the court intervene and void the arbitrator's ruling. Normally, a motion to vacate must be filed within thirty to ninety days after delivery of the award. However, if one party moves to confirm the award after three months, the other party may cross-move to vacate it without regard to these time limits. Otherwise, time limits are strictly enforced. If a judgment has been issued that affirms the arbitration award, or if an out-of-state court has agreed to recognize the award, localizing it and issuing a judgment, the only path left is to attack the judgment, as you would in any other situation where you believe you might have the grounds to have the judgment stayed or vacated.

Here's an experience that clearly demonstrates the possible downside to arbitration and the difficulty in affecting an appeal to the courts.

In 1982, I was asked to allow Kool Cigarettes (Brown and Williamson Tobacco Company) to sponsor a jazz concert I produced each year at the international recording industry trade show, MIDEM, in Cannes, France. B. B. King, Dave Brubeck, the Heath Brothers, and Pat Metheny were to perform.

Metheny was the final addition to the lineup chosen from a list of names submitted to Kool. The plan was that once the video and audio recordings of the event were completed, the recordings would be distributed worldwide to promote Kool cigarettes. (Unfortunately, when Kool changed its corporate thinking about the use of music as an advertising vehicle, their promotional plans for the project were scuttled.)

Obtaining name performers, who are usually under exclusive contract to record companies, is not easily accomplished. However, MCA Records was happy to have B. B. King perform at an industry trade show and MCA's president signed off on an agreement for King's cameo appearance on a recording. Dave Brubeck was between contracts and willing to make a cameo appearance on the record, provided that the amount of material used was limited and that his producer had sufficient control of the sound mix of the finished product to satisfy his quality concerns.

However, Pat Metheny's manager was an extremely hard-nosed negotiator, and the negotiations were probably the most difficult of my career. A deal was finally struck, Metheny was paid $25,000 for a 20-minute live performance of which no more than two selections were to be used on the finished recording. In addition, there were myriad other contingencies and clauses that turned a simple concept into a contract whose demise was almost predestined.

The live performance went off without a hitch before an audience of 2,500 of the world's recording executives and French citizens of Cannes. The concert turned out to be a spectacular musical feast with some of the finest jazz performances I have ever heard. Although most jazz concerts have a jam session at the end with all the performers playing together, only Brubeck and King participated. Metheny's manager went to the Heath Brothers' dressing room and told Percy Heath, "Whitey is trying to take advantage of you, you were not contracted for a jam, so don't play in it." Metheny simply refused outright. Luckily, the audience didn't mind the missing artists, for King and Brubeck making music together was a first-time-ever treat for all music lovers.

Although Metheny's manager refused to comply with certain terms of the contract and delivered his master tape too late to secure Kool's marketing support before they changed their corporate advertising policy, the recording was released in 1984 on the Kool Jazz label and was titled *Kool Jazz at MIDEM*. A third-party licensee in Germany took the material, including the two Pat Metheny songs, and falsely marketed the recording as a "Pat Metheny recording." Metheny's manager was furious, and after attempts to have the German licensee withdraw the recording from the market failed, he invoked the arbitration clause in our original labyrinthine contract.

From the beginning of the arbitration, it was obvious that there was a cozy relationship between the arbitrator and Metheny's attorney. The two were on a first-name basis, and continually joked with each other. This made our side very uncomfortable. Then, after two and a half days of intense sessions, it was discovered by sheer chance that the arbitrator had been the attorney representing B. B. King on the original contract for the Kool recording four years earlier. We immediately protested the arbitration to the AAA, claiming that the arbitrator had been involved in the transaction and should have been replaced. (We were hoping that a dismissal of the proceedings would result in either a new, and in our opinion more equitable, arbitrator, or an agreement with Metheny's attorney to drop the proceedings.) The AAA, however, decided differently; it felt that the arbitrator's previous role in the case was not significant for the present dispute and would not color his opinion in the Metheny matter.

The expensive and time-consuming lesson herein is that you should be extremely cautious about agreeing to an arbitration clause in a contract. The courts have held, and continue to hold, that only the most serious and outrageous actions on the part of an arbitrator can provide grounds for an appeal that would hold a prayer of being upheld or even heard by a judge. In the Metheny case, even the past acquaintanceship of an arbitrator to one side's attorney and to an uninvolved but related former client and principal in the transaction was not enough for the AAA to disqualify the arbitrator. There was little chance of a court altering the position taken by the AAA, and the expense of taking the case to court was too great for our company, anyway.

Thus, you should view arbitration as an alternate dispute resolution system whose outcome will receive widespread judicial support and should be considered final. In the case of an agreement that does not have an arbitration clause, the courts will recognize your legal rights to a review by the judicial system. But in the words of Robert Coulson, president of the AAA:

> I think there is going to be continuing need for private dispute resolution, because the courts are, on the one hand, swamped with cases and on the other hand . . . are underfinanced, there are not enough judges, there are not enough courtrooms, and the system itself is obsolete. In view of that, I think it is quite unlikely that the courts will ever be able to satisfy the public need for prompt and expert dispute resolution and so I think many parties will continue to turn to professional mediators and also to organizations that can provide expert arbitrators and simplified rules.

Settling a dispute by arbitration or mediation will save the time, expense, and heartache of a trial. No matter how tense the bargaining becomes, less damage to your nervous system will occur than at a trial. However, there are times when the parties are too far apart for compromise. In that case, regardless of how crowded the court calendars are and how long it takes a case to come before a judge and jury, you may find it necessary to bring the disputed issue to a court for final resolution.

# CHAPTER 15

# Pretrial Procedures

*For a judge rarely performs his function adequately unless the case before him is adequately presented.*

—Louis D. Brandeis

I magine being accused of a crime and having your accuser be a member of the jury that was deciding your fate. Or even worse, imagine walking on red-hot plowshares with your guilt or innocence dependent on whether your body was damaged by the ordeal. Before 1216, if you were not a high-ranking member of society, accusation and judgment by the same individual and suffering an ordeal to prove your innocence were your lot. Our trials have come a long way since then (see Viva Voce, page 236).

In colonial America under British rule, trial by jury did more than simply provide justice; it was also an instrument of liberty, offering the colonists the chance to stand up to the British judges presiding over American justice. This freedom was so important to the colonists that when the Constitution was drafted, the words "the trial of all crimes . . . shall be by jury; and such trial shall be held in the state where the said crimes shall have been committed" were woven into the fabric of our inalienable rights (Section 2, Clause 3, Article III).

The inalienable right to a trial by jury for criminal cases is granted to every United States citizen on the federal level; it is also provided for in the constitution of each state. The fact that you might have to wait two years or more for a trial date, or that the trial's cost may overshadow any possible monetary return, or even that a trial may not be conclusive because of years of appeals, motions, and problems in collecting a judgment is not the Constitution's concern—if the grand old document could speak for itself, it would probably say, "I never said it would be easy."

# Viva Voce

*Early common law courts conducted virtually all of their business orally,
or* viva voce. *Once a lawsuit had been initiated and the defendant had been
summoned to appear in court, the plaintiff's counsel would commence the
proceedings by verbally explaining the plaintiff's complaint before the
court. This statement was called the* count *(from the French for "story").*

*Next, the defense counsel stated the defendant's position. This was called
the* plea. *The opposing barristers (lawyers) then argued back and forth until
the issues of law and fact were isolated. Issues of law would be decided by
the judge; issues of fact would probably be tried by a jury. As the trial
proceeded, an officer of the court would sit near the judge and enter the
pleadings on a parchment roll, or record.*

*Over time, the law grew more complex and the system of oral pleadings
could not keep up with it—not all that was said could be recorded, and major
points could be forgotten. The courts moved toward the use of written
pleadings that were filed with the office of the court and delivered to the
parties concerned. This, however, proved extremely time-consuming and
produced a greater volume of documents than the courts could handle.*

*Eventually, a sort of compromise evolved. Today's justice system combines
the use of both oral and written pleadings. Since written pleadings alone do
not allow for a full discussion of facts and law, the modern pretrial conference,
in which participants stipulate points of agreement and disagreement (see page
238), has taken over many of the functions of the original viva voce.*

Easy a trial is not. Satisfying, maybe—depending on the outcome. Interesting, always. Now that you have chosen or identified an actionable cause,
researched the law, drafted your complaint or answer, battled your way
through motions and countermotions, completed discovery, collected and
categorized your evidence, calculated damages, negotiated to try to avoid the
time and expense of a trial, you are finally ready for your day in court. (See
Trial Preparation, page 237.)

A modern jury trial consists of nine elements:

# Trial Preparation

*Although your preparation for trial should begin with the act that was the basis of the unsettled dispute, here are certain things to do just before the drama of the trial unfolds.*

1.  *Reread the pleadings, the products of discovery (depositions, etc.), and all exhibits and documents to be introduced. Make at least four copies of each exhibit to be used at the trial.*

2.  *Review each claim, each defense, and each piece of evidence that proves or rebuts a material allegation.*

3.  *Choose witnesses who will authenticate and identify each exhibit. Prepare a list of these witnesses.*

4.  *If you are the plaintiff, decide on the order of proof; that is, the order in which you will present your evidence.*

5.  *If you are the defendant, arrange rebuttal material in such a manner that you can quickly retrieve it, and decide on the order of proof; that is, the order in which you will present your evidence.*

6.  *Prepare in advance any charts, graphs, or audiovisual aids that you might use at the trial.*

7.  *Use relaxation or imaging techniques to eliminate pretrial anxiety.*

8.  *Confirm trial date and time.*

9.  *Review service of subpoenas for witnesses.*

10. *Contact witnesses and review their roles in the trial.*

11. *Write or outline your opening statement.*

12. *Establish an outline for your closing argument.*

*No stage play can be presented without proper rehearsal, and no trial can be handled professionally without proper preparation. Remember that the outcome of your trial depends on the quality of your preparation.*

1.  Pretrial conference and stipulations.

2.  Calendar call.

3.  Judge and/or jury.

4.  Jury instructions (charge to the jury).

5.  Jury selection.

6.  Opening arguments.

7.  Presentation of the plaintiff's case and examination and cross-examination of witnesses.

8.  Presentation of the defendant's case.

9.  Final arguments (summation).

## PRETRIAL CONFERENCE AND STIPULATIONS

Although most jurisdictions today begin the trial stage with a pretrial conference, this was not always the case. In 1929, Chief Judge Ira W. Jayne and his associate judges of the Federal Third Circuit Court in Detroit developed a simplified trial process, hoping to save time and expense. The judge, acting as a friend of the participants (at that time, not a usual posture for a judge), worked to define the issues and to obtain an agreement from both sides on as many points as possible. This provided litigants the ability to stipulate agreement on certain points, thereby cutting down the issues to be decided by trial. This program was extremely successful: Court calendars were reduced, trials were simplified, and many cases were resolved with a pretrial agreement. In 1934, a group of Boston judges, having heard about Judge Jayne's experiment, traveled to Detroit to watch it in action. The same procedures were soon instituted in Boston and the practice began to spread. A committee appointed by the United States Supreme Court to draft the Federal Rules of Civil Procedure heard about this new practice, and after some study, the advisory committee adopted this pretrial process under Rule 16.

Interestingly, the adoption of the pretrial process occurred without legislative action. It is an example of the judiciary's deciding on its own how to handle its own workload. As Judge Brandeis said (ex parte *Peterson*, 253 U.S. 300 [1919]), our courts possess an "inherent power to provide themselves with appropriate instruments required for the performance of their duties."

Since most jurisdictions now have some form of pretrial conference that generally results in a pretrial statement or stipulation between the parties, let's look at what goes on at a typical pretrial conference:

1. The plaintiff and the defendant are asked to state the substance or essence of their cases. During this oral presentation, the judge may ask questions to clarify issues.

2. The judge then attempts to find issues on which both parties agree, in an effort to determine which issues can be stipulated (agreed) to.

3. The court inquires next as to the condition of the pleadings. If they are not in order, the judge may allow amendments as may be necessary and reasonable, or may strike or otherwise limit the use of pleadings.

4. Any pending or interim questions of law are ruled upon by the court.

5. The court may then inquire into the authenticity and admissibility of exhibits and discusses the possibility of the litigants stipulating to any facts that may speed the trial process.

6. The court may inquire into the number and background of the proposed expert witnesses, and by agreement with the parties or by court order arranges the number and order of the experts to be called.

7. The respective counsel or individuals acting pro se are then requested to estimate the amount of time they think the trial will take. This is done for calendar purposes.

8. Next, the court may inquire as to the possibility of settling the case in an effort to avoid an actual trial. At the end of the conference, an order or memorandum is usually drawn that outlines the results obtained at the conference, including those items to stipulated to, the number and names of proposed witnesses, and any other pertinent details the court believes should be included.

Thus, the goals of the pretrial process include the avoidance of squandering the court's time by avoiding unnecessary proof during trial, settling procedural arguments, and in some cases determining the admissibility of evidence in advance of a trial. Be ready for this process if you litigate either with counsel or pro se. In some jurisdictions, overcrowded courts order the parties to follow a mandated outline of a pretrial stipulation. This method is all right for attorneys who are knowledgeable about the standard outline; however, if you are acting pro se, you should request (petition the court for) a hearing on the pretrial stipulation as just described. (A typical pretrial stipulation order appears in Appendix III.)

## CALENDAR CALL

In many jurisdictions, a trial date is obtained when the plaintiff notifies the defendant and the court that the case is at issue (ready for trial). The court responds and plaintiff and defendant are notified to be ready for a calendar call (docket review), a pretrial conference, and/or trial date.

## JUDGE AND/OR JURY

Although you would normally decide to ask for a jury long before this point, this is an appropriate time to discuss the all-important choice of trial by judge or trial by judge and jury.

In today's civil procedures, the jury determines the fact; it does not interpret the law. It is the court's province (the judge's responsibility) to guide the jury in the application and meaning of the law and to rule on points of law at issue. It is the jury's province to determine the truth relative to the factual discrepancies or issues of the case as demonstrated by the evidence. Questions of law are explained to the jury in a set of jury instructions. At this point, however, we will look only at the elements of the decision to employ a jury or not.

Under Federal Rule 38, in federal court a party may demand a jury trial in writing (on any claim triable as of right by jury) any time after a complaint is filed but not less than "10 days after service of the last pleading directed to such issue." The party may also specify which claims he wishes tried by the jury. This jury request ("Jury Trial Demand") is then noted on the pleading below the case number. The opposing side may then, if it wishes, ask for other counts in the complaint to be tried by the jury also. If the plaintiff desires a jury from the beginning, he can set forth the following phrase at the end of the complaint: "Plaintiff demands trial by jury."

The rules for demanding trial by jury vary in state courts. In Florida, for instance, the plaintiff must make the demand at the time the original complaint is filed, or the right is considered waived. In general, the right to a jury trial is deemed waived unless it is demanded at the appropriate time. You must check your local rules of court to determine the appropriate point in litigation to demand trial by jury.

As a general rule, actions in equity are not tried by a jury, while actions at law may be. (Equity involves having the courts make a decision that may not be readily resolved by applying particular rules or statutes. Actions at law are more often resolved by applying statutes or prior case law to the issues.) There may be exceptions in certain jurisdictions. For example, in New York, the court must grant the application of either party for a trial by jury even though no right exists in the statute. New York courts also have the power to direct that a jury trial be held on any issue or issues of fact if the court deems it in the interest of justice to do so. In federal courts, the powers are even broader, and the court, "in furtherance of convenience or to avoid prejudice, may order a separate trial of any claim, cross-claim, counterclaim, or third-party claim, or on any separate issue or of any number of claims, cross-claims, counterclaims, third-party claims, or . . . issues" (Federal Rule of Civil Procedure 42[b]).

If you are the plaintiff, in what type of case should you demand a trial by jury? Any answer should be taken as a generalization only; you must make the actual decision after further study. However, the following actions are generally considered best tried by jury if you are the plaintiff. Start by assuming you will ask for a jury in these cases, and then determine whether you have a special reason to have only a judge as the trier of fact:

- Negligence.
- Breach of warranty causing personal injuries.
- Slander.
- Libel.
- False arrest.
- Malicious prosecution.
- Assault.
- Criminal conversion.
- Action for wages.
- Recovery of commissions.
- Breach of contract against an employer.
- Most actions against large corporations.
- Actions against banks.
- Actions against stockbrokers.

Another consideration in deciding whether to use a jury is the kind of jury you may have in a given location. Sometimes jurors in a community are known to be less liberal than the judges. If a large portion of jurors have low or moderate incomes, a substantial amount of money damages may look larger to them than to a judge who may be receiving a hefty salary. Juries may not understand why such large figures may be necessary, even when the facts justify a substantial verdict, and so you might fare better in front of a judge alone. The strength of your evidence should also weigh in your decision. If a defendant's liability seems certain, it might be better for you to present the case before a judge, who is more likely to see this clearly. Conversely, if the liability is doubtful, you might have a better chance of obtaining a positive verdict from a jury that may be swayed by other factors in the case's presentation. (See Chapter 12).

If you are the defendant and the court calendars are congested, you may find it more advantageous to ask for a jury trial, not only to gain additional time, but also to obtain the intangible benefits of such a trial. The extra time becomes valuable, for as time goes on witnesses for the plaintiff may become less available or their memories may become more foggy. And don't discount sympathy. For instance, a tenant would probably find a jury beneficial in an action against a landlord. Likewise, employees who sue an employer, or a party of modest circumstances battling against a rich corporation or the government would probably prefer a jury, hoping to gain its sympathy.

In deciding whether to use a judge and/or a jury, consider these factors, too:

- The prominence of a party or witness to the litigation.
- The reputation and attitudes of a particular judge.
- The effectiveness of the opposing counsel before a judge and/or a jury.

## JURY INSTRUCTIONS (CHARGE TO THE JURY)

Why should you consider jury instructions before the jury is picked? One law book gave this interesting account from a seasoned attorney. (Scott Baldwin, Eugene Davidson, and John Lynch, Jr., *The Art of Advocacy: Jury Instructions*, New York: Matthew Bender, 1989.)

A sage old lawyer once boasted that he tried his case backward.

> . . . the first thing he did was to prepare jury instructions. The advantage to preparing . . . jury instructions in the early stages of the case are numerous. The preparation of the charge [to the jury] will require the attorney to think through the entire case from beginning to end. The attorney will obtain an overall perspective of the case and will be able to foresee how facts and the law will merge. This will give . . . insight into the strength and weakness of the case. Finally, he will know the ultimate issues to be determined by the jury and will be able to prepare his case accordingly.

By defining the legal issues first, you can more succinctly apply the facts to the law, eliminating superfluous work (investigations, discovery, and so on) not applicable to the now clearly defined case.

Looking at negligence, as defined in terms of a jury charge, shows how very clear a legal issue can be made when plain English is used to instruct prospective jurors. The following standard jury instructions on negligence, are taken from a form book, *Florida Standard Jury Instructions*, published by the Florida Bar Association (many other states have similar form books):

### Negligence Defined
### Traditional Instruction—Reasonably Prudent Person
The law requires that everyone must act as a reasonably prudent person would act and exercise that degree of care which a reasonably prudent person would exercise under the same circumstances. Everyone must do or avoid doing what a reasonably prudent person would do or would not do in order to avoid injury or damage to others. Failure to act as a reasonably prudent person is negligence.

### General Instruction—Elements of Negligence
In order to recover for negligence against the defendant, the plaintiff must prove a duty, recognized by law, requiring the defendant to conform to a certain standard of conduct; a breach of such duty by the defendant; and a causal connection between the defendant's breach of duty and the plaintiff's injuries.

### General Instruction—Unreasonable Risk of Harm
In order to recover for negligence against the defendant, the plaintiff must prove a breach of the duty, recognized by law, requiring the defendant to conform to a certain standard of conduct for the protection of others against unreasonable risks.

### Plaintiff's Instruction
### Foreseeability
Although a finding of negligence requires that it was likely injury or damage could have resulted from the defendant's conduct, such a finding does not require that the defendant foresaw that the precise injury would certainly occur. A finding of negligence requires only that a reasonably prudent person would have foreseen the possibility that injury or damage could have resulted from his conduct.

*Defendant's Instruction*
*Foreseeability*
Negligence is the failure to exercise that degree of care which a reasonably prudent person would exercise under the circumstances. The degree of care required of a reasonably prudent person under the circumstances is not based upon knowledge that could only be obtained by viewing the circumstances of the plaintiff's injury after the fact, or upon the knowledge of an expert or other person with special qualifications.

Work backward from the jury instruction (the legal issue). You need to find or develop the proof to support the instruction; if you can't find the proof or develop it through discovery, then either the case doesn't work or the jury instruction is not correct for the set of facts that you have.

Although the judge makes the final charge to the jury, both plaintiff and defendant are usually asked to present to the judge their concepts of the instructions. This usually happens at the start of the trial, with the judge using the material along with the court's own knowledge of the law at issue (as well as evidence and testimony developed at the trial) to prepare a formal charge or set of instructions to the jury panel. Jury instructions prepared at a trial's outset can also be used as a guide to the direction of the trial and the law at issue during the trial. They may also play an important role in determining the makeup of the panel of jurors that both sides will finally accept. The process of jury selection often benefits from the attorneys being able to discuss with prospective jurors the issues at stake in the trial as outlined in the jury instructions.

The text of particular jury instructions on various issues of law can be found in many form books in a law library. To complete the instructions, you must add to the law therein (as in the negligence example) the individual facts of the case in clear and understandable terms. (See Appendix II for a typical charge to the jury.) Both law and facts should be as brief as possible. The shorter the length, the more likely the jury will understand the substance of the case. Further, when drafting jury instructions, carefully consider the connotations of your words. You might have to consider the accepted use of certain words in a particular jurisdiction. For instance, the terms reasonable care and ordinary care may be interchangeable in one jurisdiction, but not in another. In order to use the correct word, check the law when preparing jury instructions.

Naturally, when preparing jury instructions, you should attempt to show your case in its most favorable light, without committing an error. Choosing applicable instructions that at the same time prove your legal theory of the case is the real challenge in preparing a well-organized set of jury instructions.

When using form instructions, apply the following tests:

1. Is the instruction correct for the case, and is it the best possible one of all the alternatives?

2. If the instructions have alternative language or options, has the right language been chosen, as applied to the facts, for your particular jurisdiction?

3. Do the instructions need to be modified, or are they adequate?

4. Has the factual component been added to the instruction, and does the evidence support the use of the instruction in the case?

5. Is the legal position as used in the instruction supported by legal authority in the jurisdiction?

*Caution:* Not every instruction is written to fit every set of facts as found in a form book or pattern jury instruction book (as many are called). If the five-point test reveals that a form instruction does not fit, you will have to draft a new instruction.

Since most jurors are laypeople and not familiar with legal jargon, you must spell out the issues and facts in everyday language. For the most part, the legal community recognizes the necessity of using plain English. It is for precisely this reason that a set of jury instructions is such a valuable tool to the individual operating pro se; if done properly, the issues will be explained in language that can be understood by those who are not trained attorneys. By using plain English, by being brief, and by giving clear and concise instructions, you will enable the jury and all others concerned with the case to more quickly understand the issues at stake.

## JURY SELECTION

Jury selection, often referred to as *voir dire* ("to speak the truth") requires a knowledge of the justice system as well as of human character. The subject is so complicated that some people now sell their expertise on who should sit on the jury to the highest bidder; thus, you can have the best chance of winning money can buy. Be that as it may, this is not only the time for choosing jurors, but the beginning of a relationship between yourself and the individuals on the jury. It's the time that a skillful presenter of a case can implant certain notions and concepts in the jury's thoughts, laying the groundwork for a successful drama of persuasion. Let's look at jury selection so that you may develop a rudimentary working knowledge of the subject. This will be the basis on which to build if you desire or need to go further in voir dire.

Before the actual start of jury selection, you must stipulate with your opponent or file with the court your motion *in limine.* This is the ruling or stipulation to withhold certain past history of the defendant from the jury during the course of the trial, to prohibit the disclosure of prejudicial—and probably inadmissible—information (prior criminal record, divorce, remarriage, alcoholism, ownership of a bar, being under investigation for tax fraud, or any other matter properly excludable). Once an improper statement is made to the jury, no admonition from the judge can erase the impression implanted in the jurors' minds. You must always be alert for attempts to disclose prejudicial facts to the jury.

The actual process of selecting a jury begins either in a special jury room or in the courtroom itself. If it takes place in the courtroom, the judge should always be present. The judge, however, is largely passive, ruling only on objections to questions and challenges to the favor (see below).

The principal purpose of voir dire is to obtain information that will provide you with reasons to eliminate jurors who may be biased in their evaluation of a case. The process also gives you the opportunity to educate jurors about the issues of the case and to begin to establish a rapport with them. This process can also provide a forum for you to experiment with the strategy and tactics to be used as the trial progresses.

As in previous cautions regarding jurisdiction, you must remember that particular rules of jury selection change from one jurisdiction to another. Some states require the court to question the jurors; in certain other states and in federal court, the judge may permit attorneys to ask the questions. Various ways to eliminate jurors exist, but most states and the federal system recognize three types of challenges to a prospective juror:

1. *For cause:* When a prospective juror is perceived to be hostile or prejudicial, or is clearly related to one of the parties, elimination is mandatory.

2. *To the favor:* This challenge is available when the juror has a relationship to the appearing party that may cause bias in that party's mind. For instance, some states will recognize the bias of an employee as grounds for this challenge. Elimination on this challenge is at the discretion of the judge.

3. *Peremptory:* This challenge is granted as a matter of right—no reason or explanation is needed to eliminate a prospective juror.

In some cases the entire jury panel may be challenged as a group. This most often happens when a constitutional question regarding the method used to select the jury is brought before the court.

Since the object of voir dire is to select an impartial jury of one's peers, there is no limit on the number of challenges *for cause* or *to the favor*. However, the number of peremptory challenges will vary from state to state and jurisdiction to jurisdiction. In federal court you are allowed three such challenges (28 U.S.C. Sec. 1870 [1970]), whereas in state court the number may be as high as six. Check the rules at each location in which you are involved in a trial.

We think of a jury as being comprised of twelve people; however, the tendency of many jurisdictions is to reduce the number in civil cases to six, or to base the size on the amount at stake. In California, parties may stipulate in open court to any number less than twelve. The Utah Code allows for eight jurors, and in Virginia, the number is seven or five if the amount, exclusive of costs, is $1,000 or less. More recently, the New Jersey Supreme Court made six jurors, as opposed to twelve, the rule rather than the exception. Many jurisdictions provide for the selection of an alternate juror, who sits with the regular members of the jury, listens to all the testimony, and reviews all evidence, right up until the end of the summation. If all members of the regular jury panel are able to participate (no one has taken ill) in deliberation, the alternate is then discharged from jury service.

For the most part, challenges *for cause* or *to the favor* are used before peremptory challenges are exercised. This is done to conserve these precious peremptory challenges. By uncovering grounds for challenges for cause or to the favor, you protect the peremptory challenges for use when you have no other grounds. Also, try to figure out who the other side is going to challenge—a correct guess could save a peremptory challenge. The plaintiff is required to challenge first, and so is at a slight disadvantage. Therefore, the more information you have about the prospective jurors and the more you know about what the opposing counsel may do, the better your chances of obtaining the jury you want.

The care and handling of jurors is both an art and a science. Information on background, values, opinions, intellect, and socioeconomic standing must be solicited in a manner that will not create hard feelings. (Remember, despite your best efforts, an individual whom you do not want may wind up on the jury.) Asking name, address, and occupation is a fairly routine starting place. In some jurisdictions this basic information is provided to each side by the court. (You should enter this data and any other information on a chart or devise some other system of keeping track of the prospective jurors, their answers, and any challenges made.)

It is usually better to question jurors individually rather than as a group. By engaging a prospective juror in conversation, you may gain a glimpse of how he or she thinks. As the great advocate Louis Nizer explained it (Louis Nizer, *My Day in Court*, New York: Doubleday, 1961, 35–36):

> By speaking individually to each juror, one can get behind the face's mask. Sometimes a hard face lights up in a warm smile, or a kindly face becomes forbidding as the lips curve during an answer. The voice and diction are always revealing. During personal questioning, one may sense a sympathetic bond or, conversely, a resistance. All the psychological arts can be employed to evaluate the juror's meanings. But when a number of jurors merely shake their collective heads in answer to the judge's formal questions, observation gives very limited clues.

To get the best reading on each juror's personality, avoid questions that can be answered "yes" or "no." Here are some tips from the experts on questioning a prospective juror:

• Know in advance the type of juror you want.
• Do not underestimate the juror's intelligence and desire to act correctly for the benefit of justice.
• Do not exaggerate the extent of injuries or liability.
• Do not joke; the entire matter is quite serious to everyone present.
• Be polite and correct at all times.
• Allow the juror to speak, too.
• Do not allow your likes or dislikes regarding the individual juror to be exposed.
• Do not humiliate or embarrass a juror.
• Cover issues in their simplest form.
• Ask questions in a logical sequence.
• Allow problems in your case to surface, but ask jurors to keep an open mind.
• Use jurors' names, if possible.
• Try to get jurors who have said they will follow the law "as charged by the court."
• Treat all prospective jurors alike.
• Explain that you do not want charity or sympathy before your opponent takes advantage of the issue.

Questioning potential jurors starts with each side describing the nature of the case as they see it. Just enough about the case is disclosed so that prospective jurors can answer questions intelligently. However, no mention of the plaintiff's or defendant's side of the facts is permitted until after the trial formally opens. The parties to the litigation are then identified, and all participating counsel are identified. You will then take the following steps for each juror:

1. Determine whether the juror knows about the particular controversy.

2. Determine whether the juror knows any of the parties (including counsel).

3. If you are the defendant, you (or your counsel) make a brief comment about the nature of the defense.

4. Determine whether the juror has a prejudice relating to any type of action or defense, such as oral contracts.

5. Examine any relationship that may be disclosed as to the extent it may affect an impartial judgment.

6. Examine the juror's previous exposure on juries, to litigation, or as a witness.

7. Gently excuse any juror you find undesirable, being careful not to antagonize the prospective jury.

Your skill in soliciting an understanding of the prospective juror's personality and in building a relationship with each individual on the jury during the selection process may very well be what turns the jury's decision for you or against you. Thus, legal textbooks go on and on with suggestions for various approaches to questioning, depending on the type of case and what prejudices may be encountered. Size of verdict, criminal records, accidents, family relationships, education, nationality, race, age, and social values and standing are just some of the areas discussed, since jury selection must be tailored to each case. For example, if the plaintiff were of English descent, you would not want to have a Northern Irish juror; the same consideration holds for Arabs and Jews. High-level corporate officers are usually good jurors, except if they are from a manufacturing company (they may be sensitive to claims relating to manufacturing defects) and you are before them with a product liability case. Older folks, who have learned to live with aches and pains, usually do not make good jurors for an injury case, so you'd be better off without senior citizens on a case involving product liability.

Once jury selection is completed, the pretrial phase is concluded. If you have been doing your homework and have prepared properly throughout the preliminary proceedings, you should now be ready for the curtain to rise on your courtroom drama. The following chapter will help you know what to expect and how to proceed at your trial.

# CHAPTER 16
# Conducting Your Trial

*A case well prepared is a case half won before going to trial.*
—George Schmutz

N ow that you have completed the pretrial conference (see Chapter 15), attended calendar call, received a trial date, learned the makeup of your jury (if you asked for a trial by jury), and have participated in the process of jury instructions (along with your opponent and the judge), you are ready to begin the evidentiary phase of the trial. Don't be startled if His or Her Honor abruptly says, "Tell me what this case is all about." Despite the existence of reams of pleadings and all that has taken place in the case prior to your actual appearance in the courtroom, the judge may have only a cursory knowledge of the issues, if any at all. The judge needs to hear succinctly and clearly what the issues are. Now is the time to tell your side of the story.

## OPENING ARGUMENTS

It is generally believed that what an individual hears first on a subject creates a lasting impression and forms the basis for his or her opinion on the matter. This is called the "primacy effect." Weyman J. Lundquist, an experienced trial lawyer, writing for the American Bar Association's *Litigation Manual*, believes that "(O)pening statements determine the outcome of trials 50 percent of the time. . . . studies indicate that it may be as much as 85 percent of the time. . . . Opening statements give the jury a basic feeling for *who is right and why, who has the better facts, what is the logical result.* This first impression is not often changed." (Emphasis added.)

Whether the advantage is 50 percent or 85 percent is of little consequence.

What matters is that there is an advantage to presenting your side first (providing both sides are competent)—an advantage that is uniformly acknowledged (unless it is imperative to keep your opponent from gaining a preview of your case). In some jurisdictions the judge in a nonjury trial may dispense with opening statements and instead rely on the written pleadings to acquaint himself with the facts of the case. Otherwise, in federal and state court, the plaintiff usually has the right to give opening (and closing) statements first, except in rare circumstances where the defendant has admitted all allegations and is relying on a counterclaim or a special defense. If a single allegation is denied by the defendant, then the plaintiff's right to open is preserved. (Since it would be unusual for a defendant to acquiesce to all allegations, our discussion will assume that the plaintiff is first and plans to use this to the best advantage.)

The opening statement permits the jury to consider the entire story, with the facts presented as part of a cohesive whole. However, in the hands of a skilled individual, the opening statement can go much further than simply outlining the case; it can also create a climate or atmosphere favorable toward the plaintiff, which should be considered at least a secondary goal of the opening statement. You might think of the opening statement as a backdrop to which the facts, evidence, and testimony will be applied as adornments are applied to a stage set. If the jury sees the "set" materialize as you said it would in your opening statement, your view, and hopefully your contention (and legal theory), will appear to be substantiated by what the jury observes in the trial.

The task is somewhat different for the defense. By concentrating on the plaintiff's opening remarks, and not on specific evidence, and by presenting defenses to accusations made by the plaintiff, you attempt to blunt the effect of the plaintiff having the first say. (See Three Strikes and You're Out . . . Maybe, page 253.)

A well-drawn opening statement is brief, clear, and direct. It tells the story in a concise and logical sequence. By testing various theses and hypotheses in advance against the facts (as discussed under Jury Instructions), you should be able to present a legal theory that encompasses the facts and is easy for the laypeople on the jury to understand. You might make your opening remarks understated, and reserve more powerful statements for your summation.

Think of the opening statement as telling a story—a story that either takes the jurors back in time to the events as you believe they happened or anticipates what will happen during the trial and how you believe the trial will unfold. Either way, your purpose is to let the jury see the facts from the plaintiff's perspective.

# Three Strikes and You're Out . . . Maybe

*Your trial is about to begin, and you're a little edgy about its outcome. You could have used a little more time for discovery, and you couldn't locate a key witness. All you can think about as the judge bangs down the gavel is "perhaps I can win on appeal." If this happens to you, you must be aware of the three main areas of error that may give you that second chance through an appeal or a new trial.*

Excluded Evidence (Failure to Make Offer of Proof). *If something is not in the record, then it does not exist (as far as the court is concerned). If evidence is excluded by a trial judge in response to an objection, then it is paramount that you present proof of the importance of the evidence, and make it part of the record. There are three ways to accomplish this:*

- *Ask to excuse the jury and attempt to convince the judge on the record of the importance of the evidence, explaining what it is as the court reporter takes it down.*
- *Tell the court, "If my witness is allowed to testify, I will ask the following questions . . . and expect to get the following responses . . . ."*
- *Narrate, summarizing what the excluded evidence is.*

*No matter what the trial judge rules, your evidence will be in the record to be reviewed by the appellate judges. The offer of proof (as to the relevancy of your evidence and your right to use it at the trial) must be made of any and all excluded evidence.*

Prejudicial Final Arguments. *Opening counsel (or litigants) addressing the jury may make statements that could be considered reversible error. However, without a trial objection, proposed corrective measure, or a motion for a mistrial, the error may as well not have happened at all. The record must show an attempt to abate the damage when it occurred.*

*Statements to the jury must be supported by evidence. If your opponent oversteps this threshold, you may have grounds for reversible error—but you must act then to protect the record.*

Defective Jury Instructions. *The rules regarding jury instructions must be followed to the letter, and it is imperative that the court reporter get every word of the proceedings. If not, your record is unprotected and your ability to use reversible error regarding jury instructions will be lost. Here is Florida Rule of Court 1.470(b) (similar to such rules in most jurisdictions) regarding jury instructions:*

*"Not later than at the close of the evidence, the parties shall file written requests that the court charge the jury on the law set forth in such requests. The court shall then require counsel to appear before it to settle the charges to be given. At such conference all objections shall be made and ruled upon and the court shall inform counsel of such charges as it will give. No party may assign as error the giving of any charge unless he objects thereto at such time or the failure to give any charge unless he requested the same. The court shall orally charge the jury after the arguments are completed and, when practicable, shall furnish a copy of its charges to the jury."*

Here is how to make a strong opening statement:

- *Prepare.* Know exactly where you are going and the legal theory on which you are relying. Examine all the available evidence. Then tell your story in a clear manner so it appears that you have control of your case and of the courtroom.
- *Use the facts to your advantage.* Present the facts so they provide the jury with a cohesive and logical conclusion—your conclusion.
- *Identify with the jury.* You must understand the jury's need to grasp the case and the facts, so help the jury understand what is happening. The jury needs to know why they are there and what the trial is all about.
- *Set a direction.* Setting a course early on can place you in a position of control. Continuing with the theme or course set in the beginning can contribute substantially to the cohesive picture you are trying to paint for your side.

- *Remember the jury is comprised of laypeople.* An opening statement is a prime opportunity to help educate the jury and acquaint them with the process that is taking place, hopefully winning friends at the same time.
- *Use theatrics.* Your persuasive ability to reach out to the members of the jury is extremely important. Simply reading a prepared statement is not the way to make an opening statement. You must be so familiar with the case, the facts, and your legal theories that you can speak convincingly and extemporaneously to the jury and judge and convince them of your point of view.

Remember that an opening statement is an opportunity. It gives you a chance to gain an advantage, if you execute it properly. Don't promise what cannot be produced, and do not put your own credibility on the line with a jury (such as by asking them to evaluate your performance). Clearly establish in their minds the issues from your vantage point. The jury is at the very peak of attention prior to the opening statement, a pregnant moment that can, if handled correctly, give birth in their minds to the plaintiff's view of the case.

Any individual in the music business learns early on about the songwriting "hook"—the magical sequence of words and notes that grabs listeners and makes them want to hear the composition again and again. In developing a good storytelling technique for your opening statement, use a hook to spark the jury's curiosity.

Take, for example, this opening statement in a fictitious nautical accident case:

> On the moonlit evening of June 15, 1985, the Smith family set out in their 46-foot sailboat for a trip to the Caribbean, the family's first vacation in years. Although Frank Smith was an experienced captain, the family never made it past the entrance to the harbor. All perished in the depths of the murky intracoastal waters . . . .

Such an introduction almost guarantees attention (and hopefully sympathy). The remainder of the opening should contain the following sections:

1. *Introduction:* Introduce the parties.

2. *Body:* Tell what, how, and why. Define the issues.

3. *Closing:* Use the magic words: "I intend to prove" or "the evidence will show."

When you have completed your opening, it's your opponent's turn to speak. Now is not the time to make frivolous objections. First, you are trying to make a good first impression. If you are overridden by the judge, you may look foolish; more important, the court has officially said "you're wrong," and that impression may have a detrimental effect. Second, nitpicking your opponent's view may only diminish your stature in the eyes of the jury. (Lundquist suggests raising certain matters *in limine* to avoid having to object to your opponent's opening remarks. This means you must anticipate any problems so you can raise them at the *pretrial conference*.) Objections of substance, however, if not prevented *in limine*, are valid and should be made to prevent the jury from receiving misinformation that could be detrimental to your case. (See I Object, Your Honor, page 257.)

## PRESENTATION OF THE PLAINTIFF'S CASE

A trial is an emotionally charged pursuit, and should never be viewed as a purely scientific endeavor with its outcome predictably based on the contents of its input. There are just too many intangibles. Because of these intangibles, the performance of a trial should be considered an art. We could not attempt in this book to teach such an art or to provide sufficient information, direction, or background to make you an accomplished courtroom advocate. We will, however, attempt to acquaint you with the trial process and some of the pitfalls to watch for in conducting or participating in a trial.

The plaintiff is the initial protagonist; therefore it seems fair that *the burden of proof* falls on the plaintiff. This burden requires proof positive— proof without a reasonable doubt. (Different standards of proof apply in different types of litigation: Beyond a reasonable doubt; clear and convincing; and fair preponderance of evidence.) In the trial process as practiced in the United States, the plaintiff in any matter is first to present evidence. This is called the *direct case, case in chief,* or *on direct.* Once the plaintiff has completed the direct presentation of evidence and announces that the plaintiff "rests," the defendant can either challenge the legal sufficiency of the plaintiff's proof (that is, whether the case, based on law and statutes, has been properly presented) or provide evidence to rebut what the plaintiff's side contends. The defendant will then rest. Next, the plaintiff is given an opportunity to challenge the legal sufficiency of the defendant's contentions, and may counter with additional evidence relating only to what the defendant has claimed or what has been covered in cross-examination. This is called rebuttal. Rebuttal may continue back and forth until the judge ends it or both sides agree to rest.

After rebuttal, either side may attack the legal sufficiency of the other side's case. If found sufficient by the judge, each side will be asked to present

# I Object, Your Honor

*You have no doubt heard this sentence time and again on television, in the movies, and perhaps in a real courtroom: "I object, your honor." However, those four words can't be used frivolously. There must be valid grounds for an objection, and the objection must fit the situation. A mistake may hurt your chances for appellate review. The following are the most common reasons for objection:*

- *The witness is being led—the question is suggestive.*
- *The question has already been asked and answered.*
- *The question is argumentative.*
- *The question or answer assumes facts not in evidence.*
- *The question calls for a conclusion on the part of the witness.*
- *No proper foundation for the question or answer has been laid.*
- *The question is unintelligible.*
- *The question goes beyond the scope of the direct examination.*
- *The question calls for an opinion by an expert. This witness has not qualified as such.*
- *The evidence is barred by the Best Evidence Rule—what is being offered is not an original document.*
- *The evidence is not germane to the issues in this case.*
- *The evidence is repetitive and has already been introduced.*
- *The evidence is immaterial to the case—it does not prove or disprove any material fact.*
- *The witness is not qualified to testify—the witness is incompetent.*
- *Hearsay—the witness is not the person involved in the prior out-of-court event.*
- *The testimony or evidence is barred by the Fifth Amendment—the witness cannot be forced to incriminate himself or herself.*
- *The question is compound—it is made up of two or more questions.*
- *The answer is privileged (husband/wife, attorney/client, priest/parishioner, and so on). See page 145.*
- *Improper impeachment—the side calling a witness is barred from impeaching that witness.*

closing arguments. In a jury trial, the court will then instruct the jury on the law and the jury will retire to deliberate their verdict.

## Presenting the Direct Case

On direct, you (the plaintiff) conduct the case by calling witnesses who are supportive or friendly and by presenting supporting documents and any expert testimony. The purpose of the direct case is to lay a factual foundation for your legal claims. This phase of the trial may provide the record with a few facts or thousands of facts, depending on the complexity of the case; you should take care, however, to select facts that support the issues you have chosen—in effect creating a theme around which to organize the trial. The purpose of direct examination is to obtain from witnesses, in a logical sequence and with as much clarity as possible, their observations that have a bearing on the issues of the case (as you have defined them). Information from witnesses become facts, and facts developed from this direct testimony should support your claims and objectives. (See To Be or Not To Be . . . A Witness, page 259.)

The believability of a witness is critical to your case, and will "play" to the jury based on the credibility of the witness, the content of the witness' testimony, and the demeanor of the witness. An impeached witness, one proven to be lying and therefore lacking in credibility, cannot help you and may damage you. Evidence or testimony whose content is not germane to the case, or worse, that contradicts your claims, is a negative. The demeanor of a nervous or uncouth witness may damage even the best set of facts elicited on examination. Thus, credibility, content, and demeanor must gel into a cohesive statement by the witness with a set of facts that support your case. You should consider not using a witness if you have an alternative source, or if the evidence is only marginally necessary to your case.

The order of presentation of witnesses, relative to content of their testimony, is quite important, also. Here are a few rules of thumb from the plaintiff's perspective:

1.  Jurors view the first witness more critically than those that follow.
2.  In accident cases, jurors will resent talk of injuries before they know whether the plaintiff will recover.
3.  When liability is disputed, the plaintiff should not testify first. Build a supporting structure for the plaintiff's position.
4.  Television has created the impression that every witness is a liar—which is obviously not true, but it must be dealt with.
5.  Jurors will wait in anticipation for the victim's testimony.

# To Be or Not To Be . . . A Witness

*"To be or not to be, that is the question." In our context, the question might be changed to "Who should or should not be a witness" in a civil lawsuit? This decision may come well before trial and could be a major factor in the outcome of your trial. When you depose a friendly witness, you are in effect preparing, rehearsing, or rejecting the witness for his or her role in the trial. However, with the lapse of time and possible development of new information between the deposition and the trial, you should once again prepare, rehearse, and possibly reject your witnesses for the trial drama following these steps.*

1. *Have the witness review his or her deposition, and those of the opponent testifying on the same general subject.*

2. *If not previously deposed, witnesses should be interviewed on all pertinent facts, documents, and evidence in their knowledge.*

3. *Familiarize witnesses with any documents or exhibits involved in their testimony.*

4. *Coach the witness in proper conduct and demeanor:*

   - *Tell the truth to the best of your ability.*
   - *Be polite.*
   - *Take your time.*
   - *If you do not understand the question, ask that it be repeated.*
   - *Never volunteer information; answer "yes" or "no" whenever possible.*
   - *Don't guess when you answer.*
   - *If you are sure of the facts, do not begin sentences with "I think" or "I guess."*
   - *Do not be evasive. Truth enforces credibility, even if the facts are damaging. Let the questioner handle that problem.*
   - *If an objection is made, stop talking immediately! Wait for the outcome of the objection—you will be told when you should begin speaking again.*

> - *Never anticipate the questioner. Answer only after the entire question is asked.*
> - *Review documents and/or evidence before answering to be sure of your answer.*
> - *If asked, freely admit that you have discussed your testimony with your attorney if that is the case.*
> - *If asked, speak freely about your background, education, employment, and so on.*
>
> *If you are still concerned about a witness' performance at trial, try role playing. Set up a mock courtroom scene and audition the testimony. If you have access to video equipment, tape the audition. A witness who sees the performance on tape may perform better.*
> *The value or importance of your case may dictate or limit the amount of time, effort, and money you invest in staging or preparation. Try to do as much as possible within your time frame and budget.*

6. Hold weak witnesses for the end of the day or before lunch, when there is a general desire to recess and a witness' credibility is less likely to be scrutinized closely.

7. Even open minds can become closed. Constantly supported testimony may create a mindset.

8. If used properly, visual exhibits can hold the jury's attention.

9. Simplicity and understatement may be more impressive to the jury, particularly in the most serious cases.

The astute advocate will learn what questions will bring forth what responses from witnesses. (Cross-examining witnesses is also an art.) However, whether on direct or on cross-examination, documents, depositions, and other pieces of evidence should be marked and ready for immediate referral and use. (You should have the appropriate number of copies ready to hand to the appropriate people at the trial. More about evidence later.)

The presentation of direct testimony gives you the opportunity to make your case; however, it also places certain restrictions on the use of evidence. Whether you are acting pro se or have competent counsel, here are some basics of trial protocol that will help you.

## Examination of Witnesses

Although you may have been living with this case for several years, remember that the case you are presenting is completely new to the judge and jury. Therefore, question witnesses in such a way that you orient the jury about both the case and the witnesses' backgrounds and reasons for being present. If the testimony concerns action, prepare the witness to use descriptive narrative in setting the scene and bringing out the action. Control the pace, drawing out small segments of the action at a time. Use open-ended questions to elicit productive answers, but don't lead the witness (which will bring an objection from your opponent). If your case has a weakness, and most do, bring it out yourself. You're in control at this point, so the detrimental aspects of a witness' testimony can be brought out with the least damage.

Concentrate on the answers your questions elicit. Although you have reviewed the testimony and you think you know the witness' answers, listen carefully for any surprises or changes—and be ready to deal with them. If a witness gets a case of stage fright or has some memory loss, follow this procedure to refresh his or her memory (Thomas Mauet, *Fundamentals of Trial Techniques*, Boston: Little, Brown, 1988, page 14):

1. Witness knows the facts, but has a memory lapse on the stand.

2. Witness knows his report or other writing will jog his memory.

3. Witness is given and reads the pertinent part of his report or other writing.

4. Witness states his memory has now been refreshed.

5. Witness now testifies to what he knows, without further aid of the report or of other writing.

Coach the witness beforehand that the phrases "do you recall" or "do you remember anything else" signal that you are about to begin refreshing his or her recollection.

If you are planning to use an expert as a witness, you must "qualify" that individual prior to the start of testimony. (See May I Present My Expert? page 262.)

# May I Present My Expert?

*Qualifying an expert in the eyes of a jury is essential to the successful use of expert testimony. Even if opposing counsel concedes the qualifications of your expert, you should have the expert's background spread lavishly on the record. In jurisdictions that will permit experts to give reasons for their opinions on direct examination (some jurisdictions exclude all opinion on direct testimony), take advantage of the opportunity. The better the foundation your expert lays for his or her conclusions, the more credible the expert will appear to the jury.*

*When qualifying a professional (accountant, doctor, dentist, etc.), every facet of educational background, experience, teachings, and memberships in professional organizations should be presented. For a non-professional expert (realtor, plumber, merchandise buyer, and the like), validate expertise with a recital of special training, employment, and experience. In the case of quasi-professionals, (handwriting, polygraph, and fingerprint experts), take special care to establish their qualifications in their fields. Jury members do not, in the normal course of their lives, come in contact with ballistics experts, forensic experts, and the like, so you must familiarize them with your expert's qualifications and work so they can understand the testimony.*

*Whether in a court or in an office interview, you can use certain questions to establish the credentials of your expert witness.*

1. *What is your occupation?*
2. *What is the address of your office?*
3. *What training do you have in the field of (name the field)?*
4. *What work experience have you had in the field of (name the field)?*
5. *How long have you been working in (name the field)?*
6. *Is this your primary occupation?*
7. *Have you testified in court before on the subject of (name the field)?*
8. *How many times have you testified in court?*

9. *Have you made reports on the subject of your expertise?*

10. *Would you name some of the more important cases or instances of your work in the field of (name the field)?*

11. *Did you in this matter examine (the evidence, circumstances, documents, test results, etc.)?*

*The rest of your questions will relate to the specifics of the case. First, show the expert the specific evidence and ask, "Have you studied (evaluated) this?" Then ask the following questions:*

1. *Can you describe the study or examination you made of (name the evidence)?*

2. *As a result of your examination, have you an opinion of (name the evidence)?*

3. *What is your professional opinion?*

4. *Will you explain to the court and to the jury what you did and what you observed that caused you to arrive at your conclusion(s)?*

*An expert whose background has been carefully placed on the record and whose testimony is backed up with logical explanation and conclusions will go a long way toward influencing a jury and judge.*

## Testimony of Conversations

Using testimony of conversation is anything but cut and dried. Normally the hearsay rule of evidence applies, but there are so many exceptions that it would be best to check your local rules or the federal rules of evidence before deciding whether to use material from a conversation. The conversation may be allowed, depending on its evidentiary basis; for instance, if it is with a party opponent (an individual or entity that has been named in a lawsuit as a plaintiff or defendant and is on the opposite side to yours), the testimony may be allowed. Telephone conversations may also be allowed, providing the witness can identify the speaker on the other end of the line. (See Hello? Anyone Home? page 264.)

# Hello? Anyone Home?

*Using telephone conversations as evidence, like so many other areas of the law, is a subject unto itself. Here are the requirements for such conversations to be admissible.*

*If the witness knows the other person, the following must be established:*

1.  *When the conversation took place.*

2.  *Where the witness was when the conversation occurred.*

3.  *Whether the witness recognized the other voice.*

4.  *How the witness knows the other voice.*

5.  *The name of the person who is the other voice.*

6.  *Whether there were any other individuals participating in the conversation.*

7.  *Who said what to whom.*

*If the witness does not know the other individual, but learns that individual's identity through subsequent conversations, the following must be established:*

1.  *When the conversation took place.*

2.  *Where the witness was when the conversation occurred.*

3.  *The fact that the witness did not recognize the other voice at the time of the conversation.*

4.  *The fact that the witness talked to the other voice personally at a later date.*

5.  *The fact that the witness now recognizes the other voice during the original call.*

6.  *The name of the person who is the other voice.*

7.  *Whether there were any other individuals participating in the conversation.*

8.  *Who said what to whom.*

*If the witness does not know the person, but learns the individual's identity through later transactions, the following must be established:*

1. *When the conversation took place.*

2. *Where the witness was when the conversation occurred.*

3. *The fact that the witness did not recognize the other voice at the time of the conversation.*

4. *The fact that the witness was engaged in a prior or subsequent transaction that caused the witness to identify the voice.*

5. *The fact that the witness now knows the other voice.*

6. *Whether there were any other individuals participating in the conversation.*

7. *Who said what to whom.*

*If the witness does not know the person, but has dialed a listed business and participated in a conversation, the following must be established:*

1. *When the conversation took place.*

2. *Where the witness was when the conversation occurred.*

3. *The fact that the witness obtained the number of the business from a current telephone directory.*

4. *The fact that the witness dialed the number that was listed in the directory.*

5. *The fact that the voice that answered acknowledged it was the business entity dialed.*

6. *Whether there were any other individuals participating in the conversation.*

7. *Who said what to whom.*

*Each jurisdiction may have its own rules of evidence as to what may be allowed in the courtroom, and under what circumstances. If a conversation is crucial to your presentation, check the local rules ahead of time so you will know how to get it admitted into evidence.*

## Adverse Witnesses

Sometimes you must call an adverse witness—a witness who from the start is known to be on the opposite side of the case. This is usually necessary to establish an element of your claim or a particular defense. Once you call the witness and announce that you are going to question an adverse witness, the court understands the witness is out of your control. This allows you to use the rules of cross-examination (see Presentation of the Defendant's Case), such as being able to lead the witness. Some adverse witnesses include party opponents and officers, directors, and managing agents of party opponents to a suit.

## Hostile Witness

In the typical Perry Mason scenario, when a supposedly friendly witness drops an unexpected bombshell (on Mason's case) Mason might say, "Your Honor, I would like to have this witness declared a hostile witness." If the judge agrees with the request, the individual is so declared and all the rules used with adverse witnesses apply. The "bombshell" must be a genuine surprise for the court in order for the hostile witness label to be issued.

## Depositions in Court

If a witness is unobtainable (because of illness or some other major obstruction to a court appearance) and if the opposing party has had the opportunity to question that witness in the deposition to be introduced, then the court will probably give its blessing to use the transcript. Here is the procedure that usually occurs:

1.  You describe the portion of the transcript you wish to read.
2.  Your opponent describes the portion he or she wants read.
3.  Objections will take place, if there are any. Once they are dealt with the court will give its okay for the reading of that specific portion.
4.  The transcript of the deposition that has been ruled admissible is read, either with an individual sitting in for the witness or the questioner reading both parts. (Obviously, it is more effective to have the reading staged.)

If the deposition is of a party to the case (as opposed to an uninvolved witness), it may be read or used as evidence to impeach the testimony of that party. However, only the section relevant to the testimony in question may be read. This is similar to using admissions obtained during discovery for the purpose of impeaching testimony.

Finally, if a deposition is used in the case in chief, then you may proceed as if the witness were unobtainable with the same rules being applied.

## Judicial Notice

If the formal proof of certain facts is time-consuming or difficult, you may ask the judge to take "judicial notice" and rule that certain facts are true. There are three categories of items that may be ruled on in this manner, providing opposing counsel's objections do not change the judge's mind:

- Facts that are generally known, such as in geography.
- Facts that can be easily verified, such as Department of Labor life-expectancy figures or the day of the week on a certain date.
- The scientific basis for accepting tests; in other words, radar, blood tests, and so on.

## Use of Exhibits

In any courtroom drama, exhibits become the center of attention. However, before items such as real or demonstrative things or documents or business records can be admitted into evidence, certain procedural steps must be taken, using a witness to authenticate and qualify the evidence. Sometimes more than one witness may be required to provide the necessary testimony for the item to be entered into evidence.

Rules may vary from jurisdiction to jurisdiction, but the following illustrates a complete procedure that may be required to obtain the admission of evidence.

1. Have the exhibit marked for identification. (Normally, the court reporter or court clerk will number each exhibit.)
2. Show the exhibit to the opposition.
3. Ask the court's permission to approach the witness.
4. Show the exhibit to the witness.
5. Lay the foundation for the exhibit (see explanation below).
6. Ask the court to admit the exhibit into evidence.
7. Have the exhibit marked as "evidence." (It was previously marked only for identification.)

8.  If the judge permits the use of the exhibit, hold, mark, and otherwise handle the exhibit for greater effectiveness with the jury.

9.  Ask the court's permission to show or read the exhibit to the jury (this is known as "publishing the exhibit").

10. If the exhibit is complicated or cumbersome, ask the witness to read or describe the important parts of the exhibit to the jury. (The jury can look at the exhibit during recess.)

11. At the end of your case in chief, review the exhibits and the numbers assigned to them with the court to ensure accuracy.

## Laying a Foundation for Evidence

There are three basic requirements for an exhibit to be entered into evidence: (1) The witness who qualifies the exhibit must be competent (in the legal sense); (2) the exhibit must be relevant to the case; and (3) the exhibit must be authenticated by a witness. The witness will usually have first-hand knowledge of the exhibit because he or she will have previously seen the exhibit within the relevant circumstances and thus be competent to testify about it. Relevancy can usually be established, in a discussion with the court, by explaining the exhibit within the context of the issues in the case. Authentication éstablishing that the exhibit is what you say it is may be the problem. The process of authentication is known as "laying a foundation" for the exhibit. The judge will look at the foundations for technical adequacy; the jury will be more concerned with its factual authenticity. There are four basic categories of evidence (see Table 16.1).

Here are some specific foundation requirements for certain exhibits:

*Tangible objects.* The exhibit must be identified by one or more of the senses and be in the same, or substantially the same, condition as when the witness saw it on the relevant date.

*Tangible objects not identified by senses.* Chain of custody must be established—the exhibit must have been secure at all times or have been in a marked, tamper-proof, secured container.

*Photos and motion pictures.* Establish that the photo is an accurate reflection of the scene on the relevant date. The witness is familiar with the scene depicted in the photo and the actual scene on the relevant date.

*Diagrams, models, and maps.* Establish that the witness is familiar with the scene depicted in the exhibit and with the scene on relevant date. This or another witness can also establish that the exhibit is useful in helping to explain testimony and that the exhibit is reasonably accurate.

**Table 16.1.** Categories of Evidence and Foundation Requirements

| Type | Foundation Requirements |
| --- | --- |
| 1. Real evidence, tangible objects. | It must be what it purports to be. |
| 2. Demonstrative evidence, evidence that represents or illustrates the real thing (photographs, diagrams, maps and models). | Okay to use if it accurately represents the real thing. |
| 3. Writings, documents that have legal significance (letters, form contracts, promissory notes, wills, contracts, etc.). | It must in fact be signed by the individual who appears to have signed the document—signatures must be genuine. |
| 4. Records (business papers, such as invoices, shipping documents, telephone memos, and diaries). | Custodian of records or another knowledgeable witness must testify that the record was actually made and maintained by the business. |

*Sound and video recordings.* Establish that the recording was securely stored. Establish that the recording machine was tested before being used and was found to be all right. Establish that the equipment used can actually record sound or sound and images and was used by an experienced operator. The witness must have heard and seen what was being recorded; the tape or film was checked after recording and actually reflects the sound and images made at the time of the recording; the tape or film was secured against tampering during storage. The recording machine in court must be normal and able to accurately reproduce the sound and images. The witness can identify the voices and images of persons on the tape or film.

*Signed instruments.* The witness must know the party's signature or must have seen the party sign the document. The signing party can be called to admit signature; if necessary, call a handwriting expert to testify as to the signature's authenticity.

*Checks.* The witness must identify the signature of the drawer; or call the drawer to state he or she gave the check to the payee (or agent); or call the payee (or agent) to prove receipt, endorsement, and cashing of the check. Call a handwriting expert to testify; or call the payee's bank to qualify microfilm of canceled check as a business record and show the check as deposited in the payee's account.

*Letters (if ruled nonhearsay), or if offer and acceptance as in a contract.*
Establish that the letter is relevant to the case, that the witness received the
letter, and that the witness recognizes signature of party. Establish that the
letter is in the same condition today as it was when first received. (If the
original has been sent out or is not available, then expect to face the requirements of the Best Evidence Rule. See Chapter 10.)

*Business records.* Establish that the record fits into the definition of a
business record. Establish that the witness is the custodian or is qualified to
testify relative to the business record. Establish that the record was made by
a person with knowledge of the facts or made from information transmitted
by a person or persons with knowledge of the facts. Establish when the record
was made relative to the information appearing on it and that the record was
made as a regular practice of the business activity or kept in the course of the
regularly conducted business activity.

Any qualified witness for a business (such as an institution, association,
profession, occupation, or entity of any kind), whether or not the business is
conducted for profit, can be called to testify as to the authenticity of a business
document. Memoranda, reports, records, or data compilation in any form, or
acts, events, conditions, opinions, or diagnosis must be confirmed by a person
with knowledge or made from information transmitted by a person with
knowledge. The witness should be able to identify the person working for the
business who has first-hand knowledge of the facts and initially received,
recorded, or transmitted the information that ultimately appears on the record.
Computer printouts or data compilations can be qualified as evidence like any
other business record, but keep in mind that the *rule of completeness* requires
that when a business record is offered in evidence all parts of that record, in
fairness, should be considered at the same time and must be offered into
evidence.

*Copies.* Establish that an executed original once existed and that a copy of
the original was made. Establish that the copy is a true and accurate copy of
the original, and establish that the original was unintentionally lost or is
unavailable, and the reason for its unavailability. Also establish that a thorough search for the original failed to produce it.

Stipulations, pleadings, and discovery responses are court documents and
may be entered into evidence if they otherwise meet the criteria necessary to
qualify them as evidence, subject to any proper objection from your opponent.
In jury trials, depending on the nature of the exhibit, tangible items that can
be held, seen, or read will garner a large share of the jury's attention.
Therefore, you must think out how your exhibits might interrupt the flow of
the testimony. Once the exhibit is exposed to the jury, give them the oppor-

tunity to examine the admitted evidence as soon as possible in order to satisfy their curiosity and to regain their attention for continued testimony. Expect your opponent to scrutinize your exhibits that have not been previously agreed or stipulated to and to cross-examine the witness on the evidence admitted during the pretrial procedures. Anticipate questions and any weaknesses in your exhibits and be ready to deal with them.

Immediately following your examination of your witnesses and before your side rests, your adversary gets a chance to cross-examine. You'd better believe that your opponent at this time will work hard to impeach or at least blunt or nullify the testimony, pushing your witnesses' statements as far into the neutral zone as possible.

## Examination and Cross-Examination of Witnesses

As we have said before, performing a trial is both science and art. During examination and cross-examination, the science involves meticulous attention to the details—facts, documents, witnesses—and being so familiar with the case that you are likely to know what each witness will answer during questioning before actually hearing the answer. The art has to do with detecting the subtleties of human behavior, and responding to changes in direction that may suddenly take place as you question and probe for the facts and attempt to elicit the truth. Body language, wet palms, dry mouth, and nervous twitches can tell you that a witness may be lying or concealing something. Watching for these signs and adjusting the direction of your questioning can make all the difference between testimony that's meaningful to your side and just more words through which the judge or jury must sift through in their deliberation.

I once sat on a jury in a minor felony case. The prosecutor was out to convict a prior burglary offender and get him off the streets. Material to the case was whether the suspect was in the witness' pickup truck (in which the stolen stereo speakers were found) or whether he was just in the vicinity. The young, inexperienced prosecutor failed in questioning the friendly witnesses. One witness said he "thought" the defendant was in the truck, and another witness placed the suspect in a garbage dumpster nearby. The prosecutor didn't even seem to be aware of the ambiguity.

We of the jury had no choice but to find the defendant guilty only of a lesser charge of petty theft. The conflict prevented a guilty verdict on the grand theft felony charge because of a reasonable doubt that remained in our minds because of the slipshod questioning of the witnesses.

Had the prosecutor been sensitive to the developing testimony, he would have gotten his conviction. His science was well done, but his art was not fully developed.

Here are some general rules that may help when you are examining or cross-examining a witness.

*Preparation.* A thorough review of documents, contingency questions in the event you get answers different from those you expect, color-coding copies of documents with colored highlighters, and a complete grasp of all the facts are important when examining or cross-examining a witness. Without this preparation, you will find yourself swimming upstream, if not drowning.

*The judge may question.* Be prepared for any questions the judge may throw at you or your witness. Not only does the judge have the right to question, he or she may be very skilled at eliciting the truth.

*Box in a witness.* Try to paint an adverse witness into a corner with facts, documents, or testimony you possess (that the witness does not know you have). By laying a foundation to catch the witness in a lie, the lie's importance is magnified and may help to impress the judge or jury.

*Quit while you're ahead.* If you score a meaningful admission or create a dramatic moment for your side and you don't have anything better to follow with, quit! Don't let an important point be diminished by a torrent of unimportant ones, or give the opposition the opportunity to correct or mitigate your coup.

*Move on when you score.* When you score a direct hit, be silent for a moment to underscore it, and then move on. Belaboring the point will lessen the value of the prize.

*Witnesses may believe themselves.* A witness may actually believe what he or she is saying. You may have to delicately take the person on the road to the truth.

*Con artists catch themselves.* Pathological liars, con artists, and the like frequently dig their own graves. If you have one on the witness stand, you may only have to help the lying witness along; the witness will do the rest.

*Scrap petty points.* Don't beat a dead horse is good advice here. Petty points about dead issues will only distract those trying to learn the facts and make a decision.

*Don't abandon ship.* If you are right in a line of questioning, don't give up. Twist, turn, probe, and reword until you get the truth or admission. You'll know when you've reached a point of diminishing returns.

*Finish strong.* Watch the clock and the progression of your questioning. Ending with a witness on a strong point is a plus for yourself. The impression on the judge and jury might help tip the scales in your favor.

*Keep your objective in view.* Keep your focus on the main point(s) at all times. Don't get distracted. Those listening are depending on you to lead them to the truth. Side issues only detract from the main points.

*Humanity helps.* Wit, humor, and personality contribute to the overall picture of an individual. Try to reach into your past experience, be profound, and present yourself as an educated and well-rounded individual.

There are five additional rules expressly for cross-examining witnesses.

*Concentrate on your main adversary.* Fire your most effective ammunition at your main adversary; don't waste it on the little guys or extras who are used for show. The judge is a pro, the jury astute—you will just be harming your presentation by making a mountain out of a molehill.

*Destroy the story.* Use facts and information developed in your discovery and information that you or your witnesses possess to demolish the witness' story or premise. If you cannot destroy the witness with one crushing blow, then chip away at the story until it crumbles.

*Destroy the witness.* Use any means at your disposal to destroy the credibility of the witness. With his or her story exposed as false or at least questionable, and with the weakness in the witness' character exposed, the witness will be a diminished threat to your story and your credibility, and to that of your own witnesses.

*Catch the perjurer.* Remember that the witness is under oath. Exposing a lie not only weakens the opposition but strengthens your side by default. Revealing a lie has a devastating effect, overcoming a strong witness or an otherwise convincing story.

*Do not use open-ended questions.* Don't give an adverse witness the chance to expound with a self-serving speech that benefits your opponent. Ask questions that can be answered "yes" or "no," or with very direct answers. Keep the scope as narrow as possible when questioning an adverse witness.

Finally, if you yourself are being cross-examined as a witness, answer "yes" or "no," or smile! Do not say more than is necessary, and answer directly but without embellishment. If you're in trouble, smile—that may buy you time and goodwill.

## PRESENTATION OF THE DEFENDANT'S CASE

One benefit of being a defendant in a lawsuit is that you don't have to prove anything. In fact, if you can produce enough doubt or uncertainty about your opponent's case, you may even prevail. One defensive tactic to consider using is the "smoke screen" approach. Raise as many proper issues as possible, and challenge your opponent's moves so the plaintiff tires and may actually become willing to capitulate or compromise out of sheer exhaustion. Your opponent may also slip up while trying to find a way through your legal smoke. (Be careful, for frivolous challenges may bring down the wrath of the judge and perhaps the ire of the jury as well.)

As the defendant, you have the right to cross-examine each of the plaintiff's witnesses. Compelling the presence of any adverse party is one of the rights guaranteed to a defendant, along with asking the adverse party leading questions. In other words, the court protects your right to face your adversary—and once he or she is on the witness stand you have the opportunity to use leading questions to your advantage.

You may have the natural human desire to get your hands around a witness' throat (figuratively) and ask questions until he or she chokes. Before you do this, and possibly ruin your case, think about the answers you'll be getting from the plaintiff's witness under cross-examination:

- Will the witness' answers hurt my case?
- What risk will I take in cross-examining?
- Do I really need to cross-examine this witness?
- Will cross-examination provide any favorable testimony?
- What discrediting questions, if any, can I ask?
- Can I find a way to discredit the witness' perception, memory, reputation, or conduct?
- Can I show the witness to be biased, as having prior bad habits, to be inconsistent, or as contradicting the facts?
- Can I impeach the witness?

Unless the answers to these questions are in your favor, don't even consider cross-examining a particular plaintiff's witness.

If you think you can elicit information beneficial to your side or even impeach a witness' testimony, then you should cross-examine. However, you should keep in mind these guidelines:

- Limit your cross-examination to a few basic points that support your theory of the case.
- Start strong and end strong.

- Try to keep the witness from perceiving your purpose or goal. It may help to vary your subject matter.
- Don't play, "Say it again, Sam"; get support for your case or don't go any further. The witness' original testimony does not need to be reheard.
- Play it safe—ask questions to which you know the answers.
- Stop explanations! Hostile witnesses are always looking for a way to slip in damaging material.
- Try to ask questions that would tend to agree with your statement of fact.
- Lead up to major points bit by bit.

Your basic goal is to suggest, through the witness' responses on cross-examination, that the testimony given on direct examination is less true than it initially appeared. By discrediting facts originally stated by the witness, you damage the jury's perception of the witness' story. If you can discredit the witness, his or her testimony may be called into question.

## Impeachment

Impeachment is a dramatic way to bring into question facts presented by a witness. Statutes and case law, as well as local custom, govern the procedures of impeachment. However, there are a few prerequisites before you can use the tactic. First, you must in good faith believe that what you are about to disclose is in fact true. The use of insupportable material in an impeachment attempt is forbidden. Second, for reasons of fairness and judicial economy, impeachment must be raised during cross-examination. Third, you must be able to "prove up" your position if required. Obviously, if the witness admits to the impeachment, there is no need for proof. However, if the witness unequivocally denies the impeachment, then you must put your proof on the table. In the event the witness' answer is on a matter that is collateral (those items in a case not connected with the central issue), just accept the witness' answer. However, if the witness' answer is on a noncollateral matter that reaches to the heart of the case, then the impeachment must be proved with hard evidence. Fourth, you must prove up the hard evidence (on noncollateral matters only) the very next time the witness is available for testimony.

There are seven basic areas of impeachment under the federal rules of evidence: Bias and interest, prior bad acts, prior convictions, prior inconsistent statements, contradictory facts, bad reputation or opinion of truthfulness, and treatises. All of these areas, except prior convictions, have some bearing for the civil justice system.

*Bias and interest.* This category also includes prejudice. Bias and interest are always considered noncollateral and therefore must be proven with evidence. An example of this would be to expose an employment relationship that means the witness is not an impartial or objective witness.

*Prior bad acts.* Only certain jurisdictions allow impeachment in this area. Check local rules for this category, which would include such items as submitting false loan applications or inaccurate employment applications as a basis for the impeachment.

*Prior inconsistent statements.* This is the most common form of impeachment. For this to be legally effective, the witness must have a chance to admit, deny, or explain making the inconsistent statement. If the statement is noncollateral, it is still necessary to prove the witness incorrect with tangible evidence.

*Contradictory facts.* This is usually called "impeachment by contradiction." In this instance, if an impeaching question is asked during cross-examination and the witness denies it, then it will be necessary to offer proof of the impeachment and whether the fact being discussed is collateral or noncollateral to the case.

*Bad reputation or opinion of truthfulness.* A witness' truthfulness is relevant to his or her credibility when appearing in a trial. Once a witness has been attacked, the proponent of the witness can present supporting testimony and personal opinion evidence to support the truthfulness of the witness.

*Treatises.* Expert witnesses may be impeached by using treatises, periodicals, and pamphlets if the author of the treatise is a reliable authority in the field. This may be established through the testimony of witnesses or another expert witness or by judicial notice. Once the authority has been established, the appropriate impeaching part of the treatise can be read into evidence.

As mentioned before, you must prove impeachment the very next time you call the witness. For instance, if a witness impeaches himself during the plaintiff's case in chief, you must call the offending witness and ask the impeaching question or questions after the plaintiff has rested and during your turn at bat. Next, you would call a witness who can specifically testify to the impeaching fact discovered in the original testimony by the plaintiff's witness in his direct case.

## Objections to Evidence

Since the plaintiff's case is presented first, the defendant has the first shot at objections to evidence (and testimony) used by the plaintiff. You should be aware of several possible objections to the use of evidence. (Hassles over certain testimony and evidence may have been worked out during discovery, especially when pretrial discovery was extensive.)

- *Statutory exclusion:* The law does not permit the use of a piece of evidence; for example, illegally tape recorded conversations.
- *Work product:* This evidence presented is preliminary work, such as backup notes and accounting sheets of a financial statement.
- *Hearsay:* The witness was not present during the out-of-court conversation or event. (See Chapter 10.)
- *Best evidence:* For example, the authenticity of a copy of the original document was not established.
- *Trade secret:* The information presented is proprietary, such as a chemical formula or food preparation.
- *Relevancy/materiality:* The questions do not have a direct bearing on the case and may be out of bounds relative to issues at hand.
- *Privilege:* Specially protected communications. (See Chapter 10.)

## Defense Witnesses

After cross-examining the plaintiff's witness (when it is to your advantage to do so), and after objecting to evidence (where cause can be found for a valid objection), your next salvo is calling defense witnesses. Just as the plaintiff is not permitted to hold back proof in the direct case (so as to make a big impression at a later stage), you as the defendant now have the obligation in your direct defense to produce all defensive evidence. Such proof is usually in the form of rebuttal to the plaintiff's testimony and evidence. Unless affirmative defenses, setoffs, and counterclaims are involved, you should attack the plaintiff's evidence and the credibility of the plaintiff's witnesses with the plaintiff's own evidence and witnesses. If counterclaims or setoffs are involved, you should offer supportive testimony to that end. Of course, just as you had the opportunity to rebut the plaintiff's case, so too will the plaintiff have an opportunity to rebut your direct case.

When the rebuttals finally end and the judge rules that the case is ready for final arguments, each side will have one more chance to convince the judge and jury of the correctness of its position.

## CLOSING ARGUMENTS

It is recognized that along with opening statements, closing arguments are a vital part of winning a lawsuit. The elements that make a persuasive closing argument are those that bring the testimony and evidence together into a cohesive picture projecting the theory of your case. These elements fall into two categories—classical oratory (the art of persuasion) and content.

To be successful, persuasion requires effective rhetoric. According to Aristotle, effective rhetoric contains ethos, pathos, and logos. Ethos may be regarded as the attitude of the orator in relation to the audience. Pathos speaks to the passions and emotions of life. Logos encompasses reason and logic—a rational approach to a problem. Therefore, any persuasive closing argument must contain a connection between the speaker and the audience—a degree of emotional content, a slice of life—embodied in a logical and rational package. By blending the basic elements of rhetoric, the speaker builds a framework for the closing argument. The facts of the case become the building blocks that complete the structure.

Despite the popular picture of eloquent oration swaying the minds of twelve diverse citizens, it is generally believed that eloquence alone has little bearing on the decision of a modern jury. Whereas eloquence played a major role in the simpler society of yesteryear, our society favors the analytical and scientific side of life.

Abraham Lincoln was a renowned trial lawyer before he became President. Lincoln's reputation for fairness reached legendary proportions when he was actually asked to argue an opponent's case. His style of oration was great in its simplicity and rich in its emotional appeal, and it conjured up an image of an individual who was just and fair and therefore had to be believed.

An example of Lincoln's expertise is available in the Rock Island Bridge case (1856). Here is the case, in brief.

The Rock Island railroad bridge, spanning the Mississippi River from Rock Island, Illinois to Davenport, Iowa, enabled the railroads to compete with river transportation for the lucrative freight hauling business. One day, the steamship *Effie Afton* carelessly rammed into the bridge's pilings and sank. (Some say it was deliberate; see P. C. Lagarias, *Effective Closing Argument*, Charlottesville, VA: Michie Company, 1989, Chapter 5.) A lawsuit was filed claiming that no bridge could safely be placed on the Mississippi and that the existing bridge obstructed river traffic. Lincoln was the attorney for the defendant. The lawsuit was described as follows (*The Rock Island Bridge Case*, 73 U.S. 213, 213-214, 18 L.E. 753 [1867]):

> [The plaintiff] alleged that, by law and the public treaties of the United States, the Mississippi is, for the distance of 2,000 miles a public navigable stream and common highway, free and open to all the citizens of the United States, who are entitled to navigate the same by sailing and steam vessels, and otherwise, without

impediment or obstruction; that the Rock Island Bridge obstructed the free navigation of the stream; and that by collision with this obstruction the steam vessel of the [plaintiff] had been injured.

Lincoln's final arguments in the case indicate his tremendous grasp of the facts. He began by asserting that the bridge had a right to be there and that people had the right to cross that body of water as well as to sail up and down it. He supported his argument with evidence from the record, including facts and figures on the frequent use of both the railroad bridge and the waterway. Lincoln said, "The proper mode for all parties in this affair is to live and let live. . . ." He next dispensed with the problem of conflicting testimony, doing so in a manner designed to evoke ethos. Lincoln discussed angles, size and shape, currents, and various mathematical formulas affecting speed and distance. Then, in his rebuttal argument, he turned to sarcasm (toward concepts, not individuals):

It is suggested as a way out of the difficulty that a tunnel be built under the river; but there is not a tunnel that is a successful project in this world. A suspension bridge cannot be built so high but that the chimneys of the boats will grow up till they cannot pass. The steamboat men will take pains to make them grow. The cars of a railroad cannot without immense expense rise high enough to get even with a suspension bridge or go low enough to get through a tunnel; such expense is unreasonable.

He then concluded his rebuttal by placing his adversaries on the defensive.

The plaintiffs have to establish that the bridge is a material obstruction and that they have managed their boat with reasonable care and skill. As to the last point, high winds have nothing to do with it, for it was not a windy day. They must show due skill and care. Difficulties going downstream will not do, for they were going upstream. Difficulties with barges in tow have nothing to do with the accident, for they had no barge.

The case resulted in a hung jury, which was considered by all as a great victory for Lincoln.

A closing argument is a carefully woven blend of rhetorical questions, review of evidence and testimony, judiciously worded jury instructions, and as much friendly persuasion as the orator can deliver. From the plaintiff's point of view, its content should be considered as two separate entities: The closing address and the rebuttal. Since the plaintiff initiates the action and has the burden of proof, our system allows the plaintiff not only to have the first closing argument, but also to rebut the defendant's closing argument.

It is generally considered prudent to place your main points in the closing argument rather than saving them for the rebuttal. The defense might waive its right to a final argument, or limit the argument's scope, and then those salient points that you saved for rebuttal would never be heard. Plan to use twice as much time on the closing as on the rebuttal so you will be assured of stating your important arguments (regardless of what the defense does), and you will still have time for a solid rebuttal.

Regarding the content of your argument: Argue your strengths, not your weaknesses, and emphasize affirmative evidence produced at the trial. This does not mean that you should ignore weak points; by pointing them out yourself, you may disarm your opponent and gain respect from the jury for your candor. You should then concentrate on a theme and hammer away.

Since a piece of information becomes a fact only when a judge and jury believe it to be true, you should allot time for selectively chosen testimony to be presented in a fashion that creates an oral mural that depicts your contentions. Develop a picture that will help convince the jury that the facts are on your side. "Arguing facts involves more than a simple recitation of the testimony. It involves analysis. Jurors decide cases on the basis of impressions (of) what they think the truth is based on the way the parties have presented the evidence." (Mauet, *Fundamentals of Trial Techniques*, page 272.)

Since the negative of any picture is less attractive than the positive, your summation should be filled with positive images, not defensive issues. It should develop a life of its own, with a theme, or themes, taken from evidence presented at the trial and played back for the jury with all the richness the orator's intellect can provide.

And finally, like a salesperson, you must be able to close the deal; you must effectively state, in clear and simple terms, the reasons you are entitled to prevail.

Here are some do's and don'ts to consider when constructing your closing argument.

- Present your theory of the case and support it with facts in a logical structure.
- Do not present your personal beliefs about guilt, credibility, or quality of evidence.

- Use exhibits both as effective tools of persuasion and as a break from rhetoric.
- Weave the jury instructions into your presentation of the facts and testimony. Explain such terms as burden of proof and credibility of witnesses, and define legal terms.
- Rhetorical questions can be effective, but use them sparingly for maximum impact.
- Minimize your use of written notes. If you read your argument, you will inhibit the very important eye contact with the jurors, which will tend to have a negative effect.
- Stories and anecdotes can be effective, but must be short and to the point.
- Use understatement to change the pace and to stimulate thinking.
- Do not argue that there is additional evidence that you were not able to provide the judge and jury.
- Do not attack the court or opposing counsel for excluding evidence.
- Unsupported inferences or suggestions regarding unestablished facts are not allowed as a suggestion to the jury.
- Some jurisdictions require relevancy between evidence cited in the summation and issues in the case.
- Always be faithful to the facts as established. Do not imply the truth of facts not established by evidence.

Of all the techniques used in a closing argument, using jury instructions to make a point seems to be one of the most important. To quote Mauet, "Closing arguments that selectively utilize instructions have a greater impact on the jury. By suggesting that the court's instructions of law as well as the facts support your side, a doubly effective argument can be fashioned."

Here is an outline of a closing argument on which you can build (on page 351 appears an annotated version of an actual closing argument):

1. Introduction.

2. Review of parties.

3. Description of scene or general circumstances.

4. Damages (if defendant).

5. Legal issues.

6. Facts.

7.  Conclusion based on issues and facts (liability or nonliability).

8.  Corroboration (using evidence).

9.  Weakness of the other side's point of view.

10. Jury instructions.

11. Damages (if plaintiff).

12. Final points.

13. Conclusion.

The case is now placed in the hands of the jury, with the basic assumption that the truth will win out. Or will it? It may be comforting to believe that it will, just as it may have been comforting to believe that ordeal by fire would bring out the truth. But you must acknowledge that we live in age of jury specialists, consultants, big legal budgets, and the like, and that the system now, more than ever, is less than perfect. Still, we continue to believe in it and try to make it work or to make it work better.

Yet it's not really a question of how well the system works, but of how well you use the system. As we have detailed in this book, before the case is placed in the hands of the judge or jury, there are many facets of the process (some in your control, some not) that ultimately influence the result. Thorough discovery, careful research, meticulous attention to rules, thoughtful analysis and presentation of legal theory, and meaningful opening and closing statements are just steps along the way to what we hope will be a successful conclusion for you.

# CHAPTER 17

# Reconsideration—Appeals

*There must be a final tribunal somewhere for deciding every question in the world.*

—Joseph P. Bradley

The United States appellate system has been described as having "no equal today or in ages past in terms of utility and breadth of review, accessibility to the populace, and structure of deliberation." (F. Coffin, *The Ways of a Judge*, Boston: Houghton Mifflin, 1980.) This was not always the case.

Section I of the Constitution establishes a court system, but does not specifically mention an appellate system: "The judicial power of the United States shall be vested in one supreme court, and in such inferior courts as the Congress may from time to time ordain and establish. . . ." It was left to Congress and state legislatures, as empowered by this clause, to devise a system of appeals. With no specific mandate, the appellate process "in both the federal and state systems became procedural mine fields." (Robert Martineau, *Modern Appellate Practice*, Rochester, NY: Lawyer's Cooperative Publishing, 1983.)

Our early system of appeals, derived from the vestiges of two English systems of review—error and appeal (see Development of the Appeals System on page 284)—was fraught with technicalities, from simply preserving an issue for review to the balance of the procedural requirements. As Professor Roscoe Pound states (*Appellate Procedures in Civil Cases*, Boston: Little, Brown, 1943): "Appellate procedure in the last century was largely taken up with rules as to what the appellate court could not do in the way of insuring that there had been a right decision on the law and evidence below [in the

# Development of the Appeals System

*In the ancient civilizations surrounding the Mediterranean, if a decision by an official went against you, your only recourse was to appeal to the king, the ultimate authority. In Greek and early Roman times, the prevailing philosophy was "juries decide all." To attack a judgment, you had to start a new action in the original court. As the Roman justice system became more sophisticated, appeal to the emperor was allowed in cases of death penalties and imprisonment only. Between then and the development of English common law in the Middle Ages, about the only review of a formal judgment or penalty was provided in the canon law of the Roman Catholic Church.*

*By the 1700s, the English review process was developing two distinct types of action: The writ of error and the appeal. In the former, the plaintiff in error (as the appellant was called) arranged for a copy of the lower court record to be sent to the court of review. If a matter to be raised was not in the record, a bill of exceptions had to be prepared, citing alleged errors of law made in the trial and not shown on the record. This bill was approved by the trial judge and appended to the record. The defendant in error then had a chance to respond to the plaintiff's filing before the court of review.*

*In the latter system, the appellant filed a document called a petition and appeal. (A bond was also required to cover costs.) The appellee was ordered to file an answer, and oral arguments were heard. Any matters in the case, whether or not they were in the trial record, could be reviewed. Then a judgment was rendered by the reviewing body—the House of Lords.*

*The difference between the two systems was that under a writ of error, only errors of law could be reviewed, whereas under an appeal, matters of both law and fact could be explored.*

lower court]." Obviously, reform was necessary, and such efforts finally began in the early twentieth century. The appellate process continues to change, becoming more accessible and emphasizing deciding cases on their merits rather than on procedural technicalities.

## APPELLATE COURT PROCEDURE

The United States Supreme Court has found that due process does not have to include appellate review. "We Americans have no right to appeal except by statute" (*National Union of M.C. & S. v. Arnold*, 348 U.S. 37, 99 Led. 46 75 Sct. 92 [1954]). However, our lawmakers have now provided most of us with a system of appellate review incorporating such important criteria as the following:

- Timely review by a body of judges.
- Review of the merits of the trial court's final judgment .
- Statements of reason by the appellate court (written decisions after parties involved have submitted their views on the issues, when applicable).
- Due consideration of the issues based on the complexity of the case.

Because of the streamlining of the appellate process, and the growing complexity of our society, appellate courts have seen a huge increase in activity since the early 1960s. Along with that increase in activity has come an increase in publicity, making the general public much more aware of the process. Most of us have come to think that if we lose a lawsuit, we have another chance to win on appeal. What the legal professionals know, and laypeople don't, is that in order to appeal a lost case to a higher court, you must have an appealable issue. You might find an issue in your trial that meets the criteria for review by a higher court, but it's neither certain nor guaranteed. Therefore, to make review by a higher court possible, you must find in the proceedings an error of law that has resulted in a miscarriage of justice.

Since there are no due process rights involved in the appellate process, and all requirements are determined by statute and court rules, you will have to understand the rules and follow them rigorously. The lack of due process rights also eliminates much of the case law that builds up around constitutionally mandated law. Therefore, the appellate process has only nine common law principles that are generally considered to apply to most of the appellate jurisdictions in the country. Along with the legislative requirements and each district's rules of court, these nine principles are what you should understand and follow.

*Note:* If you are contemplating an appeal, you must review your jurisdiction's rules, the appropriate state or federal statutes, and the rules of the court to which you wish to appeal.

Let's look at and discuss the nine principles.

1. Before an appeal can be heard, a lower court decision must be final.

Justice Sullivan has indicated the general attitude of the court system regarding the fact that a decision must be final before an appellate court will act: "There is a strong policy against piecemeal adjudication of controversies." Not only would any other policy, if implemented, disturb the normally uninterrupted proceedings at the trial level that permits a single complete review (of an issue), but the inconvenience, expense, and delay resulting from fragmentation of the trial process would be untenable. Although no exact definition of final action exists, a frequently quoted decision (*Catlin v. United States*, 324 U.S. 229, 233 [1945]) states that a final judgment, when entered, "ends the litigation on the merits and leaves nothing for the court to do but execute the judgment."

2. New issues (those not covered in the original trial) cannot be raised on appeal.

The term *scope* is used to designate the depth or breadth of review considered proper by the appellate system. Since the scope, relative to review, is limited, appeal aspirations must be considered during the original proceedings. In other words, you must cover all the bases in your original proceedings to ensure the possibility of an appeal. If you don't make the proper preparations, you might receive a ruling like this: "Since this issue is raised for the first time on appeal, the trial court has not been afforded an opportunity to determine the merits of appellant's assertion. If the issue had been presented to the trial court . . . its ruling thereon would, of course, be subject to review by this court" (*Number GAC Corp. v. Beach*, 308 So.2d 550 [Fl.2d DLA 1975]). There are valid reasons for this principle:

• To prevent a party from deliberately holding back an issue to provide grounds for appeal.
• To prevent the cost in time and docket congestion for appeals that border on the frivolous.
• To provide the original trial judge and parties to the case the opportunity to take remedial action on an issue brought to their attention.

3. Issues of jurisdiction may be decided by the appellate court at its own discretion.

There are but two exceptions to the rule regarding an appellate court hearing a matter that has not yet been finalized in a lower court: (1) An appellate court will usually hear a matter of jurisdiction; (2) the appellate court may act to correct *fundamental error*, *manifest injustice*, or *plain error*. In other words, if there is a ruling in an ongoing case in a trial court and a jurisdictional issue goes against a party, that issue may be brought to an appellate court forthwith. Fundamental error is such that the error in law is apparent on the face of the record or proceeding and is clearly reversible. The doctrine of plain error encompasses those errors which, if uncorrected, would be an affront to the integrity and reputation of the judicial proceeding (the same for manifest injustice).

4. The time frame for filing an appeal is rigid.

In all jurisdictions, the appellate process is started when a party files a notice of appeal. The filing of this notice, however, is governed by very strict requirements (both statutory and as a matter of court rule). Certain factors can affect when the clock starts to tick on the allotted time to file the notice. If a party to a case timely files a motion for a rehearing with the original trial court, the case is not over and the time to file an appeal is effectively extended, preserving the right until the motion is resolved and the case can be brought to a final judgment. If an application for a new trial affecting multiple defendants or plaintiffs is filed, the question affecting all concerned must be satisfied before the case can be concluded. In most instances, no notice of appeal can be filed until all questions affecting all plaintiffs and all defendants are answered (except when a final judgment is rendered by the court to one or more of the parties).

In some jurisdictions, the allotted time within which to file the notice of appeal is usually considered to begin with the court's oral announcement of the judgment. A notice of appeal may also be given orally (*Brooks v. Goaden*, 318 S.E2d 348[N.C. App. 1984]). Even service of the notice of appeal may have requirements attached to it, so our caveat regarding statutes and jurisdictional rules must be well respected.

5. The appellant must be a party with standing in the original action.

Only those persons who are actually parties to an action may file an appeal. Sympathizers, witnesses, and even those with the official status of *amicus curiae* (friend of the court) cannot be considered a party with status. The accepted definition of a party is "a person who commences or against whom relief is sought in a matter" (42 Pa. C.S. Section 102).

6. Review of appellate issues is confined to the record of the lower court.

Nowhere in appellate law are the vestiges of ancient tradition as visible as in the appellate court's refusal to consider anything beyond the record in its review of a lower court decision. This is the best place to explain the purpose and intent of the appellate system. In simple terms, it is error correction.

The original *writ of error*, on which so much of the appellate process is based, was originally considered a new lawsuit filed by the losing party. It was a lawsuit against the judge attacking the error made by the judge at the trial. Since the judge could hardly be held accountable for making a wrong decision on an issue that was never presented at trial, the new lawsuit excluded anything that was not on the record in the original lawsuit. Hence, from a historical perspective, only issues raised at the trial level qualified for appellate review.

This principle is still followed today, and here are some reasons. If a losing party were permitted to raise an error during appeal that was not raised at the original trial, the party could "build in" an error to guarantee a successful appeal. (A good way to bring an error to the trial court's attention is a posttrial motion. You might have the motion granted, or at least you would have done everything possible at the trial level before approaching the appellate level.) Also, if it were not the practice to exclude new issues, the need for a thorough, well-prepared trial would be diminished by an "I'll catch it in appeal" attitude. That attitude would reduce the quality of trials. The principle of what is required for an appeal is well stated by Judge Ruggero Aldisert:

> For a reviewing court to determine that there is reversible error, three critical prerequisites must be implicated in the judicial error-correcting process. It is necessary that: (a) There are specific acts or omissions by the trial court constituting legal error; (b) these acts or omissions were properly suggested as error to the trial court; (c) if uncorrected on that level, they are properly presented for review to the appellate court. For there to be reversible error, it is mandatory for the appellant properly to identify the error to the trial court and to suggest a legally appropriate course of action (*Pfeiffer v. Jones and Laughlin Steel Corp.*, 678 F2d 453 [1982, CA 3 Pa]).

This appellate court philosophy is reflected in Federal Rules of Civil Procedure Rule 46: "Mak(e) known to the court the action which he desires the court to take or his objection to the action and his grounds therefor."

England moved beyond its tradition of strict error correction within the appellate process with the Judicature Act of 1873, which provided the appellate court with full authority to receive new evidence and to render whatever judgment the appellate court believed appropriate. This broadened scope has never been accepted in the United States, although there are some exceptions and limitations to the general rule regarding what the appellate court will consider that may not have been part of the original record.

Appellate courts will usually agree to review a matter, regardless of the status of the original action, if any of the parties have a new status (i.e., death, divorce, etc.) or if a new court decision has come down that affects the case at hand. In addition, jurisdiction regarding subject matter (which cannot be given or waived by the parties) may also be subject to review by the appellate court *sua sponte* (on their own initiative).

There are several other situations that will be reviewed by a court of appeals. The court may find an error not noticed by the appellant, or it may want to change an underlying legal rule that had been accepted by the parties to the case in its old form. In an adversary system such as ours, the parties to an action control the issues presented to the court. However, the court can take control of the issues, especially if it wants to change the existing law. The court may simply raise issues the parties ignored.

Now we get to a really tricky exception that requires an understanding of the difference between issues of fact and issues of law. Appellate courts will review a case on the basis of issues of law, but will not reevaluate facts. Appellate review is concerned with the proper application of law; it is not concerned with retrying the case or determining factual issues, which is the task of the trial court.

7. The concept of waiver (that the appellant could have taken some action at the original trial) is enforced.

If a party to a lawsuit fails to make an objection, that lack of action is considered a waiver. Waiving one's rights (intentionally or out of ignorance) precludes later appellate review.

8. An all-out effort will be made by the appellate court to sustain the lower court.

It's a basic principle that appellate courts are reluctant to disturb what has transpired in lower courts. The unwritten and unspoken presumption is that the lower court was correct. Two opinions speak to the appellate court's attitude on the subject: "There is a presumption that the judgment below was correct, and the appellant has the burden in asserting error to show it by the record" (*Attwell v. Heritage Bank of Mt. Pleasant*, 161 Ga.App. 193, 194(2),

291 S.E.2d 28 [1982]). "Trial court error is never presumed. To obtain appellate reversal of a judgment, it is appellant's burden to make it affirmatively appear that the judgment is erroneous" (*Denton v. Sunflower Electric Cooperative*, 12 Kan.App.2d 262, 740 P.2d 98 [1987]).

The following are some parameters used by the courts to help them affirm trial court decisions.

When it comes to evidence, no appellate court wants to second-guess a trial court. As Hon. Walter Rogosheske writes in *The Art of Advocacy* (New York: Matthew Bender, 1981), "Any appellant should think not only twice, but a hundred times, before attempting an appeal that requires a disturbance of the finding of fact in the trial court." Here it is in strong case language from court decisions:

> In weighing the evidence, the trial court was entitled to reject certain evidence and accept other evidence. If the evidence which the trial court chose to accept is competent and credible, we may not substitute our judgment for that of the trial court and determine the judgment to be against the manifest weight of the evidence merely because there is other evidence which the trial court rejected, which would permit a contrary result, and which this court would consider to be more credible than that accepted by the trial court (*Branford Village Condo. Unit v. Upper Arlington*, 12 Ohio App.3d 120, 467 N.E.2d 542 [1983]).

And in even more positive terms, simple and to the point, the courts have held, "A jury verdict will be sustained by this Court where the record discloses a sufficient evidentiary basis" (*Girror v. Carpenter*, 136 Vt. 290, 292, 388 A.2d 831, 833 [1978]). In fact, if the verdict is justified by any reasonable view of the evidence, it must stand (*Crawford v. State Highway Board*, 130 Vt. 18, 25, 285 A.2d 760, 764 [1971]).

The doctrine of "harmless error" is also used by appellate courts to sustain lower court rulings. The court will admit an error did occur but that it did not affect the outcome of the case. Here are one court's words on this type of error: "We have held error which does not prejudice the substantial rights of a party affords no basis for reversal of a judgment and must be disregarded (*Kansas Savings and Loan Ass'n v. Rich Eckel Construction Co., Inc.*, Kan 493, Syl. Para. 1, 576 P.2d 212 [1978]).

There is one exception to appellate courts not tampering with evidence in lower courts, and its roots are historically clear. Actions in equity, equal to the old "appeal" in English law, are approached by appellate courts differently from the *writ of error* appeals from common law trial courts. Here are the words of one court on the subject: "In an action in equity . . . we are entitled to find (the) facts in accordance with . . . (our) view of the preponderance of the evidence" (*Townes Associates, Ltd. v. City of Greenville*, 266 S.C. 81, 86, 221 S.E.2d 773, 775 [1976]).

9.  Trial courts must have been given opportunity to correct the error.

Perhaps the most important element in preserving an issue for review is a litigant's obligation to make a problem known to the trial judge on a timely basis. One appellate court decision put it very well: "In objecting to instructions, counsel must state distinctly the matter to which he objects and the grounds of his objection, apprising the trial judge of the nature and substance of the objection."

Here's a list of common situations in trial that must be called to the trial judge's attention to preserve your right to appeal.

- Prejudicial and nonresponsive answers.
- A proffer of evidence that was excluded on opponent's objection. (When evidence is excluded by the court, you may "proffer"—put on the record—the evidence you want admitted.)
- Testimony of witnesses that was objected to at trial.
- Challenged statements of opposing counsel made at trial.
- Improper denial of requested jury instructions.
- Objection made to jury instructions at the time they were given to the jury by the court.
- Timely objection made in court of an opponent's alleged misconduct.
- Objection made to a special verdict.
- Challenge of sufficiency of evidence to support jury's verdict or judge's findings of fact at the trial.
- Timely objections made to all matters now claimed to be irregular or prejudicial.
- Failure to give specific grounds for objections made to opponent's evidence (allowing the judge to rule on technical correctness of evidence).
- Posttrial motions made for new trial, based on now-claimed prejudicial error or errors.

## STRUCTURE AND PURPOSE OF THE APPELLATE SYSTEM

Now that you have some understanding of the parameters of appellate court thinking and procedure (what constitutes a possibly reversible error and what is not grounds for an appeal), we can take a closer look at the workings of the appellate system.

There are twelve federal circuit courts of appeal. (Table 17.1 indicates the circuits, which states each serves, and each one's base of operations.) You probably know them as, for example, the United States Court of Appeals for the Eighth Circuit. In 1925, the jurisdiction of the United States Supreme Court was made entirely discretionary. This made the decisions of the appellate courts final in all but those few cases in which the Supreme Court exercises its discretion. The Court of Appeals decisions are usually made by three-judge panels. (Under certain conditions and questions of exceptional importance, the entire panel of active judges—eleven in Florida—may sit *en banc* to participate in a decision.)

The structure and organization of the state appellate system differs greatly from state to state. There are also major differences between the state and federal systems. In some states, the highest courts have little discretion, with an appeal to them a matter of right. Other states have intermediate courts between the trial courts and the highest court, which may cover different jurisdictions. In a majority of the states with intermediate courts, appeals end with those courts; they do not automatically travel up to their highest court. However, in certain classes of cases, a direct appeal to the state high court may be permissible. You can see that these differences will have an enormous impact on someone attempting to enter the system with an appeal. The effect that these differences have on practical matters must be considered, as methods of practice vary from jurisdiction to jurisdiction:

- The length of time required for paperwork mailed to reach the courts and be clocked in.
- Whether, where, and if a case will be argued orally and/or only with briefs.
- The size of the panel of judges that will hear the case.
- The particular judges who will hear the case.
- The past decisions that are a binding precedent for the particular court.
- Types of cases and issues that can be presented to a particular court.
- Procedural matters.

Within the appellate system two categories of courts exist: Intermediate courts and courts of last resort. (Thirty-six states plus the federal system have

### Table 17.1. Federal Circuit Courts of Appeal

| Circuit | Area Covered | Location |
| --- | --- | --- |
| District of Columbia | District of Columbia | Washington, DC |
| First | Maine, New Hampshire, Massachusetts, Rhode Island, Puerto Rico | Boston |
| Second | Vermont, New York, Connecticut | New York City |
| Third | Delaware, Pennsylvania, New Jersey, Virgin Islands | Philadelphia |
| Fourth | West Virginia, Virginia, Maryland, North Carolina, South Carolina | Richmond, Asheville |
| Fifth | Louisiana, Texas, Mississippi | New Orleans, Fort Worth, Jackson |
| Sixth | Michigan, Ohio, Kentucky, Tennessee | Cincinnati |
| Seventh | Wisconsin, Illinois, Indiana | Chicago |
| Eighth | North Dakota, South Dakota, Nebraska, Minnesota, Iowa, Missouri, Arkansas | St. Louis, Kansas City, Omaha, St. Paul |
| Ninth | Washington, Oregon, Idaho, Montana, California, Nevada, Arizona, Alaska, Hawaii, Guam, North Mariana Islands | Portland, Los Angeles, San Francisco, Seattle |
| Tenth | Wyoming, Utah, Colorado, Kansas, New Mexico, Oklahoma | Denver, Wichita, Oklahoma City |
| Eleventh | Alabama, Georgia, Florida | Montgomery, Atlanta, Jacksonville |

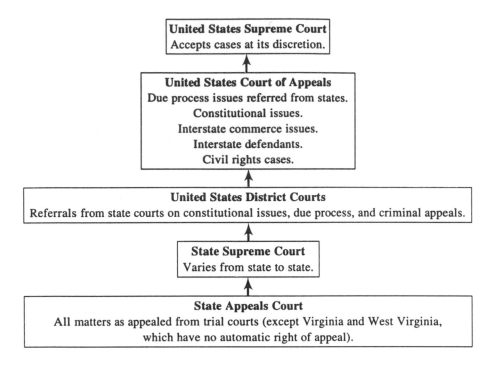

**Figure 17.1.**  How the state and federal court systems interact

intermediate courts.) Without becoming overly technical, the difference between the two categories is the stringency of their requirements for accepting
a case for appeal. Any decision that you make as to which is the proper court
for appeal should be made in consultation with a professional or, at the very
least, with considerable further study.

Figure 17.1 shows the interaction between the state and federal systems.
You should consider this information, and many additional factors—interstate issues, location of defendants, constitutional issues, and jurisdictional
issues—before choosing whether to file in federal or state appellate court.

Once it appears that you might have the makings of an appeal, use the
following checklist to help you make the final decision. Unless you can
answer all five questions affirmatively, you should not file an appeal without
a great deal of further study.

1.  Does the record clearly show an error sufficient to justify reversal?

2.  Did you provide the judge at your original trial with a chance to correct
    the alleged error or errors?

3. Is an appeal in your best financial interest?

4. Do you have an effective answer to the claims that your opponent will probably make?

5. Are the results of your legal research on the issue on your side?

According to the Honorable Walter Rogosheske (*Art of Advocacy*, New York: Matthew Bender, 1981), some understanding of how the appellate court thinks about certain issues will help you win your appeal. He states what the appellate judges think the appellate process is designed to accomplish: "It is to regulate a government's dealings with its citizens, to gain their cooperation and respect, and to permit the operation of the rule of law instead of the rule of man, through the time-honored vehicle of precedent."

In order for your appeal to have a chance of acceptance by an appellate court, it must fit into one of the following accepted categories used by the court system:

- Review for correctness.
- Trial court harmony.
- Review regarding the law.

The first category is concerned with the correctness of the trial procedure, how the decision affects the parties, and evidentiary questions. According to Rogosheske, the following questions are open to review for correctness:

- Was the plaintiff entitled to the verdict?
- Was the judge fair?
- Was the jury reasonable in its approach?
- Was the verdict adequate (too little, too much)?
- Did the judge rule correctly on the admissibility of evidence?
- Were the instructions to the jury consistent with the law covering the rights of both parties?
- Did bias and prejudice intervene to cause any unfair results?
- Were errors at the trial called to the judge's attention in posttrial proceedings?
- Overall, did a manifest injustice result?

The second category concerns discord or harmony in the trial court system on a particular issue. Various judges, even those in the same state, may interpret or apply a law differently. It becomes the duty of the appellate system to bring harmony to the court system, eliminating dissonance in the application of those laws that may be interpreted variously by different judges within the same jurisdiction.

As we have indicated, our system of law is always changing to meet the sociopolitical pressures of an ever-more-complex society. Thus, the third category concerns the court's responsibility to effect change by making law, by interpreting and applying the law, and thus by establishing precedent. An appeal may have a chance of success on the basis of the appellate judge's decision to reinterpret, change, or expand the law or statute, reversing the trial court's decision and parenthetically saying, "The trial court may have been correct based on past interpretation of the law, but after reexamination we feel the law actually means this. . . ."

## APPELLATE PROCEDURES

Now let's turn to the procedural side of the appellate system. If you or your counsel, after careful examination of your case, are actually going to file an appeal, here are the steps that will lead to possible appellate acceptance and decision:

1. File a timely *notice of appeal* with the correct court.

2. Be sure the *record* of the trial is transcribed.

3. Arrange for the *record* (consisting of the transcription of the trial, all court papers, filed discovery, and documents and evidence that had been admitted into evidence) to be transferred to the appellate court. Some jurisdictions may have an automatic procedure within the system for transferring documents.

4. Expect mediation as an attempt by the court to lessen the onslaught of new cases and eliminate congestion.

5. As the appellant, you will need a *brief* carefully stating your claim and citing authorities to back up your legal theory or claim.

6. The appellee must answer your brief with a counter-argument in his *reply brief* (including authorities to back any claim or legal theory).

7. The appellant gets a chance to reply to the appellee's arguments in a second brief. (The process in a cross-appeal—when the winner of an

action also decides to appeal, perhaps for a greater award—is similar, except the court may call for several additional briefs.)

8. Motions may be made, if appropriate, and may include motions for attorneys' fees, depending on the nature of the issue or on what is stated in the contract or statute under which claims are being made.

9. Oral arguments may be heard. (Appellate courts now have "sorters" who decide which cases warrant oral arguments.)

10. An opinion is rendered—the appeal is affirmed or denied.

11. A written opinion may be published providing insight into the appellate judges' decision and what they relied upon as authorities to make the decision. Decisions are published only when the judges believe there is some reason to do so.

12. Mandate—equivalent to final judgment in trial courts.

The mine field of procedure, practice, and rules of court—varying from jurisdiction to jurisdiction—requires the utmost care and professionalism when dealing with appellate matters. It takes an expert not to be thrown out on procedure alone—even before any consideration is given to the issues or evidence in a case. Here is a procedural checklist to follow (adapted from *Art of Advocacy*):

1. Do I have a final order that I can cite in my notice of appeal (a judgment as the final act of the court below, as distinguished from findings of fact, conclusions of law, and orders for entry of judgment; or an adverse ruling on a motion for partial summary judgment that furnished the grounds for an *interlocutory appeal*)?

2. Have I adhered to the prescribed time limitations for filing my notice of appeal?

3. Does my notice of appeal meet all the technical requirements of this particular appeals court?

4. Do I have sufficient copies of my notice of appeal?

5. Do I have the correct fees, bonds, and so on to get my appeal properly entered?

6. Do I need to file a docketing statement, or any other document, to alert the appellate court to the type of case I present and the type of relief I ask?

7.  Do I need to file an appropriate motion to preserve the status quo and prevent the execution of the judgment during the appellate process (supersedeas bond, injunction, injunction bond)?

8.  Do I fully understand what my appellate court requires for the record on appeal (partial transcript; statement of issues; complaint, exhibits and other original papers in those courts that use the Appendix format)? Have I worked out an agreement with opposing counsel on the contents of the Appendix? If my court does not use the Appendix format, have I complied with all other requirements for making the Record on Appeal?

9.  Do I understand what can happen to my case after I meet all the formalities of launching the appeal, so that I can make the right strategic and tactical moves in every step along the way, from notice of appeal to final decision?

10.  Am I prepared to write a dramatic, entertaining, persuasive brief?

11.  Do I know how to react to a cross-appeal if the respondent seeks to inject an affirmative, offensive maneuver at this early stage?

## WHY APPELLATE REVIEW?

Keeping in mind that the United States Supreme Court has never held that a system of appellate review is required by due process (in either civil or criminal cases) Judge John Parker, then a justice of the Fourth Circuit Court of Appeals, stated:

> The judicial function in its essence is the application of the rules and standards of organized society to the settlement of controversy, and for there to be any proper administration of justice these rules and standards must be applied, not only impartially, but also objectively and uniformly throughout the territory of the state. This requires that decisions of trial courts be subjected to review by a panel of judges who are removed from the heat engendered by the trial and are consequently in a position to take a more objective view of the questions there raised to maintain uniformity of decisions throughout the territory. ("Improving Appellate Methods," 25 NYU Law Rev. 1, 1950.)

The appellate courts accomplish something else, too: They provide society with a psychological escape hatch. An aggrieved party has an option with an appellate court system that appears to be providing justice, and this is as important as any of the system's real functions. This option may keep the lid on a situation that otherwise might be blown out of proportion.

No one should rely on anticipated results of an appeal. My earliest recollection of the appellate process is an attorney telling me (regarding a client), "I am going to win the case on appeal but he [the client] doesn't deserve it." He was wrong on both counts: He lost the appeal, and he displayed a very unethical stance toward his client. My second encounter with the appellate process was more gratifying. When my recording business was young, my attorney said to me, "I think we should appeal" after we had lost a decision. We did appeal, and we won!

After this case, my attorney told me, "We've made law on your appeal." It's a great feeling to know that you actually had an effect on the laws of society, regardless of how insignificant to civilization the issue may be. The right issue at the right time can make a difference when appealed and sustained and published by an appellate court, and it can make a difference in the future to your fellow citizens.

## CHAPTER 18

# Civil Enforcement (Collecting a Judgment)

*Let me tell you the secret that has led me to my goal. My only strength lies in my tenacity.*

—Louis Pasteur

Congratulations! You won your case. The judge has made an award to you, a judgment against your opponent. Counsel has advised your opponent that an appeal would be too costly and probably counter-productive. You leave the courthouse and call some friends to gather at your favorite watering hole to celebrate. Ah, the sweet taste of victory!

Now it's a week later. You have just received a copy of the court's "final order"—the judgment of money in your favor, and the reality of collecting the judgment sets in. You remember that, as he left the courtroom, your opponent said, "You can use it [the judgment] for wallpaper!" You didn't care at that time because victory was still fresh, but now those words resound in your brain as you contemplate how to turn the piece of paper you are holding into cash.

In many cases, your opponent will not have the ready cash or won't be willing to pay the judgment, and you'll have to find some other way to get the money. At one time, your next step might have been calling a collection agency. However, what used to be fair game for the collector and credit agency is now protected by the Fair Debt Collection Practices Act of 1977, as supplemented by the Debt Collection Act of 1982 (Title 15, Sec. 1692). Although the wording of the Fair Debt Act indicates that it is concerned with debts that "are primarily for personal, family, or household purposes," it indicates the thinking of society toward collection practices. In three important sections (806-808), the act forbids, among other things:

- The use or threat of violence.
- The use of obscene or profane language.
- Publication of a list of consumers who allegedly refuse to pay debts (except to consumer reporting agencies).
- Intent to annoy, abuse, or harass any person at the called number.
- False representations that the individual calling is an attorney or that any communication is from an attorney.
- Implication that nonpayment of any debt will result in arrest or imprisonment.
- The solicitation by a debt collector of any post-dated check.

These are but a handful of the many restraints on collectors. (See Table 18.1 for a list of states that license collection agencies.)

Here is a story that is typical of the limitations (sometimes bordering on fraud) that can thwart normal collection procedures in the business world. The music industry's distribution system for recorded products is notorious for its bad credit practices and hence its collection problems. In the early 1960s, Textile Banking Corporation lent the owner of Riverside Records (which included the Jazzland and Wonderland Children's Records labels) money for every sale made. (This is called factoring.) When Riverside Records wanted to create large receivables before going public, it filled its distributors' warehouses with hundreds of thousands of children's records (a commodity that does not go out of date).

These distributors, or perhaps we should call them depositories, had the right to return what they didn't sell, a fact Textile Banking didn't know (which in this case was tantamount to fraud). Riverside's owner passed away suddenly and the company never went public. Textile exercised its security interest in the receivables (see Securing Payment Before the Transaction, below) and sent out a proper, white-haired banker to collect the money owed. I happened to be present when the gentleman arrived at the National Record Mart headquarters in Pittsburgh. After being asked for payment, one of the principals of the record store chain escorted the banker to the basement warehouse, and with outstretched arms said, "Here are your records, sir." There were more than 100,000 children's LPs in that basement, stacked up to the ceiling. The principal added, "I imagine you will find it this way throughout the country." The banker's face turned as white as his hair. He received no money from National Record Mart that day!

Even if fraud is not involved, frustration can force you into some strange collection procedures. Once I was badly in need of money for my business and was making an extra effort to collect my receivables. Beta Records owed me

**Table 18.1.** States That License Collection Agencies

| | | |
|---|---|---|
| Alaska | Maine | North Dakota |
| Arizona | Maryland | Oregon |
| Arkansas | Massachusetts | Tennessee |
| California | Michigan | Virginia |
| Colorado | Minnesota | Washington |
| Connecticut | Nebraska | West Virginia |
| Idaho | Nevada | Wisconsin |
| Illinois | New Mexico | Wyoming |
| Indiana | North Carolina | |

about $500, but the company was in decline and I was panicked at the thought of suffering another loss. I used extraordinary means to secure payment.

A young man working for us at that time, Richard, with all due respect, could have passed for a gangster. I told Richard to wear his black leather jacket, which made him look like a real hood, and prepare for a trip to New York City. I also told him that when we got to Beta, he was not to say a word and was to remain a few steps behind me. When we arrived at Beta, Richard played his part with all the intensity of a method actor. I asked the owner of Beta for the money owed. He hesitated a moment, then gestured at Richard and asked, "Who's he?" I coolly said, "He's with me." Richard ad-libbed, "Yeah, I'm with him." It took the gentleman about thirty seconds to make out the check in full.

## SECURING PAYMENT BEFORE THE TRANSACTION

Not counting actions born out of frustration and desperation, there are two basic ways to extend credit and receive payment (or collect a judgment): Secured transactions and unsecured transactions. The definition and inherent risk of an unsecured transaction is explained quite well in Eldon Reiley's *Guidebook to Security Interests in Personal Property* (New York: Boardman, 1982):

> When a debtor makes a bare agreement to pay, the obligation to the creditor is unsecured. If the debtor later fails to pay as promised, there is a breach of contract. The creditor has a legal action on the broken promise, but the creditor has no right to move immediately against any of the debtor's assets.

Establishing a security interest or obtaining a lien against the debtor's property when you extend credit and prior to any payment or collection problem gives you a better chance of obtaining payment.

> A valid security interest means that your rights in the collateral are enforceable against the debtor. A valid and perfected security interest places your rights in the collateral ahead of the debtor's trustee in bankruptcy's rights. If your valid and perfected security interest is prior in time to any other perfected security interests or to any lien, your rights in the collateral will be ahead of almost everybody. If there are some other security interests or lien claimants ahead of you, you will, of course, still have to face the resolution of the conflicting claims between you and those claimants. (Reiley, page 8.)

Therefore, the safest way to ensure payment is to prepare for problems in advance by arranging for a security interest in tangible property or having a guarantor on the debt.

A judgment from the court, if not confirming a secured interest in property, creates a lien similar to a secured obligation. Either secured or unsecured transactions, in judgment form and in accordance with due process, may require civil enforcement after you have attempted to collect through the normal course of business. You can then use the court system, the sheriff's department, and the full faith and credit clause of the Constitution in the collection effort.

Since a security interest or guarantee is a recognizable interest in or to property, the terms, conditions, or scope of the guarantee, mortgage, or other security agreement should be established by the parties upon first entering into the transaction. In order that it be publicly recognized (to protect other potential creditors as well as the parties to the transaction), the details of the transaction should be recorded by the appropriate clerk's office or secretary of state, depending on the jurisdiction and type of transaction.

One method of recording an interest in property is to use a Uniform Commercial Code (UCC) filing. First established in 1952, the UCC has been adopted by all fifty states, the District of Columbia, Guam, and the Virgin Islands. It prescribes the code for the operation of business in the eyes of the judicial system, and the courts make their rulings based on the code's prescribed procedures. For instance, in Chapter 11 we spoke about the use of written purchase orders (in the K Mart case). Article II, Sec. 201 of the UCC states that "a contract for the sale of goods for the price of $500.00 or more is not enforceable by way of [legal] action or defense unless there is some writing [written agreement] sufficient to indicate that a contract for sale has been made between the parties." The code is extensive and covers everything from banking to beans. With nine articles and hundreds of subparts, it is the ultimate rule book for commercial transactions.

Once your secured interest is documented and publicly proclaimed, if it is necessary to exercise the security interest, you must file a lawsuit to enforce your rights. Obviously, you must have a properly documented and recorded secured interest affirming that interest in the property for your claim to be enforceable through litigation. In a lawsuit, there are considerably fewer defenses against a secured transaction than against an unsecured claim, which must be proven beyond a reasonable doubt with documentation and testimony.

Probably the most familiar form of a secured transaction is a home or business property mortgage. Provided that the exact legal description of the property and the terms of the secured interest are stated accurately and filed in the appropriate jurisdiction (usually with the courthouse in the county where the property is located), enforcing the secured interest (taking the property by foreclosure) should be relatively simple. It is important to mention here that any document or set of documents filed for the purpose of securing an interest in property must conform to the particular jurisdiction's requirements as to signature, witnesses, notarization, and other details necessary for the document to be recognized by the court.

As government moves toward a more humanitarian approach, the tendency of many courts is to give the individual being foreclosed upon every chance in the world to save the property. Brian Duff, a federal judge in Chicago, said, "We make sure that every mortgage foreclosure is called in open court and after the clerk calls it and the lawyer for the plaintiff comes up, then I personally call it from the bench in (a) loud tone, so that if some person is sitting back there . . . and is either afraid or unsure or doesn't know or wasn't paying attention, they can come up."

## COLLECTING A JUDGMENT

Except in cases where a federal statute governs a situation, collecting a judgment (federal or state) is accomplished according to state law (FRCP Rule 69). In most jurisdictions the first step after a state judgment is to record the judgment in the same county in which the debtor resides or where the debtor owns property. In the case of a federal judgment, you would record it within the federal district where the judgment was entered.

In order to take advantage of the Constitution's full faith and credit clause and collect on a judgment in another jurisdiction, you must enroll the judgment in the court docket of the jurisdiction in which the property is located. Jurisdictional rules should be followed for this procedure. (When final, federal judgments may also be registered in other federal districts; 28 U.S.C. Sec. 193.)

Once your right has been established, your position in respect to other creditors becomes a matter of public record, hopefully anywhere the debtor has property. Creditors filing after your lien is recorded must wait until your claim is satisfied before collecting anything on theirs.

If you are collecting a federal judgment, you would use the services of the United States marshal. In a state judgment, you would use the services of the local sheriff's office or appropriate court officer to execute on a writ of attachment, garnishment, foreclosure, or other procedure as issued by the state court.

Describe very precisely to the court clerk the property on which you wish to execute. The court clerk will know the correct writ to issue. In the federal system, there are different forms for executing on personal property, goods, chattels or credits, or garnishment of wages, earnings, salary, commissions, and pensions.

Your judgment may be enrolled or registered in each jurisdiction where you believe your debtor has assets. Once registered with the court clerk in a "foreign" jurisdiction, writs of attachment can be issued until your judgment is satisfied. This is allowed in any state that has adopted the Uniform Enforcement of Foreign Judgments Act. (Currently, thirty-eight states have adopted the act. California has not, but it has its own Sister State Money Judgment Act, which accomplishes much the same thing.) Another way of executing a judgment in a foreign jurisdiction is with a writ of execution obtained by a federal administrative agency, which may be executed in any state or territory or in the District of Columbia (*U.S. v. Thornton*, 672 F2d 101 [D.C. Cr. 1982]). Under certain circumstances, this long-arm type of execution may be used by a private party if the basic cause of action is within the United States and the judgment is for the use of both parties (*United States ex rel. Marcus v. Lord Electric Company*, 43 F.Sup. 12, 13 [W.D.Pa. 1942]; *United States v. Palmer*, supra, 609 F2d at 547).

Depending on the nature of the property, you may have to record a levy (a lien or security interest established by the court) with a government agency in addition to the appropriate court clerk. For example, under the Federal Aviation Act (49 U.S.C. Sec. 1403) an attachment or levy should be recorded with the Federal Aviation Administration's registry division (Oklahoma City, Oklahoma). In maritime law, if a ship of twenty-one tons or more is involved, according to the Ship's Mortgage Act (46 U.S.C. Sec. 921), you must file documentation with the collector of customs or with the United States Coast Guard Vessel Documentation Office.

Whether your attachment employs United States marshals or the local sheriff's office, you must instruct the executing officer on the proper method of attaching and levying each item of the debtor's property. I once had two corporations with the same name that operated in two states, Florida and New

Jersey. A judgment existed against the inactive Florida corporation, and the Broward County Sheriff's Office Division of Enforceable Writs executed against the active New Jersey company, which had property. This was deemed by us to be a violation of our federal civil rights. After several years of federal civil rights court action, the violation was finally settled in our favor, and we were awarded a token payment of $5,000. The violation occurred because the sheriff's office had received instructions from an overzealous collection attorney. (The sheriff's office has since changed its procedures for enforcing writs.)

Once property is seized and is in the hands of the civil justice system, the debtor is notified and a judicial sale takes place. The proceeds of this sale are applied to the judgment, and the overage is then applied to other lienholders of record. If no other lienholders are recorded in the jurisdiction, the balance of the funds from the sale (over and above the judgment amount, costs, and usual attorneys' fees) are returned to the debtor. If there is a shortfall, the balance of the unpaid judgment remains open and on record for the collection process to continue by other means (attachment of other assets).

This area of law is complicated enough to sustain "creditor's rights specialists"—lawyers who devote their practice to collection. These attorneys, as well as some who do not so specialize, know how to unearth assets and how to proceed in an advantageous manner in their jurisdictions. Allen Stokes, Jr., of Denver, is such an attorney. Stokes filed this report about a simple garnishment used in an attempt to collect on a judgment; it shows how complex and tenuous collection work can be, and the time frame involved:

> We have obtained the writ of garnishment—judgment debtor other than natural person and have sent it for service on the debtor's bank. Assuming the bank account is both current and has a balance, we should have the first payment within 45 days.
>
> We must obtain a court order directing the bank to send the account balance to the court. The bank must then send a check to the court, the court clears it for 21 days, then we receive it and remit forthwith. Advance file 60 days for remittance.

In Broward County, the court clerk's office details, for the benefit of the public, the precise procedure for attempting to collect on a judgment. Although the specific procedures may vary from jurisdiction to jurisdiction, the following Broward County procedures will give you a general idea of what is involved.

1. *Record Your Judgment.* We suggest you first obtain a certified copy of the

judgment from the clerk of the court and record it in any county in which the debtor owns real estate. The judgment then becomes a lien on any real estate the debtor owns in that county. The lien acts as a defect on the title to the real estate and normally must be paid off if that property is ever sold.

2. *File a Writ of Execution*. Ten (10) days after the judgment has been entered by the court, the clerk will issue a document called a writ of execution upon your request. Take this document to the sheriff's office located in the county where the debtor has personal property or movable goods. When the writ of execution is filed with the sheriff, the sheriff will then have authority to seize and sell the property of the debtor to pay off your judgment. At the time of the sale of the property, the sheriff will pay the judgments in the order in which the writs of execution were filed. Therefore, it is important to file your writ with the sheriff as soon as possible, in case there are many creditors.

3. *Levy and Execution*. If you can locate personal property of the debtor, you can then give the sheriff written instructions (the form is usually called Instructions for Levy) to seize specifically identified personal property of the debtor. You must also give the sheriff the exact location of the property. After the sheriff has seized the property, he will publish a notice in the newspaper announcing the date of a public sale of the goods that he has seized. At that sale, people will bid on the property. Any money received at the sale, after payment of the sheriff's expenses for the seizure and sale, will be given to you to pay or partially pay your judgment. If the monies received do not pay the entire judgment, you can repeat the process. If your writ was not the first one filed against the defendant, you may not be paid in full, for the sheriff must pay off all writs according to the order in which they were filed.

4. *Locating the Debtor's Property*. There are many ways to find out what property the debtor owns. The county tax collector can tell you if the debtor owns a vehicle registered in the state. You may also write to the Department of Motor Vehicles to see what vehicles the debtor owns.

The official records of the county will also show you what real estate a debtor owns in the county. These records can be complicated, and you may want an experienced person to help you with this.

If you do not find any property of the debtor through research, you may file a request with the court for a supplementary proceeding. To do this you must have first filed your writ of execution with the sheriff. You must then file an affidavit with the court stating that the judgment has not been paid, and the sheriff has been unable to collect on your writ of execution. The court will then set a hearing requiring the debtor to appear before the judge and answer questions under oath as to property, income, employment, and the like. If the debtor refuses to come to court after being given proper notice, the court has the power to hold the debtor in contempt until he or she appears and answers the questions.

Another way to locate the debtor's property is a deposition in aid of execution. In this method, the debtor is subpoenaed to appear before a court reporter or a notary public and is made to answer questions under oath about property. This procedure is somewhat complicated, and you may wish to consult a lawyer to assist you.

5. *Garnishment.* Your debtor may also be owed money by a third person, such as an employer or bank where the debtor has an account. In such a case, you may wish to file a garnishment suit.

   To obtain a writ of garnishment, you must file a motion for a such a writ with the clerk of the court and pay a filing fee. The sheriff would then serve the writ on the third person, who would be required to make a written report of the amount, if any, owed to the debtor, and to reveal any property of the debtor in the possession or control of the third person. Then, unless the debtor is entitled to exemption (see below), the third person would have to pay the money to you or give the property to the sheriff for execution to satisfy your judgment. Please note that garnishment procedures can be quite complicated. You may wish to seek the advice of an attorney.

6. *Exemptions.* Some state constitutions provide that certain property of a debtor may be exempt from forced sale and execution. Exempt property may include the real estate that is the residence (homestead) of a person or his or her family, as well as an amount of personal property. A debtor who is head of a household may also be entitled to claim an exemption on wages. There are also certain federal exemptions that limit the amount of wages that may be garnished. The debtor must show that he or she is entitled to these exemptions by claiming and meeting certain requirements.

## COLLECTING FROM "JUDGMENT-PROOF" INDIVIDUALS

A judgment-proof individual is one who claims to have assets so well protected that a judgment against him will not be collectible. For example, all assets may be in the spouse's name. However, the law provides for *supplementary procedures* that may help you overcome such a condition. By reciting to the court the facts concerning your judgment, including a request to examine the judgment debtor (including documents), a petition for supplementary proceedings may be granted allowing a new phase of discovery relative to assets. In *The Litigation Manual*, attorney James J. Brown lists the documents you should ask for, especially if the debtor is a business:

1.  All documents relating to any leasehold or freehold interest of the debtor in real property, in tangible or intangible personal property, including any options to purchase any property that the debtor owns or leases as a member of a partnership or with any other personal business entity.

2.  All canceled checks, check stubs, bank statements, ledgers, and correspondence showing disbursements and receipts of the last five years.

3.  Copies of all federal and state tax returns for the last five years.

4.  All records relating to any transfer to others of title to or any other interest whatsoever in any real or personal property within the last five years.

5.  All documents relating to any cause of action pending against the debtor, or any loans or advances of money to the debtor.

6.  Master payroll file.

7.  All documents relating to the funds, other assets, liabilities, ownership, capitalization, and incorporation of the debtor. (This shows the importance of an up-to-date corporate minutes book.)

The information you have already developed about the debtor will help you determine whether to expand or contract this list of documents. Also, regardless of whether the debtor is an individual, a partnership, or a corporation, you should carefully consider the list of answers and documents requested, as each may reveal some clue to the whereabouts of assets. If a company is publicly held, you can secure copies of annual reports, and probably other disclosure documents, that are in the hands of local, state, or federal agencies. All of these public information documents may provide clues to the whereabouts of assets.

## DEALING WITH RELUCTANT DEBTORS

Reluctant debtors are subject to sanctions by the court if they do not cooperate. Federal Rule 37 provides for sanctions, and many states provide for them as well as for the threat of contempt of court. Despite this, the debtor, having seen financial difficulties coming, probably took steps to hide, transfer, or otherwise place assets in a safe haven. Here are some steps a smart collector might use to unearth assets:

1.  Subpoena the debtor's accountant, if the debtor has one. Under bankruptcy law, the accountant/client privilege is not recognized, even though that privilege may exist in state law. The accountant's file would probably have financial statements and tax returns. If the accountant can't produce them, then move the court for an order allowing you to request them directly from the Internal Revenue Service.

2.  If you know the name or names of the debtor's bank account, you can subpoena the records directly. The banking records may provide clues to assets that could be claimed to have been transferred, sold, or exchanged in violation of creditors' rights.

3.  Credit card records may tell of a lifestyle that will lead to assets not visible on the surface. For instance, a simple charge for fuel at a marina might indicate the existence of a floating asset. Credit card transactions may go a long way toward proving a corporation is an individual's alter ego, making one responsible for the other's debts. According to Brown, "judges find it hard to stomach that kind of abuse and will usually allow you to 'pierce' the corporate veil, when it is shown that the corporation exists mainly for the purpose of protecting the debtor's assets."

4.  The debtor's family members are also potent sources of information. A fraudulent transfer of assets may be unearthed, forcing a settlement or the possible attachment of property. However, recovering assets that have been transferred to third parties may require lengthy litigation. In order to prevent any further movement, you may have to obtain an injunction or writ, freezing the movement of property or assets until the court has had the opportunity to reassess the situation.

5.  Under certain state and federal laws it may be possible to have a receiver appointed to administer and protect the assets of a business until the outcome of litigation is known. The receiver will freeze salaries, protect the movement of assets, and prevent the dissipation of the business pending a court ruling.

6.  In federal cases, you can rely on Federal Civil Procedure Rule 62 to restrain the movement of assets. In the event that it is impractical to post a bond, the court, at its discretion, may allow the freezing of assets pending the outcome of litigation.

The last maneuver in this list comes from *Trans World Airlines v. Hughes* (314 F.Supp.94 [S.D.N.Y. 1970]). This is a fascinating tale of corporate intrigue and monopoly. In this case, the reclusive Howard Hughes cost his company, Hughes Tool Company (Toolco) a third of its total net worth just by refusing to appear at a deposition. As Chief Appellate Judge Lombardi wrote in his opinion, "Counsel for Toolco informed the District Court that Toolco had made a 'business decision' not to proceed further with discovery proceedings. . . . consequently, counsel for Toolco stated, 'Hughes would fail to appear for the deposition ordered'. . . . Toolco was aware of the sanctions which could be imposed." Hughes' refusal to appear was responsible both for Toolco's counterclaim against TWA being denied with prejudice and for TWA's successful motion for summary judgment against Hughes. This finally resolved into a judgment, in favor of TWA, for $145,448,141.07. This award was comprised of a judgment of $45,870,478.65 that was trebled (per the provisions of the Clayton Anti-Trust Act) to $137,611,435.95. The balance of the award was for a claim of 64,000 hours of attorneys' time and other out-of-pocket expenses.

The preceding exemplifies a number of legal principles that we have discussed previously: The use of mandatory depositions; the request for sanctions; and ultimately the restraining of assets.

There is no guarantee that using any of the above measures will provide the funds to which your judgment states you are entitled. Post-judgment litigation is time-consuming, expensive, and sometimes devious. Discovery at the outset of your collection attempts should provide at least a clue as to what lies ahead.

The specter of bankruptcy always looms as a threat to the collector or creditor. When someone seeks bankruptcy protection, all adverse actions stop instantly. At the moment the bankruptcy is filed it becomes a matter of law, and creditors are looking at potential contempt of court if they proceed in any way against the debtor without obtaining *leave of court*, or permission of the bankruptcy court. Even a creditor holding a secured interest must first enter the bankruptcy court and obtain the court's permission to enforce a judgment to seize the property. I have seen banks reverse transactions, ferocious collection lawyers become meek pussycats, and legitimate debts turn into worthless pieces of paper—all because of the bankruptcy stay.

## A VIEW FROM THE DEBTOR'S SIDE

Life is not always as we want it to be. Uncertainties are pervasive in business, especially for the small business owner or entrepreneur. Sometimes, despite all the hard work, the entire operation goes down the drain. The safest way to protect your assets is to plan ahead, and establish a mechanism for protection in advance.

A corporation is considered to have a life of its own and, except in very few instances, it protects the shareholders from personal liability. (Withholding taxes and federal copyright infringement are two items that are not protected by the corporate shield.) Many small corporations are set up by individuals for protection, tax advantages, and the like. If you have such a corporation and don't operate it properly, you may be leaving yourself and the other principals open to the charge that the corporation is your alter ego—the claim that the individual and the corporation are one and the same. If this claim is sustained by a court (known as "piercing the corporate veil"), it defeats the very purpose of your corporation's protective umbrella.

The following are a few tips on proper corporate etiquette aimed at thwarting an alter ego charge. These suggestions apply to claims of alter ego between individuals and corporations or between different corporations and their principals.

1.  Keep the minute books up to date, with major decisions recorded (even if with a simple handwritten memo inserted in the book).

2.  At least once a year, hold a meeting and elect the officers.

3.  Document checks and the use of funds, and avoid the use of "cash" checks as much as possible. If they are necessary, then have backup paperwork for the expenditures.

4.  Do not commingle (mix) personal money and corporate monies. This is the easiest route for your opponent to pursue in proving that there was no real corporate entity in the first place.

5.  Always try to sign checks, documents, and letters using a business title after your name; for example, president, secretary, treasurer, and so on.

6.  If the corporation is going to pick up certain expenses for officers or employees, don't try to hide it. (Remember the available discovery procedures.) Instead, justify it with paper work, agreements, or entries in the minute book.

7.  Maintain separate bank accounts for each corporation. If there are intercompany transactions, such as loans, document them and keep ledgers of the loan accounts and balances. The accounts should be as separate as if they were unrelated businesses.

8.  Two or more businesses that share the same offices and/or other spaces

should have their own occupational licenses, sales tax licenses, and local business licenses as the particular jurisdictions require. All such licenses should be displayed at or near the entrance to the building or office.

9. Lease agreements, equipment rental agreements, and contracts representing assets should clearly be in the correct corporate name in its exact form.

There is precious little else that can do as much to protect assets as using the limited liability benefit of incorporation. Joint ownership of assets may help, but use or disposal of an individual's share of the assets may be limited by a lien. Trusts and individual retirement accounts/pensions will protect assets under certain conditions; but again, a lien may restrict use of the assets.

An item of value or an asset that is already encumbered may provide a measure of protection. A car financed by a bank and with a limited amount of equity is not very attractive to a collector. Even if a creditor takes possession and sells the vehicle for its appraised value, it has to pay off the bank (first lienholder), and pay costs and legal fees (even if later charged to the debtor). What is left may not be worth the trouble. The same goes for equipment and machinery financed and used in business (or pleasure). If the equipment is not substantially more valuable than the outstanding loans, it does no good to seize it unless you are the first or primary creditor, and even then you will have to find the property and change it into cash.

Some jurisdictions give landlords an automatic first lien on property on their premises. Therefore, if a lessee is behind on the rent, a third-party creditor would not be able to touch the contents of the premises without the consent of the landlord—a measure of protection of your assets if you are on good terms with your landlord. Hidden assets, numbered bank accounts, foreign accounts, and investments may provide some degree of safety. However, this method is becoming more and more difficult as some of the former "havens" give way to governmental pressures to make the presence of foreign assets known and collectible.

# CHAPTER 19
# Summation

*The law: it has honored us; may we honor it.*
—Daniel Webster

A lawyer was retained by a longtime client to write a will. The charge was $100. When the client picked up the will, she paid the lawyer with a crisp new $100 bill and left. While the lawyer was on the phone, he began fiddling with the bill in his hand. Suddenly, it separated into two $100 bills. (The client had inadvertently made a double payment.) The lawyer, quite astonished, thought to himself, "Should I do the right thing . . . and share this with my partner?" The extensive circulation of this story exemplifies the dilemma of the legal profession today: Self-enrichment or moral conduct.

Is our society providing access to the civil justice system in an ethical manner? Does it offer fair distribution of quality services to those who are not rich? A strong argument can be made for a negative answer. The drive for wealth in our society, and the high charges for often shoddy legal work, can make life in business miserable. This situation is typified by the remark made by small business owner Jack Kelly, Jr. when he suffered what he felt was incompetent representation by several lawyers: "It gives you a helpless feeling when you have entrusted your faith to someone who basically drops the ball." ("Victims, Clients Lose When Their Lawyers Abuse," *Los Angeles Times*, June 7, 1980.) He continued with the significant comment: "It took a few cases for me to realize that I could do the job myself."

Even the American Bar Association (ABA) has recognized the movement of average citizens toward taking on more responsibility for their own problems. In its introduction to *Dispute Resolution Papers Series #2* (December 1983), the ABA said, "In America we have been characterized as a litigious society. . . .

(T)here is a movement afoot for individuals to take more responsibility for their own problems. It is not uncommon for individuals to avoid the legal system because they find it costly, time-consuming, and inaccessible."

All over America, the backlash against the inaccessibility, cost, time-consuming nature, and, as Mr. Kelly has expressed it, incompetence of legal representation is festering under the surface of what should be one of the best legal systems in the world. One Los Angeles lawyer is offering do-it-yourself court appearances, with his paperwork, his tutoring, and your time at the bar of justice (Legal Action Workshop, Los Angeles). The New Hampshire Bar Association is distributing a do-it-yourself divorce kit and is investigating the availability of a self-help bankruptcy kit, which they also plan to distribute. Steve Scudder, the New Hampshire Bar Association's director of legal services, said, "We can't get enough lawyers to do pro bono [free legal work for the poor or indigent], so self-help is the next best remedy." The book you are reading is a product of the growing demand to provide the public with tools for self-help. More and more court calendars are displaying the words pro se after the case title, instead of a lawyer's name.

Self-help books do not typically have heroes. This one is an exception, and there are two. Their intertwined stories demonstrate many of the problems of our legal system today. Yet, in contrast with the indictment of the system that opened this chapter, their stories also demonstrate "the wonderful justice," as one of our heroes called it, that was the solution to the other hero's legal dilemma.

Our two heroes are about as far apart on the socioeconomic scale as they could be. Yet each deserves our respect and admiration for his deeds and the manner in which he carried them out.

Eugene Wzorek, one of our heroes, was the victim of lawyer dropout. He engaged and paid several attorneys in succession to plead his case for the unfair loss of his city job. Finally, penniless, out of work, and psychologically disturbed at his decline in life (knowing the loss of his job was not his doing), he was left to his own devices on his day in court. His response: "Judge, I'll do the best I can."

Judge Brian Barnett Duff is our other hero—a man with a compelling sense of justice, who presided over *Eugene Wzorek v. The City of Chicago*. One of a family of ten children, Judge Duff received his legal education at night while working by day to pay for it. An experienced Illinois Circuit Court Judge, he was sworn to the federal bench in 1985. One of Judge Duff's earliest remembrances sheds light on this compassionate man:

> One day a young friend of mine in school asked me to come play
> at his house. I was probably nine. My mom brought me in the car

about nine in the morning. Sometime around lunch, my friend's mom came out and asked him to come in to lunch, and I sat on the stoop. At 4:30, Mom picked me up. We were some miles from our house. She said, "Did you have a good time?" I started to cry. I said, "I don't think my friend's mom likes me." "Why not, dear?" "Well, she didn't ask me in for lunch." And my mom as quickly as that said, "Dear, that's my mistake. I'm sorry. I didn't think. Your friend's mom didn't have another hot dog." I have never forgotten that day and that circumstance or the sensitivity that we must have to what is really going on in other people's lives.

Eugene Wzorek was a sewer department truck driver, a real-life Ed Norton (the fictional sewer worker and friend of Ralph Kramden on the television show *The Honeymooners*), who became a victim of the notorious Chicago political patronage system. Wzorek made a campaign donation, but unfortunately to the wrong side. The city bosses found out and his firing was engineered even though his supervisors had given him a performance rating of 85 (out of 100). The firing was a breach of the Shakman decree, which was supposed to put an end to the age-old patronage abuses in Chicago. (This was a consent decree reached in 1976 between the federal courts and the city: *Shakman v. Democratic Organization of Cook County*, 533 F 2nd 344 [1976]. It prohibited political firings.)

Two years after the trial, Wzorek was described by Judge Duff:

About 5'5" or 5'6", probably weighs 200 pounds. He's a very, very rotund, not unattractive man, a man with a nice little smile, when he feels like smiling; very emotional, cries easily, beautiful blue eyes, just come right out at you, curly, kinky, almost afro-type hair; he's eastern European . . . a canny man, not a dumb man; not a person you would say that man's got a great IQ, but been out there in the city neighborhoods growing up, making his way. . . .

It is 10:00 a.m., June 29, 1988 (four years to the day since Wzorek was fired). In United States District Court, Chicago, the minute clerk enters and addresses the courtroom: "Hear ye, hear ye, the United States District Court for the Northern District of Illinois is now in session, the Honorable Judge Brian Barnett Duff presiding. God save the United States and this Honorable Court. Please be seated."

*Judge Duff:*    We are going to try the case . . . but I want to be sure that everything is done right. . . . I have a pro se plaintiff. I will be depending on the city, to some extent, to do things, to get things done.

Against the lone sewer truck driver, the city has put three of its corporate counsels, Darka Papushkewych, Charles Ex (his real name), and Mary Smith. Before the trial even starts, the city, having previously been ordered by Judge Duff to make a witness available, informs the court as to when a former city commissioner says he can be available.

*Judge Duff:*    Mr. Barnes is not going to pick the day. And his wife is not going to avoid the process. I want him subpoenaed.

The city lawyers protest that Barnes is now a political lobbyist in the state capital.

*Judge Duff:*    Mr. Barnes may think he is doing something important in Springfield. . . . Tomorrow the session is over. . . . There isn't a lobbyist in the world that can influence any major issue between now and tomorrow night at midnight. And, if there is, it isn't Mr. Barnes.

The plaintiff asks the court in all naïvete if he can testify in a narrative style.

*Wzorek:*    Your Honor, may I testify as a narrative witness?
*Judge Duff:*    Yes.
*Wzorek:*    Because no one to cross-examine me. I will put myself on first then.
*Judge Duff:*    You may.

Next, the city tries to bar one of Wzorek's witnesses.

*Ex:*    It is the city's position that anybody who is fired at the same time can only talk about their own particular set of circumstances.
*Judge Duff*
*(to plaintiff):*    Why did you want to call him?
*Wzorek:*    He was my foreman. He could relate to what I was rated [as an employee]. I am not going to call him about his case, just mine. There was rated 85.

*Judge Duff:*      That's relevant. The objection is overruled.

In a standard request, the city asks to bar witnesses from the courtroom (the equivalent of sequestering).

*Wzorek:*          Pardon me? Would my witnesses have to wait outside?
*Judge Duff*
*(explaining):*    Yes. That is so each witness can testify without being over-
                   heard by the other witnesses.
*Wzorek:*          I am sorry.
*Judge Duff:*      Don't be apologetic. Let's just move along here.

Wzorek, who describes himself as having only an eighth-grade education and "one year high, but I didn't pass that one year," proceeds to try his own case, to prove that political patronage is responsible for his firing and "not . . . anything I did," and why his job meant so much to him. "They don't want nobody with no education [at the union hall]."

*Judge Duff:*      Now, Mr. Wzorek, do you want to make an opening state-
                   ment?
*Wzorek:*          Your Honor, I will try to do the best I can. I will try to prove
                   I was fired politically and not for anything I did . . . to prove
                   it was a Shakman . . . to show at that time I had 85, and I was
                   a good employee and shouldn't have been fired.

The Court inquires, as it has a right to do.

*Judge Duff:*      What does 85 mean?
*Wzorek:*          That is 85 percent on your rating.

Smith, in her opening statement for the city, explains, in part, the mechanism the city used to control the fate of 8,000 workers.

*Smith:*           In late December 1983, the city of Chicago passed an ordi-
                   nance which was part of the annual appropriation ordinance
                   for 1984, which placed approximately 8,000 city employees,
                   including Mr. Wzorek, on probation for six months. If he
                   successfully completed the probation period they would be-
                   come career service employees on July 1, 1984 . . .

The court instructs Wzorek to begin his case in chief.

*Judge Duff:*     Mr. Wzorek, you may put on your evidence.

Wzorek asks the court, in his own way, for a ruling on relevancy.

*Wzorek:*     Can I ask you one thing? What I was speaking about the rating cards is because Mr. Barnes had to have the rating card, and it told the ward and the political affiliation you were on the rating card. That's why they were destroyed.

The court rules on the question and then prompts the start of testimony by Wzorek.

*Judge Duff:*     It is relevant . . . do you want to take the stand?
*Wzorek:*     Okay.
*Judge Duff:*     Do you want to be under oath?
*Wzorek:*     Yes, sir . . . Okay. My name is Eugene Wzorek, 3751 West 75th Place. I started for the city about 1973, as a motor truck driver for Sanitation. After working on and off there and collecting compensation from the city when I was laid off, I joined the Sewer Department in 1977.

     I didn't do anything that was relevant to my discharge. I was also told a lot of political things when I gave Richard Daley a check for $1,000. Me and William McDermott brought it down to Daley's. After that he was transferred off my truck with me and I was warned not to, I should never donate for Daley. I was warned by Mr. Sommerford.

The city tries to object to Wzorek's damaging statements.

*Ex:*     Objection, your honor. Hearsay.
*Judge Duff:*     Mr. Sommerford worked for the City at the time?
*Wzorek:*     Yes, he did.
*Judge Duff:*     Objection overruled.
*Ex:*     If I could just finish my objection. The reason I say hearsay is that although he was a city employee, I don't believe that, for the purposes of this case, which he must show it was the decision-maker who knew of his motivation; that by merely showing Mr. Sommerford had knowledge, could be imputed

|            | to the decision-maker. There must be some showing that Mr. Sommerford had some influence or was, in fact, part of that actual decision itself, and therefore . . . |
|------------|------------|
| *Judge Duff:* | Your objection was on hearsay. It is overruled. |

Wzorek makes reference to testimony from a deposition. The judge helps.

| *Wzorek:* | Your honor, what I was trying to say in the deposition, Mr. Sommerford states that he was the one that fired the people. You know, stamped the names and did all that. |
|------------|------------|
| *Judge Duff:* | What page in the deposition? |
| *Wzorek:* | Well . . . |
| *Judge Duff:* | If you can't remember, check it later. |
| *Wzorek:* | Okay. I know it is hearsay, but . . . |
| *Judge Duff:* | Don't decide what is hearsay. That is my job. |

Again, the city tries to stop the testimony of Wzorek's supervisor.

| *Wzorek:* | Okay. I was told by Mr. Sommerford to straighten out in my ward; that I wasn't paying the dues. See, a new committee-man was taking over the ward, and he was . . . |
|------------|------------|
| *Ex:* | Objection. Same grounds. Hearsay. |
| *Judge Duff:* | It is not hearsay. If Mr. Sommerford is the person that fired him, the person that warned him, and he is the supervisor, then it is not hearsay. Continue, sir. |
| *Wzorek:* | Like I said, Mr. Sommerford's name is on both firing slips so he was there with Barnes. If it was just Barnes alone that fired me, it would have been just Mr. Barnes' name on there. That is why I am bringing Mr. Sommerford into this. He is also on the note that requested me to be fired for poor performance. And then also, Mr. Sommerford told me about my ward because Mr. Molaro was taking over the ward. He was a lot younger man than Mr. Swinarski, so he said beat that Polack, and he said . . . |
| *Ex:* | Objection, your honor. Just for the record, the same continuing objection. |

The court exercises its prerogative to question the witness:

| *Judge Duff:* | Who was Madia? |

| | |
|---|---|
| *Wzorek:* | Madia was a district foreman. He was in the Sixth District where I used to go get oil and stuff like that. |
| *Judge Duff:* | Who did he shout it to? |
| *Wzorek:* | To Ernie Costa. He was by the door. |
| *Judge Duff:* | Who is Costa? |
| *Wzorek:* | He is like a maintenance man around there, labor, takes care of the yard. |
| *Judge Duff:* | Who else could hear it? |
| *Wzorek:* | Just me and Costa were there that day. |
| *Judge Duff:* | What did he say? |
| *Wzorek:* | He says, "Did you see what happened yesterday? . . . That is a Polish ward and they put the Italian guy in and knocked the Polack out. |
| *Judge Duff:* | How is that a threat? |
| *Wzorek:* | Okay. I am going to finish the threat now. As I am walking in, he said, "Hey, you better really shape up . . . you will have to pay your dues and knock on doors better," because I wasn't paying the dues at that time. My house burned down in 1983 and I just didn't have the money. |
| *Judge Duff:* | What are dues? |
| *Wzorek:* | Dues were three hundred some dollars a year and other tickets. I just got behind because I couldn't pay for the clothes that burned. I was behind a couple of years, you know. It was in '83, so I was starting to go like $800, $900 in debt. I had a kid going to high school and I just couldn't do it. So I told them I would try to catch up with the dues. |

Once again the city tries to object.

| | |
|---|---|
| *Ex:* | Objection to this line of testimony. . . . I believe that any particular threats, as well as being hearsay, are also irrelevant for purposes of this lawsuit unless he can somehow connect up Mayor Washington or Eugene Barnes to that Twelfth Ward. |
| *Judge Duff:* | You can argue that at the completion of the case. At the moment I can't say it is not relevant. |
| *Wzorek:* | Can I try to connect it up now? |
| *Judge Duff:* | Yes. |

The city, in order to make firing employees easier, eliminated the rating system that had been established by prior city council agreement.

| | |
|---|---|
| *Wzorek:* | My rating was 85 and John Lucille will testify to that. . . . If you get over 85, they ought to rate why you're good. |
| *Judge Duff:* | How did they change the rules? |
| *Wzorek:* | There was no more ratings. She [indicating Smith] even said when she was making her opening statement. |
| *Judge Duff:* | Was there something published to that effect? |
| *Wzorek:* | On May 3, yes, there was a memorandum. |
| *Judge Duff:* | Do you have a copy of it? |
| *Wzorek:* | Yes, I got a copy of it. |
| *Judge Duff:* | Are you going to put that in evidence? |
| *Wzorek:* | Yes, if I could . . . |

The city complains that Wzorek is misrepresenting statements from a deposition, but the plaintiff knows exactly where he is going.

| | |
|---|---|
| *Smith:* | Your Honor, if I may interject. The witness has completely misrepresented the statements in Mr. Pounian's deposition. |
| *Judge Duff:* | Well, we will see when Mr. Pounian takes the stand. He can be asked the question directly, and then if he doesn't answer it he can be impeached with it. |
| *Smith:* | That is fine. |
| *Wzorek:* | Mr. Sommerford says he was never in the First Ward and I got his precinct captain card right in my pocket, if I can present it now. So I don't lose it. |
| *Judge Duff:* | You can. |
| *Wzorek:* | So I don't lose it . . . |

The evidence begins to build, and Judge Duff finds it necessary to teach the plaintiff the correct use of evidence and how to gain its admissibility.

| | |
|---|---|
| *Wzorek:* | The exit interview, like I say, your honor, it gives an affidavit memoranda. Every employee is supposed to get an exit interview, and I never got one. They put the wrong district foreman on the exit interview. It is totally phony. I mean, I was never there. Never got it because it states in the, that I will produce later, that you are supposed to get an exit interview from your supervisor. |

| | |
|---|---|
| *Judge Duff:* | Produce it now. Why later? |
| *Wzorek:* | Well, I have got it in my papers. I didn't know if I could do it or not. |
| *Judge Duff:* | Get your papers up here. You are putting your case on. If you have any documents you want to put in evidence, put them in. . . . |
| *Wzorek:* | I can do it later when they come on. |
| *Judge Duff:* | Put on what you have to put on now . . . you don't know what the other side is going to testify to. You put on your case and let them put on their case. |
| *Wzorek:* | I meant my later witnesses could bring it out. |
| *Judge Duff:* | They may not be the right witnesses. If you have evidence, put it in. If you can't get it in we will see if some other witness can testify to it. |

Procedural snarls are the major problems for the pro se litigant. But with a judge interested in justice, the problems are judiciously resolved.

| | |
|---|---|
| *Judge Duff:* | Are you numbering this as one of your exhibits? |
| *Wzorek:* | Yes, your honor. |
| *Judge Duff:* | You have got to have some order here. |
| *Ex:* | It is very difficult for us to follow. |
| *Judge Duff:* | Yes, it is. Let us start off with a list so we keep a record for the court reporter. Mr. Wzorek wouldn't be expected to know how to do this, but we do have to keep a record. |
| *Wzorek:* | I am sorry. I am nervous. I don't know what I am doing. |
| *Judge Duff:* | Don't worry about it. We all know you are not a lawyer. Plaintiff's Exhibit 1 is the ID card. Plaintiff's Exhibit No. 2 is the City of Chicago notice of Provisional Dock. . . . |

The plaintiff is unfamiliar with the process of marking exhibits, establishing a basis for the exhibit, and requesting that the evidence be admitted into the record. Wzorek wants a doctor's letter admitted; His Honor helps.

| | |
|---|---|
| *Smith:* | If I may interject one other thing. We spent approximately three hours last night with Mr. Wzorek going over the pretrial order. We discussed in detail what exhibits he would use, what exhibits we would use. That doctor's note was never once mentioned by Mr. Wzorek. |
| *Wzorek:* | This was already put in a long time ago. |

| | |
|---|---|
| *Smith:* | No, it wasn't. It was not part of his original submission. |
| *Judge Duff:* | Well, he doesn't understand that. You asked him for it at the deposition. He gave it to you at the deposition. He has a right to believe that you have it. I am going to accept it. This is No. 3. |

In another wrestling match over admissibility, Judge Duff explains basic trial procedure.

| | |
|---|---|
| *Judge Duff:* | Were you given the name of the witness in advance? |
| *Wzorek:* | No, they didn't tell me nothing. They didn't tell me who is the witness yet. |
| *Judge Duff:* | When did this come up? |
| *Wzorek:* | This just came up in the last day. It happened when I got the thing on Monday. |
| *Judge Duff:* | You save that and object when they try to put on those witnesses. . . . If those witnesses get on and they say something you haven't put on in your case in chief, you will be given an opportunity to rebut it. If they get on. But you can raise your objection before they get on. Let us go on to other things. |

The judge expresses a little bench humor and some compassion for the lonely plaintiff.

| | |
|---|---|
| *Ex:* | I am sorry. We are having a little problem hearing, and he is speaking a little rapidly in speed, and his tone makes a difference. |
| *Judge Duff:* | Don't talk at the same time as each other because the court reporter is as good as any I have ever had but she can't take three people at once, except I know who she is going to take down when I am talking. . . . Mr. Wzorek you do speak a little quickly and Ms. Brennan has to be able to get down what you say. |
| *Wzorek:* | Sorry about it. It is just a bad habit. |
| *Judge Duff:* | Just try to slow down. |
| *Wzorek:* | I will try. |
| *Judge Duff:* | Relax. |

A discussion of the "ward card" takes place. City employees had to fill out the card with ward, age, birth date, and precinct (a political history). Mr. Ex objects to the foundation and the plaintiff reacts.

| | |
|---|---|
| *Wzorek:* | So, like I say, when they say they don't know what ward you are from or not, that is unbelievable. That's just my opinion. You will have to decide on it yourself, your honor. But they know where they are from. |
| *Ex:* | Objection. |
| *Judge Duff:* | Sustained. |
| *Wzorek:* | Sorry. I'm trying like hell. |
| *Judge Duff:* | You are doing all right. |

The judge cuts through procedural red tape again in the interest of justice.

| | |
|---|---|
| *Ex:* | Your Honor, I would object— |
| *Judge Duff:* | Object to what? |
| *Ex:* | To the tax returns. We have not had any of those documents either turned over to us, or have— |
| *Judge Duff:* | Did you ask for them? |
| *Ex:* | Yes, your honor. We asked for them prior to trial. |
| *Judge Duff:* | Show me when you asked for them. |
| *Ex:* | Well, your honor, I believe it was requested approximately a week or two before this trial started. Supplemental interrogatory questions to try and determine what damages he feels he has suffered. |
| *Judge Duff:* | I think if you only asked last week, that is pretty late. Objection overruled. |

Next, the judge deals with a problem that is not uncommon in the legal profession. An attorney starts a case, collects some fees, finds a great deal of additional work is necessary (or some other obstacle), and bills the client for additional time. The client, now in over his or her head, can't (or doesn't) pay, and the attorney holds the file hostage for payment. It's called an attorney's lien, and it is permitted in some jurisdictions.

| | |
|---|---|
| *Wzorek:* | Your Honor, Mr. Mitchell, the last attorney I had, had my tax return. That is why I couldn't even do nothing with them even if somebody asked. I'll try to get it from him. I couldn't get all my stuff. |
| *Judge Duff:* | Can you get it? |

| | |
|---|---|
| *Wzorek:* | Okay, I'll try. Is it all right if I get it, because I might owe him some money. |
| *Judge Duff:* | Yes. You tell him I want it. |
| *Wzorek:* | Okay. I couldn't get all the stuff because he told me I couldn't get the stuff unless I paid him. |
| *Judge Duff:* | Not so. Not so. If he tells you that, you tell me tomorrow morning first thing. |

In cases with pro se litigants, it's reasonable to expect the professional, the lawyer, to be helpful in the interest of justice and the search for truth.

| | |
|---|---|
| *Judge Duff:* | Do you know how to issue a subpoena? |
| *Wzorek:* | No, sir. |
| *Judge Duff:* | Help him issue a subpoena. |
| *Smith:* | That is to Mr. Mitchell? |
| *Judge Duff:* | To his lawyer. I want the records. Apparently he is claiming an attorney's lien on them. That is not going to stop me from getting them for evidence in this case. |

At this point in the trial the real crux of the case comes out in the plaintiff's testimony. Wzorek, in his political dealings, made a great end run down the field—but in the wrong direction.

| | |
|---|---|
| *Judge Duff:* | So why do you say then, in summary, that you were discharged for political reasons? |
| *Wzorek:* | Well, because I gave Daley the $1,000. And, I guess according to them I shouldn't have done it. |
| *Judge Duff:* | Who said you shouldn't have done it? |
| *Wzorek:* | William Sommerford. |
| *Judge Duff:* | What did he say? |
| *Wzorek:* | He said you can get in trouble for this. You would be better off giving it to Jane [Byrne] or giving it to Harold [Washington] because Richie Daley has enemies. Because everybody in the Sewer Department didn't like Daley. |

Now for the cross-examination of Wzorek by Smith:

| | |
|---|---|
| *Smith:* | Mr. Wzorek, isn't it true that Harold Washington was not even elected mayor until 1983? |
| *Wzorek:* | Well, the point is, if you let me just be brief on this, he was running for mayor. They were all running for it then. So, in |

other words, whoever was going to win the title was going to get the jobs. That's the name of the game.

*Smith:* Isn't it true Mr. Sommerford specifically stated to you that you could get in trouble with the incumbent by making that donation?

*Wzorek:* No, he says, "you can get in trouble further down the line. . . ." He said, "Hey, Gene, can I talk to you?" And he put his arm on my shoulder and he says, "I heard you gave Daley some money, a grand." I says, "Who told you?" He didn't want to say. He says, "Word goes around like that." And I says, "I didn't." And he says to me, "You might have made a mistake there because Jane Byrne is the incumbent."

When I said I didn't, I was going to try and hide it from, but he knew that I knew it so I admitted it then. I said, "Yes, I gave it to him." I knew what was going on now. So I was going to try and tell Mr. Sommerford, but I couldn't hold back. They had me for giving the money."

In his continuing legal "lessons," Judge Duff teaches something of great historical interest. A few moments later, the judge explains the trial procedure to the plaintiff.

*Judge Duff:* Mr. Wzorek, I would like to show you what has been marked for identification as Respondent's Exhibit 13, and ask you if you recognize that document.

*Smith:* Your Honor, I have a copy for the Court.

*Judge Duff:* Counsel, will you hand those things to the court reporter? There is a reason for that, historically. That is the recognition of the bench and the bar. It is a symbolic separation. That is the bar, and you should not go around the bar. Same thinking with the jury bar by the way. Lawyers should really not intrude into the jury bar. That is why we have marshals and other people go for the jury instead of lawyers. A lot of people don't know the reasons for that.

Now, there is a system, Mr. Wzorek, called direct examination, cross-examination, and redirect examination. That means at this time you can testify on matters that were discussed, or just asked in cross-examination which weren't covered in your direct examination. If it was already covered in your direct examination, you can't repeat it.

Now our unschooled plaintiff becomes a regular Perry Mason and begins the arduous job of calling witnesses and eliciting testimony.

| | |
|---|---|
| *Judge Duff:* | Who is your next witness? |
| *Wzorek:* | I think Ron Gorski. Would you state your name. |
| *Gorski:* | Ronald Paul Gorski. |
| *Wzorek:* | Would you give your age and address? |
| *Gorski:* | My age is 34. My address is 4431 North Wolcot, Chicago. |
| *Wzorek:* | Where do you work? |
| *Gorski:* | I work for a private contractor. I am a carpenter. |
| *Wzorek:* | Have you ever worked for the Sewer Department? |
| *Gorski:* | Yes, I have. |
| *Wzorek:* | From what year to what year? |
| *Gorski:* | April 4, 1982 until June 30, 1986. |
| *Wzorek:* | Do you know Eugene Wzorek? |
| *Gorski:* | Yes, I do. |
| *Wzorek:* | Were you present during a conversation between Eugene Wzorek and William Sommerford? |

After the city has had its turn to defend the charges of illegal firing, corruption, and patronage, the court explains the rebuttal procedure to the plaintiff and queries him on taking the stand again.

| | |
|---|---|
| *Judge Duff:* | You were going to take the stand in rebuttal, Mr. Wzorek. Go ahead. |
| *Wzorek:* | Can I make an argument? |
| *Judge Duff:* | No, it's not argument. You should understand there is a difference between argument, which I'm going to give you a chance to argue, and testimony, which is evidence. Now, you're under oath and you took the stand earlier. |
| *Wzorek:* | Okay. |
| *Judge Duff:* | And some other people took the stand and said some things in their questions you wanted to argue with them. |
| *Wzorek:* | Oh, that kind of stuff. |
| *Judge Duff:* | And you wanted to say that it wasn't so. So, what you're being allowed to do is to testify, not to argue. |
| *Wzorek:* | Okay. |
| *Judge Duff:* | Not explain things, but testify about specific things that you say other people said that you don't think are true. |
| *Wzorek:* | Oh, okay. |

Following is the plaintiff's closing argument (in part).

*Wzorek:*        In conclusion, your honor, the original charges are irrelevant
                 and a pretext to hide the real reason for my firing, my
                 thousand dollars to Daley, the wrong, and my loss of political
                 protection. . . .

The corporate counsel starts to summarize the city's position, and Judge
Duff interrupts and reduces the whole controversy to its simplest common
denominator.

*Ex:*            . . . I believe Section 6 of that ordinance and Rule 9, section
                 3 of the personnel rules, all of which are part of our exhibits,
                 your Honor, in evidence—
*Judge Duff:*    Why are you talking about all this stuff? You say yourself
                 the whole question is whether he was fired for political
                 motives. They didn't have a right to fire him for political
                 motives, and if they did, you lose and if they didn't, you win,
                 right?
*Ex:*            That's correct, your Honor.
*Judge Duff:*    Then why are we going into all this other stuff?

The city, in its arrogance, takes the position that all Wzorek had to do was
show his union card and obtain other employment.

*Judge Duff:*    Do you know of any hiring halls for truck drivers?
*Ex:*            Well, your honor—
*Judge Duff:*    That was the question you asked him.
*Ex:*            Well, your honor—
*Judge Duff:*    All I have got is his testimony. I don't have anything from
                 you to the contrary.
*Ex:*            Your honor, that point aside, I still think that the overriding
                 point is that there is a lack of competent evidence showing
                 that this man was incapable of ascertaining any type of work,
                 even truck driving related work, which he himself testified
                 that he had been doing for a number of years with the city of
                 Chicago.

Wzorek explains in his closing that only five additional days would have
prevented his firing, and that he actually had those days but the city jerry-

rigged the system and did not pay him for the sick time to which he was entitled.

| | |
|---|---|
| *Wzorek:* | So, in other words, if I would have had the five days which they did not pay me for, which I'm entitled to from 1983, not from '84, '83, I would have made career service, you're not taken off the roll. I wouldn't have been fired until July 5th, and I would have had the right to a hearing. It's as simple as that. |
| *Judge Duff:* | They didn't argue that in their rebuttal, so they don't think you should argue it now. |
| *Wzorek:* | So, would I be career service then? |
| *Judge Duff:* | Good point. |
| *Wzorek:* | If I'm career service I shouldn't be fired. |
| *Judge Duff:* | Okay. |
| *Ex:* | Your Honor, just on the point of vacation that has just been brought up. . . . I believe state law actually is clearly to the contrary—that your vacation time is not a factor, is not part of any consideration of accrual of probationary career service. |
| *Judge Duff:* | It says the custom and usage was that it wouldn't be—he wouldn't be taken off the payroll until after the five days has expired. He was never paid for the time. |
| *Ex:* | Well, and I believe the reason he wasn't was because that the city fired him for poor performance and under that particular standard, that they were not obligated to pay him for vacation time. |
| *Judge Duff:* | It says right on the exit interview that they're obligated to pay him. |

After both sides have pleaded their case, entered evidence, examined and cross-examined witnesses, and argued their cases before the judge, Judge Duff recites his findings.

| | |
|---|---|
| *Judge Duff:* | . . . I think there is no question at all that the [plaintiff] has proven that he was fired for political reasons beyond—with clear and convincing evidence. The petitioner was fired for political reasons, period. |

What you have just read was taken from the transcript of *Wzorek v. The City of Chicago.* With each change in the leadership of Chicago came retributions to those employees who supported the wrong side—retributions that were against the law. In this case, the city marshaled its legal forces to try to uphold, in federal court, the illegal and immoral actions of its leaders, and to attempt to quash a citizen in the process. Members of the bar were paid by Wzorek for their services but, for reasons unknown, dropped the case. Yet the little guy didn't give up, and the patient judge was more interested in truth and justice than in accolades from his peers. The city attorneys complained to the *Chicago Sun-Times* that Judge Duff seemed to "bend over backwards" for Wzorek while keeping them within tight procedural bounds. But on July 13, 1990, the Seventh Circuit Court of Appeals affirmed Judge Duff's findings of fact and law and the award of $180,408 made to Eugene Wzorek.

The Wzorek case is unique in many ways, but its lessons are important for all. We can't expect all judges to help a pro se litigant through the labyrinth of procedure, but it is refreshing to know that it is possible that justice in its purest form is still achievable in the United States. As Judge Duff said, "[Wzorek] was going after the truth, you have to understand that his damages hurt him, hurt him a lot. . . . This was a gutsy little guy, just giving it his best shot. Frankly, it was wonderful justice."

I asked Judge Duff if he would encourage people who found themselves stuck between a rock and a hard place to represent themselves in court. He replied:

> I don't know. I often, in my court, never let the little guy get hit, but the law itself says both sides have the right to their equal shot, so if the little guy deserves to lose, he should lose. But he shouldn't lose just because he's a little guy. Now the problem is, and I've said to some of them, I've begged some of them, please get a lawyer. . . . You're living in a world where there are pitfalls of statutes of limitation, and rules of procedure, and they must be lived to because no matter what I might want, in terms of personal justice, I have to follow the rules and the Seventh Circuit [Court of Appeals] has to follow the rules. So, the chasms are deep, I sometimes tell people that it's like walking through a cow field with a blindfold on . . . you may get to the other side okay, but it's so difficult to win one's own way. I've had some pro se's and we've been able to get to the other side. . . .

## TOOLS YOU WILL NEED FOR PRO SE ACTION

There are some other useful tools besides this book to help you get to the other side, to help balance the scales when you enter the legal arena. These publications are available at most law libraries, or from the publishers.

A copy of *Black's Law Dictionary* (or other suitable substitute) is a must for the pro se individual or businessperson involved in any area of the law. Black's contains over 10,000 definitions and includes case situations for further study. It's published by West Publishing Company, 50 West Kellogg Boulevard, St. Paul, MN 55164-0526. Many quality booksellers carry Black's.

For instruction on legal research, I recommend a colorful and informative booklet from West that is available free for the asking, *West's Law Finder: A Legal Research Manual.* It takes you from the history of case reporting right up to electronic research.

If you are going to submit your research to a court or tribunal, you must follow a special format for quoting authorities. A handy spiral-bound publication prepared by the Harvard Law Review Association called *A Uniform System of Citation* (Gannett House, Cambridge, MA 02138) covers this subject very well.

If you want an overview or an in-depth study of certain aspects of the law, look to *The Art of Advocacy*, a thirteen-volume set from Matthew Bender Publishing Company. This informative and easy-to-use looseleaf set covers preparation of the case, discovery, cross-examination of lay witnesses, settlement, jury selection, opening statement, demonstrative evidence, summation, appeals, documentary evidence, and direct examination, as well as cross-examination of medical experts. Each volume of *The Art of Advocacy* is a detailed study of its subject with supporting case law, and is written in easy-to-understand language.

You will be amazed at the subjects covered in this set. For instance, Chapter 3 of *Preparation of the Case* is almost a complete course in how to become a private detective. The would-be Sherlock Holmes is even provided with a list of electronic gadgetry for gathering and storing information:

1. Camera with 50-mm lens.

2. Wide-angle lens for scene photography.

3. Telephoto lens for close-ups and surveillance.

4. Precision mirrored lens for detail photos.

5. Polaroid camera for identification shots and close-ups of evidence.

6. Video recorder and camera.

7. Cassette tape recorder for interviews.

8. Nagra-recorder (precision recording device capable of recording three hours on reel-to-reel tape).

9.  Portable radios for communication.

10. Mobile telephone.

11. Scanners (50-frequency UHF/VHF radio frequency monitor).

12. Binoculars.

13. Magnifiers.

14. Tape measures.

You may go broke buying all this equipment, but you will be prepared to be a regular sleuth, capable of the most sophisticated surveillance modern technology can supply. You never know when your legal case may depend on collecting intelligence.

In Chapter 6 of the same volume, "Mining the Sources," the author provides one of the most complete sources of available reference material we have ever come across. This listing lets you know the incredible range of material you can access. Here is the contents of the chapter:

Sec. 6.10 Sources on Liability
Sec. 6.11 The Basic Reference Library
Sec. 6.12 Technical Publications
Sec. 6.13 Association Publications
Sec. 6.14 Federal Government Sources
Sec. 6.15 Local Government Agencies
Sec. 6.16 News Media Sources
Sec. 6.17 Standards and Codes
Sec. 6.18 The Parties as a Source
Sec. 6.19 Specialized Liability Areas

Sec. 6.20 Sources on Damages
Sec. 6.21 Governmental Sources
Sec. 6.22 Medical Works for the Lawyer
Sec. 6.23 The Basic Medical Library
Sec. 6.24 The Advanced Medical Library
Sec. 6.25 Medical Research for Lawyers
Sec. 6.26 Information about Doctors
Sec. 6.27 Information about Hospitals
Sec. 6.28 Medical Films

Sec. 6.30 Electronic Sources of Information

When it comes to wills, West Publishing again has the right book. Requirements for all fifty states, plus information on trusts and related documents, are provided in *West Legal Forms: Estate Planning with Tax Analysis.* On the subject of probate, Macmillan publishes the now-famous *How to Avoid Probate* by N. Dacey. If probate is necessary, check your local law library for information relating to your jurisdiction's rules, as this can be a very complicated subject requiring the services of an expert.

For an in-depth discussion of trial techniques, I recommend Thomas A. Mauet's *Fundamentals of Trial Techniques,* published by Little, Brown & Company (Boston, MA). This book is relatively easy to understand and covers the subject well. While we're on the subject of trials, I enjoyed reading *Effective Closing Arguments* by Peter C. Lagarias, published by the Michie Company (Charlottesville, VA). It has a wealth of fascinating stories along with the eloquent arguments made by some of the most famous litigators. In the same general area, the American Bar Association's *Litigation Manual: A Primer for Trial Lawyers* provides more advanced detail than Mauet.

If you have questions about arbitration or alternative dispute resolution, the American Arbitration Association (AAA) provides many pamphlets on the subject and will be more than willing to help. Their address is 140 West 51st Street, New York, NY 10020-1203; telephone (212) 484-4000. The AAA publication *Facts About the American Arbitration Association* will provide you branch addresses, telephone numbers, and persons in charge of thirty-five AAA offices around the country. One of the AAA's pamphlets, *Resolving Your Disputes,* quoted in Chapter 14, also lists all the AAA offices.

For the task of determining what possible action and what possible remedy is available for a given legal situation, I recommend *Action and Remedies* by Charles E. Friend (Callahan, 63201 Old Glenn View Road, Wilmat, IL 60091), and *Shepard's Causes of Action* (Shepard's/McGraw-Hill, Colorado Springs, CO). If you are interested in the study of jurisdiction as it applies to civil actions, you might be interested in looking at *Jurisdiction and Civil*

*Actions* by Robert C. Casad (Warren, Gorham & Lamont, Boston). As you become more deeply involved in research for a case or legal action, the list of publications found in most law libraries will be of great help.

For basic reference (government information centers, lists of experts, government organizations, etc.), use *Lawyer's Desk Reference* by Harry Philo (Lawyers Cooperative Publishing Company, Rochester, NY). For negligence and accidents, see *The Accident Prevention Manual* by the National Safety Council; *Highway Collision Analysis* by Collins and Morris (Charles C. Thomas); *Manual of Accident Prevention in Construction* by the Associated Contractors of America; *Product Liability* by Frumer and Friedman (Matthew Bender), and *Damages in Tort Actions* (Matthew Bender).

For chemicals and poisons, read *Clinical Toxicology of Commercial Products* (Williams & Wilkins). For health, contact the Health Physics Society in McLean, Virginia. For air travel, contact the Flight Safety Foundation in Arlington, Virginia. For highway travel, contact the National Highway Users Conference in Washington, D.C.

If you plan to obtain a ship's mortgage (similar to a house mortgage) or need to provide a customer with a disclosure statement for a loan note that conforms to truth in lending regulations, look for a book entitled *Simplified Consumer Credit Forms* by Carl Felsenfeld and Alan Siegel (Warren, Gorham & Lamont). The book has 132 forms, and they are not limited to credit. For instance, Chapter 10 provides a complete set of marriage dissolution documents. Other forms included are personal lending application, permission to secure credit reports, combined disclosure statement and loan note, transfer agreement for sale of personal or real property, hypothecation agreement, car loan advertisement, apartment lease agreement, note, mortgage, second mortgage loan set, truth-in-lending, real estate sales contract, agreement to hire a lawyer (retainer agreement), fiduciary powers, and assignment of discoveries and inventions. For the individual acting pro se, this form book is well worth its $64 list price (1992).

Many federal agencies, under authority of specific statutes, issue regulations that, if violated by regulated parties, provide the basis for a possible claim. Here are a few examples of some of the more consumer-oriented statutes that may be found in the Code of Federal Regulations:

- Consumer Product Safety Act: 15 USC Sec. 2051.
- Federal Food, Drug and Cosmetics Act: 21 USCS Secs. 301-392.
- Federal Firearms Act: 15 USCS Secs. 901-909.
- Flammable Fabrics Act: 15 USCS Secs. 1191-1200.

- Child Protection Act: 15 USCS Secs. 1261-1265.
- National Traffic and Motor Vehicle Safety Act of 1966: 15 USCS Secs. 1391-1425.
- Federal Hazardous Substances Labelling Act: 15 USCS Secs. 1331-1339.
- Fair Packaging and Labelling Act: 15 USCS Secs. 1451-1461.
- Refrigerator Safety Devices: 15 USCS Secs. 1213-1214.
- Lanham (trademark) Act: 15 USCS Sec. 1127.
- Civil Rights Act.
- False Claims Act.

Has justice gone awry? Is access to the legal system restricted to those with deep pockets? To quote Judge Duff again, "I think Congress said to us all get out there and do this law and so we're supposed to. . . . That's really our heritage, but you know when you access the courts, it's overwhelmed by stature and money and dignity and it [the heavy use of the courts] is breaking down the system."

There are, however, some bright spots for public use and access to the court system. In Broward County, a poll of all county court judges indicated that 50 percent of cases brought to trial by a pro se plaintiff against a defendant with an attorney resulted in victory for the plaintiff. The ABA's publication *A Report on Self-Help Law: Its Many Perspectives*, by Steven R. Cox and Mark Dwyer and sponsored by the ABA's Special Committee on the Delivery of Legal Services (a quote from which began this book), indicates some strong statistics in favor of the do-it-yourself legalist. Here are some of the salient points that resulted from a Phoenix and Maricopa County, Arizona, study:

- The incidence of self-help [Bar Association term for pro se] divorce virtually doubled from 24 percent to 47 percent between 1980 and 1985.
- 4.5 percent of self-help cases (26 out of 586) [had] contested post-decree action, whereas almost 10 percent of attorney-handled cases (56 out of 572) involved some enforcement or modification action.
- Average duration of attorney-handled default divorce cases was actually greater than that of self-help default divorce cases. In two-thirds of those cases [where changes in representation took place] the change was from attorney to self-representation.
- Self-helpers, due to their personal involvement, may possess greater motivation to maximize case benefits.
- Evidence presented . . . shows that attorney and self-help completion and

dismissal rates for divorce cases varied by no more than one percentage point.

- Self-helpers are reported to encounter concerns (regarding) service of process, especially out-of-state service. As several interviewees pointed out, however, even lawyers have problems when attempting out-of-state service.

Perhaps the solution to an improved civil justice system lies in a court system that is trained to provide greater public access, a public more educated in the workings of the judicial system, and a legal community that exercises significantly better control of its members, all helping to protect the public from the types of problems that make pro se action necessary. For now, though, self-help may be the answer.

I rest my case!

# Glossary

*The language of the law must not be foreign to the ears of those who are to obey it.*

—Learned Hand

Although the English language is changing at an alarming rate, the legal profession has followed a more prudent course, maintaining a precise means of expressing itself throughout the ages.

Understanding the meaning of the law begins with understanding the words and terms used to express its specialized concepts. As the Talmud states, "The beginning of wisdom is to call things by their right names." In order to get the most out of this book, review the definitions and concepts in this glossary and refer to them as needed.

Some of the words that follow may seem strange at first, but you need to know and understand them as you navigate your way through the pages of this book and attempt to engage or defend an action. Knowing and understanding these terms in their legal context will help you to better comprehend legal principles.

**acknowledgment.** As used in a document, confirms the truth or veracity of the content of the document with a signature that may be sworn to. In the general sense: Confirming or admitting to the authenticity or correctness of a set of facts.

**action.** The word used to describe the underlying circumstances that justify and establish the basis for filing a lawsuit. It may also be used to denote a lawsuit.

**actionable.** A word that describes a set of circumstances that may be considered the basis for legal relief or for filing a lawsuit.

**ad litem.** "For the purpose of the suit." A person appointed specifically to perform a limited function within a particular lawsuit: Guardian ad litem.

**administrative law and procedure.** An area of law enacted by a governmental body, usually establishing board or commission, which is granted the power to impose rules, regulations, and procedures affecting a relatively narrow area of activity, such as the Federal Communications Commission or the Food and Drug Administration.

**ADR (alternative dispute resolution).** Methods of resolving conflicts without resorting to the court system, such as conciliation, mediation, and arbitration (see Chapter 14).

**affirmative defense.** New matter that constitutes a defense to a charge that has been asserted in the complaint; it must be raised in the answer to the complaint (see page 90).

**amended complaint.** Corrects faults, errors, and omissions of an original complaint.

**answer.** The formal written statement made by a defendant stating the defense. The answer is used by the defendant to resist the plaintiff's allegations of fact, or to confess to the facts and allege new information to avoid the plaintiff's attempt to win on facts presented.

**appellate.** Relating to a legal appeal from a decision of a lower court or from alternative dispute resolution, as appellate court. The appellant is the party appealing the lower court's judgment; the appellee is the opposing party in the appeal.

**arbitration.** The assignment of a dispute to an impartial third party chosen by the parties to the dispute, who have agreed in advance to abide by the arbitrator's decision rendered after a hearing.

**attorney's lien.** The right of an attorney to retain or keep a portion of a client's money or property until fees and costs have been paid.

**attestation.** Executing (signing) a document as a witness.

**avoidance.** Formally distinguishing or denying allegations made in the adversary's pleading, to indicate why the facts alleged should not be actionable as claimed by the other party.

**brief.** A written summary of the facts, laws, and arguments of a position in a lawsuit; appellate brief.

**burden of proof.** The obligation of a particular party to establish a sufficient level of proof in a lawsuit.

**certiorari.** The certifying to or acceptance of a lower court's record for review by a higher court.

**chancery.** Predecessor to courts of equity. May still be used in certain jurisdictions to designate courts of equity.

**chose in action.** A right to an action for recovery that becomes enforceable only after a successful lawsuit.

**citation.** Written reference to statutes, cases, texts, articles, and opinions that are authorities for the subject matter under discussion.

**civil contempt.** Usually applied to a willful failure to comply with a court order, such as an injunction or the appearance at a deposition or other judicial process as directed by the court.

Punishment for civil contempt may be a fine or imprisonment; the object of such punishment is ultimate compliance with the court order.

**competent.** As to an individual, one who is legally capable; qualified to act in a legally acceptable capacity—to draw a will, to be served in a lawsuit, to testify.

**complaint.** The original pleading or paperwork filed within a jurisdiction, by which an action is commenced. The document sets forth a statement or claim for relief, and usually contains (1) a short statement of the reasons the court has jurisdiction, (2) a short statement showing why the pleader is entitled to a favorable decision, and (3) a demand for judgment to which the pleader feels entitled for the relief sought in the alternative.

**complainant.** The party that initiates a lawsuit.

**continuance.** Postponement or adjournment of a legal proceeding (session, hearing, trial) to a later date or time.

**costs.** The out-of-pocket expenditures involved in a lawsuit, usually other than attorneys' fees. Certain costs are awarded to the party that prevails in the action. Costs usually include filing fees, court reporter fees, witness fees, sheriff's fees, and expert fees. In a foreclosure action, you will see abstract and title fees, and so on.

**counterclaim.** A claim asserted by a defendant in opposition to or as a deduction from the claim of the plaintiff. Counterclaims are either compulsory or permissive. If compulsory, a pleading should state any claims that, at the time the pleading is served, the pleader has against any opposing party's claim. (That is, of course, if the court has jurisdiction and the matter is not subject to other litigation at the time). If permissive, a pleading may state in a counterclaim only claims against an opposing party not arising out of the transaction or occurrence that is the subject of the opposing party's claim. Counterclaim is the generally accepted word for offsets and setoffs.

**criminal contempt.** An action that may be construed as obstruction of justice. Conduct directed against the dignity and authority of the court (see civil contempt).

**cross-claim.** A claim by one party against any other party with the same designation (i.e., another defendant), named in a particular lawsuit. The claim must arise out of the transaction or occurrence that is the subject of either the original action or of a counterclaim relating to any property (or dispute) that is the subject of the original action.

Cross-claims involve parties with the same designation (plaintiff or defendant) in the litigation, whereas counterclaims involve parties on opposite sides.

**damages.** An amount of value that is claimed or intended as compensation or reparation for a loss or injury (see Chapter 12).

**de facto.** The acceptance of a fact that appears to be legally or otherwise not so.

**default.** An omission of that which ought to be done. Specifically, the omission or failure to perform a legal or contractual duty, to observe a promise, or to discharge an obligation.

**default judgment.** When a party against whom a judgment is asked of the court fails to answer or otherwise defend the action, that party is in default and a judgment by default may be entered by the clerk of the court.

**defendant.** The person or entity in a lawsuit named by the plaintiff as being responsible. The defendant has certain rights and obligations in a lawsuit.

**deposition.** The process of taking oral testimony under oath, recorded by an officer of the court, and used as discovery along with interrogatories, request for admissions, and production prior to a trial or hearing.

**dictum.** The holding or opinion in a case that is not the primary issue, but is often gratuitously inserted. A comment or apparent decision on a side issue; as such, it is not a controlling precedent.

**direct case/case in chief/on direct.** The initial presentation of the plaintiff's case during trial through the introduction of evidence to support his or her claim.

**discovery.** The stage of litigation that allows each side to obtain information, documents, and other materials to help them determine and ready the facts of the case (see Chapter 7).

**docket.** The court's calendar of legal activities or the court's record of individual documents filed within a particular case.

**duces tecum.** See subpoena.

**ejectment.** An action to restore to a person or entity entitled to it the possession of a premises or property.

**eminent domain.** A government's right to take or use any real property within its jurisdiction.

**equity.** Justice administered by applying standards of fairness rather than formal rules and regulations.

**estoppel.** When a party is prevented from raising a particular issue or claim, or where an issue or claim has been conclusively resolved and a party is charged with direct knowledge that the matter was so resolved (see page 92).

**et al.** "And others."

**et seq.** "And the following."

**evidence.** Documents, testimony, and other forms of proof, whether written or unwritten, that demonstrate the truth of a litigant's statements or position (see Chapters 10, 15).

**exhibit.** A document or thing used as evidence in a legal proceeding.

**ex parte.** A judicial proceeding or hearing that has been held at the request of one party without notice to the other party, and which results in the issuance of an order or other judicial decree.

**fiduciary.** An individual who has accepted legal responsibility to act in a representative or responsible capacity for another.

**final judgment.** Judgment is considered final when it determines the rights of the parties to an action and disposes of all the issues involved so that no future action of the court will be necessary to determine the entire controversy. The final judgment leaves nothing for the court to do in a case except to carry out the judgment. It is from this judgment that appeals are born.

**for cause.** A challenge that is used when a prospective juror is obviously hostile or prejudiced toward, or is clearly related to, one of the parties to the litigation, and which makes elimination of the prospective juror mandatory.

**headnote.** A summary of a legal issue placed ahead of the actual text of the case opinion or ruling in a reporter, or report, of the case.

**hearing (nonlegislative).**   A proceeding of relative formality before a magistrate, judge, hearing examiner, or administrative law judge, without jury, dealing with issues of fact or law. Witnesses may be heard and evidence may be presented in much the same manner as at trial. The session may terminate in a final order on the issues in question.

**impeachment.**   In a trial, demonstrating to the judge and/or jury, especially through cross-examination, that a witness' testimony is not credible or reliable.

**in personam.**   Having control or jurisdiction over an individual.

**in re.**   "Concerning," "regarding," "in the matter of."

**in rem.**   Shorthand reference to a proceeding or action involving tangible things or property.

**joint and several.**   One or more parties may be liable either individually or all together.

**judgment.**   The final decision of a court, rendered in written form.

**judicial notice.**   Recognition by a judge that a given fact is true, for the purpose of acceptance as evidence during trial, especially when it is generally well known but would be unduly time-consuming and difficult to prove formally.

**jurisdiction.**   The authority by which courts and judicial officers take cognizance of and decide cases, or the legal rights by which judges exercise their authority. This term encompasses the power and authority of a court to hear and determine a judicial proceeding, and the power of a court to rule concerning the subject matter in a given case. The geographic area in which a court has authority, and the types of cases it has authority to hear.

**laches, doctrine of.**   The legal principle by which a person who knows what he or she must do to assert a claim or right, but who neglects or omits to do so within a reasonable period of time, is considered to have surrendered that right or claim.

**lien.**   A legally recognized encumbrance or security interest attaching to a property.

**maker.**   One who signs or executes a promissory note, check, or other document evidencing an obligation.

**mandamus.**   "We command." A command or directive issued by court order, often called a writ of mandamus and often directed from a higher court to a lower court. It is traditionally issued in response to abuses of judicial power.

**mitigation of damages.** Limiting further damages that could occur when damages and injury have already occurred. All parties should exercise reasonable care to limit further damage or injury.

**motion.** A formal request from a party to a lawsuit (or his or her attorney) asking the court for a particular rule or order.

**motion to dismiss.** A motion requesting that a complaint be dismissed by the court, usually based on the theory that either the complaint has been drawn incorrectly or that the complaint fails to properly set forth a claim upon which relief can be granted.

**nonjoinder.** A proper party to a lawsuit who has not been previously joined, either as a plaintiff or a defendant. That party is subject to being joined upon proper motion and service.

**novation.** The act of substituting a new agreement for a prior agreement. Where there is an existing contract, debt, or obligation and the terms of the agreement evidencing that contract, debt, or obligation are materially changed or restated without releasing the original contract, debt, or obligation.

**on point.** Closely analogous; an earlier case that addresses the same issues and situation involved in a current suit is said to be on point.

**order.** The ruling, directive, mandate, or command issued by a judge, usually in written form.

**parol.** Verbal, or by word of mouth. Usually refers to an oral contract or agreement.

**peremptory challenge.** Challenging a prospective juror without the need for explanation. The number of such challenges that may be used in the course of jury selection is limited.

**perjury (civil).** A false statement under oath or affirmation, usually involving an official or court proceeding.

**petition.** A formal, written application to a court requesting action on a matter. Also, a formal written request addressed to a governmental body. The right to petition for redress of grievances is protected by the First Amendment to the Constitution.

**petitioner.** The party that starts an equity proceeding or the party that takes an appeal from judgment. In legal proceedings that are initiated by petition, the person against whom action or relief is sought or the person or entity who opposes the petition is called the respondent.

**plaintiff.**   A person or entity who brings a legal action; a complaining party seeking remedial relief for damage or injury to rights. The plaintiff has certain rights and responsibilities in a lawsuit, such as presenting the case first and summing up first. The plaintiff also pays the court filing fees to start the lawsuit.

**pleadings.**   These contain the formal allegations of the parties, including the complaint, the answer, counterclaim, cross-claim, third-party complaint, and their respective answers. The Rules of Civil Procedure establish which documents are pleadings.

**precedent.**   The results of cases that have been tried and decided. The rulings and rationales from previous cases are often used in deciding later cases, particularly where no statute directly addresses the situation at issue.

**preponderance of evidence.**   Evidence that is more convincing and holds greater weight than the evidence that may be offered in opposition.

**presumption.**   A presumed fact that is recognized by the court, and which will be accepted by the court unless it is convincingly overcome.

**pretrial conference.**   Usually called by the court, this is used to narrow the issues to be tried in order to facilitate a settlement or otherwise help dispose the case.

**probate.**   The formal procedure used to establish the validity, correctness, or truth of a will. Wills are generally required to go through this process in a probate court, which uses a set of laws or rules often called "the probate code."

**quash.**   Voiding, nullifying, vacating, overthrowing, or abating of (usually) indictments or original service in a civil lawsuit. The setting aside of the original action or pleading.

**replevin.**   The statutory action intended to return or retrieve specific goods or property to the rightful owner, where another party has wrongfully retained the property.

**reporter.**   A volume or set of volumes, usually continually updated copies of court or administrative law decisions. Usually found in law libraries.

**res.**   A thing; an object or the subject matter of rights. All law relates to persons (*persona*), actions, or things (*res*).

**res judicata.**   The principle of law that holds that once a matter is judicially decided, it is finally decided.

**respondent.**   The party in an equity action, similar to a defendant in a civil action, who makes an answer to an equity action. In appellate actions, the respondent is the party that is against the appeal (the appellee).

**setoff.** In the situation where a plaintiff is entitled to a recovery from the defendant but where, in a separate matter, the defendant is owed money by the plaintiff, the amount owed by the plaintiff to the defendant may be deducted from the plaintiff's recovery.

**statute.** A law enacted by legislative process.

**stay.** The stopping of a judicial proceeding by order of the court. The suspension of or cessation of some designated proceeding.

**stay of execution.** The stopping or arresting of the act of executing on a judgment or other order of the court.

**stipulation.** An agreement between two or more litigating parties.

**subpoena.** A command to appear at a certain time and place to give testimony regarding a certain matter. A *subpoena duces tecum* requires the recipient to produce books, papers, and possibly other things related to the subject matter of the action, and usually to give testimony about the items requested.

**subrogation.** The formal substitution of one party for another, where the new party takes on all the rights, remedies, or claims of the original party. Most often used when an insurance company substitutes as a party in a lawsuit after it has paid its insured and then seeks reimbursement from a third party as if it were in the place of the insured party.

**surety.** A party who obligates himself or herself to be responsible for another party—the principal—pursuant to the original contract or obligation. Similar to a guarantor.

**summary judgment.** A party to a civil action may move the court for a decision in its favor on a claim, counterclaim, or cross-claim when he or she believes that there is no issue of material fact and that the law is clearly on his or her side. Outside material, evidence, and affidavits may be used in support of this motion.

**summons.** Document utilized at the beginning of civil action. It is a means of acquiring jurisdiction over an individual or entity. When a complaint is filed, the court clerk issues a summons available for delivery to the marshal, sheriff, or a person specially appointed to serve it on those named. The following may be requirements for a summons: (1) Signed by the clerk of the court; (2) be under the seal of the court; (3) contain the name of the court; (4) indicate the names of the parties; (5) be directed to the defendant; (6) state the name and address of the plaintiff's attorney or the plaintiff; (7) state the time within which rules require the defendant's appearance or response; (8) give notification that if the defendant fails to defend, judgment by default will be rendered against the defendant for the relief sought in the complaint.

**supplemental complaint.** Under the Federal Rules of Procedure and in most states, this is filed to bring to the attention of the court and the opposing party matters occurring after the commencement of an action that may affect the rights asserted in the original complaint.

**third-party claims.** A complaint filed by a defendant in an action against a person or entity not presently in the lawsuit (a third party) alleging that the party is or may be liable for all or part of the damages involved in the matter.

**tort.** An action arising from a violation of a duty, a civil wrong, or injury not involving a contract, which is committed upon another person or property. A personal injury lawsuit is a tort action.

**tort-feasor.** A person who commits an intentional or unintentional act against another that causes mental or physical injury.

**to the favor.** Grounds for challenging a prospective juror who has some relationship to one of the parties to the litigation that may cause bias, such as an employer/employee relationship.

**ultra vires act.** An act committed by a corporation or officer of a corporation that is not authorized either by virtue of the corporate charter or state laws establishing the corporation's powers.

**usurious.** A rate of interest that is greater than that allowed by statute within a given jurisdiction.

**venue.** The particular city, county, state, or federal district in which a court with jurisdiction may hear and determine a case. Venue deals with the locality of a suit and relates only to the place where or territory within which either party may require a case to be heard.

**voir dire.** Literally "to speak the truth," this can refer to the process of jury selection or the initial qualifying questioning of an expert witness.

**waiver.** The relinquishment, abandonment, or cessation of a right or interest that one possesses. Though generally an intentional, unilateral, or voluntary act, a waiver may occur unintentionally or involuntarily.

**with prejudice.** A final order or judgment that is intended to be conclusive or dispositive as to the rights of the parties in the action. Such an order would require an appeal in the event of a dispute with its conclusion.

**without prejudice.** When a case is dismissed where the dismissal is not meant as a final or dispositive declaration of rights or privileges in the action, the action may be refiled thereafter, assuming all other factors are suitable for refiling, e.g. the statute of limitations has not expired.

**writ.** The form of a court order requiring or directing a specific act or performance to take place.

**writ of execution.** A document issued by the court following an award of damages which, when filed with the appropriate authorities, permits those authorities to seize and sell certain property to make payment toward the damages and any assessed costs.

# APPENDIX I

# Anatomy of a Final Argument

The following case took place in 1981. The annotated condensed summation from the actual trial is presented here as an example of an excellent final argument. Studying this summation may enable you to apply some of its strategies to your own case.

John Smith filed suit in a California court against Gold Shield of California in an action for an alleged bad-faith denial of payments on a medical insurance policy. The plaintiff became sick and was diagnosed as anemic. His physician, concerned about a possibly serious condition, immediately hospitalized his patient. After tests revealed no demonstrable illness, the plaintiff was discharged from the hospital. A claim for medical expenses was submitted to Gold Shield of California, the insurer. Gold Shield denied payment on the grounds that their doctors reviewed the case and found that there was insufficient reason for hospitalization—in effect, second-guessing Smith's physician. Arbitration followed, and Smith was awarded $1,200 for the hospital bill, $12,000 for emotional distress, and $300,000 in punitive damages. Gold Shield cried foul (or "bias," in legal terms), and managed to get the whole affair into court. Before the final arguments began, the judge ruled that Gold Shield had indeed breached its duty to Mr. Smith. The remaining issues for the jury to decide were whether the breach had caused emotional distress and other damages, and whether an amount of punitive damages was warranted.

The plaintiff's attorney, William Shernoff, in his closing argument (and rebuttal), is trying to convince the jury that emotional distress occurred and should be compensated for, as well as that punitive damages are called for.

*Shernoff:* Counsel, ladies and gentlemen of the jury. . . . [*Shernoff refers to a financial statement he wants the jury to be aware of before he begins his closing argument in earnest. Then he describes his concept of what a closing argument is for.*] This is the time when the lawyers let loose a little bit because in closing argument, both counsel have the opportunity to sum up, and more or less let the jury know what we think about the evidence as it came in, and argue the significance of it and the interpretations of it.

*Shernoff explains to the jury his thoughts about divergent views and a society that has an open and free justice system.*

You are just deciding this case from what you have heard on the witness stand and the documents and the court's instruction, and that's what is really great about our jury system and about the fact that people such as yourselves can decide important issues of the day.

*Shernoff now moves into an explanation of punitive damages as punishment and the duty of good faith and fair dealing.*

You will see from the jury instructions that the purpose, one of the purposes, of punitive damages is to punish and to deter conduct of this company in the future for sake of example of others. The punitive effect of your verdict may have an effect on the way they conduct business in the future, affecting other people, and that's a very important issue. You are going to set the punishment, if you think it is warranted in this case. [*He now picks up on the key issues.*] I think the issues are whether Gold Shield did violate their duty of good faith and fair dealing and did they consciously disregard the rights of Mr. Smith.

Whether it's the treating doctor's decision, there really is no controversy. We say it should be the treating doctor's decision as to whether or not a patient should be hospitalized. (Dr. Van) knew the patient for a long time. He thought his patient was dying and did what a good doctor should do.

*Now Shernoff, the plaintiff's counsel, uses existing testimony from an adverse witness to hit on the point he has been trying to make by reading actual trial testimony.*

*Opposing Counsel:* Can I have page and line number, your honor? [*Shernoff agrees.*]
*Shernoff:* This is Dr. Kleig, page 74, lines 24 through 28. [*Reading*] "Question: Doctor, you just indicated in response to my question that you felt that Dr. Van's feeling was that the patient was sick enough to be in the hospital. Is that correct? Answer: Yes."

Page 78, lines 9 through 25. "Question: In other words, what you are saying is if a treating physician sincerely feels that his patient is sufficiently sick to be in the hospital, he should not put him in the hospital? Answer: That is not correct. He should put him in the hospital. Question: Okay. And then when you—What you are saying is once he is in the hospital, appropriate care should be administered? Answer: Yes, sir. Question: And in this case, you—you have some criticisms of the care that was administered while he was in the hospital? Answer: Yes, sir. Question: But you are not quarreling with the fact that Dr. Van at the time exercised proper judgment in putting him in? Answer: That's correct."

*Shernoff now identifies another issue—the review process.*

If they are going to have some Monday-morning quarterback review the process, at least go about it in a way that was calculated to get the treating doctor's reasons for hospitalization so that they can make an intelligent judgment. [*He brings in evidence to support this newly identified issue.*] Now, let's look at this review process. On March 19, the very day (the complete hospital chart) came in, Dr. Fox made his initial decision to reject the claim. There is no contest. That is the first step to get the doctor's orders, or get some information from the doctor. Both Dr. Zee and their own witness, Dr. Barry, at the end of this case testified as to the proper method of getting information. You get a consent. You won't see that [one] in this case.

*Shernoff now argues a conclusion that Gold Shield did not carefully review the decision to hospitalize Smith, and uses factual support.*

You know the truth of the matter is they didn't care what the (treating physician's) impressions were. Remember Dr. Fox saying there was nothing in the hospital chart that in any way referred to an admitting diagnosis of anemia, then I pointed out to him that the nurse's admitting note says, "Anemic. Doctor trying to find out why."

*Shernoff weaves witness credibility into his argument as he contrasts the actions of Gold Shield to those of Smith's physician.*

He didn't even know that Dr. Van had been a Gold Shield member physician since 1948, three years after the war. I can hardly remember back then.

A question put under oath before trial: List all the people that in any way processed the claim, but nowhere in there did they mention Dr. Jackson being involved, Dr. Lowell being involved, Beverly Jones being involved. Now, I don't know which under-oath testimony we are to believe; signed under oath [deposition], or testimony under oath from the witness stand.

*At this point, defense counsel objects to one side failing to call a witness that is available to both sides. The judge rules the objection is off point and admonishes the disruptive nature of the objection.*
*Shernoff moves his argument to the area of jury instructions. He treads carefully, as this area is usually the province of the court.*

*Shernoff:* Ladies and gentlemen, I was simply referring to a jury instruction. Incidentally, you will be read all the jury instructions and we have made separate sets of jury instructions so each of you will have his or her own instructions in the jury room, and you can read them for yourself.
*Judge:* Why don't I go into that briefly. [*The judge indicates to the jury that each member will be given a set of jury instructions.*]

*Shernoff goes back to expert testimony regarding the review process, and uses pathos.*

*Shernoff:* Peer review to make the doctor now a bad guy and apologize for the insurance company tears down the physician-patient relationship. Think about that for a second. You go into the hospital and you come out and you are presented with the bill and you get a letter from your insurance company. Your doctor made a mistake. Now, what does that do to the doctor-patient relationship? Yeah, your doctor is a dummy.
[*Shernoff reasserts the case for punishment as deterrent.*] Now, we are getting to the heart of the dispute in this case, hopefully your verdict will speak loud enough to force a reevaluation of this whole process. The hospital's utilization review committee, as you will recall on several occasions, felt the hospital payment was justified and all Gold Shield did was argue with them.

*A closing argument should integrate the jury instructions with the factual evidence. The court's rulings set the stage for Shernoff to pursue emotional distress and punitive damages.*

When we talk about this peer review, listen to the court's instruction, or read it carefully. They had a duty to inform John Smith of peer review. . . . [*Shernoff quotes from the instructions and then continues.*] That's the law, not from me, from the court. The court made a ruling: In this case, as a matter of law, the conduct of Gold Shield of California in disagreeing with the judgment of the treating physician to hospitalize his patient solely on the basis of retrospective review of hospital files is a violation of the duty of good faith and fair dealing where the subscriber is not clearly informed of this procedure in the health plan. . . .

*Understatement is an effective method of reaching out to a jury, particularly in damage cases. Shernoff uses this approach, as well as exposing a weakness in his case—the lack of psychiatric care.*

Emotional distress, as used in those instructions, is often described as including all highly unpleasant mental reactions, such as humiliation, anger, worry. Mr. Smith was disillusioned. He finally dipped into his savings and paid the $1,200 hospital bill. He was proud of his financial record. He always paid cash. I don't know how to put a monetary value on emotional distress, but I will offer you a guideline that I think would be a reasonable range I think for suffering in the last five years, something in the range of $5,000 to $25,000. Some of you might think that's a little too little. He didn't go to a psychiatrist, but he was frustrated and was angry and deserved some compensation.

*Now Shernoff devotes a lot of time to discussing the jury instructions relative to punitive damages.*

Now we ask about punitive damages as punishment, as a penalty, as a fine, as an example. I have to read to you at least a portion of the jury instruction on punitive damages. [*Reading*] "If you find that plaintiff suffered damages as a proximate result of the conduct of the defendant on which you base a finding of liability, you may then consider whether you should award punitive or exemplary damages against defendant Gold Shield of California for the sake of example and by way of punishment. You may in your discretion award such damages if, but only if, you find a preponderance of the evidence that said defendant was guilty of oppression, fraud, or malice in the conduct of which you base your finding of liability."

*Malice* means conduct that is intended by the defendant to cause damage to the plaintiff or carried on by the defendant with a conscious disregard of the rights of others.

*Oppression* means subjecting a person to cruel and unusual hardship in conscious disregard of the rights of others.

A corporation acts with conscious disregard of the rights of others when it is aware of the probable consequences of its conduct and fails to avoid those consequences.

Nonintentional conduct, nonintentional conduct comes within the definition of malice punishable by the assessment of punitive damages where a party performs an act that it knows or should know is highly probable to cause damage to another.

Let me first say, you don't have to find fraud, malice, or oppression. It could be one of the three and I haven't even defined fraud for you yet, and I will get to that in a minute. But there is no question that the conduct of Gold Shield—that they knew or should have known (it) was highly probable to cause John Smith damage.

(*Fraud* is) intentional misrepresentation, deceit, concealment of a material fact known to the defendant with the intention on the part of the defendant of thereby depriving a person of property or legal rights or otherwise causing damage.

*Now Shernoff combines facts with the instructions about punitive damages.*

They concealed this whole review process. Wouldn't you like to know within the plan that the question of medical necessity is not going to be determined by your doctor? [*Reading from transcript*] "Dr. Zee: To my knowledge, the only other insurance companies that do retrospective review based on hospitalization or diagnostic purposes is Gold Shield or Gold Cross."

You don't even know whether you have insurance until after you get out. Who would buy that policy if it stated the truth? So, besides conscious disregard you have got concealment. You have got deceit. You have got almost punitive damages on every basis imaginable under the law and you only need one.

*Shernoff switches to the amount of damages, reviews previous arguments in support of his case, and touches on a reasonable relationship of the defendant's financial condition to the amount of the award.*

Here's what the instruction says. It says: "The law provides no fixed standard as to the amount of such punitive damages, but leaves the amount to the jury's sound discretion, exercised without passion or prejudice. In arriving at an award of punitive damages, you are to consider the following: One, the reprehensibility of the conduct of the defendant." *Reprehensibility* means how reprehensible. It was how bad it was.

"Two, the amount of punitive damages that will have a deterrent effect on the defendant in light of the defendant's financial condition." That's why we put in the balance sheet and the net equity figure.

"Three, that the punitive damages must bear a reasonable relationship to actual damages."

You are going to vote on a decision that will have an effect on the health care system in this state. That's important. That's democracy. That's your job.

Where a company takes premiums to protect somebody, a subscriber, and then through the very important procedure it sets up, it makes them victims for following their doctor's orders. Not informing millions of people, including Mr. Smith, of what should be in that brochure, that's quite reprehensible.

Punitive damages must bear a reasonable relationship to actual damages. There are no further guidelines on that. The amount of punitive damages that will have a deterrent effect on the defendant in light of the defendant's financial condition, net equity of some $56,206,000. Now, if you were to say punish them $56 million, you would have every right to say that's not punishment, that's persecution; wipe them out. That's silly. We are talking about an appropriate punishment: $28 million, ridiculous. A quarter, $14 million, ridiculous. Too much. Ten percent would be $5.6 (million) . . . five percent would be $2.8 (million), and two percent would be $1.12 (million). Two percent, five percent, ten percent. Ladies and gentlemen of the jury, I think that a reasonable range to punish somebody to have the proper deterrent effect, on somebody that has the wealth, the net equity of $56 million, would be somewhere in the two to five percent category of net equity.

*Shernoff now goes into his closing, reminding the jury of the tremendous burden they carry in terms of the outcome of the case and fairness to the parties.*

Everybody is to be judged by the same standard, rich or poor, and I don't think two to five percent of the net equity would be unreasonable in anybody's book. If you come in with a verdict where they can just walk out of this courtroom back in San Francisco and smile and say, "Well, we don't have to change this; business as usual," we have lost everything. If you come out with a verdict that is meaningful and speaks and is a proper punishment, and let somebody look at it in the position of responsibility and say maybe our conduct should be deterred in the future, that's what this case is about. It's about changing the way the company handles claims of its subscribers in the future. Listen to both sides. Decide for yourself who is telling the truth. I do appreciate your listening to me all this time. I have been told by many people that you should never keep a jury past lunch and I certainly do not want to do that in this case. We believe in this system. I particularly believe in the system of letting the jury set the punishment. Let's turn democracy back to the people where it belongs. Thank you very much.

# APPENDIX II

# Hypothetical Case and Judge's Instructions to Jury

*Automobile collision; comparative negligence; single claimant and defendant; no counterclaim; seat belt defense.*

## FACTS OF THE CASE

John Doe was injured when the automobile he was driving collided with one driven by Richard Rowe with the consent of its owner, Sam Bell. Doe sued Rowe and Bell. They pleaded contributory negligence and also that Doe's damages would have been reduced had he used his available and fully operational seat belt. Questions of negligence, causation, and damages are to be submitted to the jury.

## THE COURT'S CHARGE

Members of the jury, I shall now instruct you on the law that you must follow in reaching your verdict. It is your duty as jurors to weigh and consider the evidence, to decide the disputed issues of fact, and to apply the law to the facts as you find them from the evidence.

In determining the believability of any witness and the weight to be given the testimony of any witness, you may properly consider the demeanor of the witness while testifying; the frankness or lack of frankness of the witness; the intelligence of the witness; any interest the witness may have in the outcome of the case; the means and opportunity the witness had to know the facts about which the witness testified; and the reasonableness of the testimony of the witness, considered in the light of your own experience and common sense.

The issues for your determination on the claim of plaintiff, John Doe, against defendants Richard Rowe and Sam Bell are whether defendant Rowe was negligent in operating Bell's car; and, if so, whether such negligence was a legal cause of loss, injury, or damage sustained by plaintiff Doe.

If the greater weight of the evidence does not support the claim of Doe, then your verdict should be for the defendants.

If, however, the greater weight of the evidence does support the claim of Doe, then you shall consider the defense raised by the defendants.

On the defense, the issues for your determination are whether Doe was himself negligent and, if so, whether such negligence was a contributing legal cause of the accident complained of.

If the greater weight of the evidence does not support the defense and the greater weight of the evidence does support the claim of Doe, then your verdict should be for Doe in the total amount of his damages.

However, if the greater weight of the evidence shows that both Doe and Rowe were negligent and that the negligence of each contributed as a legal cause of the accident, you should determine what percentage of the total negligence of both parties, Doe and Rowe, is chargeable to each.

"Greater weight of the evidence" means the more persuasive and convincing force and effect of the entire evidence in this case.

Negligence is the failure to use reasonable care. Reasonable care is that degree of care that a reasonably careful person would use under like circumstances. Negligence may consist either in doing something that a reasonably careful person would not do under like circumstances or in failing to do something that a reasonably careful person would do under like circumstances.

Negligence is a legal cause of loss, injury, or damage if it directly and in natural and continuous sequence produces or contributes substantially to producing such damages, so that it can reasonably be said that, but for the negligence, the damage would not have occurred.

In order to be regarded as a legal cause of loss, injury, or damage, negligence need not be the only cause. Negligence may be a legal cause of damage even though it operates in combination with the act of another if such other cause occurs at the same time as the negligence and if the negligence contributes substantially to producing such damage.

If your verdict is for defendants, Rowe and Bell, you will not consider the matter of damages. But, if your verdict is for Doe, you should determine and write on the verdict form, in dollars, the total amount of damages that the greater weight of the evidence shows he sustained as a result of the incident complained of, including any such damages as he is reasonably certain to experience in the future. You shall consider the following elements:

Any bodily injury sustained by Doe, and any resulting pain and suffering experienced in the past or to be experienced in the future. There is no exact standard for measuring of such damage. The amount should be fair and just in the light of the evidence.

The reasonable value or expense of medical care and treatment necessarily or reasonably obtained by Doe in the past or to be so obtained in the future.

If the greater weight of the evidence shows that plaintiff Doe has been permanently injured, you may consider his life expectancy. The mortality tables received in evidence may be considered in determining how long Doe may be expected to live. Such tables are not binding on you but may be considered together with other evidence in the case bearing on Doe's health, age, and physical condition, before and after the injury, in determining the probable length of his life.

Any amounts that you allow in damages for future medical expenses or loss of ability to earn money in the future should be reduced to their present money value and only the present money value of such amounts should be included in your verdict.

Rowe and Bell contend that some or all of Doe's damages were caused by his failure to use a seat belt.

The automobile occupied by Doe was equipped with an available and fully operational seat belt. [In this model charge, this preemptive charge is appropriate. In other circumstances, the issue should be submitted to the jury.]

The issues for your determination on this question are whether the greater weight of the evidence shows that Doe did not use the seat belt, that a reasonably careful person would have done so under the circumstances, and that Doe's failure to use the seat belt produced or contributed substantially to producing the damages sustained by Doe. If the greater weight of the evidence does not support Rowe and Bell on each of these issues, then your verdict on this question should be for Doe. If the greater weight of the evidence supports Rowe and Bell on these issues, you should determine what percentage of Doe's total damages were caused by his failure to use the seat belt.

In determining the total amount of damages, you should not make any reduction because of the negligence, if any, of plaintiff Doe or any reduction because of Doe's failure to wear a seat belt. The court will enter a judgment based on your verdict and will reduce the total amount of damages by any percentage of negligence that you find is chargeable to plaintiff Doe and also by any percentage of Doe's total damages that you find were caused by Doe's failure to use the seat belt.

Your verdict must be based on the evidence that has been received and the law on which I have instructed you. In reaching your verdict, you are not to be swayed from the performance of your duty by prejudice, sympathy, or any other sentiment for or against any party.

When you retire to the jury room, you should select one of your number to act as foreman or forewoman to preside over your deliberations and sign your verdict. Your verdict must be unanimous; that is, your verdict must be agreed to by each of you.

You will be given one verdict form, which I shall now read to you. When you have agreed on your verdict, the foreman or forewoman, acting for the jury, should date and sign the verdict form. You may now retire to consider your verdict.

## SPECIAL VERDICT FORM

### Verdict

We, the jury, return the following verdict:

1.  Was there negligence on the part of defendant, Richard Rowe, that was a legal cause of damage to plaintiff, John Doe?

    YES____          NO____

If your answer to question 1 is NO, your verdict is for defendants, and you should not proceed further except to date and sign this verdict form and return it to the courtroom. If your answer to question 1 is YES, please answer question 2.

2.  Was there negligence on the part of plaintiff Doe that was a legal cause of the accident? (In answering this question, do not consider plaintiff's use of or failure to use a seat belt.)

    YES____          NO____

If your answer to question 2 is YES, please answer question 3. If your answer to question 2 is NO, skip question 3 and answer question 4.

3.  State the percentage of all negligence that was a legal cause of the accident that you charge to:

    Defendant Rowe ____%     Plaintiff Doe ____%

    (Total must be 100%.)

Please answer question 4.

4. What is the total amount (100%) of any damages sustained by plaintiff Doe and caused by the accident?

Total damages of plaintiff Doe       $____

In determining the total amount of damages, do not make any reduction because of negligence, if any, of plaintiff Doe. The court in entering judgment on your verdict will make the appropriate reduction.

5. Did the plaintiff Doe fail to use reasonable care under the circumstances by failing to use an available and fully operational seat belt?

YES____         NO____

If your answer to question 5 is NO, you should not proceed further except to date and sign this verdict form and return it to the courtroom. If your answer to question 5 is YES, please answer question 6.

6. Did the plaintiff Doe's failure to use the seat belt produce or contribute substantially to producing any of the plaintiff Doe's damages?

YES____         NO____

If your answer to question 6 is NO, you should not proceed further except to date and sign the verdict form and return it to the courtroom. If your answer to question 6 is YES, please answer question 7.

7. What percentage of plaintiff Doe's total damages were caused by his failure to use the seat belt?

____%

Do not make any reduction of total damages because of Doe's failure to wear a seat belt. The court in entering a judgment will make the appropriate reduction.

SO SAY WE ALL THIS ____ day of _____,19 ____.

_____
Foreman or Forewoman

# *APPENDIX III*
# Pretrial Stipulation

A joint pretrial stipulation must be filed by all counsel of record not less than twenty days before the beginning of the trial period. These stipulations should contain the following in separately numbered paragraphs (based on Broward County Rules of Court; the form may vary from jurisdiction to jurisdiction):

1. Concise, impartial statement of the facts of the case.

2. List of any stipulated facts requiring no proof at trial.

3. Statement of disputed issues of law and fact to be tried.

4. Exhibits, listed by number and description on a separate schedule attached to the stipulation and initialed by all counsel prior to trial.

5. Witnesses (including "rebuttal" or "impeachment" witnesses) and their addresses, listed numerically on a separate schedule attached to the stipulation, with all expert witnesses so designated.

6. Agreed jury instructions and disputed jury instructions.

7. Agreed verdict form or disputed verdict forms.

8. Number of peremptory challenges for each party.

9. List of all pending motions requiring action by the court.

At trial, the parties shall be strictly limited to exhibits and witnesses disclosed and objections reserved in the pretrial stipulation (or at the pretrial conference). A party desiring to use an exhibit, examination, test result, or witness discovered after the pretrial conference must immediately, upon discovery, notify all other counsel and the court. Use of these may be allowed for good cause shown or to prevent manifest injustice.

# APPENDIX IV

# Sample Litigation Forms

The following forms are some of the most common pleading forms. They have been reprinted from *Florida Rules of Court—State* (West Publishing), and are presented here only as a guide to typical form pleading. The Florida Supreme Court has approved these forms, thus prohibiting a challenge to their form in individual cases in Florida. These forms vary from state to state, and it is important to use the accepted form in the jurisdiction in which you plan to litigate. However, most states take the approach that a court-approved form cannot be challenged, except on its substance.

These forms do not show the "style" of the case (see page 60), i.e., the format for showing the names of the plaintiffs, the defendants, the courts, the case number and court division, as well as the certificate of service (see page 84) and signatures.

### Form 1.931 Jurisdictional Statement—Law. Actions for Damages

Action for Damages

This is an action for damages that
(a) do not exceed $2,500.
(b) exceed $15,000.
(c) exceed $10,000 but do not exceed $15,000 (if filed after July 1992).

**NOTE:** Choice (a) is for the small claims division of county court, (b) for circuit court, and (c) for county court without summary procedure.

Added June 19, 1968, effective Oct. 1, 1968 (211 So.2d 174).
Amended Oct. 9, 1980, effective Jan. 1, 1981 (391 So.2d 165).

#### Committee Notes

**1980 Amendment.** The form has been modernized by inserting the amounts that are now applicable under the constitution and general law. Formerly the number of courts and varying jurisdictions did not make completion of the blanks for the amounts practicable.

## Form 1.932   Open Account

### Complaint

Plaintiff, A. B., sues defendant, C. D., and alleges:

1.  This is an action for damages that (insert jurisdictional amount).

2.  Defendant owes plaintiff $____ that is due with interest since _____ , 19 ___, according to the attached account.

WHEREFORE plaintiff demands judgment for damages against defendant.

**NOTE:** A copy of the account showing items, time of accrual of each and amount of each must be attached.

Added June 19, 1968, effective Oct. 1, 1968 (211 So.2d 174).

## Form 1.933   Account Stated

### Complaint

Plaintiff, A. B., sues defendant C. D., and alleges:

1.  This-is an action for damages that (insert jurisdictional amount).

2.  Before the institution of this action plaintiff and defendant had business transactions between them and on _____ 19___, they agreed to the resulting balance.

3.  Plaintiff rendered a statement of it to defendant, a copy being attached, and defendant did not object to the statement.

4.  Defendant owes plaintiff $____ that is due with interest since _____ , 19___, on the account.

WHEREFORE plaintiff demands judgment for damages against defendant.

**NOTE:** A copy of the account showing items, time of accrual of each and amount of each must be attached.

Added June 19, 1968, effective Oct. 1, 1968 (211 So.2d 174).

## Form 1.934   Promissory Note

### Complaint

Plaintiff, A. B., sues defendant C. D., and alleges:

1.  This is an action for damages that (insert jurisdictional amount).

2. On _____19 __, defendant executed and delivered a promissory note, a copy being attached, to plaintiff in _____ County, Florida.

3. Plaintiff owns and holds the note.

4. Defendant failed to pay (Use A or B)
   (A) the note when due.
   (B) the installment payment due on the note on _____ 19___, and plaintiff elected to accelerate payment of the balance.

5. Defendant owes plaintiff $_____ that is due with interest since _____19___, on the note.

6. Plaintiff is obligated to pay his attorneys a reasonable fee for their services.

   WHEREFORE plaintiff demands judgment for damages against defendant.

   **NOTE:** A copy of the note must be attached. Use paragraph 4A, or B, as applicable and paragraph 6 if appropriate.

   Added June 19, 1968, effective Oct. 1, 1968 (211 So.2d 174).
   Amended Oct. 9, 1980, effective Jan. 1, 1981 (391 So.2d 165).

### Committee Notes

**1980 Amendment.** Paragraph 3 is added to show ownership of the note and paragraph 4 is clarified to show that either 4A, or 4B, is used, but not both.

## Form 1.935   Goods Sold

Plaintiff, A. B., sues defendant, C. D., and alleges:

1. This is an action for damages that (insert jurisdictional amount).

2. Defendant owes plaintiff $_____ that is due with interest since _____, 19___, for the following goods sold and delivered by plaintiff to defendant between _____, 19___, and _____, 19___: (list goods and prices)

   WHEREFORE plaintiff demands judgment for damages against defendant.

   Added June 19, 1968, effective Oct. 1, 1968 (211 So.2d 174).

## Form 1.936   Money Lent

### Complaint

Plaintiff, A. B., sues defendant, C. D., and alleges:

1. This is an action for damages that (insert jurisdictional amount).

2. Defendant owes plaintiff $_____ that is due with interest since _____, 19___, for money lent by plaintiff to defendant on _____ , 19___.

WHEREFORE plaintiff demands judgment for damages against defendant.

Added June 19, 1968, effective Oct. 1, 1968 (211 So.2d 174).

## Form 1.937   Replevin

### Complaint

Plaintiff, A. B., sues defendant, C. D., and alleges:

1. This is an action to recover possession of personal property in _____ County, Florida.

2. The description of the property is:

   (list property)

   To the best of the plaintiff's knowledge, information, and belief, the value of the property is $_____.

3. Plaintiff is entitled to the possession of the property under a security agreement dated _____, 19___, a copy of the agreement being attached.

4. To plaintiff's best knowledge, information, and belief, the property is located at _____

5. The property is wrongfully detained by defendant. Defendant came into possession of the property by (describe method of possession). To plaintiff's best knowledge, information, and belief, defendant detains the property because (give reasons).

6. The property has not been taken for any tax, assessment, or fine pursuant to law.

7. The property has not been taken under an execution or attachment against plaintiff's property.

WHEREFORE plaintiff demands judgment for possession of the property.

## Form 1.942   Check

### Complaint

Plaintiff, A. B., sues defendant, C. D., and alleges:

1. This is an action for damages that (insert jurisdictional amount).

2. On _____19___, defendant executed a written order for the payment of $_____, commonly called a check, a copy being attached, payable to the order of plaintiff and delivered it to him.

3. The check was presented for payment to the drawee bank but payment was refused.

4. Plaintiff holds the check and it has not been paid.

5. Defendant owes plaintiff $_____ that is due with interest from _____, 19___, on the check.

WHEREFORE plaintiff demands judgment for damages against defendant.

**NOTE:** A copy of the check must be attached. Allegations about endorsements are omitted from this form and must be added when proper.

Added June 19, 1968, effective Oct. 1. 1968 (211 So.2d 174).
Amended Oct. 9, 1980, effective Jan. 1, 1981 (391 So.2d 165).

### Committee Notes

**1980 Amendment.** Paragraph 4 is divided into two paragraphs to properly accord with Rule 1.110(f).

---

## Form 1.943(a)   Petition for Dissolution of Marriage

The petition of A. B. shows:

1. This is an action for dissolution of the marriage between petitioner and respondent, C. D.

2. Petitioner has been a resident of Florida for more than six months next before filing the petition.

3. Petitioner and respondent were married to each other on _____, 19___, at (place of marriage).

4. The marriage between the parties is irretrievably broken.

WHEREFORE petitioner demands a judgment dissolving the marriage.

**NOTE:** Allegations about joint property, alimony, custody, attorneys' fees, and temporary relief are omitted from this form and must be added when proper. Similarly, a demand for judgment for these items must be added when proper. Verified allegations or an affidavit must be used when child custody is an issue. See 61.132, Florida Statutes (1979).

Former Form 1.943 added June 19, 1968, effective Oct. 1, 1968 (211 So.2d 174). Amended Sept. 29, 1971, effective Dec. 13, 1971 (253 So.2d 404); Oct. 9, 1980, effective Jan. 1, 1981 (391 So.2d 165) redesignated as Form 1.943(a) Dec. 8, 1983 and Feb. 17, 1984 (450 So.2d 810), and May 3, 1984, effective June 1, 1984 (450 So.2d 817).

**Committee Notes**

**1980 Amendment.** The form is amended to change the demand for judgment to comply with Rule 1.110(b) and to make editorial changes.

---

## Form 1.943(b)   Petition for Simplified Dissolution of Marriage

The petition of Husband and Wife shows:

1.  This is a petition for dissolution of marriage.

2.  The Husband and the Wife or one of them has been a resident of Florida for at least six (6) months immediately prior to filing this petition.

3.  Husband and Wife were married to each other on _____ 19___, at _____.

4.  The marriage between the parties is irretrievably broken.

5.  There are no minor or dependent children of the parties and the Wife is not pregnant.

6.  The parties have made provisions for the division of their property and the payment of their joint obligations. They are satisfied with those provisions. [The property settlement agreement entered into by the parties and a financial affidavit from each party are attached.]

7.  The parties understand that they may have legal rights against each other arising out of the marital relationship and that by signing this petition they may be giving up those rights.

8.  Each party certifies that he/she has not been threatened or pressured into signing this petition. Each understands that the result of signing this petition may be a final dissolution of the marriage with no further relief.

9.  The parties understand that they are required to appear before the judge to testify as to the matters contained in this petition.

10   The address of each party is as stated below.

11.   The Wife wishes to have her former name restored to her. (Yes ___ No ___) If "Yes," state Wife's former name: _____

WHEREFORE, Husband and Wife ask the Court to dissolve the marriage existing between them.

UNDER PENALTY OF PERJURY, WE CERTIFY THE FOREGOING FACTS ARE TRUE.

_____          _____
Wife's signature                          Husband's signature

Wife's name typed          Husband's name typed

Wife's residence address   Husband's residence address

SWORN TO AND SIGNED before me this ____ day of ____, 19__.

CLERK OF THE CIRCUIT COURT

By_____
DEPUTY CLERK

**NOTE:** The property settlement agreement and financial affidavits should be used only when the circumstances are appropriate for their inclusion in the proceeding. Added Dec. 8, 1983, to be effective June 1, 1984 (450 So.2d 810). Amended May 3, 1984, effective June 1, 1984 (450 So.2d 817).

## Form 1.943(c)   Certificate of Corroborating Witness

UNDER PENALTY OF PERJURY I CERTIFY that I am a resident of the State of Florida; I have known (insert name of Husband or Wife) for more than six (6) months preceding this date and I know of my own personal knowledge that such person has resided in the State of Florida for at least that period of time.

Witness' Signature

Witness' Name Typed

Witness' Residence Address

SWORN TO AND SIGNED before me this ____ day of _____ , 19__.

CLERK OF THE CIRCUIT COURT
OR  NOTARY PUBLIC

Added Dec. 8, 1983, to be effective June 1, 1984 (450 So.2d 810)
Amended May 3, 1984, Effective June 1, 1984 (450 So.2d 817).

## Form 1.943(d)   Financial Affidavit for Simplified Dissolution of Marriage

STATE OF FLORIDA
COUNTY OF _____

Before me, the undersigned authority, personally appeared _____, who was sworn
and says that the following statement of affiant's income, assets, and liabilities is true:

Occupation _____

Employed by _____

Business address _____

Pay period _____

ITEM 1: INCOME (Averaged on _____ Basis):

| | | |
|---|---|---|
| Average GROSS Wage | | $____ |
| Less Deductions | | |
| Federal Income Tax | $____ | |
| Social Security | $____ | |
| Other | $____ | |
| Total Deductions | | $____ |
| Average NET Wage | | $____ |
| Other Income | | |
| _____ | | $____ |
| _____ | | $____ |
| TOTAL NET INCOME | | $____ |

ITEM 2: ASSETS

| | |
|---|---|
| Cash on hand or in banks | $____ |
| Stocks, bonds, notes | $____ |
| Real estate | $____ |
| Home | $____ |
| Other | $____ |
| Automobiles | $____ |
| Other personal property | $____ |

Other assets

_____      $____

_____      $____

TOTAL ASSETS      $____

ITEM 3: LIABILITIES

Real estate mortgages      $____

Automobile loans      $____

Other notes and loans      $____

Other

_____      $____

_____      $____

TOTAL LIABILITIES      $____

_____
Affiant

Sworn to and subscribed before me this ____ day of ____, 19___.

_____
CLERK OF COURT
OR NOTARY PUBLIC

**NOTE:** A financial affidavit may not be necessary in every case, particularly where the parties have already completed a division of their property. A financial affidavit would be appropriate, however, where there is a continuing obligation of one or both parties because of the property agreement. Added May 3, 1984, effective June 1, 1984 (450 So.2d 817).

## Form 1.943(e)    Property Settlement Agreement for Simplified Dissolution of Marriage

We, _____ (the Husband) and _____ (the Wife) were married on _____.

Because irreconcilable differences have caused the permanent breakdown of our marriage, we have made this agreement to settle once and for all what we owe to each other and what we can expect from each other. Each of us states that nothing has been held back, that we have honestly included everything we could think of in listing the money and goods that we own; and each of us states that we believe the other one has been open and honest in writing up this agreement. Each of us agrees to sign and exchange any papers that might be needed to complete this agreement.

*Division of Property*

We divide our property as follows:

1. Husband transfers to Wife as her sole and separate property:

   A.
   B.
   C.
   D.
   E.
   F.
   G.

2. Wife transfers to Husband as his sole and separate property:

   A.
   B.
   C.
   D.
   E.
   F.
   G.

*Division of Debts*

1. Husband shall pay the following debts and will not at any time hold Wife responsible for them:

   A.
   B.
   C.
   D.
   E.

2. Wife shall pay the following debts and will not at any time hold Husband responsible for them:

   A.
   B.
   C.
   D.
   E.

Dated: _____          Dated: _____

   _____                _____
   Husband                         Wife

Added May 3, 1984, effective June 1, 1984 (450 So.2d 817).

## Form 1.944  Mortgage Foreclosure

### Complaint

Plaintiff, A. B., sues defendant, C. D., and alleges:

1. This is an action to foreclose a mortgage on real property in_____County, Florida.

2. On _____, 19___, defendant executed and delivered a promissory note and a mortgage securing payment of the note to plaintiff. The mortgage was recorded on _____, 19___, in Official Records Book _____ at page _____ of the public records of _____ County, Florida, and mortgaged the property described in the mortgage then owned by and in possession of the mortgagor, a copy of the mortgage containing a copy of the note being attached.

3. Plaintiff owns and holds the note and mortgage.

4. The property is now owned by defendant who holds possession.

5. Defendant has defaulted under the note and mortgage by failing to pay the payment due _____ , 19 ___, and all subsequent payments.

6. Plaintiff declares the full amount payable under the note and mortgage to be due.

7. Defendant owes plaintiff $_____ that is due on principal on the note and mortgage, interest from _____, 19___, and title search expense for ascertaining necessary parties to this action.

8. Plaintiff is obligated to pay his attorneys a reasonable fee for their services.

WHEREFORE plaintiff demands judgment foreclosing the mortgage and, if the proceeds of the sale are insufficient to pay plaintiff's claim, a deficiency judgment.

NOTE: This form is for installment payments with acceleration. It omits allegations about junior encumbrances, unpaid taxes, unpaid insurance premiums, and for a receiver. They must be added when proper. Copies of the note and mortgage must be attached.

Added June 19, 1968, effective Oct. 1, 1968 (211 So.2d 174).
Amended Oct. 9, 1980, effective Jan. 1, 1981 (391 So.2d 165).

## Form 1.945  Motor Vehicle Negligence

### Complaint

Plaintiff, A. B., sues defendants, C. D., and E. F., and alleges:

1. This is an action for damages that (insert jurisdictional amount).

2. (Use A or B)

A. On or about _____ , 19___, defendant, C. D., owned a motor vehicle that was operated with his consent by defendant, E. F., at _____ in _____, Florida.

B. On or about _____, 19___, defendant owned and operated a motor vehicle at _____ in _____, Florida.

3. At that time and place defendants negligently operated or maintained the motor vehicle so that it collided with plaintiff's motor vehicle.

4. As a result plaintiff suffered bodily injury and resulting pain and suffering, disability, disfigurement, mental anguish, loss of capacity for the enjoyment of life, expense of hospitalization, medical and nursing care and treatment, loss of earnings, loss of ability to earn money, and aggravation of a previously existing condition. The losses are either permanent or continuing and plaintiff will suffer the losses in the future. Plaintiff's automobile was damaged and he lost the use of it during the period required for its repair or replacement.

WHEREFORE plaintiff demands judgment for damages against defendants.

NOTE: This form, except for paragraph 2B, is for use when owner and driver are different persons. Use paragraph 2B when they are the same. If paragraph 2B is used, "defendants" must be changed to "defendant" wherever it appears. Added June 19, 1968, effective Oct. 1, 1968 (211 So.2d 174). Amended Oct. 9, 1980, effective Jan. 1, 1981 (391 So.2d 165).

### Committee Notes

**1980 Amendment.** This form was changed to show that one of the alternatives in paragraph 2 is used, but not both; and paragraph 4 has been changed to paraphrase Standard Jury Instruction 6.2.

---

## Form 1.946   Motor Vehicle Negligence When Plaintiff Is Unable to Determine Who Is Responsible

---

### Complaint

Plaintiff, A. B., sues defendants, C. D., and E. F., and alleges:

1. This is an action for damages that (insert jurisdictional amount).

2. On or about _____, 19___, defendant, C. D., or defendant, E. F., or both defendants, owned and operated motor vehicles at _____ in _____, Florida.

3. At that time and place defendants, or one of them, negligently operated or maintained their motor vehicles so that one or both of them collided with plaintiff's motor vehicle.

4. As a result plaintiff suffered bodily injury and resulting pain and suffering, disability, disfigurement, mental anguish, loss of capacity for the enjoyment of life, expense of

hospitalization, medical and nursing care and treatment, loss of earnings, loss of ability to earn money, and aggravation of a previously existing condition. The losses are either permanent or continuing and plaintiff will suffer the losses in the future. Plaintiff's automobile was damaged and he lost the use of it during the period required for its repair or replacement.

WHEREFORE plaintiff demands judgment for damages against defendants.

NOTE: Allegations when owner and driver are different persons are omitted from this form and must be added when proper. Added June 19, 1968, effective Oct. 1, 1968 (211 So.2d 174). Amended Oct. 9, 1980, effective Jan. 1, 1981 (391 So.2d 165).

### Committee Notes

**1980 Amendment.** Paragraph 4 is changed to paraphrase Standard Jury Instruction 6.2.

---

## Form 1.947   Tenant Eviction

### Complaint

Plaintiff, A. B., sues defendant, C. D., and alleges:

1. This is an action to evict a tenant from real property in _____ County, Florida.

2. Plaintiff owns the following described real property in said county: (describe property).

3. Defendant has possession of the property under (oral, written) agreement to pay rent of $____ payable ____.

4. Defendant failed to pay rent due _____, 19___.

5. Plaintiff served defendant with a notice on _____, 19___, to pay the rent or deliver possession but defendant refuses to do either.

WHEREFORE plaintiff demands judgment for possession of the property against defendant.

NOTE: Paragraph 3 must specify whether the rental agreement is written or oral, and if written, a copy must be attached. Added June 19, 1968, effective Oct. 1, 1968 (211 So.2d 174).

---

## Form 1.948   Third-Party Complaint. General Form

### Third-Party Complaint

Defendant, C. D., sues, third-party defendant, E. F., and alleges:

1.  Plaintiff filed a complaint against defendant, C. D., a copy being attached.

2.  (State the cause of action that C. D. has against E. F. for all or part of what A. B. may recover from C. D. as in an original complaint.)

WHEREFORE defendant, C. D., demands judgment against the third-party defendant, E. F., for all damages that are adjudged against defendant, C. D., in favor of plaintiff.

NOTE: A copy of the complaint from which the third-party complaint is derived must be attached.

Added June 19, 1968, effective Oct. 1, 1968 (211 So.2d 174).
Amended Oct. 9, 1980, effective Jan. 1, 1981 (391 So.2d 165);
Oct. 6 and Dec. 30, 1988, effective Jan. 1, 1989 (536 So.2d 974).

### Committee Notes

**1988 Amendment.** This change was made to eliminate the words "third-party plaintiff."

## Form 1.949   Implied Warranty

### Complaint

Plaintiff, A. B., sues defendant, C. D., and alleges:

1.  This is an action for damages that (insert jurisdictional amount).

2.  Defendant manufactured a product known and described as (describe product).

3.  Defendant warranted that the product was reasonably fit for its intended use as (describe intended use).

4.  On_____, 19___, at _____ in _____ County, Florida, the product (describe the occurrence and defect that resulted in injury) while being used for its intended purpose, causing injuries to plaintiff who was then a user of the product.

5.  As a result plaintiff was injured in and about his body and extremities, suffered pain therefrom, incurred medical expense in the treatment of the injuries, suffered physical handicap, and his working ability was impaired; the injuries are either permanent or continuing in their nature and plaintiff will suffer the losses and impairment in the future.

WHEREFORE plaintiff demands judgment for damages against defendant.
Added June 19, 1968, effective Oct. 1, 1968 (211 So.2d 174).
Amended July 26, 1972, effective Jan. 1, 1973 (265 So.2d 21).

### Committee Notes

This form is changed to require an allegation of the defect in paragraph 4. Contentions were made in trial courts that the form as presently authorized eliminated the substantive requirement that the plaintiff prove a defect except under those circumstances when substantive law eliminates the necessity of such proof. Paragraph 4 is amended to show that no substantive law change was intended.

## Form 1.951   Fall-Down Negligence Complaint

Plaintiff, A. B., sues defendant, C. D., and alleges:

1.  This is an action for damages that (insert jurisdictional amount).

2.  On_____, 19___, defendant was the owner and in possession of a building at _____ in _____, Florida, that was used as a (describe use).

3.  At that time and place plaintiff went on the property to (state purpose).

4.  Defendant negligently maintained (describe item) on the property by (describe negligence or dangerous condition) so that plaintiff fell on the property.

5.  The negligent condition was known to defendant or had existed for a sufficient length of time so that defendant should have known of it.

6.  As a result plaintiff was injured in and about his body and extremities, suffered pain therefrom, incurred medical expense in the treatment of the injuries, suffered physical handicap, and his working ability was impaired; the injuries are either permanent or continuing in nature and plaintiff will suffer the losses and impairment in the future.

WHEREFORE plaintiff demands judgment for damages against defendant.

Added July 26, 1972, effective Jan. 1, 1973 (265 So.2d 21).

## Form 1.965   Defense. Statute of Limitations

Each cause of action, claim, and item of damages did not accrue within the time prescribed by law for them before this action was brought.

Added June 19, 1968, effective Oct. 1, 1968 (211 So.2d 174).

## Form 1.966   Defense. Payment

Before commencement of this action defendant discharged plaintiff's claim and each item of it by payment.

Added June 19, 1968, effective Oct. 1, 1968 (211 So.2d 174).

## Form 1.967   Defense. Accord and Satisfaction

On_____, 19___, defendant delivered to plaintiff and plaintiff accepted from defendant (specify consideration) in full satisfaction of plaintiff's claim.

Added June 19, 1968, effective Oct. 1, 1968 (211 So.2d 174).

## Form 1.968   Defense. Failure of Consideration

The sole consideration for the execution and delivery of the promissory note described in paragraph _____ of the complaint was plaintiff's promise to loan defendant $1,000; plaintiff failed to loan the sum to defendant.

**NOTE:** This form is for failure to complete the loan evidenced by a promissory note. The contract, consideration, and default of the plaintiff must be varied to meet the facts of each case.

Added June 19, 1968, effective Oct. 1, 1968 (211 So.2d 174).

## Form 1.969   Defense. Statute of Frauds

The agreement alleged in the complaint was not in writing and signed by defendant or by some other person authorized by him and was to answer for the debt, default, or miscarriage of another person.

**NOTE:** This form is for one of the cases covered by the Statute of Frauds. It must be varied to meet the facts of other cases falling within the statute.

Added June 19, 1968, effective Oct. 1, 1968 (211 So.2d 174).

## Form 1.970   Defense. Release

On_____, 19___, and after plaintiff's claim in this action accrued, plaintiff released defendant from it, a copy of the release being attached.

**NOTE:** This form is for the usual case of a written release. If the release is not in writing, the last clause must be omitted and the word "orally" inserted before "released."

Added June 19, 1968, effective Oct. 1, 1968 (211 So.2d 174).

## Form 1.971   Defense. Motor Vehicle Contributory Negligence

Plaintiff's negligence contributed to the accident and his injury and damages because he negligently operated or maintained the motor vehicle in which he was riding so that it collided with defendant's motor vehicle.

Added June 19, 1968, effective Oct. 1, 1968 (211 So.2d 174).
Amended Oct. 9, 1980, effective Jan. 1, 1981 (391 So.2d 165).

## Form 1.972   Defense. Assumption of Risk

Plaintiff knew of the existence of the danger complained of in the complaint, realized and appreciated the possibility of injury as a result of the danger and, having a reasonable opportunity to avoid it, voluntarily exposed himself to the danger.

Added June 19, 1968, effective Oct. 1, 1968 (211 So.2d 174).
Amended Oct. 9, 1980, effective Jan. 1, 1981 (391 So.2d 165).

### Committee Notes

**1980 Amendment.**   This form is amended to show the substantive changes caused by the substitution of the doctrine of comparative negligence for contributory negligence. The form is paraphrased from Standard Jury Instruction 3.8.

# Index

Page numbers in bold type indicate definitions of terms.

# About the Authors

*Robert W. Schachner* studied at Carnegie-Mellon University and Duquesne University Journalism School. He is the president and chief executive officer of RTV Communications Group, which represents New Age music, Gateway Recordings, and the Who's Who in Jazz record labels, among others. Robert is the author of *The Official Scrabble Word Finder* (Macmillan, 1988) and *Lost Words in the English Language* (Bob Adams, Inc., 1989). He resides in Hollywood, Florida.

*Marvin Quittner, Esq.*, is an attorney who has been in private practice since 1971. He was the moderator and production coordinator for "The World at Law" television show on Southern Florida's Channel 6. Mr. Quittner and his wife, Shelley, served as directors on Broward County's Children Education Association. They reside in Plantation, Florida, with their two children.